CW00591781

Mamerto Gueritz

Sacristy
Press

Mamerto Gueritz

A Country Catholic
1823–1912

— DAVID GUNN-JOHNSON —

Sacristy
Press

Sacristy Press
PO Box 612, Durham, DH1 9HT

www.sacristy.co.uk

First published in 2023 by Sacristy Press, Durham

Sacristy Limited, registered in England & Wales, number 7565667

British Library Cataloguing-in-Publication Data
A catalogue record for the book is available from the British Library

ISBN 978-1-78959-310-5

Contents

List of illustrations

Dedication

When the late Bishop Geoffrey Rowell was chaplain of Keble College, Oxford, he supervised some work on the Oxford Movement that I was engaged in at the time. As others might bear witness, his supervision had about it a kindly firmness which made for interesting tutorials. For my part, I recall the day at Hawarden in St Deiniol's Library, as it was then known, when he put his blue pencil through 10,000 of my hard-written words with the blunt statement: "The examiners will not want to read your vague lucubrations on the nature of history!" I had to look up lucubrations; "Any literary effort especially of a pretentious or solemn nature usually undertaken at night."

"I have ever considered and kept the day" as the beginning of a friendship that lasted the rest of Geoffrey's life and, I trust, beyond. Our infrequent meetings kept the excitement of discovery and of telling the tale alive and only a little before his death Geoffrey was still encouraging and steering my further explorations in the lesser trodden pathways of the nineteenth-century Church. It was his prompting one convivial evening in Great Torrington that I should follow up the work on, as he put it, "your man" that has led to this further study. The man in question is Mamerto Gueritz.

I have done so in thanksgiving to and for Douglas Geoffrey Rowell, scholar, bishop, mentor and friend, hoping that he would approve of what I have managed to write and wishing that he were here to warn me still against "vague lucubrations".

David Gunn-Johnson
Exeter, February 2023

Preface and acknowledgements

This is more of an exercise in storytelling and detection than a scholarly work, although it may appear scholarly by the appearance of copious footnotes, references, bibliography and an appendix that will verge on peritonitis. However, this is simply the story of Mamerto Gueritz, a priest of the Church of England. It is a work of detection, because the story has to be pieced together from fragments; there are no great repositories of correspondence, and the reader may find the frequent use of words such as "probably" or "likely" and phrases such as "the balance of evidence" frustrating, as did the author.

The story of Mamerto Gueritz cannot be told *in vacuo* as a series of actions and events because understanding his life and ministry is particularly dependent upon the context, both historical and contemporary. There is the personal and familial history of Mamerto Gueritz which reaches back into the political turmoil of eighteenth-century Spain, but this is also a tale told in the setting of what we have come to call the Oxford Movement. Perhaps the analogy of a stone in its setting is not too extravagant. If Mamerto Gueritz were a stone polished by the passing of the years, then the setting we have is a complex filigree of his personal history, the movement which claimed his loyalty, and the roles in which he was cast. His "fiery Spanish temperament" also played a not inconsiderable part.

Gueritz' personal history and that of his forbears we shall set out as well as we may. The Oxford Movement, to which he gave his commitment, is seen here not as something that began with a particular sermon on a particular day, but rather as a flowing of ideas and actions from well before the Tractarians up to and beyond the exuberant Ritualism of the late nineteenth and early twentieth century. The continuities and discontinuities of that flow are still worthy of study although, among others, Peter Nockles in his *The Oxford Movement in Context*[1] and George Herring, both in his doctoral thesis "Tractarianism to Ritualism" and his published work *The Oxford Movement in Practice*,[2] have illuminated the process well. Then in the later evolution of the Movement the distinctions between the early Tractarians and those who promoted Ritualism, and the differences between both of them and the so-called "Romanizers", have been rightly explored; so much so that the differences and departures have sometimes been taken for the fragmentation of the Movement itself. It is not to the present purpose to offer yet another in-depth analysis of the emergence and evolution of Anglo-Catholicism; even that term meant different things to different generations. Let it suffice to say at the outset that the presupposition here is of an underlying continuity, issuing from which some very different manifestations of the forces at work in the Church of England are to be seen. A brief description of that process is offered in the introduction simply to add substance to the context.

Then there are the roles in which Mamerto Gueritz was cast. If the Oxford Movement is part of the setting, then contemporary evidences of that movement in the places where Mamerto exercised his ministry will be of considerable importance. The diocese of Exeter was the setting for all but one of the curacies Mamerto Gueritz served and for his first and only incumbency. Similarly, the parish of Colyton where he laboured for almost 42 years was the place where the forces at work in the Church Revival, as he habitually called it, and the forces at work in the local community came face to face with, quite literally, incendiary results. Gueritz was at the interface of that engagement; more than that, he was the interface! Therefore, some awareness of the community into which Mamerto Gueritz arrived as parish priest in 1860, especially regarding its religious life and traditions, will be essential to complete the setting.

As in the telling of any story or the unfolding of any drama, there are characters to be developed other than that of the leading man. They may be minor members of the cast in this story, but each will have been the central character in other narratives. It would not be to the purpose to interrupt the telling of this tale, which will already have substantial contextual interpolations, with lengthy asides about famous, almost famous, and scarcely known figures either of the Oxford Movement or of Colyton who here appear as walk-on parts. It would, however, be lacking in generosity to those who are not already aware of such players to leave them with no real substance to the encounter. Therefore, while some of those supporting characters are introduced in the text, several vignettes of other characters in the tale are provided in the final chapter under the title "The

Supporting Cast", in the hope that this will lend greater depth and understanding to the story as a whole. The lesser known the character the longer the vignette. The best known of the Oxford Movement characters, John Henry Newman, John Keble, Hurrell Froude, Edward Bouverie Pusey and Henry Parry Liddon among them, are omitted entirely from that section on the dual basis that, firstly, better scholars and writers have already done them justice and, secondly, this is a story and not a *magnum opus*.

In acknowledging a debt to those long-departed participants in the story, I must also acknowledge the debt to those whose present help and support has made the telling of this little history possible. I have acknowledged in the dedication my gratitude to Bishop Geoffrey Rowell. The late Rear Admiral Edward (Teddy) Gueritz of Salisbury was kindness itself when this journey was first begun and provided copies of manuscript accounts, letters and other original documents. Other members of the Gueritz and Mortimer families have given generously of their time, their memories and their family records. Such help was also given by the late Miss Pamela Rattray of Colyton, a member of the Liddon family.

Of course, nothing could be done without libraries and record offices and here the extent of indebtedness can only be inadequately expressed. To the staff of the Bodleian Library, the Librarian of Pusey House, the staff of the Morrab Library in Penzance, and the staff of the Lambeth Palace Library much thanks. To those who opened the archives of Magdalen College and Keble College, Oxford, again great gratitude. The patient and helpful people who work in the Cornish Studies Library in Redruth and the Record Office in Truro (now amalgamated in the Kresen Kernow), the South West Heritage Centre, incorporating the Devon Record Office, the West Country Studies Library and the Somerset Record Office have all been most supportive. The kindness and patience of the Librarian and the Archivist of Exeter Cathedral, who have allowed me to delve in unlikely places, are most gratefully acknowledged.

Time and space to go aside and read and write is essential. I am therefore greatly indebted to the Revd Canon Dr Robin Ward, the Principal of St Stephen's House, Oxford, and his staff who have welcomed me for sometimes extended stays. Also special thanks to H. E. J. "John" Cowdrey, of St Edmund Hall, who, although he has departed this life, leaves behind him both the memory of his encouragement and his delight in the Gueritz story. Further support was given by the Anglo Catholic History Society in the form of a grant, which was very gratefully received.

As Sabine Baring-Gould discovered, the accumulated memories of folk in rural communities, especially those who can claim uncounted generations in the same place, are quite remarkable. There were, and still are, people in the community of Colyton who can make such a claim regarding Mamerto Gueritz. When the author first went there as rector in 1988, there were those living who could remember him and one even claimed to have been a 12-year-old server at his requiem in 1912. The stories which have been handed down through the generations, while not always uncritically received, are of great value.

The most unexpected treasure of all, however, was the discovery of a collection of notes and records in the parish chest which quite evidently had not been touched for decades. These are all now safely bestowed in the South West Heritage Centre, but the first finding of them brought to sudden and highly coloured life an episode in the history of Colyton which had all but faded from memory. At that time, the chest was situated against the wall of the northeast corner of the church, now known as the Lady Chapel. Gueritz called it "the Morning Chapel", because when he first went to Colyton for him to use the title Lady Chapel would have been deemed part of his "Jesuitical plot to lead good Protestants to Rome". Mamerto's modest memorial brass still stands on the wall between the sanctuary and the chapel where the discovery was made and just across the sanctuary the rather more impressive memorial to Henry Parry Liddon is set in the tower wall. The finding of those records gave birth to the desire to know more of the person at the heart of it all and made this exploration seem at first possible and then inevitable.

When studying the development of the Oxford Movement in the towns and cities, there are collections of letters and papers to draw upon far in excess of the collection found in Colyton. The doings of the leaders were of national interest and were well reported, which created considerable resources for the researcher. It is not so much the case for the explorer who would step off the main highway into lesser-known paths. However, parish life in Colyton was comparatively well documented by secular observers, though little of their work is published, and the church records themselves give a further perspective. The service registers after 1868 provide a commentary on developments in the parish in the form of marginal asides, but before that the recording of services was embryonic. The later controversies in the parish produced files of correspondence between diocesan authorities and Gueritz' opponents. They also contain some of his own replies. Faculty applications for the reordering of the church tell their own story, especially where they concern the removal of pews and galleries. The local newspapers, several of which were in the hands of Unitarian proprietors, were transparently partisan, which makes for entertaining if necessarily selective reading.

Finally, to all of these acknowledgements I must add in special place the name of William Gueritz. William is a descendant of Mamerto Gueritz through Mamerto's second son, Jose Fortescue Lawrence Gueritz, and Lucy Octavia née Elton, and is also the great nephew of Rear Admiral "Teddy" Gueritz. From the time of our first conversation in July 2019, William has provided much information and many newspaper references, some from the far corners of the earth, in order that I might give as full and accurate an account as I may of his ancestor. He has also patiently read several chapters and drafts and without his kindly corrections and suggestions this work would be much less than it is.

The early attempts to tell the story of individual characters of the Oxford Movement sometimes verged on hagiography. This attempt to tell the story of Mamerto Gueritz in his personal, ecclesiastical and historical context is not such. It is the tale of a parish priest who, though perhaps no saint, strove for sanctity in himself and in others and it is affectionately offered in memory of a man upon whose ministerial foundations the author was privileged to build.[3]

Notes

[1] Peter B. Nockles, *The Oxford Movement in Context* (Cambridge: Cambridge University Press, 1994).

[2] George W. Herring, "Tractarianism to Ritualism", DPhil thesis (2 volumes), Oxford University, 1984. Also, *The Oxford Movement in Practice: The Tractarian Parochial World from the 1830s to the 1870s* (Oxford: Oxford University Press, 2016).

[3] Actually, quite a lot of saints were very difficult to live with and were formidable in conflict, so perhaps .

Introduction

One of the many images that provided both background and inspiration for this study is that of

> Alfred Augustus Peregrine Marley, who was relieving the vicar of such-and-such a parish (when he) collapsed and died at the altar while administering Holy Communion.[1]

This is from *Lark Rise to Candleford*, the autobiographical reminiscences of Flora Thompson.[2] Writing of her early childhood she remembers A. A. Marley in a scene which dates from around 1885:

> He was surely as strange a curate as ever came to a remote agricultural parish . . . a fanatic where his Church and his Creed were concerned, otherwise he was the kindest and most gentle of men . . . He was what is now known as an Anglo-Catholic. Sunday after Sunday he preached "One Holy Catholic and Apostolic Church" and "Our Holy Religion" to his congregation of rustics. But he did not stop at that, he dealt often with the underlying truths of religion, preaching the Gospel of love and the forgiveness of sins and the brotherhood of man. How such a preacher came to be, in his old age, but a curate in a remote country parish is a mystery. His eloquence would have filled a city church.
>
> . . . when officiating he openly genuflected to the altar, made the sign of the cross, made known his willingness to hear confessions, and instituted daily services and weekly instead of monthly Communion.[3]

The manner in which Flora Thompson records her memories reveals her awareness of the controversies which surrounded such men and of how Alfred Marley in particular managed to gain such freedom:

> The Rector by that time was bedridden and a scholarly, easy going, middle aged son, was deputising for him, otherwise ... this in many parishes would have caused a scandal, but the Fordlow people rather enjoyed the change, excepting the Methodists ... and a few other extremists who said he was a Pope's man.[4]

As we see him in *Lark Rise to Candleford*, Alfred Marley, the elderly curate who worked himself to death, sets before us an example of the "Country Catholic". Marley unswervingly proclaimed the Church's teaching regarding the sacraments and the search for personal holiness but was equally unswervingly committed to the care of his parishioners; a commitment that ultimately cost him his health and his life.

Marley stands as an exemplar of Anglo-Catholic parish priests who laboured long, often at best ignored by their bishops and at worst hounded from office. In spite of this, they were to be found the length and breadth of the land. It is an encouragement for this study that the first three examples in Michael Yelton's *Outposts of the Faith* are found in Devon and Cornwall.[5] Where could be further out of the way than the village of Throwleigh, tucked away on the edge of Dartmoor? The parish priest who began the hidden work of "Church Revival" in that parish was Gambier Lowe, a nephew of Fr Wainright of St Peter's, London Docks. The relevance of that relationship will become clear as St Peter's appears again in the story.

Priests like Marley and Lowe won the affection of their people, often after overcoming initial opposition, but they were sustained in their labours and preserved from total isolation by the networking of like-minded clergy whose capacity for letter-writing and just staying in touch astounds today. This level of communication was costly both in terms of time and of energy and bears no comparison with the ease of exchange in a technological age.

As he appears in this story, Marley is also the fulfilment of prophecy. Thomas Sikes was rector of Guilsborough and a leader of the Hackney Phalanx, a group of pre-Tractarian High Churchmen. Sikes once said to W. J. Copeland:

> Wherever I go about the country I see among the clergy a number of very amiable and estimable men, many of them in earnest and wishing to do good. But I have observed the universal want in their teaching . . . there is no account given anywhere as far as I can see, of the One, Holy, Catholic and Apostolic Church . . . and by and by, those who live to see it, will hear of nothing else, and just in proportion, perhaps, to its present suppression, will be its future development.[6]

Copeland had been curate of Hackney before he went to Oxford, where he emerged as a firm supporter of Tractarianism and served at Littlemore under John Henry Newman.

It is salutary to have these images from history and literature before us as the journey begins. Flora Thompson's writing is particularly refreshing because she records the things she saw and the people she knew just as they were. There is little, if any, of the reading back into an earlier period the effects of later developments, which so bedevils the writing of history, especially the history of the Oxford Movement. It is a fitting memorial to Alfred Marley that his teaching of "One Holy Catholic and Apostolic Church" was engraved upon Thompson's memory lifelong.

Flora Thompson found the presence of Alfred Marley in a country parish a mystery. It is with another such mystery that this work is concerned. This is a study, using a hitherto scarcely remarked example, of the way in which the Oxford Movement spread into the remotest places and there took root.

In the place of Fordlow or Throwleigh, we have the town of Colyton in East Devon.[7] In the place of A. A. Marley or Gambier Lowe, we have Mamerto Gueritz, incumbent for just short of 42 years. The keen student of the Oxford Movement will be aware of many characters in many settings, but who has ever heard of Mamerto Gueritz? Interestingly enough, Professor Owen Chadwick, in conversation with a member of the Gueritz family, is reported to have said: "I used, quite often, to come across the name of Gueritz."[8] The reasons for that will become clear.

That conversation is gratifying in that it lends weight to one of the presuppositions of this study, namely that the Oxford Movement is not to be understood solely through the lives and deeds of the great leaders, hugely rewarding and essential though that study is, neither can it be compassed by focussing just on the controversies surrounding its key figures. The conflicts which enveloped the first leaders—John Keble, John Henry Newman, Richard Hurrell Froude and Edward Bouverie Pusey—at frequent intervals and for a variety of reasons also broke upon those who followed them. A balance is to be gained by sometimes taking a lesser trodden pathway and finding at its end the full flowering of Tractarian theology shaping the religious life of some small and out of the way community. As George Herring wrote, "The loneliness of the country retreat was an essential feature of the Tractarian experiment after 1845."[9]

Herring was referring, among other events of that year, to the effects of the departure of John Henry Newman for the Church of Rome and the ongoing persecution by the university authorities of Edward Bouverie Pusey. This initially engendered an atmosphere of discouragement if not despondency among the Tractarians. However, Pusey in Oxford and Keble in Hursley stood firm and others emerged to stand with them; men such as James Mozely, then of Magdalen College; R. W. Church, at the time a Fellow of Oriel; and Charles Marriot, another Oriel man.

While Oxford was aflame with the controversy and while they empathized entirely with their friends and fellow alumni caught up in the battle, many rural Tractarian clergy could do little other than get on with the task of restoring Catholic teaching to their people. A rural, sequestered ministry was not an entirely negative thing. W. E. Heygate, the author of several Anglo-Catholic novels and devotional works, wrote:

> Nor can anything better for us be imagined than hopelessness of preferment, which takes away our worldly and second motives and makes our purpose single and our affection pure.[10]

Mamerto Gueritz is valuable because he is an example of this great body of almost hidden country Catholics and yet he stands sufficiently in view for his story to be told. His name appears on attendance lists of meetings, as signatory to a number of petitions, on membership lists of clerical societies, in national and provincial newspaper articles which either vilified or lauded according to their own agendas, and all this happened often enough for Professor Owen Chadwick to recognize the name. It has additionally to be noted that some of those reports of the doings of Mamerto Gueritz, and the actions they recorded, warranted mention in Parliament and were published as far afield as the Antipodean newspapers!

It was through the agency of priests such as Gueritz that the Oxford Movement permeated the life of the English Church as completely as it did. The effects of that were profound, especially in the locations here in view: principally the diocese of Exeter and the parish of Colyton. Gueritz stands out from this body and offers rather more than an example of the typical rural Tractarian, if ever there was such a being. He was one who first encountered the Oxford Movement in the dark days following Newman's departure for Rome and then experienced just about every facet of its growth and change right into the first decade of the twentieth century. His experience of that growth and change and his part in bringing it into parochial ministry make him worthy of note among "Country Catholics".

After graduating from St Edmund Hall, where he had arrived within a few months of Newman's final departure, Gueritz served his first curacy—his title—at Shepton Beauchamp and Barrington with James Coles, father of V. S. S. Coles, later known throughout the Oxford Movement as "Stuckey" and who was to become a lifelong friend. After his return to Exeter diocese, Mamerto served several curacies under interesting circumstances until he finally went to Penzance as a sort of *locum tenens* for the ailing incumbent. There he witnessed, took part in, and can be said to have promoted the early manifestations of Ritualism in Cornwall. In 1860, he arrived in Colyton in East Devon and began his long and colourful ministry there. In Colyton he was loved and hated, championed and vilified. All that his more famous brethren in the Movement endured or enjoyed, Gueritz in his country fastness experienced the same; not that he always remained sequestered. Friendships from university days and acquaintanceships made in London were sustained and developed so that, far from being isolated from the mainstream, Gueritz was more than ordinarily aware of national developments. The priests who were the London vanguard of the battle, particularly in Margaret Street and Stoke Newington, grew to know and value him and he them.

Seeing Mamerto Gueritz through the lens of the material available and against the background of the Oxford Movement immediately raises questions concerning the ways in which the origins of the Movement and the manner of its dissemination have been recorded and understood. It has in some quarters been tacitly assumed that the process of change and the spread of Tractarian ideas, and then the transmutation (or warping, as some of the earlier Tractarians saw it) of those ideas into Ritualism, was all through well-defined channels, each having its source in Newman, Pusey, Keble, Froude or others who took centre stage after 1845. Real history is simply much messier than that and such a view ignores the earlier contribution of men like Thomas Sikes and the Hackney Phalanx, already briefly mentioned. This group was named for what was then the village of Hackney, northeast of London, where one of the leading figures, Archdeacon John James Watson, was incumbent. It was his younger brother, Joshua Watson, who was seen as the central figure around whom the circle gathered. The men of Hackney were active for around three decades from the early years of the nineteenth century to the middle of the 1830s. The Watsons in turn were closely linked with several members of an earlier body of High Churchmen which included men like William Jones of Nayland, and through him to a number of earlier Oxford divines who held a high doctrine of the Church and church principles. A goodly number of these men rather resented the tendency of the Tractarians to ignore or undervalue the work they had done to lay the foundations for this new generation of Oxford men. John Burgon wrote:

> The smouldering materials for the cheerful blaze which followed the efforts
> made in 1832–3–4 had been accumulating unobserved for many years;
> had been the residuum of the altar-fires of a long succession of holy and
> earnest men.[11]

Later, when the first histories of the Movement began to be written, the authors were people who had known the first leaders and who had a personal involvement in the account they were constructing. These records were partisan and personal; inevitably so while memories were fresh and loyalties still strong. Some later champions of the cause, lacking that direct and personal experience of the first Tractarians, assumed that the way in which the Oxford Movement developed into Ritualism reflected the mind of the Movement from the outset. This was patently not the case.

It was also inevitable that the zealous clergy who set out to restore the visible Catholic character of the Church of England in its doctrine, its ritual and its buildings, should leave behind them a rather partisan record of their success. Readers of *The English Gentleman's Magazine* of 1865 were informed that:

> The present religious movement seems to leave no part of the religious life unsupplied, taste and feeling have their appetite satiated in the ritual, architecture and music of the house of God, while the true spiritual life is maintained by the frequent and constant celebration of the sacraments.[12]

It is something of an irony that this was the same year in which the Church Association was formed, with the specific intention of opposing all manifestations of Ritualism and the Oxford Movement. No mention is made in the article of the turmoil which surrounded attempts to supply the religious life in this manner, the accusations which were levelled at the "Ritualizers" and the persecution they endured. There is no hint of the long battles beginning in Plymouth in 1848 with those who opposed the " . . . chanting and bowing, turning east, preaching in a surplice, using the offertory sentence and the prayer for the Church militant",[13] all of which were then in use at St Peter's, Plymouth. There is here no indication of the earlier surplice riots in Exeter or of the violence at St George in the East in 1860. The author seemed blithely unaware of the storm that was about to break in the form of Church Association-inspired prosecutions.

Later scholars still, alert to the dangers attendant on uncritical acceptance of earlier accounts, have stressed the elements of discontinuity within the Movement, claiming that the Tractarians and the Ritualists had little in common and that the latter did not develop naturally from the former. It is outside the scope of this work to deal fully with the question of whether, for example, the Ritualist of 1880 could legitimately claim to be an inheritor of the first Tractarians, but for the present purpose it is of considerable importance to understand something of the underlying continuity of motive between the generations and something of the processes by which the Oxford Movement spread and changed. This in turn will allow a grasp of the milieu within which the central character of this study played his part, for as the Movement changed so did Mamerto Gueritz.

Gueritz stands before us as one who spans not only the differences between old and new elements of the Oxford Movement but also as one who experienced a personal migration from Evangelical to Catholic theology; a transition he shared with Newman and several other Tractarians. He is, therefore, ideally placed to speak to us of that experience of change and continuity. He stands in a process which had its roots in, emerged from, and in some sense continued in relationship with the earlier High Church party. The Oxford Movement did not arrive *ex nihilo*. Later Tractarians, such as Henry Parry Liddon, with whom Gueritz had an ongoing acquaintanceship, differed from the first Tractarians and also from the emergent Ritualists, yet they all appeared within the same historical continuum. There was an essential continuity, but where that was to be found and how discerned has often been obscured by focus on external differences between, for example, the restrained Tractarian at the altar in scarf and academic hood and the priest in full Roman panoply surrounded by clouds of incense. However, before we attempt to discern that continuity of motive between the various developments of the Oxford Movement, we shall need a passing glance at nomenclature.

Be the intention and method of a study never so clear one thing that above all else requires clarity, especially when looking at the Oxford Movement, is terminology. What one person will today label Anglo-Catholic might historically be more closely defined, for example, as Tractarian or Ritualist. Another will speak of the second wave of Puseyism without adequately defining whether this actually meant an early Ritualist or one who still wore a surplice and perhaps a stole instead of the hood, yet lived a generation later. John Henry Newman himself in his *Lectures on the Prophetical Office of the Church* wrote:

> It still remains to be tried whether what is called Anglo-Catholicism, the religion of Andrewes, Laud, Hammond, Butler and Wilson, is capable of being professed, acted upon, and maintained on a large sphere of action and through a sufficient period.[14]

Newman was referring to a much earlier body of men, who preceded even the High Churchmen of the Hackney Phalanx by a century, and he used the term "Anglican" interchangeably with "Anglo-Catholic". Thus, the term itself predated the later terms, Tractarian and Tractarianism, and was then applied not only to these seventeenth-century divines but also to the later old-fashioned High Churchmen of the Hackney Phalanx. Both groups were quite distant by more than just separation in time from those whom Flora Thompson labelled "Anglo-Catholic".

The waters were further muddied by the tendency of some of the first Tractarians to adopt Hurrell Froude's whimsical labelling of the various parties. The old-fashioned pre-Tractarian High Churchmen had immediate ideological descendants in men like Hugh James Rose. He was one of the few who met with John Keble in the immediate aftermath of his Assize Sermon in 1833. Froude called Rose and his peers "Zs", describing them as "high and dry". Evangelicals were termed "Xs" while the Tractarians themselves were labelled "Ys" or "Apostolicals". Such an attempt to categorize or pigeonhole people who were perhaps in a process of transition themselves, within a body of thought which was itself growing and changing, was not terribly helpful.

For the sake of clarity then: in this work the term Tractarian is applied not only as when first used by Christopher Benson in a sermon at the Temple Church in 1839 to refer to the writers of the *Tracts for the Times* in the narrowest sense, but also in a wider sense to apply to those who overtly espoused their teaching and supported their aims. This latter use of the term became more widespread once the series of *Tracts* ended with *Tract 90* in 1841. Being afforded the name did not imply that the supposed Tractarian had any commitment to externals in a ritualistic sense, although many espoused the wearing of the surplice and stole for the celebration of Holy Communion.

Puseyite was a label attached to Tractarians, often by unsympathetic commentators after Newman departed for Rome, and is used when quoting them here. Even before that departure Pusey's intellectual stature, his restraint in externals and his personal spiritual discipline commended him to many. Both terms, Tractarian and Puseyite, therefore appear in relation to those who chose to retain a level of restraint in liturgical externals, and who may have chosen not to espouse the development of Ritualism. To describe a priest as a Tractarian in, say, 1880 may be taken to indicate one who had not followed the ritual road and whose celebration of the liturgy would resemble that of Pusey rather than that of All Saints Margaret Street or St Matthias, Stoke Newington at the same date.

Opponents of the Movement were later wont to use the label "Puseyite" indiscriminately as a term of opprobrium for anyone or anything that looked vaguely Catholic.

The label Romanizer was applied widely, inaccurately and as a term of censure by opponents of the Oxford Movement to anything and anyone perceived as a threat to their understanding of the Church of England as a Protestant body. It was applied to men like Gueritz who had no intention of leading anyone to Rome, unless the whole English Church could be reconciled. It was properly given to those who, like W. G. Ward, appearing in the 1840s and 1850s, believed that the Church of Rome was the only true repository of Catholic authenticity and of whom Newman was writing when he lamented that they "cut into the Movement at an angle, seeking to drive it Romewards".[15] Romanizer is, therefore, more a political term in the history of the Oxford Movement than descriptive of the Romanizer's liturgical behaviour.

The labels Ritualist and Ritualism are more widely applicable than they might at first appear and therefore offer another potential source of confusion. The so-called Ritualists of, for example, the Margaret Chapel, before the building of All Saints Margaret Street, were very little different in appearance from the mid-twentieth-century Conservative Evangelical, presiding at the Eucharist in surplice, scarf and hood.[16] However, if the priests were not apparelled in "Romish" garb, the altar most certainly was. So, early Ritualism was more about the liturgy and the sacrament and what the priest did, than about what the priest wore. Later Ritualism championed the "six points" which were set out at the annual meeting of the English Church Union in 1875 and were supposed to be the acid test of an authentic liturgy. These were: the use of vestments, lights on the altar, incense, wafer bread, the mixed chalice, and the eastward-facing president. To these were eventually added the hearing of sacramental confession and the reserved sacrament.

Those who came rather later, like Stuckey Coles, could look back at the days of trial and persecution from the early years of the twentieth century, when what he termed "Catholic privileges" were almost beginning to be taken for granted. People such as Coles tended to use terms like Catholic Revival or Church Revival and, with them, embrace the sweep of history from John Keble's Assize Sermon in 1833 to their own present day; in the main giving little weight to all the work that had been done before 1833.

The drawing of hard and fast boundaries between any of these definitions is not really possible, for there was much shading off between them and much depends on who was using them, when, and why.

There was also movement in both directions, as we shall see when we look at the curates at work in Penzance. We shall also see that Gueritz himself in 1860 was still, by these measures, essentially a Tractarian in theology and externals, but one who was moving to emulate the ritual he had experienced in London. He still wore a simple surplice, but his liturgical innovations were lights on the altar, the provision of a robed choir in the chancel and the use of Helmore's *Manual of Plainsong*. This, to the opponents of the Oxford Movement in 1860, would mark him unmistakeably as a Ritualist. By 1866, his use of vestments, indeed of the six points of ceremonial, left both his detractors and his supporters in no doubt that he had become an advanced proponent of the Ritual Revival.

Of course, all this simply underscores the fact that, while some internal clarity in the use of labels is useful in a study like this, it is still dangerous to assume that the various factions used those terms with any consistency. *Caveat lector!*

There was another group of people and a movement at work in the late 1850s led, among others, by Frederick George Lee. Lee will appear at several points and in different guises in this story. He helped to found the Association for Promoting the Unity of Christendom in 1857 and 20 years later, in 1877, the rather more arcane Order of Corporate Reunion. The first was a body which had a widespread membership, both Roman and Anglican, for some considerable time and which sought to bring the Church of England and the Church of Rome into some kind of mutual acceptance. The second organization differed considerably. By dint of irregular and secretive ordinations and episcopal consecrations, it attempted to oblige the See of Peter to acknowledge the validity of the orders of a substantial body of Anglican priests. However, the orders thus created were not Anglican orders and while they might have been considered valid under Roman canon law, they were completely irregular. Thus, such orders would not be recognized in the Church of England and could not be allowed to be exercised in the Church of Rome. This coercive process may have prepared the ground in a minor way for the Papal Bull of 1896, *Apostolicae curae*, which declared Anglican orders to be "absolutely null and utterly void".

Although the Association for Promoting the Unity of Christendom was espoused initially by many adherents of the Oxford Movement, Tractarians and Ritualists alike, the later characteristics of Lee's work sat uneasily with them. The leaders of the Order of Corporate Reunion, F. G. Lee, J. T. Seccombe and T. W. Mossman, having themselves received irregular ordination and consecration, proceeded to ordain others, some already in Anglican orders but others not. This led to many disputes over the validity of the ministers and their ministry. Indeed, Gueritz' son, Fortescue, would become entangled in such a dispute with a visiting priest in Scotland.

Lee, Seccombe and Mossman seemed to many to have already taken the view that Rome later formalized, that Anglican orders and Anglican catholicity were not valid, or at the least, were in doubt. The belief that the Church of England was both Catholic and Reformed, and that its clergy were in true orders, was at the very heart of the Oxford Movement.

Although the people, ideas and events we have in view were from the beginning closely associated with Oxford and the university, the term the Oxford Movement was not often used before 1880 and then rarely without inverted commas. That perhaps legitimizes its use here as a term to include that development of High Church Anglicanism which was refocussed in the public mind by John Keble's sermon of 1833, which held within its permeable bounds all the phenomena we have in view in this story and continues in the present in ways that its inceptors could scarcely have imagined.

Several times thus far it has been asserted that what held, or rather what holds, the Oxford Movement to a coherent whole, in spite of the many developments and changes that have taken place down the years, is continuity of motive.

It may seem that the outward appearance of discontinuity between the old and the new is the story of the fragmentation of the Oxford Movement. There were without any doubt considerable differences between the Old High Church party, the "Zs" as Froude had it, and the Tractarians, between the Tractarians and the Ritualists, and certainly between them all and the Romanizers. In all justice, the early Tractarians did much to reinforce this understanding. Their seeming dismissal of the earlier High Churchmen and their distance even from some of the later pre-Tractarians such as Hugh James Rose fed the fear that continuity had been lost. The behaviour of some, perhaps Newman and Froude first among them, has been likened to that of

> [m]odern-day teenagers who cannot imagine their parents and elders ever being as deeply moved as they, as deeply passionate as they, as fervently wedded to a cause as they. It is as if they invented feeling itself and just because the "fuddy duddies" choose not to make a display of those feelings they are assumed to have none.[17]

Yet there were, in spite of the differences, also evidences of the sharing in an inheritance which began well before 1833. Joshua Watson was a High Churchman of the old style. He helped found the Additional Curates Society in 1837 and was its first treasurer. In 1839, Pusey wrote to him:

> One had become so much the object of suspicion that I cannot say how cheering it was to be recognised by you as carrying on the same torch we had received from yourself, and those of your generation, who had remained faithful to the old teaching.[18]

Watson was not entirely a supporter of the Tractarians and found himself out of sympathy with later developments, but here he afforded Pusey a recognition of their common ground and inheritance.

That ground lay in their shared conviction, inherited from the earlier seventeenth-century Anglican divines, that the doctrine of the Church of England was that which was proclaimed by the Church of the early centuries and was passed through the generations in the writings of the Church Fathers. That teaching was to be found in the formularies and teaching of the Church enshrined and summarized in, but not exhausted by, the Book of Common Prayer. This belief placed the teaching of the nature of the Church and its relation to the world and to society close to the heart of what was to become the message of the Tractarians. Keble's sermon of 1833 demonstrated precisely that. Three years later, in a sermon which he preached at Hursley, Keble said:

Christ's Holy Catholic Church is a real outward visible body, having supernatural grace continually communicated through it by succession from the Apostles, in whose place the Bishops are.[19]

Baptismal regeneration was an ineluctable part of that teaching, as affirmed in Article 27 in the Book of Common Prayer:

Baptism is not only a sign of profession and mark of difference, whereby Christian men are discerned from others that be not christened, but it is also a sign of regeneration or new birth.

Baptism is, of course, but one of the two Dominical sacraments, but the message was not concerned with sacraments alone. It was only six years after Keble's sermon at Hursley that William Ewart Gladstone wrote of the

great Catholic principles which distinguish our Church from many other Protestant bodies: such, for instance, as the doctrine of grace in Baptism, of the real sacramental presence in the Eucharist, of absolution, of universal or Catholic consent, of the Apostolical foundation of the Episcopate, and its being the source of lawful Church power and of a valid ministry.[20]

If Church principles and Anglican doctrine were thus validated what, if anything, was lacking in what the Tractarians were to carry forward? What would make all of this more than abstract doctrinal teaching? It was one of Newman's fears for the *via media* he proposed that it would be seen as an empty paper exercise.
    Geoffrey Rowell wrote:

At the heart of Tractarian Spirituality and at the centre of Tractarian theology was the doctrine of the Incarnation issuing in the doctrine of the Divine indwelling.[21]

This holding together of spirituality and theology was to become the key to all that followed and to provide the motive and intent which was and is the ground of continuity; the fire which was to light the way for successive generations. In one of his sermons on the subject, the passion with which Pusey held this conviction was crystal clear:

> Through God indwelling the soul we have our spiritual and eternal life begun in us; we think all the good thoughts we have. Our good is not merely ours, not chiefly or primarily ours, but His . . . But then what an existence, aweful for the very greatness of the love of God! What a tingling closeness of God! "Christ in you, the hope of glory".[22]

The catholic doctrine of the Church tended to this one end. Christianity must be more than speculation about faith and more than mere philosophy but also a lived experience. The inevitable outcome of such a conviction was to make the pursuit of holiness the common ground and true hallmark of the Oxford Movement. It marked the first Tractarians profoundly, so much so that their earnestness was a byword and, although disconcerting to some, won them followers of the heart just as their *Tracts* seized the mind and the intellect of their readers.

Many followers of Keble, Froude and Newman and then, a little later, of Pusey, felt that the kind of devotion they aspired to should be expressed in a disciplined and methodical approach to worship. Evidences of this were not confined to the Tractarians themselves. John Keble's brother, Tom, was a member of an earlier group which became known as the Bisley School. Thomas Keble was vicar of Bisley and with friends such as Isaac Williams developed a pattern of disciplined prayer and public daily offices. They were thought by later Tractarians to be typical "Zs", rather strict and rigid, and they were certainly doubtful of Newman's charismatic influence, but they had that deep devotion and desire for holiness which was the mainspring of the whole Movement.

For Thomas Keble and his circle, the outward signs of faith were to be found primarily in disciplined, prayerful lives. Later developments, almost inevitably, added other, more material evidences of the sense of the numinous. Such things would become necessary aids to and expressions of worship, for humankind cannot focus for long on the eternal verities, at least at the beginning of the spiritual journey. Therefore, one almost inevitable outcome of John Keble's great challenge in the Assize Sermon of 1833 was that attempts would one day be made to provide a tangible beauty of holiness in the worship of the Church.

It is often asserted that one effect of the development of glorious ceremonial was to attract the poor and the underprivileged. This was certainly true, but it was not the whole story:

> The great "slum priests" such as Mackonochie, Lowder and Dolling certainly ministered to enormous congregations, though it could be argued that the crowds were attracted not so much by the advanced ceremonial as by the saintliness and charismatic personalities of the priests in question. They were successful because their lives were so self-denying and their enthusiasm so forceful.[23]

There is a most telling image which brings together early and later elements of the Oxford Movement, the Tractarian and the Ritualist, around the person of John Keble. At Keble's funeral in April 1866, Dean Church noted among the followers "a crowd of younger men who no doubt have as much right in him as we have, in their way—Mackonochie, Lowder and that sort".[24]

Church was well aware that, in some measure, these "younger men" viewed the older Tractarians as just as staid and inflexible as they, in their day, had viewed the men of Hackney. He suspected that they saw him and his peers as "rather dark people who don't grow beards and do other proper things".

The picture of Church and these young men assessing each other across Keble's grave brings to mind an assertion made by G. W. Herring that "the difference between the generations was a key to understanding the new Ritualism". This does not, however, mean that there was great dislocation, simply a difference to be understood. Contrast this sense of difference between the generations with the understanding of Henry Newland, incumbent of St Marychurch, Torquay from 1855 to 1860. In his *Brighton Lectures*, he said:

> I have no objection to tell you how it was I came to be a Tractarian. Not that I mean you to infer from this, that at any known time of my life I *began* to embrace the doctrines held by the Tractarians. Theirs are the doctrines of the English Church, and I cannot tell you how and when I learnt them. I always held them—they grew with me . . . there was never a time in my life that I had them not.[25]

Henry Newland had a sense of belonging both to the past and the present, a span which embraced men like Sikes, Isaac Williams, the Tractarians, and those who came later and did "grow beards and do other proper things".

When the Tractarian and the Ritualist were motivated by the same rooted desire for holiness and the offering of devotion, they existed in the same continuum. Both appealed to tradition as their authority; the Tractarian to the Church Fathers in order to renew and affirm Anglican doctrine and the Ritualist to less ancient traditions to renew the worship of the Church. Both were part of a revolution which appealed to antiquity for its validation: a revolution by tradition.

This phrase, which is so powerfully descriptive of the Oxford Movement, was coined by Michael Hill in his work on religious orders, where he uses the term specifically in relation to what he describes as the "religious virtuoso". It is a concept which answers, at least in part, the challenge often levelled at the champions of the Oxford Movement that they were obsessed with the past. They did indeed look to historical authority but only so that the Church of the present could be authentically Catholic and the Church of the future be true to its foundations:

> The religious virtuoso follows what he takes to be a pure and rigorous interpretation of normative obligations which already exist in a religious tradition. He is an extremist . . . Virtuosi take as their central point of reference a period in the early history of their religion which can be seen as particularly authentic. Their response (to a seeming decline) is to practice a style of religious observance which aims at reinstating the valued tradition. Although in the limited historical context in which this occurs the activities of the virtuosi may resemble innovation, they do not claim to be following a novel religious style . . . it is possible to speak of a revolution by tradition.[26]

Although in this passage Hill was writing about religious orders, he also explored the concept in relation to what he called "mass religion" or the religious life of the main body of church members. Thus, it can be seen how this applies not only to men like Keble and Newman, Froude and Pusey, but also to those who came before and to those who came later. It applies to those who were intent on recalling the Church of England to its ecclesiological and theological inheritance and to those who focussed on the renewal of worship as a means to that end; men such as John Purchas and then others who stood at the centre of the Ritualist storm, like Arthur Tooth of St James', Hatcham; men like C. J. Le Geyt of Stoke Newington, A. C. Le Geyt of Beer in Devon and Mamerto Gueritz of Colyton.

If a renewal of worship was to be an authentic outworking of the Movement, arising from the marriage of spirituality and doctrine already noted, there would be needed serious liturgical scholarship and study of the history of the English liturgy. Alongside this, a renewed understanding of the liturgy would provoke a rethinking of the setting in which it took place—the churches themselves. And if this renewal was to be for all worshippers and not just the pious few, it would lead to a new involvement of the congregation through music and hymnody. Thus, if the shared motive was devotion and the desire for holiness, the shared intention was a renewal of the English Church that would inflame everyone, whether they dwelt in slums or palaces, with the same motive and desire.

At the heart of the Oxford Movement there was a marriage of spirituality and theology, there was an appeal to the inheritance of faith, doctrine and tradition, and the whole was bound together by a conviction that if the Church were truly to be One, Holy, Catholic and Apostolic, then its members and its shepherds must also be thus.

This conviction endured and became the hallmark of authenticity as the Movement itself grew and developed from its Tractarian beginnings. Almost three decades after Keble's Assize Sermon, an example is to be found in the correspondence of Richard Meux Benson, the founder of the Society of St John the Evangelist (SSJE); the Cowley Fathers as they became known. The SSJE would not be formally established until the Mission House in Marston Street was built in 1868; however, by 1861 or 1862 the religious lifestyle which would ultimately mark the rest of Benson's ministry was already being developed, particularly in his leadership of the Brotherhood of the Holy Trinity. The Brotherhood began several years earlier as a small devotional society, but by 1861 it had grown and taken an almost monastic shape. It was in December 1861 that Benson received a letter from Robert Reynolds Winter, a great friend who was at work in the Delhi Mission. Winter wrote:

> it does appear of the most vital importance that the Clergy should continually stir up the Spiritual life within them if they would have any

influence over their people . . . as you say, this wants something more than multiplied offices, or a minute attention to Ritualism, however important both may be in their way.[27]

A hundred and twenty years later, among the many papers and addresses given to celebrate the 150th anniversary of the Assize Sermon, F. H. Borsch wrote:

> The responses of the Oxford leaders to the challenges of their times in terms of single-hearted discipline, sacrifice and devotion, their sense of God's sacramental presence and their . . . awareness that the authenticity of Christian faith had to be tested through serious commitment in the examples of their lives together with their call of a church to holiness— these deeply rooted themselves in many hearts and imaginations, sending up shoots to bear fruit in subsequent generations.[28]

Mamerto Gueritz was among those who, in the generation which followed the first Tractarians, became the bearer of such fruit. However, before we can see how that came to be we will need to understand his personal history. And so the tale begins.

Notes

[1] Flora Thompson, *Lark Rise to Candleford* (Oxford: Oxford University Press, 1945 and Harmondsworth: Penguin, 1973), p. 229.

[2] *Lark Rise* (1939), *Over to Candleford* (1941) and *Candleford Green* (1943) were published in one volume in 1945.

[3] Thompson, *Lark Rise*, p. 225. The complete picture is given in pp. 224–9.

[4] Thompson, *Lark Rise*, p. 225.

[5] Michael Yelton, *Outposts of the Faith* (Norwich: Canterbury Press, 2009).

[6] Part of this conversation is quoted in S. L. Ollard, *A Short History of the Oxford Movement* (London: Mowbray's, 1915), p. 13. The whole appears in *The Letters and Correspondence of J. H. Newman*, ed. Anne Mozely (London: Longmans Green & Co., 1891), vol. ii, appendix pp. 483–4.

[7]   Colyton is a town rather than a village because Henry VIII made it so by charter. Even so, with a population of around 2,000 people, it was a metropolis compared with Fordlow or Throwleigh.

[8]   Notes of a meeting with Vice Admiral E. Gueritz, Salisbury, January 1993. Author's papers.

[9]   George W. Herring, *The Oxford Movement in Practice* (Oxford: Oxford University Press, 2016).

[10] W. E. Heygate, *Ember Hours* (London: Masters, 1857), pp. x–xi.

[11] J. W. Burgon, *Lives of Twelve Good Men*, vol. 1 (London: John Murray, 1889), pp. 154–5.

[12] *The English Gentleman's Magazine of Literature, Religion, Science and Art* 1 (1865), p. 11.

[13] *The Guardian*, 20 December 1848.

[14] J. H. Newman, *The Via Media of the Anglican Church: Illustrated in Lectures, Letters, and Tracts written between 1830 and 1841*, vol. 1 (London: Longmans Green & Co., 1891), pp. 16–17.

[15] J. H. Newman, *Apologia Pro Vita Sua* (London: Longmans Green & Co., 1864), edition used: (London: Dent, 1942), p. 59.

[16] Ollard, *A Short History of the Oxford Movement*, p. 233. The illustration of "The Last Eucharist on the Feast of the Epiphany at Margaret Chapel in 1850". Also, G. Rowell, *The Vision Glorious* (Oxford: Oxford University Press, 1983). Illustrations following p. 120. The provenance of the illustration is given as a watercolour by Thomas S. Boys.

[17] From a lecture given to the Exeter Chapter of the Society of Catholic Priests in 2005. The author has since had cause to regret the comparison but allows it to stand as an apology for his earlier intemperance.

[18] E. B. Pusey to J. Watson, 30 October 1839. Pusey MSS (Pusey House). Also quoted in Geoffrey Rowell (ed.), *Tradition Renewed* (London: Darton, Longman & Todd, 1986), p. 40.

[19] John Keble, *Sermons, Occasional and Parochial* (Oxford: J Parker, 1868).

[20] D. C. Lathbury, *Correspondence on Church and Religion of William Ewart Gladstone*, vol. 1 (London: John Murray, 1910), p. 240.

[21] Rowell, *The Vision Glorious*, p. 14.

[22] E. B. Pusey, *Parochial and Cathedral Sermons* (London: Walter Smith, 1883), pp. 476–7.

[23] B. Palmer, *Reverend Rebels* (London: Darton, Longman & Todd, 1993), p. 2.

[24] M. C. Church, *The Life and Letters of Dean Church* (London: Macmillan, 1895), p. 173.

25   Henry Newland, *Three Lectures on Tractarianism*, 4th edn (London: J. Masters, 1855), p. 2.

26   M. Hill, *The Religious Order* (London: Heinemann, 1973), p. 3.

27   S. James, *The Cowley Fathers* (Norwich: Canterbury Press, 2019), p. 31.

28   F. H. Borsch, "Ye Shall be Holy", in Geoffrey Rowell (ed.), *Tradition Renewed* (London: Darton, Longman & Todd, 1986).

1

Antecedents, childhood and Mamerto Gueritz the scholar

The name Mamerto is thought by some to be derived from Mamers, the Oscan or Sabine name for the god Mars. The Mamertines were a company of mercenary warriors in the third century BC. Others discern a link with St Mamertus of Vienne in Gaul, who died around the year AD 475, but even that saint's name had to have an origin somewhere. In the absence of a more plausible theory then, we have a name which has its roots in the life of a warrior and yet is overlaid with hints of sanctity, which in this case is singularly apt.

"Scion of a line of warriors, it is small wonder that this Mamerto, this 'fiery Spaniard', had a distinctly combative quality in his priestly ministry. A keen awareness of his heritage, held from his earliest days, helped to form the nature and character of Mamerto Gueritz."[1] At a later date, this was to take him on a journey to visit the people and country of his grandfather's birth, and for many years he had his widowed mother to remind him of the life that she had shared with his father and to tell the stories of his grandfather. Therefore, in order to understand the personality of the priest who is at the heart of this exploration we must share that heritage inasmuch as we can.

The grandfather: Juan Gueritz

To begin, as it were, before the beginning, Mamerto Gueritz' grandfather Jean Guericke (as we shall call him for the moment) was born in the early 1770s in Louvain, which was in Wallonia, the south of what we now call Belgium. The name Guericke is attested principally by family lore, but that is not to be disregarded and gives us the name we shall use. Wallonia had been separated from the Protestant north for almost two centuries and, in spite of many political changes, had retained several characteristics that the north had not. The Dutch northern provinces had won independence from Spain, but in the 1579 Treaty of Arras the south and Wallonia had recognized the Spanish King Philip II.

The links between Belgium and Spain ran deep. Charles V of Spain, who died in 1556, well before the separation, was said to have been "surrounded by grasping Flemish favourites" and that "born a Fleming he grew up to be a Spaniard". However, by 1770 Wallonia was largely French speaking, with several local dialects, while the northerners used mainly Dutch, again with local dialects. The Dutch Protestants held sway in the north while the Walloons remained largely Catholic. There remained several important points of cohesion between Wallonia and Spain, and one such was the Royal Walloon Guard. Philip V of Spain had raised the regiment in 1702 believing, as did a number of other European monarchs, that a personal guard, recruited from outside the homeland and with absolute loyalty to the monarchy, would be a good insurance against the fickle tides of internal politics and the power of the aristocracy. In a letter to Louis XIV dated 18 May 1702, he wrote:

> I see clearly that so long as I do not have any troops of my own, and above all a regiment of Guards, I can get nothing done.[2]

By 1714, the Spanish Netherlands had been ceded to Austria, but recruitment to the Royal Walloon Guard, while not officially encouraged, still continued. Then, in 1794, the Netherlands, including Wallonia, were overrun and annexed by the First French Republic and open recruitment to the Guard ceased. We know that Jean Guericke left for Spain and the events of 1794 might have had some part to play in that decision, but there was another, more pressing, reason.

Until 1794, there was a recruitment office of the Royal Walloon Guard in Liège which, at its peak, supplied between 400 and 500 recruits each year of the strongest and tallest men available.[3] These recruits were originally intended to supply both officer material and the ordinary foot soldier, but that changed as the years passed and there were fewer and fewer Walloons in the rank and file. The officer *cuerpo* was intended by Philip V to be fully Walloon and drawn from the upper classes, but that aim had never been fully realized and by the first two decades of the nineteenth century, a time when the regiment was being reduced, a good many officers were second- or even third-generation members of the Guard; Walloons by descent but with mothers and wives drawn from among the Spanish gentry. Serving alongside them were Italian and Swiss officers who had migrated from other wars and other regiments.

So it was that when Jean Guericke found himself in some difficulty in Wallonia, there was an obvious and honourable direction of departure. It has been assumed, with justification, that he "fled" to Spain or that he "found refuge" there. That departure for Spain was made necessary because he had engaged in a duel which he won, with fatal consequences for his opponent.

If this was before the date of the French annexation, then Jean Guericke may well have been in mortal danger from a vengeful friend or relative of the dead opponent but not necessarily from the forces of law. It was not until 1841 that the government passed a law which attached specific penalties to duelling and to the wounding or killing of an opponent. As late as 1833, there was a duel fought in Luxembourg between the Baron de Tornaco and a Dutch captain. The captain was killed, but no judicial enquiry ensued. If the duellists were in military service, the penalty for the winner of a mortal duel was simply to be cashiered. In other words, he would lose rank, related income, and station in life.[4] It appears that the same was true of the professions, especially the legal profession. Guericke was a lawyer and, effectively, would have cashiered himself, and as a result be without a profession and station in life.

The second possibility is that this happened not long after 1794 and that Guericke's opponent had been French. If Guericke, a native Walloon, had killed a Frenchman in a duel so soon after the French had taken control of Wallonia, he would indeed have been in mortal danger. The recruitment office may have closed but the road to Spain was still open. So it was that Jean Guericke departed for Spain and there became Juan Gueritz, the name by which recorded history knows him.[5]

There is, of course, a certain romance attached to the story, but for the young Gueritz this was no easy option. Life as an officer in the Royal Walloon Guard did involve a certain amount of looking wonderful in a uniform, but it was far from being merely ceremonial. The regiment was there to provide the honour guard for the king in peacetime, but in battle they were expected to be the best and most feared of fighters, to be both the spearhead of assaults and also there to cover retreats. "First in and last out" was their *cri de guerre* in every engagement and the history of their battles shows that they lived up to their motto, often at great cost of life and, quite literally, limb.

In 1770, in order to house the Royal Guards fittingly but also to ensure they could the more easily attend the king in emergencies, two splendid barracks were constructed next to the Royal Palace at Aranjuez, just a little outside Madrid. On the right side of the road were the Royal Spanish Guard and on the left the Royal Walloon Guard. Both buildings were connected to the palace by tunnels.[6]

Having established himself in the Guard, Juan took a wife, the lady Antonia Fabre, with whom he had two sons, one of whom was Jose Francisco Gueritz, the father of Mamerto. Sadly, Jose's brother Manuel died an infant. Jose, who will prove essential to our story, was born at San Roque in Andalusia, near Gibraltar, in 1798. Meanwhile, Juan Gueritz was ascending the ladder of promotion and had achieved the rank of captain. In addition, he was made "Serjeant of the Brigade", a grade afforded to officers in the overall command structure.[7]

Ten years later, in 1808, the world had changed yet again. On 16 February, while ostensibly sending troops through Spain to reinforce the French forces which had occupied Portugal since the previous year, Napoleon Bonaparte seized the moment and began his invasion of Spain.

Although four battalions of the Walloon Guard were still active, two in Barcelona and two in Aragon, the invading French were in Madrid and the units of the Guard and other regiments stationed nearby were either disarmed or confined to barracks during emergencies. On 2 May an uprising of the citizens of Madrid was sparked by the news that the French were intending to remove the Spanish royal house, which is exactly what Napoleon did. He forced the abdication of Charles IV and his heir, Ferdinand VII, and then named his brother Joseph Bonaparte king of Spain. This served only to fan the fires of resistance and the insurrection spread throughout the city, with some Spanish troops breaking their confinement to support the people. They were dealt with mercilessly. The French commander ordered the Imperial Guard and his regiment of Mamelukes to charge the relatively unarmed civilians. The carnage was recorded by the artist Francisco Goya in his eponymous painting, "The Second of May 1808". The reprisals were dreadful. Any citizen arrested as a result of the affray and found to be carrying arms of any kind, including, for example, a carpenter's chisel or a leatherworker's awl, was to be shot. The following day hundreds were executed. This was just one of many uprisings which unsettled the French and prompted Napoleon to take action. In June, he sent 20,000 men towards Cadiz, where a French naval squadron was endangered. The Spanish forces moved to counter-attack, deployed at the battle of Bailén, and against all expectations, especially those of the French, it turned into a rout and the Spanish were victorious. It was a temporary reversal in the ebb and flow of war, but it gave hope to the Spanish forces that the defeat of Napoleon's armies was not an impossibility. In the battle at Bailén, Juan Gueritz died. First in, last out.

The father: Jose Gueritz

Juan's son, Jose Francisco, had already been enrolled as a child of the regiment, and being ten years old in 1808, he could be formally enlisted. In this way, the Walloon Guard supported the children of its dead, children who might otherwise have had few prospects. Two years later, at 12 years of age, Jose Francisco was in the field with his regiment and spent the next six years on active service. This was to include service with the Spanish forces supporting Wellington during the Peninsular campaign. He was 14 years old at the time of the siege of Badajoz and that of Ciudad Rodrigo, but the battle where the Spanish troops were most involved, and therefore probably Jose, was the siege of Burgos which ended in October 1812. As we shall see, this period of active service was of particular value in later life.

In 1814, Napoleon released the heir to the Spanish throne, and the Spanish Bourbon monarchy, in the person of Ferdinand VII, son of the deposed Charles IV, was restored by a French force. Ferdinand's first target was the constitution and the *Cortes*. The *Cadiz Cortes* was the first national assembly to claim sovereignty in Spain, and it had its initial meeting in September 1810. In March 1812, it promulgated the Constitution of Cadiz which enshrined civil liberties such as freedom of the press and free enterprise; it also provided for a constitutional monarchy and an electoral parliamentary system. Although the constitution affirmed the Roman Catholic Church as the only permitted religion, it took the radical step of banishing the Inquisition. The Roman Catholic hierarchy feared that the freedoms and liberalities espoused by the *Cortes* would lessen their own power, and fear begets enmity. This constitution was the first of its kind in the world, and Jose Gueritz was a committed Constitutionalist.

Had he been a wiser and stronger king, Ferdinand's return might have heralded the dawn of a more settled and prosperous period for the troubled country. It was not to be because Ferdinand would not consent to be a constitutional monarch; he wanted absolute rule. It was, after all, the Bourbon way. The Constitution had specifically banished the Inquisition; Ferdinand immediately recalled it and instead of building on what was in place he revoked the Constitution of Cadiz and the country was plunged into "an orgy of reaction". The supporters of Ferdinand, the absolutists, were aware of liberal opposition in any number of army units, the Royal Guards among them. An appreciable number of the officers of the Royal Walloon Guard had become identified with the *Cortes* and were open Constitutionalists, Jose Gueritz among them. As a way of mitigating the perceived threat the Guard was to be reformed. The flow of officers from Wallonia having long since dried up, on 1 June 1818 the Royal Walloon Guard was renamed as the Second Regiment of the Royal Guards of Infantry.[8]

The king, the absolutists and the Church, in an expedient political alliance, made every effort to foment hostility against the Constitutionalists. The Catholic Church discerned in the liberal policies of the Constitutionalists an anti-clericalism which echoed the French Revolution. The resulting antipathies permeated every level of society and were revealed in the life of the Regiment in the highly charged tension between some of the officers and the members of the rank and file.

The widespread and often violent suppression of political and personal freedoms had an entirely predictable outcome in the proliferation of secret societies within the army. A network of cells sprang up whose members shared a common, twofold purpose. They were there to protect the Constitutionalists who belonged to them, but the wider aim was the restoration of the civil liberties previously enjoyed. Their solution was the removal, preferably permanently, of Ferdinand VII. It seemed, briefly, that such a radical solution would not be necessary. Fortunes were again reversed in 1820 when "the flag of freedom was unfurled at Cadiz and Ferdinand, feeble as he was cruel, made abject surrender".[9]

This refers to the mutiny in Cadiz of a body of liberal officers who led their forces around Andalucía, seeking and gaining support from the various garrisons. They were demanding the restoration of the freedoms and civil liberties they had lost. Other units around the country joined them, and before it could become a full-blown revolution, Ferdinand agreed to their demands and signed the Constitution of 1812.

In 1820, a banquet was given to mark the restoration. As the youngest officer in the Regiment, Jose Gueritz was chosen to recite patriotic verses written for the occasion. This must have seemed to Jose and his companions to herald a new security for those of their convictions. Perhaps it was because of this assurance that he felt able to establish his future, and in 1821 Jose married Antonia Josepha Hermogenes Moxica Iperagheri, a lady of Madrid. However, the imagined security was an illusion, and those who had hoped that Ferdinand was in earnest in his acceptance of the Constitution were to have those hopes crushed.

By the time he was 25, Jose had already been decorated several times for bravery and outstanding service. The way in which such service was materially rewarded was to increase entitlements by the award of additional years of service. So it is that the last entry in his regimental record shows that, when he was aged 25, Jose was deemed to have 22 and a half years of service, with the grade of first serjeant and the rank of lieutenant,[10] but the world in which these honours had been won was falling apart around him. In spite of the capitulation of 1820, the absolutist supporters of Ferdinand were still in positions of power in the provinces, their followers were everywhere, and leading Constitutionalists were still being assassinated.

One incident stands out above others because had it fallen out differently this story would never have been told. On or near 2 July 1822, Jose Gueritz and a fellow officer and friend, Mamerto Landover, were returning to the barracks on horseback from a patrol when Landover was shot and killed by one of the soldiers.[11] Evidently the soldier had intended to kill Jose Gueritz, whose liberal convictions and Constitutionalist loyalties were well known, but shot Landover instead. This was not an isolated incident and other officers were similarly endangered. Aranjuez was no longer safe so later the same year Jose Gueritz left the Regiment which, although its name had changed, had been his home since infancy, and transferred to the Provincial Militia of Jativa in Valencia. At the same time, a corps was being raised for the protection of endangered Constitutionalists and Jose was given the rank of captain in the corps and made second in command.

The year 1823 saw two major events in the life of Jose Francisco Gueritz. On 31 January, in a convent in Jativa, a son was born whom he named Mamerto after his murdered friend, Landover. The second event was to affect the whole nation, and for the second time in as many years, the political world of Spain was turned on its head. A French army, under the Duc d'Angouleme, marched into Spain and, at the battle of Trocadero, put Ferdinand back in power on his own terms: absolute rule. The duke was given the princedom of Trocadero for this service to his cousin, but revolted by Ferdinand's abuse of power, he refused all honours offered him and returned to France. The acts of cruelty and reprisal which had so sickened the duke grew unchecked and the "orgy of reaction" rose to new heights.

Life was becoming increasingly perilous for the Constitutionalists, so the *Cortes* returned to Cadiz, where lay such strength as they still had, and Jose left Jativa and travelled to the far north of Spain to join the regiment of Navarra. He travelled alone,[12] the family records indicating that Antonia Josepha and the infant Mamerto returned to the convent in Jativa where Antonia had kept her confinement and had given birth to her son.[13] It would certainly have been the safest option. However, Jose's attempt to find a new life in a northern setting was doomed from the outset.

The absolutists were determined to eradicate all opposition, and the remodelling of the army was aimed specifically at removing any safe havens that were left to Jose and his fellow Constitutionalists. The Navarra regiment was disbanded, and the so-called rebels were identified and sentenced to life imprisonment. Jose Gueritz was among those so condemned. He and several companions immediately left their stations in Navarra and made their way to Barcelona, intending to escape through France, but Ferdinand's agents were close behind and no sooner had Jose arrived in Barcelona than he was recognized and, pursued by armed police, chased from one hiding place to another. At one point, he found refuge by hiding in a house and crouching in a corner under a window while musket balls smashed into the room and his pursuers shouted "Bring out the rebel" over and over again. One account tells us that "the cheerful feelings of hope and self-possession never forsook him".[14] Jose's history to that point makes such an assertion highly credible!

The pursuers gave up and went their way and later Jose, and several of his fellow officers, found temporary refuge with supporters of the liberal cause and were dispersed around the city. Here Antonia Josepha and the infant Mamerto joined him, but the danger was still very great. Stay or leave? Neither was a good option. An anonymous letter arrived. Several of his brother officers had been betrayed to the Spanish authorities and arrested. It would be only a matter of days, if not hours, before Jose suffered the same fate.

This episode is significant especially in attempting to understand the religious loyalties in the later life of Jose Gueritz. The account from which this is largely drawn records:

> His concealment could no longer be preserved from the intelligence of the absolute partisans whose antipathy was stimulated against the liberals by religious fanaticism as well as by religious hatred.[15]

The Constitution may have affirmed the place of the Church in relation to the State, but to the conservative Roman Catholic Church the liberalism being established in Spain was comparable with that of the French Revolution, which was anti-clerical and therefore to be feared and hated. Jose may have been Catholic by birth and by descent and probably, after the manner of a soldier, by personal practice, but that same Church was now, through the agency of the Inquisition and its manipulation of fanatics, persecuting him and those who in all conscience had followed a different path and aspired to greater political freedom. Whether or not she shared in those aspirations Antonia Josepha shared in the persecution and danger. Small wonder then that it might prove no great wrench for either of them to leave Catholic religion behind and eventually find a new expression for faith once they were established in England. What was Liberal in Spain might very well transmute into Protestant in England. We should also remember that religious affiliation, while not in every case an expression of personal commitment, was also, at this time, a means of defining a person's place and acceptance in English society.

But all of that lay in the future. Jose, having unsuccessfully tried a number of avenues of escape, resolved to hazard everything on one last gamble for life or death. He would go to the French general commanding Barcelona and hope that the general, being set apart from the frenzy of Spanish reprisal and bloodshed, would treat him as an officer and a gentleman. Amazingly, it worked! The general provided him with an order of banishment, effectively placing him under French protection. Local authorities had to allow, even facilitate, Jose's compliance with the order which specified where he should go and how long the journey should take. He was to take ship for Marseilles and, from there, travel through France to Calais, Dover and London. The journey was eventful, with various local officials not quite understanding that the order of banishment was effectively a one-way passport, but at the end of the journey Jose Francisco Gueritz found himself in London. There he also found many other Spanish political refugees and discovered that, because of his service with the Duke of Wellington in the battles of 1812, he was entitled to a pension according to his most recent rank of captain; this was £2.8.0 monthly. It was a great help, but it did not go far in London.

Jose had left Barcelona early in 1824, probably arriving in England later in the same year. As Jose set off for Marseilles from Barcelona, the city commander also provided that Antonia Josepha and the infant Mamerto should take a vessel bound for Alicante, where there were friends who would shelter them. Once established in London, Jose wrote asking for his wife and child to join him.

The son: Mamerto Gueritz

In 1826, the arrival of an orange boat in a tiny harbour in Devon would have been a welcome if relatively unremarkable event. It is remarkable for us for two reasons: the passengers and the landing place. If this small vessel, described many years later as a "Scotch fruit boat",[16] had collected Mamerto and his mother from Alicante, it would have had to sail through the Bay of Biscay and then the Straits of Gibraltar to reach them. It is more likely that they made their way to Cadiz, where they could wait for passage in relative safety. The little ship had no accommodation for passengers, so the captain and mate of the vessel gave their own berths to the women going into exile. The other adult female passenger was the wife of General Navarrete, whose family had seen distinguished service in the Americas. Yet another refugee was a child, the daughter of a member of the *Cortes*, who had been left behind as her parents fled the country. This was a vessel which carried in it the memory of loss and abandonment, hope in an uncertain future and, of course, oranges. The second matter of note; Antonia Josepha carried her infant son ashore in the then thriving harbour at Axmouth to lodge briefly at the Ship Inn. From the hill above the inn, just in sight along the valley running inland, was the unusual tower of Colyton Church, an octagon on a square Norman base. In years to come, Mamerto was to become very familiar with that sight. In fact, octagonal towers would feature twice in his story.

In 1826 the family was reunited in London and there, on 15 February 1828, a daughter, Adelina, was born. Evidently the family had not yet been much influenced by English society and religion. Adelina was baptized at the Roman Catholic Church of Our Lady of the Assumption and St Gregory in Golden Square. In his novel *Nicholas Nickleby*, Dickens describes the square as "a great

Colyton Parish Church seen from the north-west with
Axmouth a mile along the valley to the right.

haunt of foreigners". Significantly Adelina's godparents were Isidoro Navarette and his wife Asunción Ruiz, she who shared the journey from Spain with the infant Mamerto and Antonia Josepha, also to join her husband.

Shortly afterwards,

> Señor Gueritz with his family removed to Plymouth where with the best English Society, the necessities and even the comforts of life were to be procured in a more economical scale of expense than in the metropolis.[17]

Asunción Navarette, with her daughter Maria, also moved to Plymouth and lived not far from the Gueritz household. However, Jose, Antonia Josepha and their family began a remarkable process of integration into the life of their new community.

We have to note that the typescript account of that process, handed down through the family, cannot be received uncritically. There is an evident keenness to claim the Gueritz family as converts to Protestantism: "they embraced from conviction the protestant religion". However, when it is noted that a large part of the document is comprised of a letter from the vicar of Charles Church, Dr James Carne, to Jose Gueritz during a later illness, and if we recognize that not long afterwards Charles Church was described as distinctly Calvinistic, we may begin to have something of a perspective on the record. Be that as it may, Dr Carne was a good friend to his new parishioners, interesting himself in the education of the two children, Mamerto and Adelina. He also helped Jose to supplement his military pension by offering lessons in Spanish to the children of the local gentry and teaching French at a nearby school. Carne's support and their membership of his congregation also ensured that the family of exiles were received into local society. Indeed, we are told that Jose Gueritz, being a man of amiable and fascinating manners, became a particular favourite. However, we are not told how well this lifelong soldier and combatant adapted to his new life. What happened when the war horse scented battle will give us an indication.

In July 1830, the erstwhile Captain General of Catalonia, General Mina, left his exile in London and went to Bayonne to raise an army. The French government, now opposed to Ferdinand VII, was encouraging, even funding, a campaign. The dispersed supporters of the Spanish Constitution were called to arms and gathered at Bayonne. Jose joined them but before he left Plymouth a third child was conceived. When Edward Anselm Peregrine Gueritz was baptized on 5 April 1831 his father's place of residence was given simply as Spain.

The Bayonne uprising was a brave but quixotic venture, an ill-conceived and ill-fated plan. Soon enough the French reached an accord with Ferdinand and abandoned the Spanish Constitutionalists. Some were taken and killed or imprisoned. Others, after suffering much hardship from cold and exposure, made their way back to their places of exile.[18] The experience severely weakened the health of Jose Gueritz, but he was not yet seriously unwell when he finally returned to his family.

Jose's health deteriorated, and on 23 June 1832 Dr Carne wrote a long and affectionate letter to him, offering prayers for his recovery and urging him to "seek to enjoy more of the spirit and the power of vital religion. Be ever living in the heartfelt enjoyment of the truths you have embraced."

Only six weeks later, James Carne died in the cholera epidemic in Plymouth. In the meantime, Jose Gueritz' illness had developed into pulmonary consumption. Exactly four months after the death of his friend, Jose succumbed to the sickness which had been growing in him since Bayonne, and he was buried next to James Carne in the graveyard of Charles Church. The gravestone has an added poignancy:

> Sacred to the Memory of
> Jose Gueritz
> Of the Second Royal Guard of Spain
> Captain in the Service of the Constitution,
> Who died December 12th 1832, aged 34 years.
> Also
> Edward A.P. Gueritz his son, who died 5th
> November 1832 aged 20 months.

Such heartbreak for Antonia; the loss of a child, widowed at 31 and needing to provide for the young Mamerto, almost ten years old, and Adelina, who was just five. There is a sense of history repeating itself in that Jose had endured the same experience of losing his father at exactly the same age. The military pension awarded to Jose continued, but for a widow was reduced from £2.8.0 per month to just £2. This, especially given the loss of income from Jose's teaching work, was not sufficient to give the children anything other than the most basic opportunities of life. However, just before Jose died, several close friends, fearing the outcome of his illness, had promised him that his family would be cared for. It seems the promises were well kept. As the Walloon Guard had cared for Jose in his childhood, so the friends in Plymouth did the same for Antonia, Mamerto and Adelina.

Mamerto Gueritz—the scholar

Jose Gueritz had taught French in the Classical, Mathematical and Commercial School run by Mr R. W. Needham in Hampton House in Plymouth. Richard William Needham was later ordained and, before leaving Plymouth for Australia, served for a time as perpetual curate of St Paul's, Dunford Street. At his school, Mamerto was able to continue his education without any financial burden on the family. Adelina too was given schooling which equipped her to take her place later as a governess or private tutor. At 13, Mamerto was apprenticed to a friend of his father, the wine merchant W. H. Hawker of Plymouth. The apprenticeship lasted seven years, after which he continued in Hawker's employ for a while. Also, during this period Mamerto had been teaching voluntarily in a Sunday school for the poor children of the parish, an activity in which he thrived.

There are connections here to the earlier history of Charles Church which help us to understand the setting in which Mamerto and Adelina found themselves and the sources of their support. James Carne's immediate predecessor at Charles Church was the Revd Robert Hawker. Robert Hawker and his wife had eight children and many grandchildren, the most famous of whom was R. S. Hawker of Morwenstow. It would have been a happy coincidence to be able to report that W. H. Hawker, the wine merchant to whom Mamerto was apprenticed, was also one of those grandchildren, but there were several quite distinct Hawker families in Plymouth at that time, and W. H. Hawker was from another branch altogether.

The Sunday school was started by Robert Hawker in 1787. He quite literally gathered poor children from the streets and taught them literacy from the Bible.

It was one of the first such schools in the country and, when the pupils numbered over 300, it warranted and gained a permanent building. It was in that building, some 50 years later, that Mamerto Gueritz began to teach and to find a vocation. Clearly at this stage Mamerto was not educationally equipped for ordination, and a university degree was quite beyond his financial means. His grandson, Ernest Mortimer, describes him as having been "absolutely poor at the time".[19] Once more the friends of the family came to their aid. Accounts vary as to who was involved and how the aid was given. The certainties are that Mamerto was supported by a Bristol-based "Protestant Society for helping candidates for Holy Orders"[20] and that this was specifically influenced by the Revd Dr Meshach Seaman, by then incumbent of St James', Colchester but who had previously been at Charles Chapel, the daughter church, from 1834. He was supported in this by the Revd Septimus Courtnay, who had moved from Charles Chapel to Charles Church following the death of James Carne. Both of these eminent clergy were closely acquainted with the circumstances of the Gueritz family. The cost of a university education was thus defrayed, but there was a great deal of preparation needed before Mamerto was academically ready for matriculation and that too would incur a cost. Mamerto undertook what we might now call a crammer course at Hatherleigh for a year under the tutelage of the Revd R. S. Feild. Before he went to Hatherleigh in 1831, Field had spent some years as headmaster of Westbury College, having graduated from Worcester College, Oxford. He was, therefore, both an educationalist and a parish priest; an ideal combination for the task of preparing Mamerto for university. We may infer from his appointment that both the clergy of Charles Church and the trustees of the "Protestant Society" found Field to be acceptable both in academic terms and in his churchmanship. Certainly, Hatherleigh parish had a long tradition of Evangelicalism which was still in evidence throughout the twentieth century.

To this point, Mamerto Gueritz' experience of the Church of England had been exclusively Protestant or what would also come to be called Low Church or Evangelical. The clergy with whom he had most contact were all of that tradition. There were later claims that he had been "brought up an anti-catholic by the universally respected John Hatchard, vicar, of St. Andrew's Plymouth", a claim that Mamerto robustly refuted:

I never lived in his parish, nor attended his church, nor was I even known by sight to him.[21]

This notwithstanding, Mamerto Gueritz' church life to the point of his sensing a vocation to priestly ministry was clearly and unequivocally Anglican and Protestant. However, like most churchgoers in every age, he would only have known what he had experienced and believed that what he knew was normal for the Church of England. The fact that there were other traditions in the Church of England and other concepts of Christianity were to impact upon him soon enough.

At Michaelmas 1845, aged 22, Mamerto Gueritz went up to Oxford. It is a far cry indeed from the undergraduate passing through the archway of St Edmund Hall for the first time, to the Anglo-Catholic and Ritualist who became vicar of Colyton. However, it would not have taken long for Mamerto to become aware of the tumult then raging in the university and to have taken some note of the secession of John Henry Newman to Rome. That took place within days of Mamerto's arrival in Oxford. Those were dark days for the leaders of the Oxford Movement. Most of the heads of the colleges and halls had joined in a morally dubious alliance to eradicate Tractarianism. As a result, Dr Pusey had already been suspended from his roles in the university. The Prime Minister, Robert Peel, had declared his opposition to any of the Oxford Party, as he called it, gaining any preferment. However, during Mamerto's first term the doings of the Tractarians seemed to have concerned him little and his memories of those early days focussed most clearly on the nature of life at the hall. There were, however, those in St Edmund Hall who would have been outraged by and at the same time rejoiced in Newman's secession to Rome, the vice principal among them:

The Chapel altar was quite bare and all the services very plain indeed as the Vice-Principal, Mr. Hill, was a rigid Calvinist.[22]

The usual length of one of John Hill's sermons was around two and three-quarters hours, at the end of which it was his custom to ask for a text to support his argument. After a sermon of some length on the doctrine of predestination, he made his customary request for biblical quotations in confirmation of his argument. Instead of this he received an unaccustomed rebuttal from a young man who called out, "who will have all men to be saved and come to the knowledge of the truth."[23]

Evidently the speaker deemed this text to be the scriptural antithesis of Hill's teaching. That outspoken youngster was Frederick George Lee, who came to play an important if idiosyncratic part in the unfolding of the Catholic Revival and whose activities certainly impacted on Gueritz in later years. If this encounter took place while Mamerto was himself an undergraduate, then Lee was not yet a student at St Edmund Hall: Lee matriculated in 1851, well after Gueritz had left. E. C. Mortimer, reporting his grandfather's words verbatim, refers to him as an "enterprising youth", which suggests that he was younger than the undergraduates attending the sermon. Lee's home was in Thame, and access to Oxford and his friends there was comparatively easy and frequently exercised. His father, the vicar of Thame, was a Tractarian of some note, and there were frequent pulpit exchanges between Thame and the Oxford churches and college chapels. It is an entertaining possibility that the vicar of Thame might have been preaching at one service in Oxford while his already combative son was attending another. This precocious outburst fits well with the character that later emerged.[24] At this stage, however, the young Gueritz considered the outburst an "unprecedented piece of rudeness". In his *Memoirs*, Lee also recalled his days as a student. That memory has particular relevance to our understanding of Mamerto's time at St Edmund Hall:

> A few of the men at St. Edmund Hall were said to have been placed there by some so-called Evangelical society, in order to provide suitable ministers for certain Simeonite benefices. The Rev John Hill an excellent and kind partisan, was said to manage the business ... Many of them were lost to their patrons by reason of the persistent aggression of adversaries and the air of the University: some afterwards became open and fierce Tractarians; others, again, wandered off into the dark and dreary desert of mere deism.[25]

This is, at least in part, such an accurate description of the experience of Mamerto Gueritz that it is possible to believe that he was among those in Lee's mind as he was writing. Lee was, both then and later, among those whom Newman earlier accused of cutting across the line of the Tractarians and trying to push the Movement in their own direction. Also among the students who Mamerto remembered was T. W. Mossman, later to play a part with Lee in working towards reuniting the Church of England and the Church of Rome and in the formation of the Order of Corporate Reunion.

Apart from these, peripheral at the time, connections, a friend from Plymouth, J. C. K. Saunders, was also up at St Edmund Hall at the same time. Gueritz and he had been boyhood friends in Plymouth and the memory of his quiet, steady presence stayed with Mamerto lifelong. Such a friendship would have been invaluable in an environment where he was rubbing shoulders with young men from the aristocracy and those who had been through public schools or had private tutors; all with far more advantages than he. Mamerto seems simply to have got on with his studies and quietly enjoyed the life of the hall. Once when he was disturbed at his studies by carousers outside his rooms, he dispersed them by pouring water over their heads from his window and went back to his studies. He also took advantage of other opportunities and heard some of the great preachers of his day:

> The men seem to have been very fond of sermons and always went to hear the "Varsity Sermon" at St Marys … My grandfather particularly remembers a sermon delivered there (Holywell) by Bishop Wilberforce. Also, he had the keen pleasure of hearing Dr. Pusey, in his first sermon after his suspension, resume his teaching just where he had left off.[26]

This was a sermon preached on 1 February 1846 on "The Entire Absolution of the Penitent". At the time, this was just as contentious as the sermon which was the cause of Pusey's suspension, "The Holy Eucharist, a Comfort to the Penitent", preached in 1843. Pusey's restriction was lifted just a term after Mamerto Gueritz arrived in Oxford.

Having been nurtured in the Calvinist ethos of Charles Church, Plymouth, for the young Gueritz to find keen pleasure in the preaching of Pusey either some change had already taken place, or both Gueritz and his grandson were reading back into his early days in Oxford convictions that he would only later make his own. As we have noted, that process of reading back has been the cause of considerable distortion in the history of the Oxford Movement. Whenever it began, the change that swept over Mamerto Gueritz took hold, not only in the hearing of sermons, although they would have had considerable influence, but most profoundly in the silence of St Edmund Hall library. It was here that Mamerto began to discover the centrality, for him, of "One Holy Catholic and Apostolic Church", and the doctrine of baptismal regeneration:

> About 1847 a change came over the spirit of the Hall which, from his words, one would judge my Grandfather to have started. In the library one day he discovered Bishop Sumner's *Apostolical Preaching* which he read with very great interest as this was the first occasion on which it occurred to him that St Paul addressed *all* the baptized as regenerate. He passed the book on to his friends, including Morsman (sic) Page and others to whom the occasion was absolutely the beginning of Catholic learning.[27]

For Gueritz at this stage Catholic learning did not include asceticism or ritual. The latter did not yet form part of his experience and as for asceticism at St Edmund Hall, as he later recalled, "Fish was only given on Good Fridays and then it was served in *addition* to the ordinary dinner."

Gueritz began his exploration of the great structure of Catholic belief with the doctrine of baptismal regeneration. This was precisely the point at issue in the battle waged by Bishop Henry Phillpotts of Exeter in the Gorham controversy, although that was not finally adjudged until March 1850. This, quite naturally, led to a close identification by Gueritz with the trials of his bishop and called to the fore the formidable loyalty of which he was capable. It was in his blood! It also may serve to help us understand the reputation he was to gain, especially during a series of troubleshooting curacies, of having Henry Phillpotts' particular trust. It is even more interesting to note that baptismal regeneration, or the assumed lack of it, would be one element in a legal battle in which Gueritz himself would be embroiled years later.

Another experience at Oxford which was to shape Mamerto's later ministry came one Easter vacation when he had stayed up to carry on with his studies. During Mattins at St Peter's, he heard the service intoned for the first time. To those who have never known any other, this may seem trivial, but it was an entirely new experience for him. To a lover of music and song, and Gueritz had a fine tenor voice, this brought the liturgy even more fully alive. The incumbent of St Peter's at the time was Edmund Hobhouse, who was, a decade or so later, to become Bishop of Nelson diocese in New Zealand. Mamerto remembered the kindness shown him by Hobhouse for the rest of his life.

While music had opened the door to liturgical beauty and study had begun the process of discovering Catholic learning, work had still to go on. Mamerto studied hard, too hard, and as his grandson recalled:

> It was here (the Common Room) during a lecture that my Grandfather suddenly fainted and was good for no work for a long time afterwards. Not, that is, until he was well out of his Oxford career.[28]

Although overwork was clearly the primary and stated cause of this breakdown, it would be entirely likely that Mamerto's personal changes in theological understanding and conviction created a serious conflict of loyalties. He was consciously departing from the Calvinistic Protestantism of his Plymouth supporters and of the Evangelical Society which had funded him, a faith which his father seemed wholly to have embraced. He was launched on a voyage into what he was beginning to see as universal truth as opposed to sectarian interpretation and that, inevitably, was leading him away from his Calvinist roots. It seems that this initial experience of tension and breakdown left behind a vulnerability which was to show itself in later, repeated illnesses; not that it ever prevented Mamerto from entering into conflict when his convictions or loyalties bade him do so, but there would be times when he needed to step aside and rest awhile. Unable to sit examinations, he had to be content with a pass degree which deprived him of the "Hons" after his BA.

Very much later V. S. S. Coles was to write of him:

> The Catholic Revival has never been at a lower ebb than in the years following Newman's departure, but it was in the three first of these years that the young Spaniard, who had every reason to love English Protestantism, learned that the English Church was, after all, Catholic and emerged as a zealous servant of the revival.[29]

Here Stuckey Coles is allowing his memories of Gueritz as a curate in Barrington, where Coles was the son of the parson, and also later memories of Devon and London, to colour his understanding of Mamerto Gueritz as he left Oxford for ordination. Although he did indeed later emerge as a zealous servant of the revival and one who bore all the hallmarks of an Anglo-Catholic priest, all that can be rightly said at this juncture is that Gueritz left St Edmund Hall convinced of the truth of the teaching of the Tractarians and aspiring to put those truths into practice in his ministry. Moreover, that ministry would be shaped by a profound love for and growing awareness of church music and the beauty of holiness that could be expressed in the liturgy of the Church. It was a process that would continue through several curacies and would finally come fully to fruition when Mamerto Gueritz returned close to the place where he was first carried onto English soil; to Colyton.

Notes

[1]   From a lecture given by the author to the Exeter Chapter of the Society of Catholic Priests in 2005.

[2]   Philip Mansel, *Pillars of Monarchy: An Outline of the Political and Social History of Royal Guards, 1400–1984* (London: Quartet Books, 1984), p. 102.

[3]   The argument against "covert" recruitment after 1794 is that it would mean that candidates would be much more likely to be those who had fallen foul of the law in various ways and thus not seen as an entirely welcome presence in Spain. The argument for such recruitment is that candidates were more likely to be from among those opposed to the French occupation of Wallonia and whose loyalty to Spain in the conflicts with France would be assured.

[4]   John Gideon Millingen, *The History of Duelling*, vol. 1 (London: Bentley, 1841), pp. 368ff. The law of 1841 was only repealed in 2018.

[5]   The name "Jean Guericke" is a reading back from the name we have. Jean would be the French equivalent of Juan, and Guericke or Guerick is the closest we have been able to get in contemporary names. For example, Otto von Guericke was a German scientist, and there was a Guerick family living at this period and earlier in France in the Moselle region. Much earlier, in 1642, there was a M. de Gueritz who was Aide de

Camp général to Maréchal de Guebrian. De Gueritz presented to the king the flags which de Guebrian had carried from the enemy. *Biblioteque Historique de la France avec notes Critiques et Historiques Édition revue, Corrigée et Augmentée par fue Feuret de Fontette*, vol. 4 (Paris: Herrisant, 1775), p. 56. Any links to Wallonie and the late eighteenth century remain to be unearthed.

[6] Today the barracks are sadly in a state of complete ruin. A report from the *Lista Roja Del Patrimonio* states that they are, "In a state of complete abandonment and total ruin. They are in grave decay and on the way to complete ruin. Subject to exploitation and vandalism."

[7] The term "serjeant" here does not equate to our contemporary rank of sergeant. In this context, it is used in the way in which the title would have been afforded at court. For example, "serjeant of the larder" would simply have meant the person given royal authority to have charge in the larder.

[8] As the inscription on Jose Gueritz' gravestone reveals: "Jose Gueritz, of the Second Royal Guard of Spain, Captain in the service of the Constitution."

[9] Ms. a/c G2 (see primary sources).

[10] Ms. a/c G2.

[11] Two sources are used in this account. Ms. a/c G2 (see primary sources), from which the name Landover is taken, and Mansel, *Pillars of Monarchy*, p. 105. In the latter, Mamerto Landover is identified as Lt Colonel Landabaru; Mansel does not give his source. The Spanish mingling of the letters "b" and "v" gives Landavar(u). A third spelling "Landauer" is equally valid with "v" and "u" interchanged.

[12] Notes of an interview with Rear Admiral E. Gueritz, 1992 (see primary sources).

[13] V. S. S. Coles, Obituary of Mamerto Gueritz, *Church Times*, 16 February 1912.

[14] Ms. a/c G1 (see primary sources).

[15] Ms. a/c G1.

[16] V. S. S. Coles, Obituary of Mamerto Gueritz, *Church Times*, 16 February 1912.

[17] Ms. a/c G1 (see primary sources).

[18] Lluis Barbé, *Francis Ysidro Edgeworth: A Portrait with Family and Friends*, tr. M. C. Black (Cheltenham: Edward Elgar Publishing, 2010).

[19] H. E. J. Cowdrey, "St Edmund Hall in the 1840s", an article on a letter, reprinted in full in the magazine, from E. C. Mortimer, a grandson of Mamerto Gueritz, to S. L. Ollard, vice principal 1903–13, *St Edmund Hall Magazine* 1987–8 (The letter is referred to here as E.C.M. Ms.). See Appendix 1.

[20] V. S. S. Coles, Obituary of Mamerto Gueritz, *Church Times*, 16 February 1912.

21   *Western Times*, 17 September 1880 and 24 September 1880.

22   *St Edmund Hall Magazine.*

23   *St Edmund Hall Magazine.* Cf 1 Timothy 2:4.

24   This disparity in dates requires further comment. Gueritz graduated in 1848. Lee
     did not matriculate until 1851. The memories which the letter of E. C. Mortimer (cit.
     supra) records were gleaned from his grandfather under trying circumstances when
     Mamerto Gueritz was 86. It was in a roomful of people who were all creating a lot of
     distractions. However, the incident itself was so clearly remembered that it is unlikely
     to have been imagined. It is possible that memories at that distance became conflated,
     but there are two clear alternatives. The first is that Lee was visiting the hall socially
     before he matriculated. This interruption took place during a sermon not a lecture,
     and several of Gueritz' contemporaries were also friends of Lee. The second is that
     this took place during a visit to his old college by Gueritz after his curacy at Shepton
     and Barrington.

25   This quotation is taken from the unfinished manuscript *Memoirs* begun by F. G. Lee and,
     in turn, quoted by H. R. T. Brandreth, *Dr Lee of Lambeth* (London: SPCK, 1951), p. 5.

26   *St Edmund Hall Magazine.*

27   *St Edmund Hall Magazine.*

28   *St Edmund Hall Magazine.*

29   V. S. S. Coles, Obituary of Mamerto Gueritz, *Church Times*, 16 February 1912.

2

Shepton Beauchamp and Barrington:
Ordination and first curacy

1848–50

Mamerto Gueritz was ordained deacon in Wells Cathedral on 17 December 1848, evidently having recovered sufficiently from his breakdown in the early part of the year. In his case, ordination was not quite as straightforward as for most of his contemporaries, because there were legal obstacles to be overcome. Mamerto's parentage and nationality of birth raised questions about his legal capacity to take the canonical oaths. There was a dispensation given which required him to abjure any allegiance to either the Pope or the King of Spain.[1] It was at this point also that Mamerto met George Anthony Denison, the examining chaplain to Bishop Bagot of Bath and Wells, who would become a major figure in the battles that were still to come, and would himself be tried for doctrinal error. That storm had yet to break. Whatever his personal allegiances within the Church of England were at the moment of ordination, Mamerto Gueritz was entering the diaconate of a Church in turmoil.

In the previous two decades, the Church of England had undergone considerable changes, not only due to the influences brought to bear by the Tractarians but just as profoundly in its relationship with the State. Indeed, the changes in that relationship may be said to be one of the motive forces for what became the Oxford Movement and most certainly for the Assize Sermon of 1833. For generations, the old High Churchmen and the Non-Jurors before and alongside them had maintained an understanding of the Church-State relationship which included a concept of sacral monarchy as the pivot between religion and government. The concept itself flexed and changed as the tides of political and religious feeling

Mamerto Gueritz—Ordination photograph 1848

ebbed and flowed, but in some form it remained. This, in turn, gave validity to an understanding of Church and State as being in an interdependent partnership. These men looked back to Charles I, the martyr king, as their ideal. Certainly, the first Tractarians shared this view in some measure, for it secured the Church against the threat of the Erastian or Hobbesian heresy in which the civil authority has the power to order the life of the Church in all its aspects. Their confidence in this view had faltered under the first two Georges, and indeed before that, but on the accession of George III in 1760, it seemed possible for there to be a renewed authenticity in the relationship. George III was the first monarch of the house of Hanover to be an unqualified adherent of the Church of England. However, under George IV and William IV, successive Acts of Parliament had eroded the basis of this so-called interdependent partnership sufficiently for John Keble to preach the 1833 Assize Sermon under the title "National Apostasy".

The first major step in this erosion of the relationship at the time passed almost uncontested. The 1828 repeal of the Corporation Act of 1661 and the Test Acts of 1673 and 1678 meant that many restrictions on those who could hold public office were lifted. Prior to this, every holder of public office was necessarily a communicant member of the Church of England. That repeal, incidentally and ironically, also removed the requirement on the part of would-be office holders to deny transubstantiation, the invocation of saints and the sacrament of the mass. Thus, the long-held assumption that the relationship between Church and Parliament was that of two bodies made up of members drawn from the same ecclesial family was made untenable. This was followed by the Catholic Relief Act of 1829 and then the Reform Bill which again changed the face of the House of Commons. To many the Church as they had known it seemed doomed and at the mercy of nonconformists and Catholics. To add to the growing sense of outrage at government interference in matters ecclesiastical in 1833, there was a Bill before the House of Lords to reduce the Irish bishoprics by half. This Bill proposed that the income of the ten suppressed sees be appropriated to pay the Irish Church rate or the "cess" as it was known. The Bill passed within weeks of Keble's sermon.

Fifteen years later, in 1848, the feared collapse of the Church under the weight of civil authority had not happened, but all was not quiet on the western front, or rather, in the west of England. Just as Gueritz was moving towards ordination, Bishop Henry Phillpotts of Exeter was entering the lists in defence of Anglican doctrine, refusing to institute George Cornelius Gorham to the living of Bramford Speke. Gorham did not believe in and would not teach baptismal regeneration. As we have seen, in exploring the thought world of the Tractarians and in his own studies, Mamerto Gueritz had already discovered this teaching and moreover had learned much of the dangers which threatened the Church he was about to serve. He had become convinced that he would best serve that Church by defending "Church Principles", the principles elucidated by the *Tract* writers and established in the Book of Common Prayer.

As our attention moves from the national arena to Wells Cathedral and Shepton Beauchamp, we recall that the same Book of Common Prayer requires that, at the morning and evening office, prayer is made for "Bishops, Curates and all congregations committed to their charge".

In its original and most authentic sense, the term "curate" applies to any priest who has the cure or care of souls in a parish. Such a priest may also be termed "vicar" or "rector" or "priest-in-charge". In later usage, the title has been afforded to a priest who is in a subordinate role; one who is assisting the incumbent of a parish and is in the early stages of ministry, assimilating the basic skills required of a *pastor in parochia*. In Trollopian terms, he would be termed a member of the "inferior clergy". A curate in his first appointment was said to be "serving his title".

Gueritz served his title with the rector of Shepton Beauchamp and Barrington, the Revd James Coles. This, like so many first curacies, was to be one of the most formative experiences of Mamerto's life as a priest, and the friendships forged in this period were to last lifelong. When Gueritz went to Shepton late in 1848, the rector, James Coles, had been incumbent for 12 years and the young Vincent Stuckey Stratton Coles was just three years and a few months old. Stuckey, as he was affectionately known, was to become a lifelong friend and supporter of Mamerto. In later life, Stuckey was to become a byword for loyalty and devotion to his friends, but there was more than common friendship underlying this particular relationship which extended beyond Mamerto himself to all his family.

Soon after Mamerto's arrival in Barrington, his mother and Adelina came to live with him. It was not long before Adelina began work as tutor to the children of James and Eliza Coles, Stuckey among them.

Just five months after his curacy began, Mamerto was married to Anne Derby Lawrence of Plymouth. The ceremony took place on 29 May 1849 in Charles Church, where he had grown up and where Anne was still a parishioner.[2] They returned to the curate's house at Shepton and Barrington where, for the time being, Adelina was continuing her work as a governess at the rectory.

The influence of the "holder of the title", or the training incumbent, on a newly ordained curate is often profound. We are told that James Coles' "ideal of the priestly life and duty must have been far in advance of that of the country parson of his day, and in later life he was greatly influenced by the Tractarians".[3]

There had been 12 years for Coles' ideal of the priestly life to have impacted on the people of Shepton Beauchamp and Barrington; 12 years since Coles became incumbent and before Mamerto Gueritz arrived on the scene. Near the beginning of his incumbency, Coles had increased the frequency of Holy Communion services and ensured that young confirmands were encouraged to become regular communicants as soon as they were able. This may not seem very radical, but if we compare it with the contemporary church life of, for example, Colyton over the border in Devon, where Holy Communion was only celebrated a few times

Barrington Church, Somerset, with its distinctive octagonal tower

each year, Shepton was comparatively Eucharistic. As the years passed, it became more so. Soon there were both early and later celebrations of Holy Communion and, as Stuckey later wrote of his father:

> He taught the blessing of Holy Communion to the sick and the dying, so that very few grown-up people died without it.[4]

This teaching of the value of the *Viaticum* was but a part of the increased teaching of what Coles' son Stuckey was later to call "The Faith", but at the time and in context it was simply what the first Tractarians had advocated, namely the practical and pastoral application of the doctrines and practices that could be interpreted from the Book of Common Prayer. Mattins was said daily at ten o'clock, and there was a sermon each Wednesday evening, for which Coles had been careful to gain episcopal approval. Hymns became a regular part of the services, which may seem unremarkable now but then was seriously innovative. Coles ceased wearing the black gown for preaching, thinking it as much a symbol of Protestantism as the surplice had become the mark of the Puseyite. These changes in the liturgy were further marked by the institution of a Harvest Thanksgiving procession, during which a hymn was sung. One local farmer wrote on his hymn sheet:

> I am of the opinion that things are being brought into our Harvest Festival which are only acceptable to those who hold High Church views.[5]

The initial disquiet of the farmer, John Phelps, at this encroachment of Tractarianism notwithstanding, his comments do have ramifications for our understanding of the impact that rural Tractarians would have on events which had hitherto been on the margins of Church life and often dismissed as mere folk religion. Here was an early example of the development of a liturgy for Harvest Thanksgiving services. Phelps was complaining about the alteration—almost hijacking—of an existing festival. It seems likely that this was in the period 1840 to 1845. This is very close to the time in 1843 when Hawker of Morwenstow is credited for having introduced the first Harvest Festival into a church service. It matters little who was first. This was an idea whose time had come. This idea was not limited to Harvest Festivals, but it stands revealed in the work of Tractarians like Hawker and Coles, on the one hand holding fast to Church principles and on the other reaching out to folk whose faith was expressed in the rhythm of their daily lives.[6]

An occurrence of certainly more import to the curate and his wife than the question of who was first with Harvest Festivals was the arrival in 1850 of Mamerto George Gueritz, the first child of Mamerto and Anne.

The birth of the firstborn brings instant domestic changes, but while Mamerto was in his first curacy, the process of liturgical change was still moderate and slow-moving. It was not until the restoration of Shepton Church in 1863–4 that Stuckey claimed for it "many marks of the revival", by which time Mamerto Gueritz had completed several other curacies and was securely in his first and only benefice. However, when we later reflect on his ministry in Colyton it will be well to have this image of the 1863 liturgy at Shepton Beauchamp in mind.

There was a choral celebration of Holy Communion on the day of reopening with a choir robed in cassocks and surplices. There was a festal altar frontal, and indeed frontals for other seasons. Standard lights were on the altar and a new chalice had been purchased to replace the common cup. However, it was the music that was a major part of Mamerto Gueritz' legacy to the parish, even though he was some years removed. The music was plainsong, and it should be recalled that this was taking place when a number of bishops had made public their disapproval of choirs in surplices:

> The chief outward mark left by Mr. Gueritz on the parishes where his ministry began was the beginning of Church music. He had a most beautiful tenor voice, and a true musical gift. He taught the Barrington people to sing and chant with no accompaniment and created in the village a delightful fellowship which centred in the choir.[7]

This mirrors, with considerable accuracy, the kind of liturgy that Mamerto later exercised in Penzance and then established in Colyton. In the meantime, while Mamerto was growing into his priestly identity and teaching the folk to sing, Adelina was quietly exercising her own influence and herself being shaped in return. "The hand that rocks the cradle . . . " Eliza Coles, the rector's wife, was a force to be reckoned with. She was very much attracted to the Tractarian movement which she encountered and then nurtured by her reading of *The Christian Year*, a book of poetry written by John Keble. The volume has been called "Keble's greatest contribution to the Oxford Movement and to English literature",[8] which is a remarkable claim considering that Newman felt Keble's Assize Sermon to be the start of it all. Nevertheless, it is a justifiable claim. If one book can be said to have placed Tractarian ideals into the heart of the nation—the heart as well as the head—*The Christian Year* is a serious contender for that distinction.

Adelina was sharing the Coles family's domestic and working life, and it appears that the relationship between the two households, Coles and Gueritz, was intimate and mutually formative. The effect of all this on Stuckey Coles will be explored elsewhere in greater detail than is appropriate at this point in the story,[9] but one anecdote told of him is apposite. Stuckey's sister recalled:

> He always took a great interest in religious matters . . . as a very small boy
> he said he wished to be ordained, and used to induce the servants to listen
> to his sermons.[10]

As a member of the household, whether as visiting tutor or resident governess, it would have been hard for Adelina to escape hearing the infant Stuckey expound the faith which was to become his life's work. Later generations of Oxford undergraduates would, in their turn, find Stuckey Coles' exposition of the faith inescapable.

In this first curacy, Mamerto Gueritz developed skills and attitudes which were to become the hallmarks of his ministry. His musical capacities, so effective especially in Barrington, were soon to be in demand well beyond parochial boundaries. His effect on and affection for the people of Barrington and their church was evident. He could little know at that stage how the silhouette of its octagonal tower would be repeated in another place. In parochial ministry, the pastoral and sacramental disciplines that he learned from the elder Coles became his own. Just one example is found in that everywhere Gueritz went to minister, Holy Communion taken to the sick and dying became a regular entry in the service registers, often appearing in the records, in his hand, for the first time.

Although James Coles' early departures in introducing the Oxford Movement to Shepton Beauchamp and Barrington were cautious and focussed more on teaching the essentials of the faith than on liturgical externals, they were, inescapably, the foundation upon which Gueritz' own ministry was built. His continuing links with the Coles family, through Adelina and his lifelong friendship with Stuckey, provided him with both an example of how the principles of the Movement could be embraced and expressed in a country parish and also an ongoing connection with developments on a national scale.

That sense of national connection was, in 1851, still part of an unknown future. Then the western peninsula did indeed feel remote from the centre of ecclesiastical and political activity in London. That sense of distance, a distance greater than mere geography, was greatly alleviated by the coming of the railway and yet, as late as the 1980s, a canon of Truro Cathedral was heard to comment: "I can get from Edinburgh to London quicker than I can get to London from here!" Distance notwithstanding, the turmoil which resulted from both the political upheavals in London and the impact of the Tractarians in Oxford had been felt even in that western fastness.

After a little over two years, Mamerto, Anne, baby George and Antonia Josepha were preparing to move back to the diocese of Exeter, which at that time included both Devon and Cornwall.

Adelina, having lived and worked with the Coles family for almost two years, temporarily departed for a new role as governess to the children of the Newman family in Glastonbury. There she had the nurture of five children, from the two-year-old Edmund to the eldest, Cecilia, aged eight. After her time in Glastonbury, Adelina returned to Shepton to continue educating the children of the rectory. The Coles family and the affection in which she was held was an obvious draw. That affection was entirely mutual and over two years in the Coles household left its mark on her, on them, and especially on young Stuckey Coles. However, among the other relationships that she had established in Shepton, it seems that her friendship with the Bartlett family was a particular tie of affection. There are indications that, sometime in her second period in Shepton, she boarded with them before she finally moved away. This was a friendship that was to stay with her and was to have an unlooked-for outcome years later.

Adelina's work with the Coles children continued for a short while after she had moved from the vicarage and after Mamerto, Anne and Antonia Josepha went to Brixham in Devon. An account dating from just after that move states:

Adelina lives in the same village, educating the children of the Rector of the parish for whom Mamerto had served as curate.[11]

Notes

1. Ms. a/c G3 (Gueritz family papers).

2. Anne Derby Lawrence was the daughter of Commander George Lawrence R.N. and Mary Spettigue. Mary was the daughter of Robert Fortescue, descendant of Martin Fortescue (d. 1472), Lord Chief Justice of England. Ms. a/c G3.

3. J. F. Briscoe, *V. S. S. Coles* (London: Mowbray, 1930), p. 36.

4. Briscoe, *V. S. S. Coles*, p. 4.

5. Briscoe, *V. S. S. Coles*, p. 35.

6. The claim for Hawker is widely made. Just two sources are S. Baring-Gould, *The Vicar of Morwenstow: A Life of Robert Stephen Hawker M.A.* (London: King, 1876), p. 226, and C. E. Byles, *The Life and Letters of R. S. Hawker* (New York: The Bodley Head, 1906), p. 171.

7. V. S. S. Coles, Obituary of Mamerto Gueritz, *Church Times*, 16 February 1912.

8. Gregory H. Goodwin, "Keble and Newman: Tractarian Aesthetics and the Romantic Tradition", *Victorian Studies* 30:4 (1987).

9. See Chapter 16.

10. Briscoe, *V. S. S. Coles*, p. 4.

11. Ms. a/c G1 (Gueritz family papers).

3

The diocese of Exeter: A contextual note

It is not entirely clear who or what induced Mamerto Gueritz to return to Exeter diocese early in 1851, or what persuaded James Coles to allow this to happen. Theories abound. The power of networking was extremely effective in the Victorian Church of England. If a bishop or an archdeacon had a staffing problem, he might well contact a colleague in another diocese. Indeed, the practice has not entirely died out 270 years later! For example, Robert Froude, Archdeacon of Totnes and incidentally father of Richard Hurrell Froude, the *Tract* writer, was well known to George Anthony Denison, later Archdeacon of Taunton, but who, at the time of Mamerto's ordination, was also bishop's examining chaplain. Denison was later to be prosecuted for his views on the presence of Christ in the Eucharist, which closely followed the teaching for which Pusey was suspended ten years earlier. The resulting conviction was ultimately quashed, but in the process, Denison resigned as bishop's examining chaplain. Gueritz' placement in curacies closely linked to archdeacon Froude lends considerable weight to the thought that Denison somehow facilitated Mamerto's return to his home diocese.

An influence even greater than that of archdeacon Froude might be discerned. From the autumn of 1847, Denison was invited each year to visit Bishop Phillpotts at his Bishopstowe residence. Denison and Phillpotts were in frequent correspondence and indeed, during the period of conflict over the Gorham controversy, Denison was a staunch defender of Phillpotts. Although they were later to become estranged, partly because Phillpotts disagreed with Denison's doctrine of the presence of Christ in the sacrament of the altar, at the time of Gueritz' move to Exeter diocese, Phillpotts and Denison were still frequently corresponding and on intimate terms.

A map of Devon showing some of the places mentioned in the text, namely:

- *Plymouth where Gueritz was brought up and Anne Gueritz was born.*
- *Stoke Gabriel, Bigbury, Brixham and Yealmpton where Mamerto Gueritz served curacies in Devon.*
- *Lyme Regis where Henry Parry Liddon was at school; Colyton and Colyford.*
- *Monckton (old spelling) which was originally linked with Colyton.*
- *Templeton where Jose Fortescue Lawrence Gueritz was incumbent.*
- *Whitestaunton where Lucy Octavia Elton and her family lived.*
- *Roborough where Reginald Mortimer was incumbent (also Mary Major, Exeter). Swymbridge (old spelling), Fortescue's second living.*
- *West Buckland School where Elton Lawrence Gueritz was at school.*

To what was Mamerto Gueritz returning? When he left Plymouth for St Edmund Hall, he seems to have had little of a wider understanding of the diocese of Exeter. Indeed, a wider perspective is mostly the privilege of those who come later and who can see the historical context. It is seldom afforded to those who are themselves in the alligators and swamp dilemma. Thus, the telling of Mamerto's story must needs pause so that the context may be better understood.

During the middle of the nineteenth century, the see of Exeter gained a reputation for being a diocese where Tractarians were appreciated and valued so long as they obeyed the law. This was almost entirely due to the attitude of Bishop Henry Phillpotts. Certainly, Tractarians did not experience the same degree of persecution as in other dioceses. Subsequently, the emergence of Ritualism from its Tractarian roots provoked a profound re-evaluation of the relationship between doctrine and worship in Devon and Cornwall, just as it did in the Church of England as a whole. Successive bishops of Exeter, each with differing motives and methods, tried to shape or suppress Ritualism, but in the time of Henry Phillpotts, particularly in the period 1850 to 1860, a considerable number of the parochial clergy could be seen to have moved from the restraint of the early Tractarians to a rather less restrained but still moderate ritual revival.[1] This was the period of Gueritz' Exeter curacies, and it was all happening as he returned to the diocese. The Gorham controversy, already briefly mentioned, was very much part of that landscape, but so were a range of other matters of concern to a newly arrived Tractarian priest, fresh from serving his title and ready for more responsibility. Therefore, this is an opportune moment to set out those matters and to place them in the context of Bishop Phillpotts' episcopacy.

When he arrived in 1830, Henry Phillpotts inherited a diocese which had undergone a long period of change, even decay. The Tractarians had not yet begun their attempt to restore the Church of England to itself. The old-fashioned High Church character, which earlier marked the diocese of Exeter, had largely given way, not so much to active Evangelicalism as to a general apathy, the "low and slow". Perhaps as a result there had been a decline in discipline among the clergy. This has been attributed not only to the fading of the old High Church emphasis on Church principles but also to "a succession of weak and latitudinarian bishops".[2]

Phillpotts was of quite a different stamp from his predecessors. His character and methods, his fierce loyalty to Church principles and the discipline of the

Prayer Book, were all soon felt throughout his extensive diocese. One example of this came rather later in 1848, when he was beset with many other controversies both national and local, and is beautifully illustrative of Phillpotts' approach. There was an exchange of letters with the churchwardens of Hennock. They complained that their incumbent used the Offertory Sentences and carried out baptisms during the service. The reply, published in the *Guardian*, a weekly national Anglican newspaper, on 12 January, was typically blunt:

> Both of these are ordered by the Rubric—and your minister does no more than his duty in observing them.
>
> P.S. It is the duty of your office to sustain your minister in the performance of his duty (if not) you incur a double measure of sin.

At the outset, one of Phillpotts' primary concerns was what he saw as an injustice partly caused by ill-managed plurality. Plurality, the holding of more than one benefice, was common and of itself not condemned. Indeed, Phillpotts could only survive financially in Exeter by retaining a canonry of Durham Cathedral, which paid £1,000 per annum more than his episcopal income. The two, added together, meant that he could maintain an episcopal household and still support his 18 children. What Phillpotts did most emphatically condemn was the refusal of some incumbents either to reside in their parish or to provide a curate in their stead. Understanding this element of Phillpotts' discipline for the clergy is most important for our grasp of how, why and where Mamerto Gueritz was deployed over the following decade. While Phillpotts would listen to argument and reason, not entirely unsympathetically, once his mind was made up, he was firm. In correspondence with his secretary, Ralph Barnes, he remarked: "Mr. Ley of St. Paul's Exeter cannot reside and asks me what I advise? I answer, *resignation*."

When the Revd Mr Wrey of Launcelles pleaded the illness of his wife's parents as grounds for non-residence, Phillpotts' comment, again to Barnes, clearly reveals his priorities:

> This may be deemed harsh; but I cannot satisfy myself with accepting such pleas. A clergyman in taking the charge of souls must really consider

that he is undertaking a duty superior to these considerations of kindness to kindred.[3]

When we look at Gueritz' curacies, especially in Stoke Gabriel and Bigbury, Phillpotts' policy in this respect will come into even clearer focus; as will his equal concern over another closely related matter, namely the mistreatment of the so-called "inferior clergy".[4] The practice of plurality or absenteeism had a consequence in the employment of curates to reside and carry out the incumbent's duties. It might also be the consequence of a freeholder's incapacity, as we saw in the case of Fordlow and its bedridden rector. However, the manner in which such clergy were employed was a point of contention for the bishop. He found that the housing and payment of many of these curates was deplorable. Phillpotts wrote to Barnes on this issue even before his consecration:

> Speaking confidentially, I have been a little startled by one or two indications of the state of the diocese in respect to curates' salaries, a matter on which I have a very strong feeling.[5]

This was written in December 1830. By March 1831, these "strong feelings" had been translated into a stated policy. Phillpotts refused to allow any title or first curacy with a smaller salary than £70 per annum unless the circumstances were exceptional. There was an example of a curate whose private income exceeded that of his incumbent tenfold: an exception was allowed in his case. Another closely related issue was the length of curacies. Phillpotts was adamant that curates should serve at least two years in their first curacy and that no deacon should be ordained priest until he had served the full year. This discipline was maintained in spite of various requests to the contrary. One young hopeful asked that he be made deacon and ordained priest simultaneously so that he could inherit his father's living. The reply was characteristically blunt!

These concerns and the measures Phillpotts took to address them did a great deal to heighten the morale of badly paid curates and of those parishes which had long suffered neglect. They did not win the unalloyed approval of the comfortable pluralists and absentee incumbents who resented this curtailment of their freedom. Phillpotts might have been a little more diplomatic in the way in which these reforms were introduced, but he had little time for those who opposed him, either in the diocese or in the House of Lords. He could indeed be persuasive and charming in private, but in open debate he was often formidable, both with tongue and pen, silencing rather than convincing his opponents. This, however, did not prevent him gaining the love and loyalty of many of the clergy who served under him. Henry Alford, later to be dean of Canterbury, was ordained by Phillpotts in October 1833. He wrote of the ordination charge:

> It was the most solemn thing I have ever heard ... may this be a lesson to me not to judge men harshly or before the time, as I certainly had of the Bishop of Exeter. I am very thankful to God for having brought me to such a place and to such a man.[6]

There is much more that could be said of Henry Phillpotts, but as the present purpose is to understand something of the life and ministry of Mamerto Gueritz, we simply note that the bishop's attitude to curates and their welfare was something which would have been highly relevant to the rapidly growing Gueritz family. Another aspect of Phillpotts' ministry, which was true also of Gueritz', was adherence to Church principles. Gueritz had come to those principles through Oxford, his studies, and the work of the Tractarians and then had seen them applied in practice in his first curacy. Phillpotts had them from his traditional High Church background and might well have said with Newland of Torquay:

> I cannot tell you how and when I learnt them. I always held them—they grew with me, there was never a time in my life that I had them not.

Phillpotts has been seen as unpredictable and inconsistent, as partisan, as pugnacious by some writers and as an enthusiastic reformer and a man of great spiritual depth by others. The truth of the matter is that his independence of mind freed him from many of the prejudices of the day and if he offended, he did so quite impartially and without malice. He could and did apply his inherited principles in his episcopal ministry without concerning himself what one party or another might think or how they would react. This set him both alongside and against Tractarians dependent upon how their teaching and actions harmonized with his understanding of the teachings of the Church:

> Let the Church of England tighten its discipline and increase its energy. Everything in Phillpotts view was already there in principle. Its doctrine, liturgy and discipline were perfect. They just needed to be applied and obeyed.[7]

This capacity for offering support and appreciation to the Tractarians without feeling in the least constrained from offering criticism and correction is clearly illustrated first in his 1839 charge to the clergy:

> but I cannot close what I have to say of them (the Tractarians) without offering my humble meed of praise to the singular meekness, charity and forbearance which they have exercised, immeasurably superior to most of those with whom they have to contend.[8]

And then later in 1842, commenting on *Tract 90*:

> The tone of the Tract, as it respects our own Church is offensive and indecent . . . its principles of interpreting our articles I cannot but deem most unsound. It cannot be a matter of surprise, that the adverse feeling provoked by it has more than neutralised in many dispassionate minds, the high estimation of him (J. H. Newman) which former services had justly acquired.[9]

Three examples of the impact of Henry Phillpotts' character and ministry are particularly relevant to the story of Mamerto Gueritz.

The first was what were later labelled "The Surplice Riots". These became a favourite subject with later Ritualists seeking to create a hagiography of martyrs for the cause and trying to claim Phillpotts as their own. As we will see, one such was the Revd W. H. B. Proby, whose interaction with Mamerto Gueritz was rich and varied.

Phillpotts had refused to accept that the wearing of the surplice was a "party badge" and in 1844, in a letter to the clergy, he ordered its use, declaring at the beginning of his remarks:

> but the more unimportant it is in itself, the more manifest is the necessity of stripping it of that factitious importance which is given to it by its being made the symbol of disunion.[10]

Francis Courtenay was incumbent of St Sidwell's, Exeter. He was a relative of the earl of Devon and also of Courtenay of Bovey Tracey, another renowned Devon Tractarian. Since 1842, Francis Courtenay and the clergy who assisted him had worn the surplice when preaching. On 3 January 1845, there was a large meeting at the Guildhall in Exeter, presided over by the mayor, at which resolutions were passed in support of the "Protestant Church of England" and against "Romanizing" uses. Courtenay was the real target of those resolutions, and a parochial meeting wrote to him asking him to cease the use of the surplice. He could not see why, when he had simply followed existing practice for three years, he should give in to such a demand. On Sunday 12 January 1845, a mob of around 600 followed Courtenay home from church. A week later, again on the Sunday, a larger mob of some 2,000 gathered and were only restrained by the police and supportive volunteers. Realizing the futility of arguing with such prejudice, on Sunday 26 January Courtenay and the visiting preacher both wore preaching gowns instead. However, three years later, on 29 October 1848, there were more disturbances. A clergyman of considerable scholarship and decidedly advanced views had preached in St Sidwell's on Good Friday and then again on 27 August. On both occasions, the surplice had been worn with only muted disapproval. However, when he attempted to repeat this in October a large crowd, which had obviously been orchestrated, packed the church and threatened violence. The service was stopped.

Henry Phillpotts certainly regretted issuing his injunction to wear the surplice, not for the principle itself but for the unforeseen and intemperate reaction. The order was simply a matter of obeying the laws which governed the worship of the Church of England.

All this was happening as Mamerto Gueritz was preparing to move from Oxford to Shepton Beauchamp, where the surplice had already become established as the priestly garb for preaching.

The second area of diocesan life of particular interest, not least for the role played in it by Phillpotts, was the ecclesiastical scene in Plymouth. As this is brought into view, we should remember that Mamerto Gueritz found his vocation at Charles Church, Plymouth which, at the time of his ordination, was markedly Calvinist. He returned there to be married in May 1849, because Anne Derby Lawrence was a parishioner, but by this time he had moved very far from the theological position of any of the clergy then in post. In fact, he was much more in harmony with the objects of their vilification, George Rundle Prynne of St Peter's, Plymouth and the Sisterhood led by Priscilla Lydia Sellon.

On 1 January 1848, Henry Phillpotts made a public appeal for help to remedy the lack of provision, both spiritual and temporal, for the vastly increased population of Plymouth and the towns of Devonport and Stonehouse. On 5 January, *The Guardian* published a summary of the appeal, and Prynne was one of those who responded to the call. He arrived already with the reputation of being a Puseyite. Prynne had first come into contact with E. B. Pusey during a curacy at St Andrew's, Clifton and rapidly became convinced of the rightness of Pusey's teaching and subsequently an avowed defender both of the man and of the message. Pusey tried to induce Prynne to go to St Saviour's, Leeds, but he declined and returned to Cornwall. It was from his incumbency of St Levan with St Sennen in Cornwall, where he had been for just a year, that he answered the call of his bishop, and on 16 August 1848 he became the perpetual curate of the new parish of St Peter the Apostle, Plymouth.

Another who answered the call was Priscilla Lydia Sellon, who had been introduced to the life of a religious community by friends, the Chambers family, in London. Near their house was the newly formed Park Village Sisterhood, and Lydia Sellon was able to see at first hand the work of prayer and service the sisters carried out. Her vision of how this ministry might be organized and harnessed for the good of the whole Church of England began to grow until eventually it became, at least in concept, a countrywide network. At this stage, however, all such schemes were of the future and the immediate need in Devonport became, as her father put it, "A call from God". Sellon, with her father's necessary support, went to Exeter to set her hopes before Henry Phillpotts. Her father's support was essential because at that time an unmarried woman was still her father's ward while he lived.[11] What the bishop thought, confronted by a young, fiercely enthusiastic woman not yet 30, is not recorded. What is clear is that Phillpotts offered both his consent and his blessing to her offer to do what she might for the religious, social and educational needs of Devonport.

Returning to the Chambers' home in London, a "council of war" was convened to discuss how this might best be done. Dr Pusey's support was gained, and his influence won the support of a Plymouth priest. A house was rented in April 1848, and the work begun. Initially Lydia Sellon worked alone, but the burden was far too great. Again with Pusey's support and with substantial financial help from her father, plans were laid for the formation of a Sisterhood. In August, the bishop gave consent and blessing to this extension of the vision, and on 16 October a small number of companions joined her. The work of education and the care of the poor moved into a new phase, and on 27 October 1848 the regular celebration of the divine office began. In all, fewer than 300 days had elapsed since Henry Phillpotts made his appeal.

Both Prynne and Lydia Sellon became the targets of vehement attacks by the local leaders of the "Protestant Church of England". H. A. Greaves, the incumbent of Charles Church, led the first wave. The mode of life adopted by the Sisterhood, their style of dress, their disciplined life of prayer, all seemed to the Calvinistic clergy of Plymouth and Devonport to be little short of papistical. Their prejudices were inflamed by stories of abuse of the orphans and young girls who lived in the home that the sisters had established. So strident were these objectors that the bishop convened a public enquiry in 1849 coinciding with the return of Gueritz for his wedding. The outcome of the enquiry was a triumph for the Sisterhood and, although Phillpotts found some of their practices questionable, he gave public expression to his "admiration mixed with reverence" for the sisters and the work they had undertaken among the poor and the orphans. Their opponents were neither satisfied nor silenced.

That year also saw another outbreak of the cholera which in 1832 had carried off James Carne, the vicar of Charles Church. The sisters worked tirelessly among the poor and sick regardless of any risk to themselves. Between July and November, 819 people died. Prynne wrote of the episode describing how he, with his curate George Hetling, and Lydia Sellon and her Sisterhood, worked in the most harrowing of circumstances. Night after night, they were in the houses of the sick and dying. In all this, only one sister died of the cholera and, ironically, she was one of those whose duties kept her in the house at Stoke. None of this sacrificial service changed the hearts of their antagonists. It did, however, seal the place of the Sisterhood in the hearts and minds of the poor of Devonport.

Early in 1852, the Revd James Spurrell, vicar of Shelford, published a pamphlet accusing Lydia Sellon and the sisters of a great many "un-Protestant" activities. Another followed, even more sensational in its accusations, penned by the Revd William Colles, *Sisters of Mercy, Sisters of Misery*. In March, feeling he had not sufficient control over the community, Phillpotts withdrew from his office as visitor. He did, however, at the same time express his continuing admiration for the work and specifically asked Lydia Sellon to continue. In spite of his clearly articulated support and encouragement, this withdrawal was seen by some as a betrayal. Entering the lists in July, Commander Sellon, Lydia's father, published a thorough rebuttal of the Protestant pamphleteers under the rather unwieldy title, *A Contradiction of the Alleged Acts of Cruelty Exercised by Miss Sellon and a Refutation of Certain Statements Put Forth in the Tracts of the Rev. Mr. Spurrell, Miss Campbell and others*.

George Rundle Prynne was also the target of Protestant attack. Led by John Hatchard of St Andrew's, Plymouth, a number of the local clergy who had attacked the Sisterhood turned their fire upon Prynne; among them, James Spurrell and Michael Hobart Seymour, both vehemently opposed to the formation of religious communities, especially Sisterhoods.

Hatchard complained of:

> [t]he use of the surplice in the pulpit; chanting the psalms and intoning the service; bowing at the name of Jesus; omitting a prayer before the sermon; reading the prayer for the Church Militant . . . and the substitution of alms bags for plates.[12]

During this first wave of attacks Phillpotts supported Prynne, but cautioned him to have "a discreet regard to the feelings of others in matters on which the law of the Church leaves you at liberty".

In 1852, Hatchard was again on the offensive; this time the central issue was the practice of auricular confession and absolution. Local clergy threatened to boycott a confirmation which was to be held at St Peter's, Plymouth and even threatened to disrupt the service. The charges against Prynne were repeated and grew in the telling. He denied any impropriety when asked by the bishop who, it seems, chose to believe him completely. Nevertheless, because of the continuing protests, Phillpotts agreed to another enquiry. Prynne did not even have to defend himself because the case of his accusers, quite literally, disintegrated. Phillpotts declared Prynne vindicated, saying:

> I pray God that every clergyman in my diocese may do his duty as well as
> Mr Prynne has done his.[13]

However, in private the bishop was not completely at ease concerning the question of the legitimacy of the confessional practices at St Peter's, as his letter to Prynne shows:

> If you have kept within the plain meaning of this my counsel you have
> a right to claim the authority of your bishop for what you have done; if
> you have exceeded it, you have not only exceeded, but run counter to it.[14]

However much Phillpotts may have sought to restrain and caution Prynne over this and other issues, he did not hesitate to defend Prynne when Dean Lowe preached a sermon denouncing the "apish imitators of Rome . . . (who) . . . have lately caused no small stir, especially in this diocese". Even though Phillpotts had himself lately been at odds with Prynne, he would not have unjust and inaccurate accusations made, especially when Lowe, in his zeal to condemn all things Roman, failed to set out the teaching of the Church of England.

The conflict rumbled on until 1853 when two events, one of local and one of international significance, supervened. There was another cholera epidemic during which the sisters were seen at their sacrificial best. Then there was the outbreak of the Crimean War. The role of nursing sisters in the battlefield gave a different vision of what these sisters in the battlefields of Plymouth might really be about. However, with cholera and the Crimea, people now had much more to concern them than local arguments about whether or not the vicar of St Peter's was a Papist.

In all this, Phillpotts was true to his vision of the Church of England. All that was needful to be true to the Church was to be found in the Book of Common Prayer, from which he affirmed baptismal regeneration, the real spiritual presence of Christ in the Holy Communion and the practice of confession. However, he objected violently to prayers for the dead and, even after it was widely accepted, he condemned the mixed chalice as something the Church of England had consciously abandoned.

The third example, of particular importance to those who held fast to Church principles, lay in the disciplines Phillpotts was upholding in the Gorham controversy. Those disciplines were not only matters of doctrine but also of authority in the Church. In several early charges to the clergy Phillpotts had given fair warning that he would invoke Canon 38, concerning authorized forms of prayer, against those who "omit or garble portions of the office of Baptism which their conscience, it would seem, is too tender to use, though not too tender to promise to use".[15]

In 1847, George Cornelius Gorham was presented to the living of Bramford Speke near Exeter by the Lord Chancellor. Of course, the appointment was dependent upon the bishop being willing to institute him, but as Phillpotts had earlier instituted Gorham to St Just in Penwith, this might have seemed a formality. However, nothing concerning priestly ministry could be a mere formality for Phillpotts. The examination was extremely thorough and brought to light that which Gorham seems never to have concealed. He would not accept the principle of baptismal regeneration as set out in the Prayer Book. His own understanding, evident from even before his ordination, was Calvinist and was later described as "naked Zwinglianism". Phillpotts refused to institute him to the living, whereupon Gorham appealed to the ecclesiastical Court of Arches. The court found in Phillpotts' favour and awarded costs against Gorham. It was stated in the judgement that "Mr Gorham has maintained and does maintain doctrines opposed to that Church of which he professes himself a member and minister."[16]

Thus far, Phillpotts had acted predictably and in a manner consistent with his known principles. It was Gorham's next step that precipitated a "perfect storm". Gorham appealed to the Judicial Committee of the Privy Council, a secular court. For such a body to rule on doctrinal matters was, to many clergy, complete anathema. To accept such a body's authority over the Church was deemed by them to be acquiescing in heresy. But perhaps the real salt in the wound was not only that the court found in Gorham's favour but that his understanding was deemed acceptable partially because, to paraphrase the judgement given on 8 March 1850, so many eminent and respected Anglican clergy had held the same opinion that their liberty to do so was proven. In other words, if enough people believe something orthodoxy can be abandoned! The Calvinist Evangelicals were delighted. One of the highest courts in the land had declared their position to be tenable in the Church of England.[17]

To the old-fashioned High Churchmen and the Tractarians alike, this seemed to be a declaration that if people got away with heresy for long enough it would stop being heresy. To some the line had been crossed and for them the Church of England could no longer claim its Apostolic inheritance; it had become a creature of Parliament. As a result, having spent a year doing what he could to recall the Church of England to its Catholic heritage, Archdeacon Edward Manning seceded to Rome. More than a dozen other clergy took the same route for the same reason.

In Exeter diocese, Phillpotts' authority was undiminished. Excepting those who had already openly opposed him, by far the greater part of his clergy supported him in his defeat, perhaps more so than in his fight. A newspaper article, published in 1849 in the period between the judgement of the Court of Arches and that of the Privy Council, declared:

> and if our Bishop is half Papist and encourages the clergy in practices which ultimately and infallibly lead to Popery, how is it that the diocese of Exeter can show but one, or perhaps two, clerical perverts? And how is it that not one clergyman ordained by the Bishop, after examination by his chaplains, has ever gone to Rome?—and how is it that the greatest number of clerical perversions have taken place in those dioceses where the Bishop of Exeter's views are most warmly abjured?[18]

Ironically, not long after the ruling of the Privy Council, William Maskell, incumbent of St Marychurch, Torquay and chaplain to Henry Phillpotts, to use the contemporary expression, "perverted" to Rome.

This then is something of the diocese and the bishop to which Mamerto Gueritz was returning after his title curacy. A bishop who had a genuine concern for the "inferior" clergy, especially with regard to their housing and stipend. A diocese in which the unfolding of the Oxford Movement was being played out just as thoroughly as elsewhere. A place where Tractarians were respected and encouraged, up to a point. A bishop who would defend his clergy against injustice, even if he had to chide them privately, and who would defend the faith of the Church of England as he found it in the teeth of national, judicial and archiepiscopal opposition.

When the pathway that Mamerto Gueritz trod in his discovery of the Catholic nature of the Church of England is considered, from his first encounter with Catholic teaching in the library of St Edmund Hall, the strength of his future loyalty to Henry Phillpotts is scarcely to be wondered at.

Notes

[1] G. W. Herring, "Tractarianism to Ritualism", DPhil thesis (2 volumes), Oxford University, 1984. Vol. 2, "Analysis of Tractarian clergy and parishes".

[2] J. F. Chanter, *The Bishop's Palace, Exeter and its Story* (London: SPCK, 1932), p. 111.

[3] G. C. B. Davies, *Henry Phillpotts, Bishop of Exeter 1778–1869* (London: SPCK, 1954), pp. 119ff.

[4] Of course, this is a label we are not allowed to use today, but it was commonly in use in the mid-1800s and not necessarily as a term of derogation. It was simply a statement, in a hierarchical system, of where a particular cleric had place.

[5] Davies, *Henry Phillpotts*, p. 116.

[6] Fanny Alford (ed.), *Life Journals and Letters of Henry Alford D.D.*, 2nd edn (London: Rivingtons, 1873), p. 91.

[7] J. Thurmer, "The Nineteenth Century: The Church of England", in N. Orme (ed.), *Unity and Variety: A History of the Church in Devon and Cornwall* (Exeter: Exeter University Press, 1991), p. 114.

[8] W. S. Bricknell, *The Judgment of the Bishops upon Tractarian Theology* (Oxford: Vincent, 1845), p. 134.

[9] Bricknell, *The Judgment of the Bishops*, pp. 547 and 553.

[10]   R. J. E. Boggis, *The History of the Diocese of Exeter* (Exeter: Pollard, 1922), p. 501.

[11]   Heather Nelson, "The Law and the Lady: Consent and Marriage in Nineteenth Century British Literature", PhD thesis, Purdue University, May 2015, p. 3.

[12]   Davies, *Henry Phillpotts*, p. 288.

[13]   A. C. Kelway, *George Rundle Prynne* (London: Longmans Green & Co., 1905), p. 91.

[14]   Davies, *Henry Phillpotts*, p. 305.

[15]   Bricknell, *The Judgment of the Bishops*, p. 373.

[16]   Davies, *Henry Phillpotts*, p. 237.

[17]   Five years later, in 1855, the Hon. Robert Liddell, vicar of St Paul's, Knightsbridge, was prosecuted for contravention of the Ornaments Rubric. Ironically Liddell, like Gorham, appealed to the Judicial Committee of the Privy Council, and in 1857 judgement was given in his favour. There was not the disapproval from the clergy that there had been over Gorham's appeal to that body.

[18]   *West of England Conservative*, 3 January 1849.

4

The troubleshooting curate:
Return to Exeter diocese

The finding of suitably equipped curates to assist in parishes where the incumbent could not or would not minister was normally the task of the archdeacon. In the days before suffragan bishops were commonplace,[1] with all of Devon and Cornwall to contend with, Henry Phillpotts relied heavily on his archdeacons for clergy management. The availability of a capable and well-trained priest was needed for a difficulty in Froude's archdeaconry and Mamerto Gueritz fitted the bill.

Brixham, 1851

The first problem Gueritz was called upon to assist with was at Brixham in Devon. The senior curate was ill and Mamerto Gueritz was asked to take his place. This was a necessity because the incumbent, J. R. Hogg, had been appointed a Justice of the Peace in December 1850 and was much taken up with hearing cases in court. As an aside, John Hogg was son-in-law to the Revd H. F. Lyte, the composer of the hymn "Abide With Me" for which W. H. Monk composed the tune Eventide. We shall hear more of them both later in the story.

The Gueritz family were in Brixham for most of 1851, and during the year Anne Gueritz' sister, Mary Fortescue Lawrence, was married in Lower Brixham on 24 June. Adelina joined them for the wedding and was one of the witnesses. The family moved on during October of that year.

Stoke Gabriel, 1852

The next need to be met was still in Totnes archdeaconry and close to Archdeacon Froude's own parish of Dartington. It was at St Mary, Stoke Gabriel, where the incumbent, Robert Hawker Bowden, had been given leave of absence following the death of his daughter in May. Bowden was a grandson of the Revd Robert Hawker who had been incumbent at Charles Church, Plymouth until his death in 1827.

For Gueritz, this appointment represented an increase in responsibility, and even if the bishop did not instigate the move himself, the temporary replacement of an incumbent would have required his approval. It was a brief stay, occupying late 1851 to late 1852, and then the family moved on again, but it was a significant year in several ways.

The first matter of note took place when the family had only just arrived in Stoke Gabriel. On 20 November 1851, in response to a request from a number of the clergy, an archdeaconry meeting was called. In the absence of the archdeacon, the Revd Richard Champernowne, at that time curate of Dartington, was in the chair. Alarm had been raised among the clergy by reports of correspondence engaged in by Archbishop Sumner of Canterbury in which he demonstrated his eagerness to affirm the ministry of "foreign pastors". This courteous affirmation was, however, couched in language which seemed to question the necessity of the apostolic succession and episcopal ordination. Whether such an interpretation of Sumner's correspondence was justified, the mere suggestion touched a raw nerve. This was the end of 1851, and Newman had been lost to the Church of England for only six years. The previous April, Archdeacon Manning had seceded in the wake of the Gorham judgement. For many clergy and not a few laity, that judgement had set a divide between those who defended the orthodoxy and catholicity of the Church of England and those who would reshape it along more Protestant, even Calvinistic, lines if they could.

This was perceived as yet another example of the continuing erosion of the doctrines which defined the Church of England. Episcopal ordination, claimed to be unbroken since the time of the apostles, was central to the claim of the Church of England to be a valid branch of the One Holy, Catholic and Apostolic Church. The outcome of the meeting was an address to the Bishop of Exeter, signed by 42 of the clergy, stating that the archbishop's correspondence might be interpreted to mean that

> the vast majority of the Clergy of the Church of England look upon Episcopal Ordination as a matter of indifference. We for our parts do not by any means so regard it; but on the contrary firmly believe that Episcopacy is of Divine institution, proved to be so from Holy Scripture, and maintained as such by the Church from the beginning . . . Neither for 1500 years did any considerable body of Christians whatsoever call into question this necessity of Episcopal Ordination.[2]

This was not entirely a Tractarian versus Evangelical division, as the list of those who signed the address to the bishop demonstrates. There were indeed names like that of Prynne of Plymouth and his curate, Oxenham of Modbury, Mamerto Gueritz and more than a dozen others who specifically identified with the Puseyites and later Tractarians. However, among the signatories there were also those who represented something of the older High Church tradition and the restraint of the first Tractarians, names such as Champernowne and Yonge.

Sixteen clergy of the archdeaconry refused to attend the summons and wrote jointly to the archdeacon lamenting that he had allowed the meeting to take place and declaring that it was unnecessary and highly prejudicial to the interests of the Church. It is no surprise to find that among them were the incumbent of Charles Church, the Revd H. A. Greaves, R. W. Needham of St Paul's, Stonehouse and John Hatchard of St Andrew's, Plymouth. As we have seen, these were clergy of a decidedly Calvinistic bent who would not have found the supposed erosion of the catholicity of the Church of England a matter of concern.

The second event of great importance for the family was the arrival in October of a second child, Jose Fortescue Lawrence Gueritz, named for the ancestry of both parents.

The third matter of note was the evident effect Gueritz' ministry had on the people of the parish. The family were not allowed to leave without several tokens of the affection they had won. Perhaps the most telling of these was a handsome home communion set, still in the possession of the family. Farewell gifts often took the form of silver tableware or vessels. The fact that this gift was for the giving of Holy Communion to the housebound, the sick and the dying is an indication that the ministry offered to the people of Stoke Gabriel was a continuation of that learned from James Coles in Shepton Beauchamp. In this relatively brief stay in Stoke Gabriel is revealed something which will surface time and again as the story unfolds. The personality behind the ministry, and the way in which that ministry was offered, were often such as to inspire great affection and loyalty from the people Mamerto Gueritz served, even after a relatively short time. Unfortunately, but inevitably, Mamerto's capacity for rigorous defence of the Church in the face of what he saw as error and heresy inspired opposition just as easily.

Bigbury, 1852–6

In 1852, the rector of St Lawrence Bigbury, the Revd Terrence Livingstone, who had been incumbent since 1821, was adjudged to be contumacious and non-resident without licence. In ecclesiastical terms, a contumacious person is one who shows contempt of the bishop's authority and is wilfully disobedient. This judgement was the culmination of a history of inappropriate behaviour and neglect of duty. In 1842, the churchwardens of Bigbury had laid a formal complaint at the bishop's visitation, citing absence from the parish and non-attendance at services. An incumbent might not necessarily reside in his parish, especially if he had more than one cure of souls and could provide a curate, but he would need the bishop's licence to live elsewhere, and Livingstone did not hold such a licence. In 1844, although his housekeeper tried to take the blame, Livingstone was fined £100 for possessing illegally imported brandy.

The income from the parish of Bigbury was around £680 per year, and the incumbent held almost 100 acres of glebe, which also provided an income. This compared very favourably with similar livings around the country. Unfortunately, this income was only available to the legal freeholder, Mr Livingstone.

It was never easy for a bishop to oust a freeholding incumbent from a parish, but in circumstances like this, and ten years after the first known complaint, there were options open to him. To appoint a curate in sole charge was one of them. Although Bigbury was in Froude's archdeaconry, this was a matter for the bishop. Several elements in the situation require note at this point. The first is that whoever was initially responsible for Mamerto Gueritz' return to Devon, at this stage and following two quite challenging appointments, the bishop had become aware of his capacities. Secondly, Bishop Phillpotts was now prepared to offer Mamerto an even more difficult task and with it considerably more responsibility. Thirdly, the curate who had held the parish together for several years was Robert Henry Fortescue, first cousin to Anne Gueritz, but it was time for him to move. How these factors are interrelated is not entirely clear. Nevertheless, in 1852 Mamerto and the family moved to Bigbury, and this time they were to settle for almost five years. The next year Mary Louisa was born. "Min", as the family always called her, maintained that her earliest memory was riding in a pannier on a donkey by the sea at Bigbury when she would have been scarcely three years old. In 1855, Edward Peregrine was born. There were evidently no great dramas in this period (at least none were recorded) and in 1856 Mamerto resigned the curacy and was briefly licensed to Yealmpton. The rector of Bigbury had still not returned at this point and a new curate-in-charge was appointed. Terrence Livingstone died in May 1861 in Surbiton, still non-resident, and a new appointment was made the following August.

Yealmpton, 1856

The incumbent of Yealmpton, James Longmore, died in September 1855, and the bishop needed Mamerto to cover the interregnum until a new appointment could be made. The significant event of the year for the Gueritz family was the birth of another son, Henry Francis (Frank) Gueritz. The next move after Yealmpton was still to be a curacy, but more senior and with more opportunities and responsibilities than hitherto and in a more urban setting. Thus far there has been no evidence that Mamerto Gueritz felt any need to disguise his growing commitment to Tractarian theology; nor has there been any indication that the congregations among whom he ministered found ought amiss in the liturgy he offered and the development of music in worship. However, it should be remembered that curates do not have the same freedom as an incumbent when it comes to liturgical innovations—at least in theory.

In addition to his parochial charge, Mamerto took on a mastership at Yealmpton School, continuing the teaching work within which he had first found his sense of priestly vocation. This was an appointment in addition to and separate from his curacy, providing additional income along the way. This was noted in one of the many reports of his later preferment to Colyton.

Less than a year in Yealmpton and the bishop called yet again. The incumbent of St Mary's Penzance, Henry Batten, was ill and had been obliged to relinquish his duties. A sympathetic bishop looked for a solution and a safe pair of hands. Evidently the need in Penzance was deemed greater than that in Yealmpton and the family was once again on the move.

Penzance, 1857–60

In 1857, to be ecclesiastically pedantic, Penzance was not an incumbency at all but a chapelry of the parish of Madron. This relationship dated back to at least 1397, when on 15 June Bishop Stafford licensed the "*Capella Sancte Marie en ville de Pensance*".[3]

The chapelry was served by a perpetual curate. For all intents and purposes, apart from lacking the authority to collect tithes, there was little difference in the status of the priest of the chapelry from that of other incumbents. Although a perpetual curate would not be inducted or installed, as would a rector or vicar, he would have to be nominated to the cure by the "impropriator"[4] and licensed by the bishop. He could then only be removed from his post by the revocation of that licence. This afforded, in effect, incumbent status but without the freehold.

The record of the priests of Penzance, compiled in 1889, gives their names as far back as 1475. Two names on the list are of importance for this study:

Henry Batten—(Third son of John Batten) Born at Penzance 1813. Matriculated Exeter College, Oxford, 2 June 1831. B.A. 1835; built St. Paul's Chapel, Penzance, of which he was minister 1843–49. Licensed to St. Mary's 2 April 1849. Died at Penzance 10 March 1860.

    Mamerto Gueritz—(Second son (sic) of Jose Gueritz of San Felipe, Valencia, Spain) Matriculated St. Edmund Hall, Oxford 7th March 1845 aged 22. B.A.Hons (sic) 1848. Was curate in charge of St. Mary's two years 1858–9 while Mr. Batten was in Brittany in search of his health. Mr Gueritz has been vicar of Colyton in Devon since 1860.[5]

The holder of the perpetual curacy in 1857 was the Revd Henry Batten. In 1844, Batten had married Anna Maria, the youngest daughter of the late Rev James Carne, who had been the vicar of Charles Church Plymouth and a caring friend of Mamerto's father Jose. Anna Maria was only two years younger than Mamerto Gueritz, and given the close friendship between the families, it is likely that they were childhood friends, or at least aware of each other. When her father died, Anna was seven years old, and she was cared for by her uncle, Joseph Carne of Penzance. She was 19 when she married Henry Batten, who was 12 years older than her. Anna Batten must have moved a long way from her Calvinist roots in Plymouth, for by the time of the wedding Batten was already a convinced Tractarian. When he arrived in Penzance, the building of houses and the growth of various small industries had moved the centre of population and commerce from Madron to Penzance. In response to this expansion, in 1843, Batten built the chapel of St Paul as "a haven for the Tractarians"; he did so from his own resources. Although it was not actually consecrated until 1866, which was after Batten's death, at the outset St Paul's represented a definite raising of the Tractarian flag in Penzance and a declaration of intent on the part of Henry Batten.

As we have seen, Henry Batten was not in good health. The baptism register, which bears the title "The Parish of Madron, Town of Penzance", reveals that Batten's last service before departing for Brittany was on 9 August 1857. Mamerto Gueritz' entries begin on the 29th of the following month.[6]

Mamerto, Anne and their family moved into a house in Regent Terrace. Originally the terrace had been a dozen small cottages, but as Penzance grew and became more prosperous, the cottages were demolished and larger houses were built commanding a superb view over the bay to Newlyn. These were intended for leasing to affluent families; people who could afford to come to Penzance for extended holidays. Number 13 was leased for the new curate-in-charge, and as the summer of 1857 drew to a close Mamerto Gueritz, his wife Anne, George, Jose Fortescue, Mary Louisa, Edward and Frank moved into their new spacious home. With five children between the ages of seven and one, it must have been quite a challenge for their mother, while her husband settled into his new and apparently congenial role in a considerably wider sphere of activity than hitherto. However, as we have seen, they were not without support. The close friendship between the Gueritz and Carne families had evidently been sustained, and two of Anne's cousins, the Fortescue sisters, lived in Penzance. One was godmother to Min Gueritz.

In 1850, the diocese of Exeter, which was made up of Devon and Cornwall, included over 800 benefices, many of them quite remote. However, even in the far reaches of Cornwall, Tractarian influence was already everywhere to be found. The rector of Falmouth from 1838 to 1869 was William John Coope, and he is described by Miles Brown as "the unchallenged pioneer of Tractarianism in Cornwall".[7]

This Tractarianism was of the early, restrained kind, not yet to be equated with later Ritualism. Coope had been up at Brasenose College when the *Tracts for the Times* began to be published and became an enthusiastic disseminator both of the *Tracts* themselves and of their teachings. The move to establish a see in Cornwall had already begun and a number of Tractarian clergy were among the activists. One of these was Arthur Tatham, of whom it was written:

> One of the chief promoters of the Cornish see was the Rev Prebendary
> Tatham to whom Cornwall was deeply indebted.[8]

Miles Brown reflects on the nature of Cornish Tractarianism around the time of Mamerto Gueritz' ministry in Penzance and in the years immediately following:

> There was a tendency for the men of the Westcountry to study at Oxford. It
> is apparent how great an influence on their students and acquaintances the
> little knot of Tractarian leaders had. Some of the clergy of Cornwall knew
> personally the Tract writers and heard Newman's series of sermons. John
> Keble and others visited Cornwall occasionally. He officiated at a funeral
> at Marhamchurch in 1845 only a month before the secession of Newman.
> He preached at St Mary's Penzance in 1863 being an acquaintance of Philip
> Hedgeland, the old fashioned High-churchman who was "incumbent",
> Keble, liked the services in the district and praised them.[9]

Hedgeland was previously curate of Madron and moved to St Mary's in 1860 following the death of Henry Batten and the departure of Gueritz for Colyton.

It is salutary to note that it was a mere ten years after Keble's Assize Sermon that Henry Batten built his "haven for Tractarians" at St Paul's. If we set this alongside the fact that the *Tracts for the Times* were written between 1833 and 1841, with the majority appearing in the first two years, and if we recall that the very term Tractarian was coined in 1839 by Christopher Benson, who was not a sympathizer, then we begin to have a sense of the timescale of the spread of the Movement in the West Country. The period of Mamerto Gueritz' curacy in Penzance began only 16 years after the storm over *Tract 90* broke on the heads of the Oxford leaders.

Gueritz was in his element. Church music was already established in both St Mary's and St Paul's, albeit not to his standards, which gave an opportunity for his considerable talents to be put to work. The principles of Tractarian teaching had already been established by Henry Batten and St Mary's and St Paul's were ready for the next stage of the Church Revival. Penzance at large, with a majority of the population being dissenters or nonconformists, was a different matter.

Public notice of Mamerto's ministry began amiably enough, although early reports of his activities occasionally misspelt his name. A service of fasting and prayer for India was allegedly led by a "Mr. Gerretis". This was the time of the Indian mutiny and news of the horrors perpetrated there began to appear in the Cornish newspapers. *The Cornish Telegraph* of 21 October 1857 carried a section headed "Pulpit Opinions on Indian Matters", which filled nearly the whole page. Gueritz' sermon occupied the centre of the page and was reported at length. This sermon provides us with an insight into his concept of the relationship between sin and suffering: the actions of the individual and the pains of humanity. The text he took was Luke 13:1 and 3, the story of the Galileans slaughtered by Pontius Pilate while they were offering sacrifices. The challenge came in his exposition of verse 3: "I tell you, Nay: but except ye repent, ye shall all likewise perish."

Having spoken in some detail about those responsible for the "atrocities perpetrated on our fellow countrymen" and reflecting upon their guilt and sin, Gueritz then took the burden of shared responsibility and shared guilt and placed it squarely upon his own shoulders and those of his hearers. Of the unspeakable deeds he said:

We had a share in causing them by our own personal sins and, as a nation, by our national sins. Of what should we repent?

The reporter summarized the answer:

> Of the sin of IRRELIGIOUS ENGLAND amongst which were particularised, Sabbath-breaking, swearing, drunkenness, unchastity, covetousness, pride, disobedience and luxury. The sins of RELIGIOUS ENGLAND, such as formality, hypocrisy, worldliness, spiritual pride, and our sad divisions. The crowning sin which seemed to call for God's judgement was our neglect of evangelising India.

Other local preachers pointed to a conspiracy between "Mohammedanism and Paganism, not so much as for the overthrow of British rule simply, as for the extermination of Christianity". Gueritz, on the other hand, was telling his hearers to look to their own sins before seeking others to blame. The smallest sin committed in England has consequences beyond the seas and beyond our imagining.

Of course, history points to other factors contributing to the Indian Mutiny, but for the present purpose Mamerto's articulation of the mystical concept of the relationship between personal sin and wider suffering, so powerfully expressed in this sermon, gives us an indication of the way in which his spirituality had developed as well as his homiletic talent. The effect on the congregation was salutary. After the sermon, a collection was taken to help provide funds for the Society for the Propagation of the Gospel for its work in India. It raised £21.10.0, which was no mean sum at the time.

This sermon, given just a month after Gueritz had begun his ministry in Penzance, added substance to his growing reputation as one "whose simple and earnest preaching has attracted . . . large congregations".[10]

As the family settled in, Mamerto looked for ways in which to supplement his curate's stipend. He returned once more to his earliest vocation, that of a teacher:

> The Rev Gueritz (St. Mary's Penzance) Receives into his family a few sons of gentlemen to be educated for Public Schools, Universities or Professions.

Three or four can be admitted after the Christmas vacation. Terms 50
Guineas per annum.

No. 13 Regent Terrace, Penzance.[11]

Possibly his own experience of an intensive study year in Hatherleigh had
convinced him of the worth and financial value of such teaching for both student
and teacher.

Not everyone was favourably impressed by liturgical developments over the
next few months, although the initial disquiet was mostly because Gueritz and his
clerical colleagues were not from Penzance, and in his case not even English let
alone Cornish. Lamenting the departure of Henry Batten for his convalescence
and that of the Revd E. Moore, his assistant, a reporter for *The Cornish Telegraph*
wrote:

> As both those gentlemen quitted the town at the same time, the crook
> passed into the hands of entire strangers. St. Mary's was handed over to
> the Rev. Mr Gueritz, who combines the double occupation of the cure of
> souls and the cultivation of the youthful mind. St Paul's was transferred
> to a Rev. Mr Fenton and he is aided by a curate—the Rev. Mr Simy. With
> new men came many changes.[12]

The writer was obviously unfamiliar with worship in either chapel; he admitted to
"dropping in" to St Paul's, just because he had a mind to see for himself what was
going on. Therefore, the charge of many changes should be received with caution.
Little had changed in two months and the shape of the liturgy in St Mary's and
St Paul's was only brought to public attention by the fact that "entire strangers"
were now in charge. It is evident that, from October onwards, a number of people
who had previously seldom attended Church of England services went with the
primary intention of seeing what the new clergy were doing. This had a dual
result. First the visitors were made aware of practices that had been in place under
Henry Batten but of which they had taken little note. Secondly this resulted in a
positive deluge of letters to the local press blaming the new men for innovation.

In October, it was not just the clergy who came in for criticism. This was a time
when seating in churches was restricted. There were some free seats, but many

were in the possession of pew-holders who paid an annual rent. In St Mary's, the annual income from pew rents and chapel fees at this time was around £150. The pew-holders' rights were guarded by the pew-opener who would let people in and out of the pews. He would also close the outer doors to prevent late and noisy access to the galleries. Evidently the pew-opener at St Mary's was accustomed to genuflecting towards the altar before carrying out his tasks. This resulted in:

> the pew opener would be better engaged opening the doors to let the congregation out (the outer doors had been bolted) after service than in performing those automaton tricks the display of which is so repugnant … especially when performed in that place where the knee should bow to one Deity only.

The author of this complaint wrote under the name "Churchman". Another prolific letter-writer adopted the pseudonym "Conservator". Another antagonist called himself "Earnest". They were intemperate in their outpourings, but they were not to have it all their own way. In his letter attacking the actions of the pew-opener, Churchman had also complained about the alteration in service times. He was joined in this by Conservator. Gueritz, in response to promptings from members of the congregation, had changed the times from 11am to 10.30am and from 6pm to 6.30pm. The barrage of complaints continued from late November into January. However, a solid rebuttal came, not from the clergy but from "A Pewholder":

> Had "Conservator" been regular in attendance at Church he would have heard from the Rev. Mr. Gueritz' own lips a most praiseworthy and reasonable explanation with regard to the alteration in the time of the service.[13]

It was simply that Gueritz had been told that the poor absented themselves from the morning service because of the lateness of the hour at which it finished. The remedy seemed obvious. When Conservator carried on with his condemnations A Pewholder carried the battle even further, inferring that Conservator and his supporters were idle and selfish: "Late comers will always be found, but I fear that in some instances this vice is wilful."

What had become evident, and was remarked on by A Pewholder, was that those prolific writers of critical letters were not regular members of the Anglican congregation at all but dissenters. As were "Zelota" and "Iota", who soon joined the fray. Such a plethora of pseudonyms! On the side of the clergy defence A Pewholder was soon joined by "A Looker On".

If their antagonists had but waited, Mamerto Gueritz and the Revd Mr Fenton were about to supply them with all the material they would need to mount a full-scale attack. On 23 December, Conservator complained of the "great innovations made in the services since the Rev. Henry Batten's departure".

On 24 December 1857, at St Paul's, Penzance, Christmas midnight mass was celebrated for the first time in Cornwall since the Reformation, or so it was claimed. Fenton presided with Simy acting as deacon and Mamerto Gueritz assisting. A report of the celebration appeared on 30 December and, being in the form of an editorial, was initially a little more temperate than the previous correspondence. The editor thought it important enough to afford the article 18 column inches! This was the same year in which the Protestant newspapers of London published a summary of the midnight masses held across the capital. The first to be selected for vilification was St Matthias, Stoke Newington, where Mamerto Gueritz was later to make lasting friendships.

By 11pm on Christmas Eve, there were between 70 and 80 people gathered in St Paul's in silent prayer and meditation, many of them women. The atmosphere of quiet devotion was a marked contrast to the drunken rendering of "Christmas Hosannas" by revellers outside the building. Gueritz was kneeling at the altar rails for this period of prayer, then just before midnight he rose and went into the vestry. Fenton and the assistant curate Simy appeared in surplices and genuflected. Facing east, they and the congregation sang the Christmas antiphons unaccompanied. There was no music at the service, the reason for which will appear. After the "psalm", as the reporter called it, the Communion service was celebrated exactly according to the Book of Common Prayer. It was noted that Mr Fenton seldom used his book. There were about 40 communicants and at one in the morning all departed. It might be thought that, in the light of developments at St Mary's in later years, when the ceremonial came to rival that of the London churches, this first midnight service would offer little offence. No incense, no vestments, no "judicious interpolations" into the rite. However, it must be remembered that, although by 1857 Tractarianism had made great advances in Cornwall, it was still early days and things that would pass unremarked only a few years later were then regarded as arrant Popery, especially by nonconformists and Calvinist Anglicans.

The service was adjudged to be "very solemn", but the editorial was not as even-handed as at first it seemed. The time of the service was criticized, as was the placing of uncovered communion vessels on the altar, but the main source of offence was the "placing of a cross above the centre of the communion table . . . three feet long and composed of evergreen and flowers . . . an innovation of the most injudicious kind". The editorial ends with dire warnings of how the people of Penzance would react to having Puseyism thrust upon them:

> We respect also the conscientious opinions of the genuine Roman Catholic; but any attempt to foist upon this town a bastard Protestantism that insidiously undermines our faith, and leads us step by step Rome-ward, that exchanges our Bibles for Prayer Books, that gives us counterfeit forms and ceremonies for genuine, simple worship, and makes our women 'Sisters of Mercy' and our men medieval apes, we will offer a strong and indignant opposition . . . The town of Penzance has once shown its indignation at clerical conduct which it did not approve, and, its suspicions once aroused, it will not be slow to make itself clearly and distinctly understood.

The town of Penzance, if only in the persons of Iota and Zelota and their allies, did its best to ensure the fulfilment of this prophecy. One of the charges levelled by Iota was that the liturgy was conducted with a "horrible faultlessness". This drew a scornful response from his opponents, who went so far as to suggest that, as the dissenters had taken it upon themselves to visit and criticize Anglican churches, so the Anglicans of Penzance should do the same in return. Zelota, in justifying the term "horrible faultlessness", wrote:

> The "style" of the midnight ceremony which I witnessed was so artistically accurate that, as I said before, the attention of both priests and people seemed to rest on *that*, rather than on the spiritual realities which the ceremony was designed to set forth. It was *not* pleasing to me to see a religious service conducted with such external perfection as to suggest the

idea that it might have been elaborately and frequently "rehearsed" for the occasion. As an exhibition it was faultlessly beautiful; as a spiritual exercise it was, to my mind unsatisfactory in the extreme.[14]

The clergy kept their own counsel and did not personally respond to the barrage of criticism in the press; a silence which enraged their opponents greatly. The correspondence on the midnight service was still going in February 1858 until it finally petered out and other causes of offence were taken up. However, Zelota's comment regarding the "horrible faultlessness" deserves consideration in the context of the Ritual Revival which was soon to unfold in Cornwall. This may have been one of the earliest instances of such a criticism being levelled, but it was not the first and it would by no means be the last. There was always a danger that the very ritual which was meant to bring the faith alive for the people would become an end in itself and would appear to some to be self-indulgent and spiritually sterile. However, as Colin Stephenson reflected, ensuring that the ritual was perfectly rehearsed freed the minds of the priests to focus on the divine action in the Eucharist and to reach for the holiness that lay behind it. The balance has always been a fine one.[15]

The Church Revival which had arrived in Penzance would take its course and a much more developed ritual would eventually become the tradition at St Mary's.[16] However, the Oxford Movement was stalled at St Paul's not so much by the voice of dissenters as by one of its earlier champions.

There was no accompaniment for the singing at midnight in St Paul's. However, there was none on Christmas Day either, which was explained in a letter written by Henry Viner the organist and published in *The Cornish Telegraph* on 30 December:

Sir—In answer to numerous enquiries as to my not fulfilling my usual duties as organist on Christmas day, and Sunday last, I think it necessary to state that it originated with the Rev M. G. (sic) Fenton (the temporary minister) having taken it upon himself to dismiss me at a few hours' notice—not on account of any misconduct, or neglect of duty, but for my firm refusal to acknowledge his right to interfere with my duties, so explicitly defined by the Rev. H. Batten, and for fourteen years closely adhered to by me . . . I contemplate taking legal proceedings.

The "temporary minister" was properly named George Metcalfe Fenton, and he discovered that the threat of legal proceedings was not an idle one. Henry Viner was in and out of court at least half a dozen times over the next few years, sometimes as complainant but more often as defendant, mostly over charges of libel. He was sometimes violent in his vilification of those who opposed him and was regarded as vexatious by more than one judge.

The point of contention was where the right to choose the hymns and the music lay and what the role of the priest should be in that. Was the music there to serve the liturgy or the reverse? Perhaps Fenton had yet to learn the skills required in establishing a working relationship between priest and organist. He certainly did not seem to be aware of the limits of the authority of a curate in such matters, but faced with a man such as Henry Viner he certainly displayed courage. The matter was eventually resolved and life at St Paul's continued without Henry Viner, but not ultimately on the same trajectory as St Mary's.

Miles Brown classes Fenton among those clergy who, having begun to follow the Tractarian line, could not continue and reverted to a less contentious style of ministry:

> There were Cornish clergy . . . who experienced a reaction to evangelicalism, as did Fenton at St Paul's Penzance. This man had been an adherent of Pusey and in his first parish, in Yorkshire, had felt the displeasure of his bishop, who refused to enter his church. Like his friend Newman, he began to feel his position was not honest and that he must choose between two directions. He met at this juncture the evangelical Hay Aitken, son of Robert of Pendeen, and decided to conform to the "accepted uses" of the Church of England.[17]

Fenton was already in the process of "conforming" at the time of Gueritz' arrival in Penzance, but this was not a complete *volte face* and the theology of the Tractarians was not completely abandoned. The Aitkens, father and son, were as much Catholic as Evangelical. This was reflected in the fact that the worst any detractor could say, with any justification, of that first Cornish midnight mass was that there were things that were "injudicious" about its presentation. The content was entirely legal, and the "horrible faultlessness" was evidence of the liturgical discipline still exercised by Fenton. Nevertheless, it was Fenton who led St Paul's to that Evangelical character that it retained for many years. It was an interesting reversal, with St Paul's becoming gradually "lower" and St Mary's beginning to be taken "up the candle", as a High Church colloquialism has it.

The lessons to be learned from this conflict with Henry Viner were not lost on Mamerto Gueritz. When John Hopkins Nunn was appointed organist at St Mary's almost two years later, his duties were spelled out in detail. The days and services at which music was to be provided were specified, the length and frequency of choir instruction was stated, and it was explicit in the contract that the clergyman was to select the hymns and the music. Only the incumbent had the contractual capacity to make such an appointment so Henry Batten, even though he was in his final illness, signed the contract. Nevertheless, it was Gueritz who guided the whole process from recruitment to final drafting. It was a good appointment. When he died in 1905 Nunn was still contributing to the musical life of Penzance.

Mamerto's work with the choir was noted by his successor. He had moved the choir from the gallery to the chancel, and his work with them had demonstrable effect on the standard of their singing. As he had striven for excellence in the music of Barrington Church, so he did in Penzance. Philip Hedgeland, who followed Henry Batten as perpetual curate, resisted pressures to move the choir back to the gallery, and in a letter to the congregation of 7 August 1860, he commented:

> Having been accustomed myself to be present at St. Mary's during evening service, I am convinced that there is a marked advance upon the singing which I recollect two or three years ago.[18]

This was just after Gueritz had left Penzance and before either Hedgeland or John Nunn had begun to make their own mark.

Mamerto's simple and earnest style of preaching meant that during his time in Penzance not only was his congregation challenged at the level of personal commitment, they also had the main tenets of the Oxford Movement placed before them in an accessible way. Baptismal regeneration, One Holy Catholic and Apostolic Church, the centrality of the Eucharist and the outworking of this in daily lives, were all taught, sometimes quite robustly as in his "Indian sermon" but more often with gentle persuasion and persistence.

Family life also continued, with the sons of gentlemen boarding as scholars in the Gueritz home and a new arrival in the form of a daughter. Mamerto and Anne's sixth child, Antonia Anne, was born on 26 April 1859. However, there were influences beginning to be felt from outside the home and from beyond the parish of Penzance, changes that would reach even to the far west of Cornwall and change the lives of Cornish folk forever.

The railway had arrived in Penzance in 1852, but London was still a long way away. Before the trains came a journey to London from the western reaches was often undertaken by sea. Overland it was a long, uncomfortable and sometimes dangerous undertaking. The Hayle to Redruth line had been extended by August 1852 to Penzance in the west and Truro in the east. Then on 2 May 1859 Brunel's bridge at Saltash was opened and, although it was necessary to change at Truro because the line changed from standard gauge to broad gauge, travel to London was comparatively quick and easy, certainly by comparison with boat or carriage. This allowed Gueritz to see at first hand all the liturgical developments taking place in the new churches, these having been built in the style of the Catholic Revival. It was also an opportunity to revive friendships made in Oxford. There was, however, a personal interest in one particular parish. The long-delayed church of All Saints, Margaret Street was finally complete and when the new building was consecrated in May 1859 preparations were already under way for the reinstatement of the residential boys' choir school. Local non-residential choristers had filled the breach since 1856 when the choir school was dissolved. Three of those former choristers headed the list of ten who, with their master, took up residence in the west wing of the vicarage early in 1860. Among the new boys was Mamerto George Gueritz. Evidently his father had been involved in those preparations and was well acquainted with Upton Richards, the incumbent, and with the other clergy. However, Mamerto's networking was not limited to Margaret Street. He was later to become greatly attached to St Matthias, Stoke Newington, which had been consecrated some years before in 1853. He would also come to know C. J. Le Geyt, the incumbent, very well. Gueritz also made friends at St John's Hammersmith, which was completed in 1859, the same year as All Saints, and later he would come to know St Alban's, Holborn, which was completed in 1863.

All Saints, Margaret Street, while George was in the choir there, was naturally Mamerto's main focus of attention when in London. Thus, he became well known to the generation of curates who were in office during those first years of the reinstated choir. These friendships were so significant that their names were recorded in Mamerto's obituary more than 50 years later. That period of his involvement at All Saints coincided with Charles Gutch, who served from 1859 to 1864 having earlier served at St Matthias, Stoke Newington and St Paul's, Knightsbridge. Gutch, who had already been offered and refused the incumbency of St Saviour's, Leeds, went on to found the Mission Church of St Cyprian of Carthage in Clarence Gate. Richard West was at All Saints from 1860 to 1864. Orby Shipley served from 1860 to 1863, became a prolific writer and later converted to Roman Catholicism.[19] Charles Christie stood out from the others, who all moved within a few years; he stayed for 30 years, from 1857 to 1887.

It was this circle, to which Mamerto Gueritz had already been introduced, which was to be a shaping influence upon his development as a priest, not only while George was at the choir school but in the years that followed. Although All Saints was not to be the only source of inspiration and formative liturgical experiences, the story of its development informs our understanding of that of Mamerto Gueritz.

Gueritz had only just matriculated when Frederick Oakeley, who had served the Margaret Chapel since July 1839, was suspended from all ministry in the province of Canterbury after a trial in the Court of Arches presided over by Sir Herbert Jenner Fust. This was on Monday, 30 June 1845. Later trials of Anglo-Catholic clergy would focus on ritual offences, but Oakeley's conviction was different. He had indeed introduced choral services and made (arguably) "the first attempt to exhibit in London the practical application in worship of the principles of the Oxford Movement".[20]

Although such ritual innovations as Oakeley introduced were restrained when compared with what came later, the Margaret Chapel was considered to be not only the first but "the most advanced exponent of Catholic ritual in the Church of England".[21]

Oakeley's offence was that he had issued a pamphlet in which he affirmed that while he personally held all Roman doctrine he did so "as distinct from teaching" it. Doctrine, rather than ritual, was the first test of catholicity in Margaret Street. However, it should be noted that Oakeley equated "Catholic" with "Roman" and this was in contrast with many supporters of the Oxford Movement who emphatically did not make Oakeley's equation. For them the catholicity of the English Church did not depend upon its relationship with Rome.

Not that such fine distinctions were made in the realm of public opinion. The principle of guilt by association was one of the major injustices of the situation. Oakeley was tarred with the same brush not only of others charged with ritual or doctrinal offences but of those whose offences were of an altogether grosser kind. *The Guardian* of 30 September 1846, a year after the trial, carried an article which challenged this injustice. It noted that under the Church Discipline Act, Tractarians were being disciplined and deprived alongside adulterers and other offenders without distinction. Sometimes the Tractarians suffered greater penalties. For example, "John Jones, for fornication and adultery was suspended *ab officio et ab beneficio* for two years." This was set alongside "Frederick Oakeley, for publishing a pamphlet . . . contrary to the articles of religion, had his license revoked and suspended *ab officio* until he shall retract his errors."

By the time the article was written, it was too late. Frederick Oakeley was received into the Roman Catholic Church on 29 October 1845 in a small chapel in Oxford.

Given such a history, woven into the mindset of Margaret Street from the earliest days was the expectation of battle and the anticipation of hierarchical displeasure. This, in turn, would dictate the kind of men, their calibre and temper, who would offer themselves as curates or openly associate themselves with the work in succeeding years. Daily mass was instituted by Upton Richards in April 1850, although that was in Great Tichfield Street because the Margaret Street site was being cleared for the new building. It should be noted that it was not until 11 August 1867, eight years after All Saints was consecrated, that full Eucharistic vestments were introduced. When Gueritz first knew the place, it was still relatively, by later standards, restrained.

As young George Gueritz settled into the life of the school in Margaret Street during the latter half of 1859, there would have been little for which he was not

Mamerto Gueritz: A portrait taken in Margaret Street c.1860

prepared, save the experience of living away from home for the first time. One facet of parish life which he may not have encountered directly in Penzance was the work of the Sisters of the Poor. His father would have had greater awareness of the work of sisterhoods, but this was an opportunity for both of them to see the work at close quarters. This was not the first such community by any means. In 1848, the Plymouth Sisterhood, under Lydia Sellon, was formally sanctioned by Bishop Phillpotts. From 1847 to 1849, Oxford and Wantage were the settings for a number of similar developments which took place during Gueritz' time at St Edmund Hall. Even in rural Cornwall the value of such communities was beginning to be recognized. Francis Caudwell was the incumbent of Carnmenellis.[22] He had been a curate in Devonport and had had connections with the Devonport Sisters of Mercy. In August 1861, he wrote to Dr Pusey:

> I have lately started a sisterhood on a very humble scale for the poor mine girls, of which there are large numbers in this parish and I am thankful to say that we have six probationary Sisters which is a great deal in a parish like mine, with seven Meeting Houses in it and methodism in every house.[23]

In accordance with Pusey's standing advice that women were best at directing the work of women, the community was looked after by the Devonport Sisters until it closed in 1865.

Although Gueritz had left Penzance by the time Caudwell wrote to Pusey, the work of sisterhoods was clearly in the public mind, as witnessed by the vilification of the midnight mass in Penzance and criticisms that such innovations "make our women 'Sisters of Mercy' and our men medieval apes".

Meeting the sisters at All Saints Margaret Street was therefore not Mamerto Gueritz' first encounter with a working community, but it was an opportunity to see the work at close quarters. Their first priority was the support of the work of the clergy, from which all else sprang. They gave residential care to orphan girls and sick and elderly women; they dispensed medicines to the poor and visited them in their homes; they found clothing for those in need; and by 1863 they and those in their care numbered nearly 140. By then George Gueritz had left to further his academic and musical education at the College of St Michael and All Angels in Tenbury Wells, under the tutelage of Sir Frederick Arthur Gore Ouseley, the founder. Gueritz and Ouseley had come to know each other years earlier when Ouseley was an undergraduate at Christ Church, Oxford. Ouseley had gone up a year before Gueritz and they first met at a musical evening organized by a mutual friend.

Mamerto Gueritz' first period of exposure to the London Ritualist scene all happened while he was still in Penzance. The friends he then made in London would continue to form part of his support network for many years to come, in fact, lifelong. However, back in Penzance, even though young George was settled in Margaret Street, the latter part of 1859 was anything but restful. Two and a half years had seen Mamerto's reputation grow considerably, not just in Penzance but across Cornwall, which brought in its wake both negative and positive reactions. We have seen how the Protestant element of the population, both Anglican and nonconformist, reacted to the emergence of High Church practices at St Mary's. In the public mind, Gueritz was unmistakeably branded as a Tractarian and a Puseyite.

Before there was even a whisper of a possible move to Colyton, Mamerto had sought once more to combine his vocation as a priest with his earlier calling as a teacher. A mastership had fallen vacant at Penzance Grammar School, and he made an application, along with a number of other candidates. In the event, the choice first fell on the Revd W. H. Drake of St Ives but, as *The Cornish Telegraph* of 15 June 1859 reported, "Circumstances prevented his acceptance of the Mastership." A second round of applications resulted in two candidates finally being considered, Mamerto Gueritz and the Revd Edward Salter of Bath. Salter was described as "moderately evangelical". The selection of the new master was in the hands of the Education Committee appointed by the aldermen, councillors and mayor of Penzance, and it seems fair to say that they made a mess of the process, even by contemporary standards. The mayor had already made known his aversion to Tractarian clergy, and when the vote was cast, it resulted in a draw between Gueritz and Salter. In spite of other councillors protesting that theological opinion should not be allowed to determine the outcome, the mayor exercised his casting vote in favour of Edward Salter and was reported to have said that "He reprobated the recent innovations at St. Mary's as tending to Romanism and said that he could not with confidence entrust his own children to anyone who held Tractarian doctrine (better at once to place them under a Catholic, and then you know exactly what to expect) as he could not vote for any one who appeared to lean that way."

A hundred and fifty years later, such blatant bias over an appointment would have caused outrage and that, combined with the complete ineptitude of the committee, would probably have resulted in a tribunal. On this occasion the chaotic process simply caused "merriment" among the members of the committee, with one of Gueritz' seconders voting for the other candidate and another councillor voting for a candidate he had earlier declared he would not pay! Such anger and disappointment as might have been felt in the Gueritz household would be rapidly ameliorated by news that Mamerto was to be offered a choice incumbency in Devon.

Another area in which Mamerto's fame had spread was, of course, the development of church music. He had been active in the inaugural gathering of the Association of Church Choirs in Cornwall in 1858, and shortly before the move to Colyton the fourth meeting of the association was held at St Ives. This was in April 1860. The Cornish press reported the meeting at some length, affording praise to those who had organized the event, Gueritz first among them: "The whole of the music of the communion office was that of the manual of plainsong ... the number of surpliced singers amounted to ninety exclusive of the clergy."[24]

Shortly afterwards the family packed up their household and moved to Colyton, where without doubt the sight of the octagonal tower would remind Mamerto and Anne of their sojourn in Barrington and Antonia Josepha of her first steps on English soil.

Twelve years of curacies, some short and some longer, were at an end. Between the quiet beginnings in the library of St Edmund Hall and the development of liturgical practice in Penzance and Margaret Street, Mamerto Gueritz had learned to make an identification between the Tractarian theology he had absorbed in Oxford and the emergent Ritualism which attracted so many of his contemporaries. His Penzance experience prepared him in some measure for the opposition that this would provoke but, nationally, the greatest battles and the time of the Church Association prosecutions was yet to come. Nevertheless, the storm clouds were massing. This was exactly the time that Bryan King, C. F. Lowder and F. G. Lee were in the news over the riots at St George in the East, riots over services which, according to Lee, were "identical with those at St Paul's and Westminster Abbey".[25]

The same West Country newspaper that, in January 1860, heralded the arrival of the new vicar carried reports of the disturbances only two weeks later.

At this stage there was still considerable variance in the practices of those who were promoting Ritualism. Some attempted to do so from a basis of the revival of old rubrics, leaning heavily on English antiquity as a model and looking towards the old Sarum or Salisbury rite. Others, like Orby Shipley and before him W. G. Ward, made a clear identification between "Catholic" and "Roman". Ward had been charged with heresy by the same cabal that had suspended Dr Pusey. In Ward's case it was over the book in which he had proclaimed his "Romanist" convictions, *The Ideal of a Christian Church*. The book was formally condemned and Ward deprived of his degrees as a further punishment.

Those who looked to the English past were hampered by the fact that liturgical research and scholarship was not yet so fully developed as would be the case only a few years later. There was a distinct lack of homogeneity in the detail of ritual practices adopted in various centres around the country—or rather they did not all achieve the same level of so-called "advancement" at the same time. Inevitably innovation became rife and was often based on individual idiosyncrasy or half-remembered Roman Catholic masses witnessed in other countries and was therefore anything but Catholic in its proper sense. As a reaction against this, as much as an encouragement to self-preservation, we know that in 1865 Upton Richards and others made attempts to persuade Alexander Mackonochie to temper some points of the ritual at St Alban's, Holborn. This is further demonstrated in one of the earlier attempts to bring disparate practices into some kind of harmony.

Before 1860 and Gueritz' formative encounters in Margaret Street, there had already been attempts to order, if not to standardize, the ritual. In 1858, John Purchas' *Directorium Anglicanum* was published, a work which he had written with the help of F. G. Lee. In his preface to that first edition Purchas said of the would-be users, or rather misusers, of ritual:

> They have thus been forced to follow the mode of "conforming to the Liturgy", as practiced in some church which most approves itself to their partially informed instincts, the selection probably being made from circumstances of proximity or from something else equally accidental.

He then made the much-quoted and now famous statement, which has been the watchword of Anglo-Catholic priests ever since, "the argument for a ritual is not within the scope of these remarks. We have a ritual, and must use it, whether we like it or not. It behoves us to use it aright and not to mar its fair proportion."[26]

In 1865, Lee published a much-enlarged version of *The Directorium Anglicanum*, which sold out three editions within a year. There was obviously a need for working guidelines and a desire for authenticity, but Lee's *Directorium* was vast and unwieldy so in 1874 he published a shortened and simplified version under the title *Manuale Clericorum*. This was the same year that Orby Shipley published his *Ritual of the Altar*, which he revised and enlarged in 1878 just before he and his wife seceded, or in the language of the day "perverted", to the Church of Rome.

So it was that when Gueritz went to Colyton in 1860, he was already among those for whom the Catholic theology of the Tractarians was becoming interwoven with the liturgical developments that would, in the not-too-distant future, be called Ritualism. It is apparent that he did not at this stage equate loyalty to doctrine with loyalty to externals. This would come in some measure but never quite to the extent of some of his colleagues. One rather extreme example of this, which illustrates the point, came 18 years later in 1878 in the dispute between Malcolm McColl, the vicar designate of St James', Hatcham (or so he thought), and Edmund Croom, the local secretary and treasurer of the Confraternity of the Blessed Sacrament. For Croom, McColl's failure to use vestments for the weekday masses was a betrayal of both the practice *and* the doctrine that he fought to maintain. Another was Orby Shipley again. Soon after the trial of Alexander Mackonochie, there was a meeting of Ritualist clergy in January 1869. Shipley, speaking of the sanctuary lamps, which had been ordered to be extinguished, said that he did not see how, if they extinguished their lights, they could teach the doctrine of the Real Presence.[27]

This was one of the points on which the Ritualist departed from the traditional Tractarian. For the early Tractarians, Catholic truth was to be expressed and taught but did not rely on externals to validate that teaching. For the Ritualist, that truth was to be expressed both in word and in liturgical action. Any suppression of ritual was, by implication, an attack on doctrine.

Notes

[1]   The Suffragan Bishops Act of 1534 provided for the appointment of episcopal assistants. The last in those early years was John Sterne of Colchester, who died in 1607/8. No more were appointed until Henry MacKenzie was consecrated Bishop of Nottingham in February 1870.

[2]   *The Royal Cornish Gazette*, Friday, 21 November 1851.

[3]   E. A. Rees, *Old Penzance* (Penzance: Private publication, 1956, Madron Library).

[4]   "Impropriator". From the time of the dissolution of the monasteries under Henry VIII. A lay rector charged with the duty of nominating a priest to the ordinary, usually the bishop, for appointment to a cure of souls. This appointment then became perpetual. In 1705, the mayor of Penzance claimed the right of appointment and was in serious dispute with the vicar of Madron over the issue. Both, of course, had only the right of nomination. The bishop would make the appointment.

[5]   Kresen Kernow (Truro Record Office). Parish files ref. D.D.P. 2/2/57–58. This list was compiled in 1860. A much more complete list was published in *The Cornishman* on 31 January 1889. However, it should be noted that the dates are incorrect. Gueritz held office in Penzance from September 1857. Two other possible errors should be noted. Gueritz did not receive an honours degree, having been prevented by illness from sitting exams. Secondly, the St Edmund Hall register is the only place in which Mamerto Gueritz is referred to as the "second son". All other mentions have their source in those records. There is no other record of a sibling currently known, and this is therefore assumed to be a clerical error on the part of a university clerk.

[6]   Kresen Kernow (Truro Record Office). Parish files ref. D.D.P. 179/1/4.

[7]   H. Miles Brown, *The Catholic Revival in Cornish Anglicanism* (St Winnow: Private publication, 1980), p. 60.

[8]   W. S. Lach-Szyrma, *A Church History of Cornwall and of the Diocese of Truro* (London: Elliot Stock, 1891), p. 123.

[9]   Miles Brown, *The Catholic Revival in Cornish Anglicanism*, p. 66.

[10] *The Cornish Telegraph*, 30 December 1857.

[11] *The Cornish Telegraph*, 30 December 1857.

[12] *The Cornish Telegraph*, 3 February 1858

[13] This exchange can be found in *The Cornish Telegraph* from 2 December 1857 to 3 February 1858.

[14]   *The Cornish Telegraph*, Wednesday, 3 February 1858. Letter dated 29 January.

[15]   Colin Stephenson, *Merrily on High* (London: Darton, Longman and Todd, 1972), pp. 88–9. Stephenson also has a splendidly whimsical analysis of the Oxford Movement which he assimilated from Fr Wagner at St Bartholomew's, Brighton: p. 25, "The Middle Ages were the high point of Christianity in England. The Reformation was a complete disaster and deprived the ordinary Englishman of the full practice of the Catholic religion which was his by right. A small group had remained in communion with the Pope and were called 'Recusants'; they were brave, but wrong minded. For two hundred years the Church of England got deader and deader and the sacraments fell into disuse. Then a gallant group of men in Oxford decided to change all this and they were subjected to terrible persecution until one of them called John Henry Newman 'went over' to Rome taking a lot of other people with him. They were very wrong, but the blame lay on those who persecuted them. A very brave old man called Dr. Pusey endured everything and gathered around him a lot of daring young priests who began to have the right sort of services and to convert people to believe the right things. There were others called Protestants who did their best to stop them and even got the law changed so that they could send right minded priests to jail, which they proceeded to do. Almost all the bishops were Protestants and not to be trusted. However, the fight was still going on and Anglo-Catholics were right and everyone else was wrong." That says it all really.

[16]   The minutes of the Royal Commission on Ecclesiastical Discipline 1904 describe St Mary's and the services on 12 June of that year: "There were two Communion Tables, one in the chancel and one at the east end of the south aisle, a brass cross and eight candles (two lighted) over the Holy Table in the chancel, a brass cross and two candles over the smaller Holy Table, a processional cross and a banner in the chancel, a red lamp burning before the Holy Table in the chancel, a sacring bell in the chancel, a tabernacle-like structure over the smaller Holy Table, and pictures known as the Stations of the Cross on the walls of the church. There were notices at the west end of the church, one giving subjects for prayer and thanksgiving which included prayer for certain departed persons, who were named and thanksgiving for confessions, especially first confessions ... The service I attended was the 8 a.m. celebration of the Holy Communion. The clergyman was vested in a green chasuble, alb, amice, girdle, maniple and stole. He also wore a biretta. He was attended by a server vested in a violet cassock and a cotta. The clergyman, having removed his biretta, and placed the vessels on the Holy Table, appeared to engage in some private service ... after this the clergyman ascended to the Holy Table and seemed to kiss it. At the reading

of the Gospel the clergyman made the sign of the cross upon the book, his forehead, his lips and his breast. At the close of the reading he closed the Gospel Book. The clergyman ceremoniously mixed the chalice, making the sign of the cross over the water cruet, and afterwards performed the lavabo. He made the sign of the cross in the air when pronouncing the Absolution. At the Sanctus the server rang the bell, and immediately after the Sanctus the clergyman repeated the Benedictus Qui Venit. During the Prayer of Consecration the clergyman concealed the manual acts by bending his body over the elements and afterwards elevated the chalice and paten to the level of his forehead. At each elevation the server rang the bell. After the Prayer of Consecration the clergyman seemed to engage in secret prayers and ceremonies, his actions were less ostentatious than in some other cases, but he was seen to make the sign of the cross over the elements and upon himself; also to genuflect before the elements. This action he repeated three or four times. He was also seen to elevate the paten to the level of his forehead . . . the clergyman turned to the people and holding in his hand a wafer said, 'Behold the Lamb of God which taketh away the sin of the world' . . . at the administration the sign of the cross was made with the wafer and the chalice before each communicant. At the close of the Communion the clergyman performed the ablutions, a practice which performed at this stage is contrary to the rubric."

[17]   Miles Brown, *The Catholic Revival in Cornish Anglicanism*, pp. 64–5.

[18]   Kresen Kernow (Truro Record Office). Parish files ref. D.D.P. 179/2/2/58.

[19]   Orby Shipley became a prolific writer and an editor of manuals of devotion and of liturgical history, especially where it touched upon the then current troubles, notably the effect of the Public Worship Regulation Act. Possibly the most widely used work was his *Ritual of the Altar* (London: Longmans, 1874, revised 1878).

[20]   W. A. Whitworth, *Quam Delicta* (London: Wells Gardner Darton, 1891), p. 37.

[21]   Whitworth, *Quam Delicta*, p. 48.

[22]   Carnmenellis is actually the name of a hill and lies between Redruth, Penryn and Helston. The ecclesiastical parish of the same name was created in 1848. The village was Penmarth, which is now (2022) part of the Stithian civil parish.

[23]   Papers of Dr E. B. Pusey, Pusey House, Oxford.

[24]   The whole was reprinted in *Pulman's Weekly News*, 25 May 1860, in order to inform the people of East Devon concerning the new vicar of Colyton.

[25]   H. R. T. Brandreth, *Dr. Lee of Lambeth* (London: SPCK, 1951), p. 24.

[26]   J. Purchas, *The Directorium Anglicanum* (London: Joseph Masters, 1st edn, 1858), p. vii.

[27]   *The Kentish Gazette*, Tuesday, 19 January 1869.

5

Colyton in 1860: Another contextual note

Colyton lies three miles inland from the coast at Seaton and is centred on rising ground beside the Coly River. It is enclosed on the other side by a steep ridge. If not entirely isolated, in 1860 it was at least away from such major lines of communication as then existed. North-south communication was along the Axminster to Axmouth road, which passed along the eastern side of the Axe valley floor with Colyton away to the west, cut off by the Coly. The coast road from Lyme Regis to Exeter passed through the parish, but more than a mile south of the town, and Exeter is some 25 miles to the west. Although these distances may not seem great today, in the days when local roads were packed flint and earth and the main roads not much better, a season of heavy rain could render transport and thus all communication all but impossible. The population of around 2,500 lived mainly in what is now the centre of the town.

In order to understand the local reactions to the arrival and subsequent ministry of Mamerto Gueritz, it is needful to have some understanding of the community which was the parish of Colyton in 1860, especially in terms of its religious heritage and practice. In order to grasp that at a deeper level than just the statistics of denominations and churchgoing, an understanding of how the community perceived itself is also necessary. In many ways, Colyton shared the characteristics of other similar communities of the same size in East Devon at the time, but in some aspects it was (and still is) unique.

The first thing to acknowledge is inherited identity. Community memory is still very strong in such places. Where there are families who have been rooted in the parish and surrounding district for centuries, in some cases for more than 400 years, their inherited memories are strong indeed. And yet, the clarity and strength of such memory which persists even today is only a shadow of what it was in the early nineteenth century. In spite of the ways in which we can see inherited or community memory to have worked in the past, it is still difficult to comprehend from within the greatly changed communities of the twenty-first century. So any attempt to record the actions of Mamerto Gueritz and his opponents would be fruitless without an attempt to understand them from within the mindset of the community of the time.

Protestant identity and the origins of nonconformity both have a long and deeply embedded history in Colyton. This was one reason behind much of the negative reaction to the ministry of Mamerto Gueritz, although within that there are nuances to be explored. We owe much of our understanding of the history of nonconformity in Colyton to Ravenor E. Rose, for 12 years Congregational minister in the town and the author of a manuscript history. That history was discovered and serialized in a local newspaper in 1953. Rose traced the roots back as far as the Commonwealth and the replacement of the incumbent, Thomas Collyns, by an "intruded" Puritan minister. The church records make the bald and disapproving statement:

> John Wilkins was intruded on the parishioners 19th December, 1647, without appointment by the Dean and Chapter: he was ejected 24th August 1662 and dying 9th October 1667, was buried 18th of the same month. Vicar Collyns was buried 13th April 1665.[1]

Rose, naturally enough, has a rather different view:

> In 1647 John Wilkins was presented to the living and continued Vicar of Colyton until Bartholomew's Day 1662 when he is said to have refused the oath of supremacy, and was ejected 24th August 1662. For some time after being ejected he preached in his own house but lived only until 1667 when he died of consumption. He was buried in the Parish Church of Colyton, in the vicar's vestry which he had built. The register contains the entry of his burial. 1667—John Wilkins, minister, buried ye xviii daye of October.[2]

As ever, a balanced understanding falls somewhere between the two. Wilkins, as far as can be ascertained, had never been episcopally ordained. Therefore, he was put out of the living not only for his failure to take the oath of supremacy but because he was not in priestly orders and could not remain. However, whether the parson is "intruded" or "legitimate", there are things about his ministry that will remain in the memory of the people. Two terse entries in the margin of the parish register, in what appears to be Wilkins' own hand, reveal much: "November 28th 1645—Here ye sicknesse began." And then, "December 22nd 1646—Here ye sicknesse ended."

The plague had come to Colyton and carried off no fewer than 458 people, over a fifth of the population, in just over one year. In all that time, all such evidence as can be found indicates that Wilkins faithfully ministered to his flock, the sick and the well, regardless of his own safety. This faithful service was rewarded by a loyal following until his death and left a markedly Protestant stamp on the life of the community. Wilkins is thus seen as the first to champion nonconformity and as the founder of Congregationalism in Colyton.

Another demonstration of the way in which Protestantism had marked the community was revealed by the research carried out by G. P. R. Pulman for his *Book of the Axe*.[3] When he went to Colyton seeking amplification of the stories, he had heard of the town's support for the Monmouth rebellion, and he asked local people for their stories. It was evident that not only were the doings of the previous generation clear in the local memory but also the doings of their families of centuries before. The events of the Monmouth rebellion, which took place less than 20 years after the death of John Wilkins, were recounted with such vividness that the feelings expressed were more than just memory. As Pulman noted, it was as if they were being experienced in the present moment. One source was W. H. Rogers of Colyton, whose great grandmother had been alive at the time of the rebellion and had passed her memory down through the family. The Duke of Monmouth passed through Colyton, and a large number of the humbler Colyton men followed him to the fight. Many of them fell at the battle of Sedgemoor; those who survived were pursued as they tried to return home. A troop of dragoons were ordered out from Ottery St Mary, others from Honiton joined them and they took up the chase. The fleeing men—and women—had varying fortunes. There were many atrocities committed as the king's forces suppressed the rebellion. Locally the worst, arguably, was against a fugitive who lived in Bull's Court in Colyton. Taken by surprise, he hid in the cabbage patch behind the house. His children, questioned by the soldiers and innocent of the consequences, told where he was hidden. The dragoons executed him on the spot. They then quartered him and compelled a nearby shoemaker to take one of the quarters around the town in a wheelbarrow. That sort of thing leaves a lasting mark on a community. However, there were two others whose fate also had a profound influence on the attitude of Colyton folk. In September 1685, George Seaward was hanged at Dorchester. On the scaffold he declared: "My whole design in taking up arms under the Duke of Monmouth was to fight for the Protestant religion."[4]

Robert Satchell, another Colytonian taken on his way home, was executed at Weymouth. In a report of his defence, or rather of his statement of defiance, it was claimed he had "always hated the name of papist and, as it fell out we did see popery advancing, as his words to divers of his neighbours can testifie".[5]

Given these events and the way community memory held and retold them in each generation, the strength of the Protestant character of Colyton, both in church and chapel, is scarcely to be remarked at. Significantly, W. H. Rogers was the author of a number of articles and letters in the Unitarian press which were acutely and imaginatively critical of Mamerto Gueritz' innovations. That aside for the moment, the manner in which dissent later evolved is even more important for our understanding of the religious forces at work in Colyton when Mamerto Gueritz was presented to the living.

Congregationalism may well have had its beginnings with the ministry of John Wilkins, but change was to come. At first, the doctrines of the nonconformist congregation were uniformly Presbyterian and thus Trinitarian. Until late in the eighteenth century, the Presbyterian Fund allowed £6 per annum towards the minister's stipend. The minister at this time was Dr Cornish, who died in 1824. Rose described him as "an Arian in sentiment".[6]

The signs of this heterodoxy lay much further back in the history of the chapel, for Pulman writes of Samuel Slater, the minister from 1745 to 1761, that he was "an Arian if not a Unitarian".[7] And to turn again to Ravenor Rose:

> After 1824 the congregation was essentially Socinian. Presbyterianism having ceased to exist, the building eventually being named and recognised as a Unitarian place of worship.

These religious labels, Arian, Socinian and Unitarian, are not entirely interchangeable, and their unwary use could cause as much confusion as the various terms in use regarding Anglo-Catholics. Arianism had its origin in the teaching of Arius, who was condemned as a heretic and exiled in AD 325. Arius had taught that God as the author of nature must be one and indivisible. Christ is his messenger and subordinate but still pre-existent and divine. He was of *like* substance with the Father and not of *one* substance as Trinitarian orthodoxy held. Socinianism began with Lelio and Fausto Sozzini in the late sixteenth century and went further than Arianism in that it denied not only the doctrine of the Holy Trinity but also the pre-existence of Christ. However, by the nineteenth century, Socinianism had become a catch-all label for any non-Trinitarian belief. Because of this rather pejorative usage the term Unitarian began to be more widely used.

In Colyton, Ravenor Rose lamented what he saw as a descent from the relative orthodoxy of Congregationalism into a doctrine he saw as a non-salvific heresy. This departure from Trinitarian religion was a national trend. There were forces at work everywhere but in most places their effect was gradual and, perhaps because of the slow pace of change, either disregarded or unnoticed by local congregations in places like Colyton. It was sudden change that attracted an instinctive opposition.

On 21 July 1813, the Unitarian Relief Act received the Royal Assent, the monarch being George III. By this time, the king had become incurably insane and the Prince of Wales, later to be George IV, was Regent. The Act merely eased the penalties laid upon "persons who infringe the doctrine of the Holy Trinity", but it was still seen as something of a watershed in the struggle for freedom of religious expression. A special meeting of the Unitarian Book Society recorded its response to the Act as "[a]n auspicious prelude to that happy day when all penal laws . . . on religious grounds shall be for ever abolished . . . and when all, without distinction, shall be entitled by law to the possession of those civil and political privileges which are the birthright of Britons".[8]

Before this Act many congregations which had become Arian or had Arian leadership retained the name Presbyterian or Congregationalist. George's Chapel in Exeter was opened as a Presbyterian foundation in 1760, the year of the accession of George III. By 1813, it had become an openly Unitarian congregation, having been so in fact for many years. The building was then called George's

Meeting House. Exactly the same history and process unfolded in Colyton at George's Meeting House in Higher Church Street.

This process of change, and the distinction between Arianism and Unitarianism, provides a background for our understanding of the religious conflicts in Colyton beginning in 1860.

The dissenting academies played a major part in this process. The academies were originally set up at a time when only members of the Church of England could attend the universities. They not only prepared nonconformist ministers for their work, but they also counted among their alumni some notable Anglicans, among them Thomas Secker, who later became Archbishop of Canterbury. These academies were originally rooted in the Calvinist theology of ministers who, like John Wilkins, were ejected from their livings in 1662. However, they began to change in character during the mid-eighteenth century.

One of the later foundations was Warrington Academy, established in 1757 by John Seddon, a local minister; Joseph Priestley was among its tutors from 1761 to 1767. This academy has been described as the first of the redbrick universities, and it took lay as well as ministerial students. Divinity was still preferred over other subjects, but it was not mandatory, and the curriculum changes represented a growing liberalization. A number of the older foundations began to close around the same time, but even in those older, more traditional, establishments "Presbyterian and Independent and not a few Anglicans had been educated together under the care of ministers of liberal sentiments."[9]

This liberality was reflected in the subjects taught, in the effect upon the students and thus upon generations of ministers and their congregations. In the hands of such tutors, Newtonian cosmology led ultimately to an Arian understanding of Christ as God's messenger and subordinate but still pre-existent and divine. Arianism thus understood, though counter to orthodoxy, could still claim a biblical foundation.

More radically modernist was Unitarianism, which was championed by men like Joseph Priestley. Priestley's first discipline was chemistry, and for him science and theology were indivisibly intertwined. Enlightenment rationalism was blended in his teaching with Christian theism. He believed that a proper understanding of the natural world would promote human progress and eventually bring about the Christian millennium. His six years at Warrington Academy meant that several hundred dissenting ministers took his message to congregations far and wide, and Priestley was not alone. It was his metaphysical writings, however, that had the most lasting influence, being considered primary sources by philosophers such as Jeremy Bentham and John Stuart Mill.

Priestley's Unitarianism was more emphatically rationalist, more completely Newtonian and far more individualistic than Arianism. Christ was not the pre-existent Word but a man commissioned by God to proclaim divine truth. Unitarianism was the means whereby his message would be reclaimed from contemporary Christianity, which was no more than the result of a progressive and sometimes deliberate corruption of the original proclamation.

During the first half of the nineteenth century, especially after 1813, Arianism and then Unitarianism grew and, in many places, supplanted the Trinitarian orthodoxy of the Presbyterians and Congregationalists. In rare cases the change was rapid and aggressive, leaving the usurped part of a divided congregation to find a new home. More often, as in Exeter and in Colyton, the change happened gradually and without too much dislocation, if any. Henry Gow expresses the changes thus:

> These Chapels and Trusts had gradually passed into the hands of the Unitarians. There had been no definite break with the past. The change of thought had been gradual, often imperceptible, from year to year.[10]

So it is that when Dr Cornish is called Arian and some 30 years later in the tale an arch opponent of Gueritz, one Harry De Spencer Kingdon, is described as Unitarian, the process and the distinction may be understood. It should therefore be no surprise that Mamerto Gueritz, holding fast to the doctrines of the Church of England and its disciplines, should find himself at odds with the proponents of a teaching which to him was heretical. However, there were more than just doctrinal differences between the Anglicans and the Unitarians.

Within the complex web of historical processes and contemporary political pressures which gave rise to the Oxford Movement, we have already taken account of the work of the earlier High Churchmen and noted the increasing tendency of the Whig government to legislate on Church matters. That latter circumstance alone may well have given rise to John Keble's charge of "National Apostasy", but another force, which had been at work for more than a decade before the Assize Sermon, had its place in stimulating both Keble's defence of the Church and the ensuing *Tracts for the Times* and then the rapid growth of Tractarianism. In 1820, the radical Unitarian John Wade first published his *Black Book* which evolved into the *Extraordinary Black Book*, published the year before Keble's charge. Wade saw the entire establishment, Church and State, as irredeemably corrupt and the first quarter of his extraordinary book was an elaboration of all that, according to Wade, was evil and corrupt in the Established Church. Of course, not all Unitarians were as radical as John Wade and by 1860 such extreme outpourings were largely in the past. Mamerto Gueritz, by that time, had clearly identified as a Tractarian. Everything that he held dear in terms of theology and ecclesiology set him completely at odds with radical Unitarianism. It is small wonder that, even though the existential threat to the Church of England might have eased, relationships between the champions of the "Church Revival" and Unitarians reflected this history.

None of this seems to have troubled the previous vicar of Colyton. Gueritz' predecessor, Frederick Barnes, was not of the same stamp, and the legacy left for Gueritz by his ministry is significant. Before we meet Frederick Barnes, however, a brief sketch of the structures of authority in the parish of Colyton will be helpful. The reason for such an excursus at this point is the rather unusual place those structures, both historical and contemporary, afforded the parish priest of Colyton.

Just as there were elements in the history of the town which contributed to the religious identity of the people, so there were others which helped create a distinctive culture of self-reliance which permeated the populace. We have already noted the effect of events during the Commonwealth and the Monmouth rebellion. Another series of events, which predated them by a century, had an even more profound and lasting effect on the character of the community.

On 9 January 1539, by order of King Henry VIII, Henry Courtenay, Marquis of Exeter and Lord of the Manor of Colyton, was beheaded. His estates were escheated to the Crown and Colyton was left without a lord. The nearby abbey fell victim to the suppression of the monastic orders and was despoiled. "No Lord, no law". The immediate effects of all this, the fields left fallow, the rise in lawlessness and the consequent sufferings of the common people, are well documented.

However, these circumstances provided the emergent merchant classes with an opportunity to change their world and even to become "landed" after a fashion:

> Like shrewd men of business, although actuated by the best and most charitable feelings that give an imperishable lustre to their memory, certain well to do inhabitants of the town collected their moneys together to the amount of a thousand pounds, and with this sum they bargained for, and bought of the Grim Monarch, a portion of the confiscated manor of Colyton, the rents and proceeds to be expended in such good, Godly and commendable uses as they should determine.[11]

More than 80 inhabitants of the town, men and women, put their resources together to find the thousand pounds with which, in the Deed of Enfeoffment dated 6 January 1546, the king acknowledged himself to be "fully satisfied and contented". In the same deed, the petitioners were not only granted the lands and properties and rents, but also the management of and tolls from the market held three times a week and the tolls and profits from two annual fairs and a Court of Pie Powder or *Pie Poudre* Court. This court sat in times of public markets or fairs with a jurisdiction limited to disputes between merchants and consumers and any other dispute arising as a result of the market or fair and on fairgrounds. This was an authority originally belonging either to the lord of the manor or to the mayor and bailiffs, and it had been ceded to the Feoffees. A remarkable shift of power but a power to be used for the community. As the deed charged the petitioners, it was for "the use of them and their heirs to fulfil and perform such intents and purposes as by twenty men of the parish of Colyton, by the parishioners of Colyton then nominated, should be declared and devised".[12]

In effect the Feoffees became a parochial corporation and most of the social functions of the town seem to have devolved upon them, except the workings of the law other than in the Court of Pie Powder. This marked, in a limited way, a transition from feudal society to embryonic socialism. The independence of spirit needed to conceive the plan, the commitment of the community needed to raise the money and the dogged courage needed to face the "Grim Monarch" and see the project through to completion became woven into the social character of the town. It became part of the expectation that the people had of their leaders.

Because the Chamber of Feoffees persisted, so the spirit which characterized the first "twentymen" infused the spirit of the whole community. Every year since, the Feoffees have held an anniversary celebration of one kind or another. Latterly, certainly throughout the twentieth and into the twenty-first century, there has been a feast or banquet held at which the names of the twentymen are recited and their history retold. Perhaps, as was claimed by a later priest of the parish, the event bears a passing resemblance to the recitation of the *Heilsgeschichte* or salvation history at the Jewish Pesach. "It will be for you as if you were there." Community memory at its most powerful.

From this point onwards, no single figure of authority could ever claim to dominate the town. This remained true even when the lordship of the manor passed to the Pole family who later left Colyton to reside at Shute. Therefore, it was a wise parish priest who tempered any temptation to influence the secular life of the town with a willingness to be allied to those who were also working for the good of the people.[13] From the outset, the Chamber of Feoffees was a decidedly secular body. With the growth of nonconformity, it gradually became also distinctly ecumenical. During the 1850s, Anglicans and Unitarians sat alongside each other to plan for the wellbeing of the town at large and the poor in particular.

In other contemporary communities of a similar size, power was often held by the parson and the squire, or lord of the manor in balance with other local worthies. What, then, did this mean for the parish priest of Colyton? Paradoxically this very spirit of independence and the lessened influence of the lord of the manor gave the parish priest a role distinctive within the community and somewhat different from the average parish priest in East Devon at the time. Other leading figures were of the community whereas the incumbent was the outsider who "belonged". An authority figure who stood out against the background. We have already noted the care with which such authority would have to be exercised and how fragile it might turn out to be, especially in a community where common folk were very conscious of their uncommon and historic freedoms.

Frederick Barnes, D.D., incumbent from 1807 until his death in 1859, seems to have managed to avoid religious controversy in Colyton for all of his 52 years in office. Such a long incumbency was by no means unusual at the time and seems to have had few of the detrimental effects now feared from clergy who outstay their welcome. Barnes was from a recently arisen but notable clerical family.

His father, Ralph Barnes, was Canon and Chancellor of Exeter and Archdeacon of Totnes. His brother was Archdeacon of Exeter when Henry Phillpotts came to the see in 1831. However, Barnes' grandfather, also named Frederick, was a physician in Colyton and Ralph Barnes was born there in 1732. When Frederick Barnes was admitted to the living of Colyton and the perpetual curacies of Shute and Monckton on 3 March 1807, in spite of the social and ecclesiastical heights to which his family had ascended, he was still the son of a Colytonian.

To Colyton folk this counted for much. In addition to his parochial cure, Barnes was also a prebendary of Exeter Cathedral, became a canon and sub-dean of Christ Church Oxford and was appointed chaplain to the House of Commons. Taken together the income from the parochial cure and the canonry of Christ Church alone came to over £1,400 together with the parsonage in Colyton and a residence in Oxford. This, with the income from his other appointments, meant that Frederick Barnes was not only a wealthy man but one with influential connections in Parliament, Oxford and Exeter and of course in Colyton.

Possibly one of the reasons Barnes was held in loving esteem by his parishioners was that they did not see enough of him to become disenchanted. He was obliged to be in Oxford to discharge his duties at the university and the cathedral. His other responsibilities also claimed him on a regular basis. In 1849, a local worthy, Samuel Seaward, wrote of him:

> He was a fine old English gentleman, with white curly hair and cravat, Dr Barnes, vicar of Colyton, Shute and Monckton and Canon of Christchurch Oxford ... he is resident at Colyton only about three months each year, leaving his curates in charge of the various parishes.[14]

The tensions created by this were to be addressed ten years later when the benefice was divided before the arrival of Mamerto Gueritz. The discontent was not to do with the extended absences of the vicar; to that the people had become accustomed. It rather concerned the perceived miserliness of the Dean and Chapter of Exeter, the patrons, in failing to provide separate appointments, with attached housing, for Shute and Monckton and instead vesting them all in one clergyman. When Barnes came to the living the parochial ministry was conducted entirely from Colyton because there were no parsonages or glebe

Frederick Barnes D.D., vicar of Colyton from 1807–59

houses in the other parishes. His curates, not all of whom shared their vicar's views or churchmanship, were housed perhaps without sufficient regard for the need for the presence of a priest within a community. Admittedly Shute and Monckton were much smaller than Colyton but during Barnes' incumbency of 52 years they grew gradually. Nevertheless, during Barnes' time, only a little discontent was expressed. It waited in the wings.

There are two aspects of the ministry of Frederick Barnes which bear directly on the story of Mamerto Gueritz. The first is Barnes' close friendships with nonconformist and Unitarian ministers and the legacy this left; the second is his relationship with the family of Henry Parry Liddon, who resided in the parish.

It may seem that Barnes held one view while in Oxford and another when in Colyton. This would not be entirely true, but appearances are more often reported than the truths behind them. In Oxford, Frederick Barnes was regarded by some as one of the High and Dry school, one whom Hurrell Froude would have labelled a "Z". In Colyton, he allowed his personal relationships to grow and flourish, unimpeded by theological differences. As a reporter from *Pulman's Weekly News*, a Unitarian-owned publication, later wrote of him, "Dr. Barnes was no rigid sectarian and although strictly true to his own belief and teaching, yet he never allowed a difference of view to be a bar to private friendship."[15]

The most significant friendship was that shared with Dr Joseph Cornish. Cornish was minister at George's Meeting House from 1772 until his death in 1823, and, as we have seen, was described as "Arian in sentiment". Cornish's ministry was already fully established when Barnes arrived in 1807. He had founded a classical school which began in the meeting house and then transferred to a house he purchased, which allowed him to take in boarding pupils. Cornish had enjoyed cordial relationships with Barnes' two predecessors, which indicates their liberality and his own often recorded charm, but with Barnes there seems to have been a particular bond, perhaps born of a sense of common purpose albeit one approached by different routes. Whist parties were held alternately at the vicarage and Cornish's house. Whenever Cornish gave the meeting house children a tea party, Barnes' butler had strict orders to carry up the spare crockery from the vicarage for their use. G. E. Evans records:

Fine afternoons would see Barnes and Cornish taking their constitutional together, arm in arm up Colyton Hill or in Shute Park: and when the last office was said, and Cornish was buried beneath his pulpit, there ... stood the sorrowing vicar of the parish and his estimable curate, Mr. Peppin.[16]

Quite aside from the emergent Unitarians, during Barnes' incumbency there was something of a renewal of nonconformity in Colyton. In 1837, a Wesleyan chapel was built in the lower part of the town. Soon afterwards a Baptist meeting began, but no records of this have been found other than the ecclesiastical census of 1851. During Frederick Barnes' incumbency, George's Meeting House received another four ministers, under whom it evolved from Arian sentiment to Unitarianism. Relatively early in Barnes' incumbency, on 24 September 1814, a new Congregational chapel was opened under the leadership of Jacob Pady, who had been exercising a preaching ministry for some years previously. Pady resigned his charge in 1852 having ministered for over 39 years. It was said of him that he was "not too bigoted to be occasionally seen at a church service".[17] The ecclesiastical census shows that Jacob Pady was simply compliant with contemporary churchgoing practices. It was common among dissenters in Colyton to attend their own places of worship in the mornings and another service at the parish church later in the day. In all this, Colyton was rather unusual. The Royal Commission on Employment in Agriculture in East Devon found that there were relatively few dissenters in country areas but that this depended largely on the "clergyman of the parish and at the chapel on the dissenting minister of the neighbourhood".[18] When the history of dissent in Colyton, from the days of the intruded Puritan minister up to the death of Joseph Cornish, is considered, together with the example of Jacob Pady and the genuine warmth towards them all of Frederick Barnes, we can begin to see something of the ecclesiastical context into which Mamerto Gueritz would bring his "High Church" views. Prior to his arrival theological differences were simply not allowed place in determining the tenor of relationships between the people of different denominations.

The Revd John B. Smith, Unitarian minister from 1830 to 1832 and a poet of some local repute, added these lines to Barnes' obituary in the *Pulman's Weekly News*:

His liberal sentiments and manners bland

Affection gain, yet reverence command,

His people hear his voice, with joy attend,

And in their pastor, view their father, friend.

This was published in 1859. By the end of 1860, few Unitarians would view the incumbent of Colyton in such affectionate terms.

Another of Barnes' relationships was to affect not only the work of Mamerto Gueritz in the parish of Colyton but also the wider unfolding of the Oxford Movement. Barnes' friendship with the Liddon family and his influence on the young Henry Parry Liddon had effects in both spheres. Liddon was later to become a leader among "second wave" Tractarians:

> almost by default and certainly not because of personal ambition, he became the leader of the second phase of the Oxford Movement...Liddon was also the one figure who bridged the gap between the first generation of Tractarians and the later men, whose opinions he did not necessarily share.[19]

In 1832, the family of Captain Matthew Liddon RN removed from North Stoneham in Hampshire and took up residence at the Grove, in Colyton. This was a substantial property, where the household included the infant Henry, his mother and the captain's sister, Louisa Liddon. Eventually another nine siblings were to arrive, six of them being born in Colyton. Captain Liddon's reputation for gallantry and as an intrepid explorer preceded him, and he and Barnes became firm friends. Thereafter Barnes took a kindly interest in the family and in the fortunes of the young Henry.

Henry Liddon began his education locally at the school run by a Mr Tett, who later became headmaster of the now famous Colyton Grammar School. In 1839, Liddon, then ten years old, was sent as a boarder to George Roberts' school in Lyme Regis. The 1851 census shows that his brother Matthew was at the same school, aged seven, and that the school was still of moderate size with 15 boys boarding. At school, Henry's strongly evangelical piety, previously inspired and fostered by his mother and to a lesser extent his aunt Louisa, was further stimulated by the preaching of the vicar of Lyme, Dr Hodges, who was given to "Vigorous and anti-Roman discourses".[20]

Liddon's early sermons, composed in this period, reflected the opinions of Dr Hodges and quite clearly the influence of his mother. Change began when, in the autumn of 1844, Henry Liddon was sent to King's College School in the Strand. The academic foundation he had been given in Lyme Regis gave him a head start, and he was soon placed in the upper school. His comments on the school motto, *Sancte et Sapienter*, made both then and often afterwards, was that the school only trained its pupils in half of it. The teenage Liddon was already fixed on the search for holiness. Captain Matthew Liddon asked Frederick Barnes to prepare his son for confirmation. In spite of his prolonged absences from the parish, Barnes took on the task, and Henry was invited to breakfast at the vicarage. During the meal, Barnes asked him if he knew the catechism, to which Liddon replied that he knew it by heart. In Barnes' view, this was all the preparation needed and arrangements were made. Liddon's diary, begun in January 1845 and maintained until his death, simply records: "Could not go to College. Confirmation." That was 29 May 1846, during his last term at King's College School. Of Liddon's time at King's, a contemporary later wrote:

> His interests even then were entirely with theology, the new Church Movement, and the preaching and teaching of the day. At seventeen Liddon was just as absorbed in Dr. Pusey and his work as at twenty-seven.[21]

The account may perhaps have an element of reading back his later loyalties into Liddon's teenage years, but even at this stage his interests were enough to cause consternation at home, at least for Liddon's mother.

Frederick Barnes had read some of Liddon's early sermons; there were quite a lot of them, and in them Barnes discerned Henry Liddon's potential for considerable scholarship. He offered to nominate Henry to a studentship at Christ Church, Oxford. This offer might never have been accepted, and the history of the Oxford Movement would have been quite changed if local and maternal influences had prevailed. We have already noted the evangelical piety of Ann Liddon. Barnes' curate of the time was an "earnest but very bigoted person who (in Dr Barnes' absence) did his utmost to prevent the acceptance of the offer". Naturally enough, the curate had the confidence of Liddon's mother and had persuaded her that to allow her son within the perilous influence of the "false teacher" Pusey would be to place his soul in peril. This warning of the danger to her son troubled Liddon's mother until just before her death. In addition to this, her son's journey into academia caused her added concern and created a slight distance between them. The heart of this sadness was revealed when she said to him: "You may become a great scholar, but will you become a true Christian?"[22]

Perhaps the mother felt she knew her son and therefore feared the danger of intellectual pride more than the influence of Pusey. Few would have placed excessive pride among Liddon's faults, but that may have been precisely because he was humble enough to heed such a warning and to take it to heart. As late as 1866, he was still recalling his mother's words and their effect on him. Ann Liddon died in February 1849.

Maternal fears notwithstanding, Captain Liddon and Dr Barnes prevailed, and, in a great fright, Liddon sat his matriculation examination. Eleven days later, on 14 June 1846, Henry Parry Liddon became a student at Christ Church, Oxford. Mamerto Gueritz was already established at St Edmund Hall at the other end of The High. The anxieties which surrounded Liddon's departure from Colyton may well be understood when it is recalled that only 16 weeks previously John Henry Newman had taken final leave of his Oxford friends.[23] That farewell had taken place at the home of Manuel Johnson, the Radcliffe Observer, and it was to this same house and company that Liddon was frequently bidden on Sunday evenings. New friends notwithstanding, Liddon held to his first friends at Oxford, and Frederick Barnes always had an open door for him. This provided an element of continuity between home and university life that would have eased the culture shock of being plunged into the foment of Oxford theological debate; perhaps conflict would be a better word. In return, Liddon would always make Barnes' house his first call at the beginning of each new term. Barnes' exercise of what might be seen as *in loco parentis* oversight seems to have been very gentle and we hear little of reproof or of too great a concern that Liddon was fast becoming a disciple of a new mentor, Edward Bouverie Pusey. There is one memorable occasion which bears on this, cited by all his biographers and recorded by Liddon in his diary. One day he was seen by the son of one of the canons of Christ Church as he waited on Pusey's doorstep. His fears that the gossip would spread were recorded in his diary, *forsan omnia omnibus relatarus*, and proved well founded for two days later he was called to see Dr Barnes.[24] Instead of the expected warning or rebuke, Liddon records that Barnes spoke "very kindly about many things". The entry in Liddon's diary, the use of Latin being a habit by then, was *de doctrina aliisque* and might at a stretch be taken to mean that they talked of everything except his visit to Pusey. The devotion which Liddon developed towards Pusey, and the influence of men such as R. W. Church and Marriot of Oriel College, began to be revealed in his thinking and writing. The few sermons that remain of Liddon's undergraduate years reflect this clearly.

When the remaining family removed from Colyton in or around 1852, only two of the children were still living with their father, some of the others being at school in either Lyme Regis or Taunton. This did not, however, sever the ties that the young Henry had with the town; indeed he was still a regular visitor into old age. Another link that was not severed by distance was that with his aunt Louisa. She had gone to live in Taunton some time earlier but had evidently maintained a considerable exchange of ideas with her nephew. Liddon even discussed with her his thoughts of taking vows of chastity in order to serve the Church, as he put it, "quite disentangled from the work of this world". Ultimately there appears to have been a better understanding between her and Liddon than he had with his mother, at least until a little while before her death when she seemed to understand and accept the path her son had taken. Twelve years of following her nephew's development had drawn Louisa Liddon along the same path. Shortly before her death on 30 March 1858, she confessed that a more complete faith in the sacraments had been a special blessing in her later years.

For a period of eight years, the progress and doings of the young Henry Parry Liddon, from his matriculation and the beginnings of his academic career until just before his ordination as deacon, were the subject of discussion in the Liddon household in Colyton and indeed in the community. The effect that this might have had on the community at large should not be exaggerated but neither should it be dismissed. What was discussed at the dinner table the servants discussed with family and friends. That such a mode of communication and the consequent percolation of ideas is not readily quantifiable does not invalidate it as a process. It happened.

It appears that over the next few years Barnes introduced, or allowed one of his curates to introduce, some features of early Tractarianism into the liturgy, but there was nothing that could remotely be called ritualistic. Not until Dr Barnes had "shuffled off this mortal coil", and his successor Mamerto Gueritz was in place, did that begin. Interestingly enough, Henry Parry Liddon was among the first to comment on the new vicar only a few months after Gueritz arrived.

Introducing even a moderate element of ritual into the liturgy was at least partially dependent on the physical setting; the layout of the church itself. For example, a procession from the west end to the altar at the east end depends on there being an available route. For a description of the challenge awaiting Gueritz in this respect, we turn once more to the memory of the church in 1849 provided by Samuel Seaward:

> [A]s we enter the porch door we notice the huge wooden pulpit in the centre of the aisle, with a long staircase to the desk and a sounding board on wooden pillars, surmounted by a golden angel blowing a trumpet. On either side below this pulpit is a large desk for the priest and a clerk with red velvet cushions, on which rest the service books. The church is filled with high pews facing the pulpit, consequently most people sit with their backs to the altar.
>
> There is a long gallery on each side of the nave, one for men and one for women; the choir occupying a portion of the men's side. The singing is led by an orchestra, consisting of violin, 'cello, double bass, flute and clarionet, and during service a curtain is drawn across the section they occupy.
>
> Above each gallery and facing the pulpit are two smaller galleries called the "birdcages" and they are used by the children of the Sunday School. The small old stone font is near the priest's door close to the Pole Chapel. (This is at the east end of the south aisle). The space under the Tower is occupied by high pews, appropriated by some of the principal residents of the town.[25]

This brief elucidation of the history and idiosyncrasies of the town of Colyton, of the liturgical setting and of some of the key personalities, is intended to offer an understanding of the milieu in which Mamerto Gueritz began his ministry there. Without doubt, he would have an effect on that setting and, eventually, it would have a shaping effect on him. However, although he had been seasoned by a number of demanding curacies, Colyton would provide Mamerto with its own unique challenges.

Notes

[1] The parish register, dating from 1538, is retained at the South West Heritage Centre (Devon Records Office) in Exeter.

[2] Ravenor E. Rose, ms. "History of Congregationalism in Colyton", published in *Pulman's Weekly News*, 28 July, 4, 11 and 18 August 1953. Rose was resident in Colyton in 1893, as evidenced by the appearance of his name in the *Parish Minute Book*, 4 November 1893.

[3] G. P. R. Pulman, *Book of the Axe* (London: Longman, 1844, also Bath: Kingsmead Reprints, 1969—edition used).

[4] Pulman, *Book of the Axe*, p. 808.

[5] Pulman, *Book of the Axe*, p. 810.

[6] Rose, "History of Congregationalism in Colyton".

[7] Henry Gow, *The Unitarians* (London: Methuen, 1928), p. 98.

[8] H. L. Short, "Presbyterians Under a New Name", in C. Bolam (ed.), *The English Presbyterians: From Elizabethan Puritanism to Modern Unitarianism* (London: Allen and Unwin, 1968), p. 224.

[9] Short, "Presbyterians Under a New Name", p. 224.

[10] Gow, *The Unitarians*, p. 102.

[11] T. R. G. C. White, *The Feoffees of Colyton 1596 to 1946* (Colyton: Private publication, 1951), p. 2.

[12] The Deed of Enfeoffment from which these quotations are taken is retained at the South West Heritage Centre (Devon Records Office) in Exeter (Colyton Archives) and is displayed annually at the Feoffees Banquet in Colyton. A grace often used before the celebration and still in use in the twenty-first century illustrates the persistence and immediacy of the community memory. "For the twenty freemen of this town, who long ago braved court and crown, For those who followed, labouring sore to aid the needy and feed the poor, For those who now stand in their place we give thee thanks O God of grace. Grant that this feast may blessed be and each who serves as a Feoffee."

[13] The Feoffees did indeed work for the good of the people. By 1673, they were providing the schoolmaster's stipend. They put in place a scheme to provide clean water for the town and maintained the supply. In 1846, they joined forces with the vestry to build and maintain a "lockup" behind the Market House, which they were also responsible for maintaining. In 1875, they were instrumental in the re-formation of the Colyton Grammar School, by which time the schoolmaster's stipend stood at £30. The balance of the Feoffees' annual income was disbursed, "among the poor who are not in the constant receipt of parochial relief". The assistance given during the year was supplemented at Christmas with gifts of coal, blankets and foodstuffs. Also, each head of household, if he were currently in receipt of the Feoffees' support, received a shilling for each dependent member of the household. In 1851, 567 shillings were disbursed in a population of 2,504. In 1895, the chamber held its ground against the newly formed parish council. According to R. G. C. White, the bailiff or clerk to the Feoffees was instructed to deny the council's right to interfere in any way with their work. This he did with considerable emphasis. As late as the 1990s, the chamber purchased a complete set of tools to allow a Colyton boy to take up an apprenticeship. As one of the Feoffees of the day said to the person charged with the purchase, "Mek shure they'm prop'r." The tools had to be of the best quality.

[14] Ms. Samuel Seaward, "Old Colyton". The manuscript was written c 1939 and purports to describe Colyton 90 years previously. A typewritten transcript is held by the author.

[15] *Pulman's Weekly News*, 23 August 1859.

[16] George Eyre Evans, *Colytonia: A Chapter in the History of East Devon* (Liverpool: Gibbons, published by private subscription, 1898), p. 22.

[17] Evans, *Colytonia*, p. 124.

[18] *Report on the Employment of Women and Children in Agriculture: Devon. 1843*, p. 25.

[19] M. J. Chandler, "Church and Ministry in the Teaching of H. P. Liddon: A Study of His Theology and Pastoral Practice", PhD thesis, King's College London, 1987, p. 8.

[20] J. O. Johnstone, *The Life and Letters of Henry Parry Liddon, D.D* (London: Longmans Green & Co., 1904), p. 5. Although Hodges' fears for his congregation in the face of "Romanizers" are dismissed by Johnstone as "The least of his parishioners' dangers", such fears should be set alongside the rising tide of suspicion directed against Pusey and Newman and the furore concerning *Tract 90*. These things were very much in the mind of country clergy who kept up with events—and most did—especially during Liddon's schooldays.

21 At the time of Liddon's death, Frederick Harrison had some reminiscences of Liddon published in the *Pall Mall Gazette*, 13 September 1890.

22 Johnstone, *Life and Letters*, p. 11.

23 Ian Ker, *John Henry Newman: A Biography* (Oxford: Clarendon, 1988), pp. 320ff. give an account of these events.

24 A recent biographer (Chandler) believes that Liddon received a "note of admonition". An earlier biographer (Johnstone) affirms that he was "interviewed" by Dr Barnes. They agree however, that when the admonition was delivered, it was "kindly".

25 Seaward, "Old Colyton".

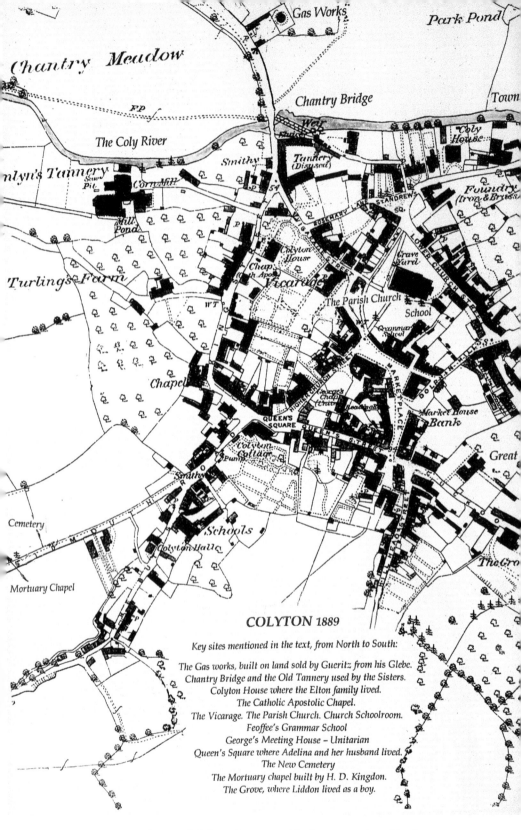

COLYTON 1889

Key sites mentioned in the text, from North to South:

The Gas works, built on land sold by Gueritz from his Glebe.
Chantry Bridge and the Old Tannery used by the Sisters.
Colyton House where the Elton family lived.
The Catholic Apostolic Chapel.
The Vicarage. The Parish Church. Church Schoolroom.
Feoffee's Grammar School
George's Meeting House – Unitarian
Queen's Square where Adelina and her husband lived.
The New Cemetery
The Mortuary chapel built by H. D. Kingdon.
The Grove, where Liddon lived as a boy.

A map of Colyton in 1889, with places mentioned in the text

6

The new vicar of Colyton: Arrival and the years to 1865

During the ministry of Mamerto Gueritz in Colyton, a number of themes emerged which illustrate both his identity as a Tractarian and emergent Ritualist and also his understanding of himself as a parish priest. Some of these elements will need to be set out thematically because at least one of them took almost his entire incumbency to achieve. For the moment, however, the tale is told chronologically.

In the months following the death of Frederick Barnes, life in the parish of Colyton went on more or less as normal. The knowledge that there was no parson to deal with, or perhaps the loss of Barnes' kindly influence, provoked minor rumblings among the dissenters. During April, there was correspondence in the papers from annoyed church members concerning the lamentable failure of the churchwardens to collect church rates from some of the leading Unitarians, but nothing really came to a head. A new graveyard had been laid out on the hill overlooking Road Green and the road to Northleigh. The Church of England section was consecrated during March. The churchyard in the centre of the town, however, was not officially closed for burials for another year, and even then it was provided in the Order of Closure that spouses of those previously interred could also be buried there, a detail that will prove to be of some importance as this tale unfolds.

The dearth of other news is perhaps illustrated by an article in the same newspaper which reported the consecration of the new graveyard: "Mr. Smith of Mounthill Farm has a . . . hen which has laid an egg weighing six ounces and measuring eight inches long and six inches round."

Such eye-watering news soon gave way to speculation as to the identity of a possible successor to Frederick Barnes. There were rumours, reported in the press, that the new incumbent might be a member of the cathedral chapter. One Exeter newspaper, seizing the opportunity to air a concern we have already noted, suggested that the dean and chapter, as patrons of the living, should untangle the "pernicious mode of managing Church property", which depleted the income of the parishes, and place "three resident, working clergymen in a situation of usefulness in these parishes",[1] namely Colyton, Shute and Monckton. It will be remembered that Frederick Barnes was vicar of Colyton and perpetual curate of the other two. It can hardly be other than that the words "working" and "resident" were deliberately chosen because of the rumour that the next incumbent might be a residentiary canon of the cathedral and thus obliged to live for some of the time in Exeter. Given the demonstrated antipathy of Bishop Phillpotts to pluralism and idleness among the clergy, it is not entirely surprising that the dean and chapter heeded this challenge, even though it would reduce their income as holders of the rectorial advowson. However, such changes do not happen quickly, and once the process had begun it was difficult to contain the news of who the new vicar would be or to correct the inevitable speculation as to what his new charge would include.

On 24 January 1860, *Pulman's Weekly News* proclaimed:

> The living has been offered to the Rev'd Mamerto Gueritz, lately resident, we understand, at Penzance in Cornwall, who has long been known in the Diocese. We should imagine from the name that he is of Portuguese or Spanish extraction.

The comment regarding his Portuguese or Spanish extraction would find resonance in at least one nearby community. The people of Beer, just a few miles away on the coast west of Seaton, were known locally as "The Spaniards". Apparently, a Spanish ship had been wrecked just off the cliffs in the 1660s during the time of the plague. The plague had all but turned Beer into a desert, so the surviving sailors simply stayed, married, and repopulated the place; not always in quite that order.

Incidentally, only two weeks later the same newspaper, *Pulman's Weekly*, was reporting the riots at St George in the East in an article highly critical of the clergy, Bryan King and C. F. Lowder. Other newspapers, making the assumption that the appointment to Colyton would follow precedent, stated in typical gazette style and with stunning inattention to detail:

> Gueritz. Rev. Mamerto. BA. Edmund (sic) Hall Oxford, to Colwton (sic) V
> w Monckton P.C. and Shute P.C. Devon. Val. £403 with residence.[2]

Yet another report commented on the musical talents of the new vicar, something which would also soon become a source of contention:

> Our new vicar, The Rev. Mamerto Gueritz, (who we hope soon to have
> residing among us) is a man of considerable attainments in this beautiful
> branch of a beautiful art, and which we think augurs well for the future
> of our church choir.

An early arrival was not to be and almost six months elapsed before the formalities were complete. The minutes of Exeter Cathedral Chapter record the process and illustrate the changes. The Order in Council to separate the parishes was made on 30 June 1860. Around the same time the curate, Mr Comins, who had managed the interregnum since the death of Barnes departed for his own cure in South Devon. On 14 July, the chapter minutes record that the testimonials of the nominated clergy were requested. On 28 July, they had been received and, in order to avoid further delay:

> The Dean and absent Canons having approved of not requiring in this case
> the Testimonials to remain the month required by Order of Chapter, they
> ordered the Presentation of Mamerto Gueritz to the Vicarage of Colyton
> and the Nomination of John Binford Selwood to the Perpetual Curacy of
> Shute to be sealed.[3]

The dean and chapter had not completely given in to popular pressure. The perpetual curacy of Monckton was still attached to Colyton, and when the appointment was finally ratified, it was announced that Mamerto Gueritz was to be priest of both parishes.[4] The avoidance of any further delay in the formalities was all the more desirable in that the Gueritz family had already taken up residence in Colyton earlier in the summer:

> The new vicar of Colyton, the Rev Mamerto Guiretz (sic) and his family arrived here on Thursday evening when the bells were rung and the town band turned out to welcome them.[5]

The new home into which the family moved was a considerable contrast to their modern Penzance house. Colyton vicarage had been the residence of the parish priest since well before the Reformation and was redolent with the history of the place, even to the extent of the legend of a ghostly monk. This story was, however, carefully kept from the children until much later. From the upper windows of the house, over the high walls of the garden, the octagonal Flemish tower of the church filled the skyline.

Being given the incumbency of Colyton and Monckton can be seen as a reward for the decade of service that Mamerto had given to his bishop and the diocese. Even in its reduced form, to be given a benefice like Colyton, when the previous incumbent had been of such exalted status academically, politically and ecclesiastically, was hardly precedented. In addition, Gueritz had been a foreign national. It is true that he had abjured loyalty to the religion and country of his birth but in those xenophobic days there would be at least one recorded instance of a racially based slur. Possibly the fact that survivors of the Spanish Armada had interbred with local women in the peninsular even before Spanish sailors had settled in a plague-decimated Beer might have had an ameliorating effect had it not been for the reputation the Beer "Spaniards" had earned over the years; that of being wreckers and smugglers!

The most demonstrable ameliorating effect, however, was the domestic scene at the vicarage, and especially the influence of Anne Derby Gueritz who, in spite of what must have been a considerable change from the amenities of Penzance, soon adjusted to her new setting and endeared herself to local people. Their children, several of whom bore Spanish names, became rather romantic figures to the local youngsters. Mamerto George, aged ten, was, as we know, at school in Margaret Street in London. Jose was nine, Mary Louisa seven, Edward five, Frank four, and the baby, Antonia Anne, had her first birthday at Colyton vicarage. To this was added the presence of Gueritz' mother, Antonia Josepha, then 63 and the survivor of great adventures, all of which added to the fascination.

Another development which affected not only the Gueritz family but the whole town was the arrival of the railway. On 17 July, even before he was legally the incumbent, Mamerto was among the first to take a train from Colyton station. Communication with his son George and the London clergy with whom he had become closely acquainted could be maintained with much greater ease.

Almost immediately, and almost by accident, some liturgical innovations began. In Penzance, given the number of church buildings in use, the ringing of a church bell was simply an indication that a service was about to begin. The same seems to have been true in Shepton and Barrington, where Mamerto learned the value of including parishioners in the recitation of the daily offices. In Colyton, however, the church bell was rather more of a public alert system. When the bell was rung outside normally expected times, folk would flock to the church to see what was happening. Prior to Gueritz' arrival the daily offices were not treated as public acts of worship, but as soon as he was in situ "some forty or fifty good people who had been used to answer every call of the bell, appeared morning by morning in Church".[6]

The Gueritz family had only been in residence in Colyton for two months when notice of his arrival began to filter through the Oxford Movement network. On 11 September 1860, H. P. Liddon wrote to Reginald Porter, who had been one of Liddon's students at Cuddesdon College and who by then was the vicar of Kenn in Devon:

> Passing through Colyton yesterday, I heard much of Mr. Gueritz (the people call him Gritz) that is very hopeful. He is training a choir: has an harmonium in the Chancel: has abolished the old Reading Desk: has weekly celebration: and—what particularly impressed one informant—has a 'Sister of Mercy staying at the Vicarage who does good all day'. She must, I think, be a natural sister of Mr. Glanville, of Sheviock. As Mr. G. only came at midsummer—this is very well?[7]

The question mark is clear on the page but quite what Liddon intended to convey by it is another matter. He had known the people of Colyton all his life, having arrived as a small boy in 1823, and had kept up his friendships in the community as this letter shows. Liddon was not himself ritualistic. Quite probably, as a follower of Dr Pusey and an emulator of his caution, Liddon wondered if Mamerto Gueritz was being a little precipitate given the nature of the people of Colyton; a nature he understood and Gueritz had yet to learn.

The presence of a Sister of Mercy at this early stage was a foreshadowing of what was to come in later years when there would be a small community of sisters, resident and working in the parish. How she came to be in Colyton in 1860 remains something of a mystery. The identity of this solitary sister is not given in the letter, save that she was the "natural" sister of Mr Glanville of Sheviock, indicating that she had been born out of wedlock. Henry Carew Glanville had been the incumbent of Sheviock since his ordination as a priest in 1855. He was also a Fellow of Exeter College, Oxford. Sheviock is in Devonport where, by 1860, the work of Lydia Sellon and her sisterhood had developed to the point where she was styled abbess and had a crozier by her abbatial throne in the oratory of St Dunstan's Abbey. We saw earlier that the Devonport Sisterhood supplied oversight to other, locally formed, communities. Perhaps, unlike the later venture in Colyton, this was a test to see how the presence of such a sister would be received and it was perhaps also a sufficiently sequestered place to labour for one who lived under the shadow of illegitimacy. The census of 1861 records an unmarried woman, aged 44, living at the vicarage. Even given the vagaries of the spelling often employed by census-takers, it is clear that this person was Frances Glanville and that she spent over a year in Colyton.[8] The only other time we hear of Henry Glanville's sister was when she was the chief mourner at his funeral in 1900.

Although the presence of the sister did not win universal acclaim, criticism of the new vicar and his actions remained muted. He won local approval over his commitment to the building of a parochial schoolroom and the minutes of Exeter Cathedral chapter record that early in October he managed to get a promise of £25 from them, provided he could raise the rest of the money. Eventually he did.

Before the end of the year a new assistant curate arrived, Kenelm Henry Smith, who had been ordained deacon that autumn. Over the next few months, the work of integration, always slow in rural Devon, continued and the Christmas season of 1860 provided an ideal time to consolidate new friendships. There was much delight when Mamerto and Anne distributed between 200 and 300 presents to the children of the Sunday school and provided a beautifully illuminated Christmas tree which, at the time, was still quite a novelty. Over the same period, there had evidently been some considerable developments in the worship because as the new year dawned the dissenters found their voice.

In Devon and Somerset, the Unitarian newspapers were strident in their criticism of the Established Church, especially if there was a hint of Tractarianism. The general practice was to employ a correspondent in each of the major towns or villages most of whom could be trusted to toe the Unitarian party line. Other, more detached and objective reports and comments were supplied by members of the public. However, to describe many of the articles in, for example, *Trewman's Exeter Gazette*, or *Pulman's Weekly News*, as partisan would not be to overstate the case. *Pulman's* had such a local correspondent in Colyton until 1874, after which point it seems no one wanted the job.

In January 1861, *Trewman's* carried reports of events in Colyton:

> Great is the distress and complaint that, since the induction of the present incumbent, the services of the parish church have been conducted in a manner eminently characteristic of those who aspire to be of the "High Church" party.

The worship was styled, Puseyite. The term "ritualist" had yet to be heard in Colyton, but the writer went on to claim that "monotonous Gregorian chants are sung and one only has to close one's eyes to fancy oneself within the precincts of St. Paul's, Knightsbridge or St. Barnabas, Pimlico".

It is hard to imagine that Mamerto Gueritz would find such a comparison anything other than flattering. The large attendance at services bears witness that not everyone experienced distress or made complaint.

The first cause of offence was not only that Mattins was being said daily at nine o'clock as a public office but that considerable congregations attended. A greater scandal was caused by the fact that "all the saints in the calendar" were being observed and that Holy Communion was celebrated every Sunday morning at eight o'clock except the first Sunday of the month. In order to consolidate matters in the public mind the reporter focussed on the Christmas celebration of the

Holy Communion in the previous month. He evidently expected the reader to be shocked that the vicar and the choir went in procession around the church and that the choir then sat in the chancel and not in the gallery, which made the service look "Popish". They sang a Christmas carol, and the vicar wore "white kids", referring to his white kid gloves. It was deemed an insult that the vicar turned his back on the congregation during the service, which illustrates the writer's ignorance of the rubrics of the Book of Common Prayer and echoes the offence taken at a previous Christmas Holy Communion in Penzance. However, the greatest cause of complaint was that the churchwardens took up a collection when the offertory sentences were being read, which did not allow those who were not staying for the Communion to leave beforehand. The fact that Gueritz wore a surplice, and soon a stole, for such services paled into insignificance compared with the attempt to relieve the parishioners of some money!

In attempting to set the conflicts in Colyton in the context of the wider battles of the Church Revival, it must be acknowledged that, while no less intense, they differed in some respects from the scenes at St George in the East in 1860, or the earlier surplice riots in Exeter of 1845 and the later disturbances in 1867 at St Matthias, Stoke Newington. This was partly due to the difference between religious life in the major cities, where there would be several Anglican parishes, and life in the smaller towns where there might be just one parish and several dissenting congregations of different kinds. In the larger centres, opposition to Puseyite practices was most often organized by people who saw themselves as loyal members of the Church of England, defending the Protestant identity of "their Church". Of course, when using mobs and fomenting riots to gain their ends, they would recruit supporters wherever they could be found. That meant, for example, that among the protestors and stone throwers at Stoke Newington there could be found Anglicans, nonconformists and people of no religious affiliation whatsoever. By contrast, in the smaller towns as we saw in Penzance, the most vigorous opposition came from Wesleyans and Congregationalists who seldom attended Anglican worship but felt themselves threatened by the renewed emphasis on the catholic heritage of the Church of England. When their attacks persisted, the defenders of the local clergy suggested that the protestors should simply mind their own business and stay in their own churches! The eventual result was a kind of armed truce with occasional flashpoints.

The religious conflict in Colyton differed from those in the cities and the towns for a specific reason. In Colyton, the lines had been considerably blurred by the steadfast refusal of Frederick Barnes and Joseph Cornish and his successors to allow doctrinal differences to affect their relationships. As a result, many nonconformists, including the Unitarians, had been accustomed to attending services in the parish church on Sunday afternoons, which made little demand on them in terms of Trinitarian formulae or Church of England doctrine. The Unitarians of the town were accustomed to thinking of themselves as Protestants, but that was a term descriptive of a branch of Christianity and in that lay the seeds of future conflict. A Unitarian, by definition, rejects the divinity of Christ and thus the doctrine of the Holy Trinity. Therefore, to the Trinitarian Anglican, and indeed to most of the rest of Christendom, Protestant and Catholic alike, Unitarians were not Christians but Deists. Local Unitarians had sufficient disregard for Anglican orthodoxy for a letter from a prominent member of the Axminster Meeting House to be published in *Pulman's Weekly News* of 2 July 1867. The writer was outraged that a clergyman in the parish church of Axminster had "preached a doctrine dishonouring to God by setting him up an equal in the person of Christ". This was a response to a sermon preached on Trinity Sunday!

In making such a protest, the writer was doing no more than emulating the work of other Unitarian propagandists, such as Samuel Thompson. Thompson followed a policy of protesting in the press whenever Unitarians had been subjected to Trinitarian formulae, such as in the marriage service. Many Unitarians, Charles Lamb the essayist among them, were profoundly unhappy at such tactics, feeling they did more harm than good. However, such outbursts can hardly be wondered at when we look at the wider picture. It is worth recalling that at this stage in its history the Church of England had not a few leading churchmen who, despite their ordination oaths, sympathized with Thompson's point of view. Dean Stanley of Westminster, when challenged over giving communion to a Unitarian in the abbey, replied: "Might it not be argued that Unitarianism is Christianity robbed of its absurdities?"[9]

Thus, the battle lines in Colyton were drawn, not between two factions in the Church of England but for the most part between Trinitarian Anglicans and the Unitarians. The doctrine of the Holy Trinity, the teaching of baptismal regeneration and the reality and centrality of the Holy Communion were at the heart of Gueritz' identity as a priest and his preaching as the *pastor in parochia*. Other nonconformists who, like the Congregationalists, still maintained a Trinitarian theology would, when their Protestant identity was threatened by the supposed Romanist teaching of Gueritz, side with the Unitarians. When the Unitarians were too strident in their denial of the divinity of Christ, they would find themselves, albeit reluctantly, alongside the Anglicans.

All that assumes some theological reflection on the part of ordinary folk, which undoubtedly did happen to a degree. However, most of the Colyton townsfolk chose sides simply on the basis of where familial and social loyalties lay, without much understanding of or regard for the theology behind it all. A few became deeply involved in doctrinal debate. Some, simply seeing their new vicar attacked and feeling themselves to be loyal Anglicans, worked on the basis of "whoever attacks my vicar attacks my Church and me". As a result, there were those who became vehement defenders of the catholicity of the Church of England without immediately grasping what it was they were defending and it is small wonder that, at the outset, they identified more with the defence of the externals of worship than the doctrinal foundation. Gueritz' patient teaching over several decades would remedy that.

The remainder of 1861 went on much as things had begun. There was the occasional flurry of Unitarian protest at either the preaching of orthodox Anglican doctrine or at the development of ritual but in the early 1860s the externals of worship were still relatively moderate.

The spring of 1862 saw some interesting developments. At that time, the provision of anything more than elementary education in Colyton was uncertain and the Feoffees' School had yet to grow into the renowned establishment that it would become. Seeing both a need and an opportunity Mamerto Gueritz decided to offer "A sound Classical or Commercial education" for residential pupils in his own household. This repeated what he had done in Penzance, but this time he had his own curate to share the work. He placed an advertisement in *Trewman's Flying Post* in April 1862 with the banner headline:

S. ANDREWS COLLEGIATE SCHOOL
COLYTON, DEVON.

Mamerto was listed as the principal, and the curate, Kenelm Smith, was to be the headmaster. It was claimed that Smith would be assisted by suitably qualified teachers in modern languages, which probably meant Gueritz himself. Prospective parents of pupils were assured that the boys would receive moral and religious training as members of the Church and that all would be under the supervision of the wife of the principal. The fee was set at £20 for the half-year, which was considerably less than the 50 guineas a year he had sought in Penzance.

In this context, the title "Collegiate", while it may now sound rather presumptuous for such a small private venture, simply meant an establishment which provided secondary education. However, it is certain that Mamerto would not have been innocent of the image of a venerable institution with ivy-covered halls that the title would evoke. Colyton vicarage was certainly ivy-covered at the time but was not then large enough to accommodate more than three or four boarding pupils. However, local families did take advantage of the opportunity. Mary Louisa, or "Min", who was born while the family were at Bigbury, later recalled:

> My father took some boys into the vicarage to educate with my four brothers and I had lessons with them . . . I grew up rather a tom-boy.

As Mary's part in this story unfolds, it will be recalled that one of those pupils was a certain Reginald Snook, who later changed his name to Mortimer.

The offering of secondary education at the vicarage did not seem to provoke contention, but something that did become a point of argument in 1862 was the election of churchwardens. At that time, it was customary for an incumbent to appoint one churchwarden and for the vestry, which was composed of ratepayers of all denominations, to vote for the other. This had happened the previous year, but in 1862 it was challenged. A long minute in the entry for 24 April 1862 begins: "We the undersigned protest . . . " The protestors believed that Gueritz had not demonstrated his right to appoint a churchwarden and that they should have been allowed to vote for both. The fact that of the five objectors four were at least nominally members of the Unitarian congregation is indicative of the reasons behind the objection. The first signatory to the protest was Harry De Spencer Kingdon, of whom we will hear more . . . much more.

In the latter part of the year, the celebration of Christmas again called forth comment, but the most telling report showed that local press awareness of matters liturgical was beginning to sharpen up:

> SIR—As saint's days have been of late very duly observed at our parish church, some of us were not a little surprised to find that there was no service yesterday, which was St. Stephen's Day. No bells were chimed, no church lighted for him! Poor Stephen! Is he not in Puseyite favour? Perhaps he was a dissenter and a schismatic.[10]

Attacked by the local press, Mamerto responded by setting out his position regarding Dissidents and Unitarians with uncompromising clarity. Nonconformists had forsaken the sacraments and therefore had lost the fullness of the Christian faith. Unitarians had no right to call themselves Protestants, and thus to align themselves with Trinitarian nonconformists, because they were, by definition, not Christians. They rejected the central tenets of orthodox faith, namely the Holy Trinity, the Incarnation of Christ and the doctrine of the Atonement. For Gueritz, the word "Christian" was not primarily an adjective, and it had a content that individuals were not at liberty to redefine. Thus, any former member of the Church of England who had become Unitarian was, again by definition, apostate.

The reporters and correspondents responsible for the attacks on Gueritz might well have felt as if they had kicked a hornets' nest! The contrast with Frederick Barnes' approach could hardly have been more marked!

Following the ironic letter regarding St Stephen in *Pulman's Weekly*, in January 1862 the Revd D. L. Evans, the "much respected Unitarian minister of this town", began a series of lectures on Puseyism. Evans could not refute the challenges concerning the Trinity and the Incarnation; their denial was a given of the Unitarian position. Instead, he focussed on the doctrine of the apostolic succession, which was at the heart of Gueritz' teaching on the difference between Anglican priests and Dissident ministers. It should be borne in mind that the reporting of these lectures was entirely in the Unitarian-owned press. Evans denounced the apostolic succession as being unscriptural and he "exposed to a grateful people the insidious design, object and tendency of Puseyism".[11]

In a later lecture in February, Evans declared:

> Puseyism, whether as the hypocritical minion of the Roman Catholic
> Church, or of her bastard sister, The Anglo-Catholic Church—has in view
> the same ulterior design, namely the overthrow of Protestantism and the
> utter annihilation of Civil and religious liberty.[12]

Those words, in the context of the centuries-old jealous defence of freedoms, religious and otherwise, woven into the mindset of Colyton folk show that Evans knew exactly which buttons to press.

There was, however, one element of Gueritz' application of Church discipline that cut across sectarian boundaries and was something of an unpleasant surprise to not a few in his first years in the parish. He would not allow marriage during Lent, and although it is not certain that he applied this discipline in his first year in the parish, he clearly did so in 1862. Coincidentally, that year Ash Wednesday fell on 5 March, while the anti-Puseyite lectures of the Revd D. L. Evans were still ongoing. This Lenten discipline might seem merely inconvenient if the practice of marriage and prenuptial activity in Colyton at the time is not fully understood. One of the difficulties in understanding the community arises from the tendency for different groups to maintain different patterns of behaviour. In Colyton of the mid-nineteenth century, it was not just a case of *aut temps aut mores* but, rather, a different street, a different ethic. The concept of a universally observed Victorian code of sexual ethics was always a myth, and patterns of behaviour in Colyton demonstrated independence of thought in this respect, as in much else. Colyton was not far from the national mean in terms of prenuptial pregnancy and illegitimacy, and the records show that between 1851 and 1881 there were 221 first live births. Of these, 107 were conceived in wedlock and 114 were prenuptial conceptions.[13] Most of the births in the latter category actually took place after marriage, thus legitimizing the offspring. It was not the case that over 50 per cent of the population were sexually incontinent but rather that they kept to an ancient custom which predated Victorian patterns of behaviour. Quite simply, a couple would declare their intention to marry following the pattern of medieval betrothal, then wait and accumulate resources until a pregnancy occurred, at which point they would wed. As already stated, this applied mainly to certain sections of the populace. For example, out of the sum of 114 prenuptial pregnancies between 1851 and 1881, farming families—always distinct from the urban community—provided nine such, labourers and agricultural workers 102 and, taken all together, schoolteachers, veterinary surgeons, shopkeepers, innkeepers and employers, just three. One of the pregnancies in the latter category was that of the fiancée of one of the trustees of George's Meeting House. He then married the mother-to-be three months after conception, to the mingled condemnation and prurient glee of the members of other sects in the town. The attitude of the Anglican clergy, Gueritz included, seems to have been very close to that of the priest of *Clochmerle*, who saw such marriages as acts of retroactive grace, setting right any unlicensed anticipation. Rigorous for Church discipline he might have been, but there is evidence that Gueritz dealt gently not only with those who married a little later than they might but also with those unfortunate girls who brought their illegitimate offspring for baptism with no trace of a father to be seen.

Fortunately for those caught up in the process Lent is only 40 days long. It is significant, however, that for Gueritz' first few years in the parish the number of prenuptial pregnancies fell to an all-time low!

Continuing the theme of Lenten discipline, 1863 brought the behaviour of the Royal Family and the convictions of the vicar of Colyton into abrupt conflict. When it was announced that the marriage of Albert Edward, Prince of Wales to Princess Alexandra of Denmark would take place during Lent, Gueritz, among many others, wrote to the Queen to protest the bad example that was being set, in the face of which he and his fellow workers were trying to instil some kind of Christian discipline into their people. The palace reply is not recorded. What is very clear, even today, is the reaction of the "Protestants" of Colyton and, it has to be said, of some church folk too.

At the top of the Market Place in Colyton, there stands a large pump. On it, cast into the metal of its sides, this declaration is set in relief:

> The Surplus of a fund collected
> To commemorate the wedding of
> H.R.H. the Prince of Wales
> *(the Prince of Wales' feathers are cast into the iron at this point)*
> During Lent March 1863
> has been devoted to the erection of this fountain

by the patriotic Protestants of Colyton

as a permanent memorial of

That National Triumph

and in vindication of their own loyalty

by vote of committee.

It seems that when Gueritz adopted High Church liturgical practices he merely annoyed the other denominations. When he applied Church discipline to every level of society, even to the Prince of Wales, he enraged the community. His attitude was thought to be treasonable. A cynical but realistic judgement delivered by a parishioner at the time was that Gueritz' action probably doubled the money that was collected for the commemoration fund.

During the year, Kenelm Smith left to return to Ely, where he had been born. He had not yet been priested, so he was ordained in Ely and served for many years simply as an assistant priest both in the cathedral and in his home parish of St Mary's. He would return to Colyton in 1867 to marry Frances Winter, the sister of Mary May Winter, the long-serving organist of St Andrew's Church, but that is another tale.

The next two years, 1864 and 1865, were without doubt the most tumultuous period that Mamerto Gueritz was ever to experience as parish priest of Colyton. It should be acknowledged that the tumult was essentially of his own making but only because he stood firm for Church principles and for his understanding, however misguided, of how those principles should be applied. And even that was not entirely his fault; the guidance he sought was not there when he needed it and the cause of the offence had long been a nagging problem for many Anglican clergy.

As early as 1850, there had been a *Memorial to the Archbishops and Bishops of the provinces of Canterbury and York*, signed by almost 3,000 clergy. The fact that clergy of all shades of churchmanship had signed it alongside men such as John Keble and Edward Pusey should have alerted the hierarchy to a serious need. Mamerto Gueritz had of course signed, as had his training incumbent, James Coles. The heart of the *Memorial* was expressed thus:

> We beg to express our conviction that the almost indiscriminate use of the
> "Order for the Burial of the Dead" as practically enforced by the existing
> state of the Law, imposes a heavy burden on the conscience of the Clergy,
> and is the occasion of a grievous scandal to many Christian people.

Fifteen years later nothing had been done to change matters.

In Colyton, the tipping point was reached over the burial of an erstwhile
Anglican who many years previously had forsaken his place in the choir of the
parish church to become a Unitarian. An unworthy thought, unwisely expressed
and soon retracted by Gueritz, was that at the time in question the Unitarian choir
paid more to its choristers than the parish church and that the move had been a
matter of "gain over godliness". That suggestion was angrily refuted and simply
added to the growing list of causes of offence. The burial of John Pavey became a
cause célèbre not only in the press but also in Parliament, in the House of Lords,
and even as far afield as the Australian newspapers.[14]

John Pavey died at the beginning of September 1864. He had been widowed
more than once but the wife next to whom he wished to be buried was interred
in St Andrew's churchyard. Although the churchyard had been closed for new
burials in 1861, parishioners still had the right to be buried there in family plots
with a deceased spouse.

In an attempt to correct the distortions that were being circulated in a hostile
press and among prominent Unitarians, Gueritz wrote a letter to the *Clerical
Journal*, setting out the events as he saw them. This was in response to an article
which concluded:

> We cannot but respect Mr. Gueritz's keen sense of the importance and
> dignity of Catholic truth but unless discretion guides our zeal in these
> times, where shall we be?

Gueritz, evidently equating discretion with unacceptable compromise, began his
reply:

> Sir—as you have inserted an account of my refusal to bury a parishioner,
> I shall feel obliged if you will now permit me to state the facts of the case.

But first let me express my utter astonishment at your raking among the scurrilities of the *Western Times* for your accounts of 'clerical doings in the provinces'. Your own article too is so carelessly written that the reader is left in doubt as to where the *Western Times* ends and the *Clerical Journal* begins, or as to whether the respective writers agree or differ.

Gueritz' anger on this point is easily understood. He might have expected an Anglican publication to check the facts before accepting uncritically the statements of an openly partisan newspaper. He continued:

John Pavey was baptized into the church and continued therein until, thinking gain to be godliness he hired himself to sing at the Unitarian conventicle now many years ago. He remained a member of the sect until his death, submitting himself and his family to the constant teaching of a minister who was in the habit of uttering the most atrocious blasphemies, even branding our Lord as illegitimate and applying the most opprobrious of all epithets to the Blessed Virgin.

Clearly, at this point Gueritz was in fighting mood and not inclined to give way on any point, save that he did later acknowledge that his understanding of John Pavey's motives for joining the Unitarians might have been better informed. His references to the blasphemies of the Unitarian minister refer to the Revd D. L. Evans, who had since been replaced by the Revd A. McCombe. Gueritz recounts how he went to see Pavey's daughter, Maria Weston, shared with her his concerns and asked if she could tell him anything about her father's faith which would allow him to set aside his scruples. He remained unsatisfied by the conversation in which Maria Weston, with complete honesty, affirmed that her father had died a most decided Unitarian. Gueritz then tried to persuade her and the family to have the burial in the Unitarian churchyard, but John Pavey had been very clear where he wanted to be buried so Maria Weston attempted to fix a date and time for the interment in the churchyard, next to his wife. According to a Unitarian source, Gueritz had informed Mrs Weston that the soul of her father was inevitably lost and that his burial in the churchyard, which was exclusively for Christians, would not be allowed, nor would he give him a Christian burial. Maria Weston's later dealings with Gueritz make that account seem unlikely, but she then asked the Unitarian minister, the Revd A. McCombe, to intervene, which he attempted to do. Various letters and messages passed between Gueritz and McCombe. Little by little concessions were made. Having been provided with proof of Pavey's baptism, Gueritz allowed that the burial could be in the churchyard but not at the family plot. In the event, he relented and instructed the gravedigger to open the grave just as the family had requested. In the meantime, he had written to his bishop, Henry Phillpotts, to ask for guidance and in a letter dated 8 September to McCombe he wrote:

> Sir—I beg to acknowledge the receipt of your letter, enclosing certificate of the baptism of John Pavey. As this gives him a legal right to a place in the Churchyard I shall not object to his interment therein on Saturday next. Your further demand that I should give him Christian burial, by using the burial office of the church, I cannot answer until I receive the Bishop's reply to my letter.[15]

McCombe was unhappy with this reply and declared that the guidance of the bishop was irrelevant in a matter where the law, as he understood it, absolutely required Gueritz to perform the service. Here stands revealed a fascinating anomaly. Unitarians and dissenters, provided they could fill the requirements of the law, had the right to be buried by the parish priest in consecrated ground using a liturgical form to which most of them would have objected while living. At the same time, there persisted the quasi belief among most parishioners, of whatever affiliation, that unless the vicar had done the funeral the deceased person had not received Christian burial. That there is little logic to the position has no relevance whatsoever.

Phillpotts was in Durham, attending to his canonry duties, and did not receive the letter in time to advise or direct, so Gueritz had to act according to his conscience and his own understanding of matters. He could not understand how Unitarians, who on the one hand took every opportunity to decry the core tenets of the Church of England should, on this occasion, demand a service which was overtly Trinitarian and full of references to the Atonement. Whatever the local and national Unitarian rhetoric might have alleged, Mamerto Gueritz was enduring a tremendous conflict of conscience; the tension between pastoral concern, the requirements of the law, and his understanding of where integrity and truth lay in his dilemma as a priest of the Church and a sworn defender of Church principles. Fortunately for local relationships the family of John Pavey eventually came to understand this.

Accounts of what happened on the day of the burial vary according to the source. All agree that Gueritz did not read the burial service. There was another local clergyman present, the Revd Mr James, and one report stated that "the vicar's lads", namely his sons and the boys of the collegiate school, were there also. One observer said that they all removed their hats for the ceremony, another that they remained covered. One report had it that the Revd A. McCombe read *a* burial service from the street just outside the churchyard and near to the burial plot, another that he read *the* Prayer Book service of the Burial of the Dead, which he had no authority to do as a Unitarian minister. The burial had been carried out, but the saga was not ended. Gueritz had received a reply from Phillpotts after the event which allowed him to end his letter to the *Journal* thus:

> I thank God that in the performance of a painful duty, amid many discouragements, I am supported by the answer of a conscience void of offence in this matter, and also by the sympathy of many valued friends; and I have the still greater happiness and comfort of knowing that this sympathy is shared by my own most venerable and honoured diocesan.

Inevitably there were those in Colyton who found their loyalties strained by these events. However, the many valued friends were found not only among his own supportive laity and the local Tractarian clergy but also in the relationships that Mamerto had been establishing wherever he went, not least in London.

Local relationships between Gueritz and the family of John Pavey and indeed the community at large might have been healed earlier than they were, had it not been for an accident of history.

Much earlier in the year, well before the death of John Pavey, it had been decided that the annual meeting of the Western Unitarian Christian Union (a contradiction in terms for Gueritz) would be held in Colyton; probably as a result of the ongoing conflict between Gueritz and the Unitarian press. The meeting was held on Wednesday, 26 October 1864 with Sir John Bowring in the chair. Bowring was an accomplished man. He had been a friend of Jeremy Bentham, an industrialist, a diplomat, Governor of Hong Kong and, since 1861, the British Commissioner to the Kingdom of Italy. He arrived at the meeting having been lecturing in Frome Selwood, where J. W. E. Bennett was rector. Bennett was a close friend of Dr Pusey and, having been in doctrinal dispute with Bishop Blomfield of London, had resigned his posts at Pimlico and Knightsbridge and accepted the living of Frome in 1852. Frome was another place where the incumbent was frequently the subject of attacks in the Unitarian press. Bowring evidently picked his targets!

It was a carefully researched and skilful speech which raised the level of antagonism towards the parish priest to new levels. An unsubtle thrust at Gueritz' antecedents came first in a jibe at his name: "a name, by the way, sufficiently un-English, for which he is not responsible, but he is responsible for the un-English spirit associated with it". And then again: "I am struck with the singular resemblance between the phraseology of the Holy Office in Spain and that employed by the distinguished vicar of Colyton."[16]

Bowring showed his knowledge of canon law by alighting on the requirement that a minister may not refuse to bury any corpse that is brought to the church or churchyard, after appropriate notice being given, unless the deceased were unbaptized, excommunicate, or guilty of "some grievous and notorious crime". This was exactly the point of tension. The law of the land, for such is canon law, required one thing, the disciplines of Anglican doctrine required another. This was the "grave burden on the conscience of the Clergy" which had been set before the bishops 15 years earlier.

Bowring claimed his motives in speaking to be "not rage, but grave and solemn reprobation; it is sorrow and shame that these things should be". He repeatedly referred to Gueritz as "our enemy". Another speaker contrasted Gueritz with Barnes, accused Gueritz of offering Papistical dogmas and lauded the local Unitarians in that "Manfully and nobly they had withstood the vicar's tyranny." The resulting uproar of applause and indignation was anything but grave and solemn.

The desired outcome was achieved. Legal proceedings would be taken against Gueritz. Mr Cox, a solicitor of Axminster, offered his services without charge and a motion was passed which confirmed that not only would the Western Unitarian Union support the process, but the British and Foreign Unitarian Association would do all in its power to sustain the committee in the steps it may be necessary to take. This was no longer a local matter; it had, to use a modern phrase, gone viral!

It has never been established that Maria Weston was content for her father's funeral to be seized upon as a *cause célèbre* by the Unitarian authorities. The legal process ground on for eight months, with costs growing all the time until, on 14 June 1865, judgement was delivered by the bishop. Phillpotts was, by then, in his late eighties, weakened in body but still strong in mind and spirit. The previous Sunday, which happened to be Trinity Sunday, Henry Phillpotts attended the ordination at Exeter Cathedral, and although most of the service was taken by the Bishop of Jamaica, "the sentences of ordination and other parts of the service spoken by our venerable diocesan, were given distinctly and with emphasis".

The following Wednesday the various parties to the suit, Weston *v* Gueritz, gathered at the Bishop's Palace. Gueritz and the complainant's agent, Mr Davies, had both already expressed their willingness to accept the judgement of the bishop in the matter without further proceedings and the bishop replied that he found it "a pleasant thing to have matters so amicably adjusted". Gueritz had admitted the charge that he had refused burial to John Pavey who had been baptized, was not excommunicate and had not laid violent hands upon himself, and the bishop accepted that he had acted in accordance with conscientious objections and that he, Gueritz, had no feeling of ill will, either to the deceased or to any of his surviving friends. The bishop also noted that the complainant had "laudably and charitably disclaimed any desire for vindictive punishment or that any should be awarded beyond that which shall show that Mr Gueritz was not justified in his refusal".

The judgement found that Mamerto Gueritz was not legally justified in his actions. He was admonished not to offend again in like manner and ordered to pay the costs of the proceedings, which were considerable, probably amounting to the equivalent of a year's income. It should be noted that the bishop did not adjudge Gueritz to be guilty but, rather, not legally justified. There was a private part of the exchange between Gueritz and his diocesan which was only shared when Phillpotts was long dead. Phillpotts had given Gueritz to understand that while the law required the performance of the service, he, personally, would not think of obeying the requirement.[17]

The changed tenor of the final proceedings, so different from the highly charged emotions of the preceding September, signalled something of a shift locally even before the judgement was given. Afterwards, honour had been satisfied on both sides, the local Unitarians were vindicated, relationships with the Pavey family were being healed, and although Gueritz had not obeyed the law, it was allowed that he had acted with integrity. They had all arrived at a place where forward movement should have been possible.

It seemed that domestic happiness might be allowed place once more in the Gueritz family. Almost a fortnight after the bishop's judgement had been given, Mamerto officiated at the wedding of his sister Adelina, as she and Samuel Bartlett were married in Colyton Church. In the vicarage garden was a pomegranate tree which, according to legend, would bloom when someone of the vicarage family was married. It was in flower when Adelina and Samuel were wedded. The legend would be fulfilled twice more as the Gueritz story unfolded but the next time would not be for more than a decade.

Samuel Bartlett and Adelina had met when she was teaching the children of the Coles family in Shepton Beauchamp, and there are indications that she lodged with Samuel and his wife, Nancy Louisa, during her second period as tutor to the children of the rectory.

On 15 May 1864, Nancy Bartlett died. Until then Samuel had been living at The Priory in Barrington village, which was part of the Shepton Beauchamp benefice. Just over a year later he and Adelina were married. Adelina was younger than Bartlett by some 18 years; he was 55 at the time of the wedding, but this seems not to have excited comment and indeed such an age disparity was common at the time. Even though Adelina stayed on at Shepton Beauchamp after her brother had moved on, returning there for a while after her appointment in Glastonbury ended, it was some time since she had lived near Barrington where her new husband still held land. How their relationship had been sustained in the interval and how it developed to the point of matrimony is not known. Although he owned land and property in Barrington, Samuel made his home with Adelina in Colyton.

This oasis of family joy was still set within the wider ripples of the Pavey controversy.

Less than a week after the wedding the case was being cited in the House of Lords as a reason to remove the compulsory use of the Prayer Book burial service from the law. Lord Ebury stated that over 4,000 clergy had lamented the demand the present situation made on their consciences. He spoke warmly of Gueritz as a man of irreproachable character who was obliged by law to read the Athanasian Creed 14 times a year, which creed consigned two-thirds of the human race to perdition, including the Unitarians! The same law compelled him to say, over the corpse of a Unitarian parishioner, that he committed "the body of his dear brother to the ground, earth to earth, ashes to ashes, in the sure and certain hope of the resurrection to eternal life"![18]

The *Western Times* printed a bowdlerized version of Lord Ebury's comments on 11 July. A comparison of the newspaper summary and the actual speech reveals just how distorted was the report and amply justifies Gueritz' comment on the scurrilities of the *Western Times*. However, the ripple effects of the case were spreading and clergy who found themselves in a dilemma where the law of the land and the teaching of the Church were in conflict discovered that they were not alone and that there were, after all, a few voices in the corridors of power prepared to speak for them. Unfortunately, in this instance, those voices were not heard from the Bench of Bishops and the plight of the conscience-stricken clergy was only eased with the passing of the Burial Laws Amendment Act in 1880 which took away the obligations which Lord Ebury lamented 15 years earlier.

Notes

[1] South West Heritage Centre (West Country Studies Library), Colyton Parish File.

[2] *Cambridge Independent Press*, Saturday, 4 October 1860.

[3] Exeter Cathedral Archives, Chapter Minutes, 1860.

[4] *The Morning Advertiser*, Thursday, 2 August 1860, reported the appointment to Colyton and Monckton in the Clerical Intelligence column but wrongly stating that Gueritz was an alumnus of Lincoln College. It should be noted that "Monckton" is the ancient spelling of the place name. Various contemporary reports have "Monkton" or even "Moncton" instead.

5   *Pulman's Weekly News*, 10 July 1860. This edition came out on a Tuesday, which dates the arrival of the family in Colyton as Thursday, 5 July 1860.

6   V. S. S. Coles, Obituary of Mamerto Gueritz, *Church Times*, 16 February 1912.

7   B. A. Orford, "Henry Parry Liddon: Correspondence on Church and Faith", PhD thesis, University of Wales, Bangor, 2000. This quotation is from a letter to the author from Dr Orford. The name of the solitary sister is not given directly in the letter, but the fact that she was the "natural" sister of Mr Glanville of Sheviock was stated.

8   The census of 1861 records two residents in the vicarage other than family and servants. There was Frances "Gleenfell" (the writing is unclear), a visitor aged 44, and Emily L. Nott, a scholar aged 15. Emily Nott's antecedents and her future after 1861 are well documented, although quite why she was in Colyton then is also a mystery. Frances Gleenfell appears in no other record found so far. It is likely that the census official misheard and miswrote "Glanville".

9   F. G. Lee, *Glimpses in the Twilight—being various notes, records and examples on the Supernatural* (London: Wm. Blackwood, 1885), p. 8. A. P. Stanley was dean from 1864 to 1881.

10 *Pulman's Weekly News*, 31 December 1861. Letter dated; Colyton, Dec 27th 1861. Signed "M---".

11 *Pulman's Weekly News*, 21 January 1862.

12 *Pulman's Weekly News*, 4 February 1862.

13 An analysis of the available information, by Jean Robin, appears in the occasional papers of the Cambridge Group for the History of Population and Social Structure. See J. Robin, "Prenuptial Pregnancy in a Rural Area of Devonshire in the Mid Nineteenth Century", *Community and Change* 1 (1986), pp. 113–24. Also, J. Robin, "Illegitimacy in Colyton, 1851 to 1881", *Community and Change* 2 (1987), pp. 307–42. Also in Jean Robin, *The Way We Lived Then* (Aldershot: Ashgate, 2000), pp. 19–26.

14 The case was reported in Australia in *The Empire* of Wednesday, 1 February 1865 and the judgement was reported in *The Gouldburn Herald and Chronicle* of Saturday, 21 October 1865.

15 The full correspondence was reported in the *Western Times* on Friday, 28 October 1864.

16 An exhaustive account of the annual meeting was also carried in the *Western Times* on 28 October.

17 V. S. S. Coles, Obituary of Mamerto Gueritz, *Church Times*, 16 February 1912.

[18]   An extract from Hansard, House of Lords Sitting, 3rd July 1865. LORD EBURY, in moving the following Resolution—"That, in the opinion of this House, the Evils arising from the compulsory and almost indiscriminate Use of the Burial Service of the Church of England, demand the early attention of the Legislature". Instances without number of painful scenes which had occurred at funerals in consequence of nothing having been done in the meantime, such as those described by the right rev. Prelate on a former occasion, had been made known to him, one of which he had mentioned to the House; but he would forbear to cite more than one, and that one of very recent date, with which probably many of their Lordships were familiar. He meant that of Colyton, in Devonshire. The incumbent of Colyton, it appeared, was a man, as he understood, of irreproachable character, entertaining rather extreme High Church views, and consequently zealous for the law. Therefore he did as the law directed: thirteen times he was required to read the Athanasian Creed—thirteen times every year, with the assistance of his congregation, he consigned three parts at least of the human race—past, present, and future—to everlasting perdition, including, of course, the Unitarians, against whom he believed this creed to have been specially directed. Their Lordships, then, would judge of this clergyman's feelings when, walking out of his church after reading this creed—on Whitsunday or on Trinity Sunday—his sexton informed him that one of his parishioners, a Unitarian, had died, and was to be buried in a day or two. Mr. Gueritz had just pronounced that this man would perish everlastingly, and he was now required to say of the same man, and before the same congregation, that he committed the body of his dear brother to the ground, earth to earth, ashes to ashes, in the sure and certain hope of the resurrection to eternal life and happiness in the world to come. Was ever an unhappy clergyman put into such a position? How long it took Mr. Gueritz to decide I am unable to say, but I have no doubt that, feeling he was acting up to the advice of his metropolitan, and that he would in so doing have the approbation of every honest man, he determined to brave the penalties of the law sooner than pronounce these words over an Unitarian; and so he did brave the penalties of the law, and the law fell upon him. He did not, because he could not, defend himself, and so he was cited before the proper tribunal, admonished, and condemned to pay the costs of the suit."

7

London and Colyton

1866 to 1870

On 2 January 1866, the minutes of Exeter Cathedral chapter recorded:

> The Chapter having learned from the Rev'd Mamerto Gueritz, vicar of
> Colyton that he was desirous of resigning the Chapelry of Monckton and
> considering that it would be advantageous to the vicarage of Upottery and
> also to Monckton that it should be united with Upottery, and having an
> application on the part of the Vicar of Upottery for such union, resolved
> that steps be taken in effecting the union.[1]

It had been hoped that the new incumbent of Colyton would be relieved of
responsibility for Monckton before Mamerto Gueritz was installed. That had
not happened. Monckton was more than 12 miles from Colyton over lanes
that, at some times of the year, were impassable. The journey could take three
hours. Providing priestly care for Monckton cost rather more than the parish
returned in income, and Mamerto Gueritz did not have the financial resources
of his predecessor. Upottery was closer to Monckton, and the petition of the
vicar seemed to offer a way forward. In the event, no such union was made. The
perpetual curacy of Monckton was given to the Revd John Fielder Mackarness,
who, aside from his other appointments and prebendal stall at Exeter, was also
rector of Honiton, just a mile or so along the Exeter Road. Mackarness had been
supportive of Mamerto Gueritz as a local colleague and, at times, proved to be
something of a friend at court both in Exeter diocese and later when he was Bishop
of Oxford. It was later noted in the cathedral chapter minutes, when they gathered

in full conclave over the election of Frederick Temple to the see in November 1869, that Mackarness was "Bishop designate of Oxford". His appointment to Monckton was effective in May 1867.

Early in 1866, the Revd William Henry Baptist Proby returned to England from the diocese of Brechin in Scotland. Proby's tale is told more fully in Chapter 16, but at this point in the story of Mamerto Gueritz we note that Proby's mother had died in January, which left him with lands and properties in and around Northleigh. His mother, Louisa Proby, had some time previously acquired the manorial rights thereof, which meant that Proby was now also lord of the manor of Northleigh. He was in the process of setting his affairs in East Devon in order and at the same time engaged in securing the senior curacy at St Augustine's, Haggerston, which was one of the growing number of churches which exemplified the Catholic Revival in London. In the meantime, in 1866 his name begins to appear in the service records of Colyton, such as they were at the time; formal service registers did not yet exist. Gueritz appears to have welcomed the assistance of a priest with local antecedents, of apparently similar convictions to his own and with some experience of managing a parish, albeit a Scottish one. There were other, formally licensed, curates slightly later. The Revd Nettleton Balme Whitby was curate in Colyton from 1867 to 1868, but in the immediate aftermath of the Pavey case and with a great financial liability laid upon him, Gueritz appears to have been glad of an additional assistant who did not need a stipend!

The liturgy in Colyton was becoming recognizably ritualistic, something which Proby supported entirely. Local opposition, carefully nurtured by an antagonistic press, boiled over into local action. The event was recorded in an article, written entirely in Devon dialect, which appeared in the *Devon Weekly Times* on 23 November 1866, just a week before St Andrew's Day. A number of attacks on Tractarians and Ritualists in Devon were couched in what the writers imagined to be local dialect. Perhaps the authors thought that by so doing they were enlisting the sympathy of those who spoke in the dialect or that they were somehow lending humour to what, if written in plain English, would have been seen by many as vulgar and offensive.

The article described the High Mass of Sunday 18 November in some detail, and although the article itself was contemptuous and, to priests like Gueritz, blasphemous, it does give some sense of the ritual. It is reproduced here with an synoptic translation to ease the strain on the brain caused by reading unfamiliar dialect inconsistently written. The translation is actually more of an elucidation at several points.

"The Meass in Colyton Church"

Deur Mr. Hedditur,—I wuz ta Colyton last Zunday an I heerd tha wuz ta be zum kungerin trix, hi mease in Church; zo zez I, I nevur zeed sich things in a Church 'eet, zo I'll go. Wal, wen I get ther tha vokes wuz all a bundling out like mad. Hallo zez I, whur be gwain tu? Why, sez Farmur Blak (ony he spoke zort a genelmun loike) thick there veller Popeboy ha ben as told uz Pope Gurtz wuz a gwain tu kunger burd an wine into vlash and bled; an we doant blive en, zo we be a kum'd out. Lor a massy, zez I, I'll go an zee en. Wul wen I got in I zeed tu gurt kanduls, an a gurt gould kros, an a lot more traps pon tap the kungerin borde. Than in kum'd a boy wi a wite shurt an a blak petikote en lited tha tu girt kanduls, than kum'd Popeboy wae a wite shurt on, an a blu strap auver ez sholdur and Pope Gurtz dres'd all za fine in grene an gould an hurd. A yung omman waz a plaiin the organ bootefule an zum boys an in or dree chaps wuz a zingin an hollerin, an than Popeboy an Pope Gurtz mead a bow tu tha gould kros az eft tu zyt how do du measter kros. Than tha moosik stayst an Pope Gurtz begun the kungerin be zayin

Dear Mr Editor, I was in Colyton last Sunday and I heard there was to be some conjuring tricks, High Mass in Church; so, says I, I have never seen such things yet, so I'll go. Well, when I got there the folks were all bundling out like mad. Hello, I said, where are you going? Why, said Farmer Black (though he spoke like a gentleman) that fellow Proby has told us that "Pope" Gueritz was going to conjure bread and wine into flesh and blood; and we don't believe him, so we have come out. Lord have mercy, I said, I'll go and see him. Well when I got in I saw two huge candles and a large gold cross and a lot more "things" on top of the credence table. Then a boy came in with a white surplice and a black cassock and lit the two huge candles, then came Proby with a white alb and a blue stole over his shoulder[4] and "Pope" Gueritz dressed all so fine in green and gold and red. A young woman[5] was playing the organ beautifully and some boys and one or three men were singing and shouting and then Proby and "Pope" Gueritz made a bow to the gold cross as if to say, "How do you do Mr. Cross". Then the music stopped and "Pope" Gueritz began the conjuring by saying zumthing tut ha kros dru iz noze, jest like an ole domman wot take snuf. The a turnd round ta wee an zed a lot more dru iz noze, an then tha boyz sing'd ever za many times but I kuden understan nort abowt et. Wal, Popeboy next gaed tu ov tha zinging boyz tu bags, just like that tu watch pakets my ole grammur us'd tu hav tut ha thed ov hur best hurd bed, an tha tu boys tuk tha tu bags tu tha vive or zix ole maids wot wos thar, an they gaed em zummit I spose tu gae on wae tha shaw, an tha boys tuk tha bags bak tu Popeboy, an he put em on his borde. The he tuk zum burd an wine an water off his borde an gied et tu Pope Gurtz tu put on his borde tu du tha kugerin wae. Hee than mixed watur wae tha wine, kaze,[2] I spose, tha ole maids didn gea en money enuf ta pay vor al wine, so he gaed em nagus. Wal, than thar wuz a lot more noze work an zinging and Popeboy went daun on ez hans and nees, wae ez noze tu tha grann, jest like a ole pig a ruting ater taties. But her, I thort twa za rude aw en turn ez hinder pearts wae ez wite shurt tew tha ole maids. Pope Gurtz then kingerd tha burd an negus; but lor a massy, I kudde zee but wat twas burd an nagus jest tha seam. Gurtz nex went on tew his nees tu wurship ez own kungerin, an than he tukt an drinkt zum o et jest tha seam ez Iziar zed, tha karpentur meaketh hiss el a image wae wun pece of a tree an wurshiped et an wormd hessel wae the chips, only Pope Gurtz

something to the cross through his nose, just like an old woman[6] who takes snuff. Then he turned around and said a lot more through his nose, and then the boys sang "repetitively" but I could understand nothing about it. Well Proby then gave the choirboys two bags, just like the watch-purses my old grandmother used to have at the head of her best hurd? bed and the two boys took the bags to the five or six old maids who were there, and they gave them something I suppose to go on with the show, and the boys took the bags back to Proby and he put them on the credence table. Then he took some bread and wine and water from the table and gave them to "Pope" Gueritz to put on the altar to do his conjuring with. He mixed water with the wine because, I suppose the old maids didn't give enough money to pay for all the wine, so he gave them "nagus".[7] Well, then there was a lot more nosework and singing and Proby went down on his hands and knees, with his nose to the ground, just like an old pig rooting for potatoes. But there, I thought it was so rude of him to turn his backside with his white alb to the old maids. "Pope" Gueritz then conjured the bread and "nagus" but Lord have mercy, I could see that it was bread and wine just the same. Gueritz next went on to his knees to worship his own conjuring, and then he took and drank some of it just the same as Isaiah said, the carpenter makes himself an image with one piece of a tree and worshipped it and then warmed himself with the woodchips. "Pope" Gueritz warmd ez inside wae tha nagus instead ev ez outzid wae tha vire. Than hee gaed zum to Popeboy, an I spose et dude en good vir a left orf ruteing an got up an helped Gurtz to gae tha kungered burd an nagus to tha ole maids. I spose et dood thay goed tu; wul ef thik thar kovetchus Gurtz diden ate an drink op all that wuz lef, an akchuley washed out tha cup twe or dree times wae zum more water an drinkd that tu cuz pore Popeboy shudden have a drap. Wel, thort I, ef this ez wot they cals a Hi Mease tis wot I cals a low mess, an a sham an a humbug, an ony vit vor vules an ole maids. Zo I waden stap no longer.

Zo no more vrom yore hever vakshurate.

Jon Stampur.

P.S. I wuz here Popeday nite.[3] There wuz a grand purseshun wae Pope Gurtz in ez vinery, and Popeboy an a lot more wae blak morter bordes an sensors an torches an a ole maid they cal'd a sistur a massy.

An then tha burned Pope Gueritz —only twadden he twar ony ez vinery—stuf'd way stra an puruffin, but twadden the same volk I seed in tha Church, 'sept twur ane ole maid I thort wuz like she in the perseshun. I lukes at she, an she luked kinder sly at I, so I thort, ef my ole dummen wuz here u wulden du that vort nort miss.

---

warmed his insides with the wine instead of his outside by the fire. Then he gave some to Proby and I suppose it did him good for he left off kneeling and got up and helped Gueritz to give the conjured bread and wine to the old maids. I suppose it did them good too; well, if that there "kovetchus"[8] Gueritz didn't eat and drink up all that was left, and actually washed out the cup two or three times with some more water and drank that too, so that poor Proby shouldn't have a drop. Well, thought I, if this is what they call a High Mass, it is what I call a low mess, and a sham and a humbug, and only fit for fools And old maids. So I wouldn't stay any longer.

So, no more from your ever 'vakshurate"

Jon Stampur.

P. S. I was in Colyton on the evening of 5th November. There was a grand procession with "Pope" Gueritz in his finery, and Proby, and a lot more with black mortar boards[10] and thuribles and torches and an old maid they called a Sister of Mercy.

And then they burned "Pope" Gueritz —only it wasn't him—it was just his finery— stuffed with straw and paraffin, but they weren't the same people that I saw in the Church except there was one old maid I thought was like the one in the procession. I looked at her, and she looked askance at me, so I thought, if my old woman was here you wouldn't do that for nothing Miss.

As to the identity of Jon Stampur: Elias Tozer was at the time joint owner of the *Devon Weekly Times*. He was also something of a poet and often published his work under various pseudonyms. Some of the poems were distinctly critical of the priesthood and of the Church and several were written in dialect form. It is, therefore, possible that the article in the *Devon Weekly Times* of 23 November 1866 was from his hand.

W. H. B. Proby, who was given the splendid soubriquet "Popeboy", acted as liturgical deacon, wearing his stole upon the left shoulder, while Mamerto Gueritz, as the celebrant, was vested in green, gold and red, being the colours of the chasuble and its orphrey. The acolytes were wearing cassock and surplice, as were the choristers present. There were large altar candles and a gold cross. The bowing and genuflecting were noted, as was the ceremonial mixing of water with the wine in the chalice and the ablutions at the end of Communion. Incense was used in procession. In fact, everything for which the Hon. Robert Liddell, vicar of St Paul's, Knightsbridge, had been prosecuted in 1855, Gueritz had introduced to Colyton by 1866. However, it was not the ritual alone that excited opposition. Proby's unsubtle presentation of the doctrine of the presence of Christ in the Eucharist had been taken entirely literally by some of the locals who claimed to be revolted at the idea that the vicar was going to "conjure" flesh and blood from bread and wine. This would not be the last time that Proby's failure to present Catholic doctrine in a manner capable of being understood by Devon country folk created havoc for Gueritz.

In the postscript to the article, the author claimed to have been in Colyton for what he called "Popeday Night", which was the local name for Guy Fawkes Night. The Act requiring a service in church to offer thanksgiving for the deliverance of King and Parliament from the "Popish plot" had only been repealed in 1859, but the self-styled Loyal Protestants of East Devon continued the custom and were wont to burn effigies of the Pope rather than of Guido Fawkes.

The anti-ritual protestors in Colyton seized the opportunity offered by the occasion and, in a manner common with all those who cried "No Popery!" on 5 November, built their bonfire in the middle of the town. However, in 1866, instead of burning the Pope, they made straw-stuffed effigies of "Pope Gurtz" (Mamerto Gueritz) and "Popeboy" (W. H. B. Proby) and consigned them to the flames.

The same evening, possibly as something of a counter-attack, there was a Solemn Evensong with a procession and incense in the parish church. It was at that procession that the presence of a Sister of Mercy was noted.

Mamerto's granddaughter, Antonia Dorothy Mortimer, the fourth child of Mary Louisa and Reginald Mortimer, although born almost two decades after the event, still recorded it in a letter in which she wrote:

> Grandpa was burnt in effigy in a Colyton Bonfire for wearing vestments! (but the curate wouldn't burn though Grandpa did).[11]

On 30 November, Mamerto Gueritz officiated at the evening service, it being the patronal festival, St Andrew's Day. The *Western Times*, or rather the local correspondent for that newspaper, did not miss the moment:

> Priest Gueritz, whose vagaries have attracted so much notice—not to say disgust—could not let an opportunity for making himself ridiculous, for showing his disloyalty to the Protestant cause, and his love of flirtation with the Scarlet Lady, pass.[12]

We have already seen the loose connection between some elements of the local press and truthful reporting; therefore the assertion in the article that a row was expected and a large crowd of protestors gathered, refusing to disperse until midnight and only held at bay by the two constables on duty, might safely be deemed an embroidering of the truth were it not for the bonfires of a week or so earlier. The article ends with the comment:

> Does that parson's conduct come under the heading of inciting people to meet together for a disorderly purpose? He is surely a kind of ecclesiastical Anglo-Fenian.

Even Gueritz' longstanding local opponents were beginning to show signs of weariness with this kind of rhetoric, and Gueritz himself was becoming increasingly affected by it; he began to experience periods of ill health. There was a vulnerability in him which seems to have dated from the time of his breakdown at St Edmund Hall. Shortly after St Andrew's Day 1866, Mamerto Gueritz left the parish for a short period of rest and recuperation. On the basis that a change is as good as a rest, he appears to have gone to friends in London, where he found sympathy for his recent trials and support for his actions.

An additional motive for going to London had previously been to see his son, Mamerto George, but George, by then aged 16, had already left the choir school at All Saints, Margaret Street and was a pupil at St Michael and All Angels College in Tenbury Wells.[13]

Although William Proby never formally held a licence to minister in Colyton, he assumed a great deal of freedom of action during the absences of the vicar. He also appeared in the service records at a time when he might have been expected to be in Haggerston, an appointment which lasted only from 1867 to 1869. Mamerto had only been out of the parish for a few days when Proby conducted what was then considered an extremely ritualistic funeral. The critics had a field day. It was claimed that there were such "goings on" at the graveside that the Pope himself would have been shocked to see it. Crosses and flowers were thrown into the grave! Actually, compared with the funeral of the vicar of Stogumber only a few years later, this ceremony was relatively low-key.

Christmas came and went and then, early in January 1867, W. H. B. Proby had altercations with two local families which fanned to a flame the dying embers of the Pavey controversy. It beggars belief that, given the experiences of the previous two years, Proby should apparently have deliberately provoked a new conflict, but so it seems.

The first instance was when Proby was called to visit a man called Sweetland who was dying. The Sweetland family had been Colytonians since before recorded history. During the visit, Sweetland's wife asked if her husband could be buried in the Church of England part of the cemetery. Proby would not countenance such a thing on the grounds that the old man had not been a "communicant". In the resulting furore, which raged not only in Colyton but also throughout East Devon, Proby was held up as a specimen of "priestly tyranny and intolerance". It was declared:

But the old man had, like many others, been driven from his church by
the detestable teachings and mummeries of our vicar and his very worthy
coadjutor.[14]

The "worthy coadjutor" did not stop there. At the end of January, John Woram died.
Woram the Bellman was a public figure in Colyton. In addition to his daily work
as a cobbler, he had been the town crier for many years and was at the heart of the
community. He even merited his own verse in local writer John Farmer's book *Poems*:

> Ha! Bellman Woram with his cheerful face,
> Leaving awhile the lapstone and the last,
> To cry some stirring news about the place.
> A character was he.

The funeral was arranged, and the widow asked for a hymn to be sung. Proby
refused. Instead, he interpolated two sermons into the Prayer Book service. The
first was on baptismal regeneration, while the second was on the Sacrament of
the Lord's Supper. Woram's funeral was a community event, and the community
turned out: Anglicans, Baptists, Congregationalists, Unitarians, and every shade
in between. The sermons offended almost everyone! The widow was asked by a
family member sitting near her if she had wanted such a service. Her answer was
an emphatic negative. Her actual words are not recorded. Proby would not tell the
family where they could contact the vicar and refused to discuss anything about
the funeral with them. He deemed it not to be their affair in either case. It was
a service of the Church, not of the individual! Perhaps, in the matter of the ill-
received sermons, Proby would have done well to heed Isaac Williams' cautionary
advice in *Tract 80*, "On Reserve in Communicating Religious Knowledge".

The outcome was almost inevitable. Without recourse to the vicar, the
complaint had to go somewhere and so, urged on by the East Devon press:

> A memorial to the Queen praying for her investigation of matters pertaining
> to the Ritualistic innovations of the present day and signed by nearly 200
> adult members of the Church of England in this town, has been forwarded
> to the proper quarter.[15]

The memorial to the Queen was sent in April. There is no recorded response. The next six or seven months were not quite so eventful, and the appointed curate, Nettleton Balme Whitby, seems to have soothed matters, either with the assistance of or in spite of William Proby. In any case, Proby should have been in Haggerston to fulfil his duties as senior curate.

Meanwhile in London Mamerto Gueritz was expanding his circle of friends and made the acquaintance of Henry Lascelles Jenner, the bishop designate of Dunedin, New Zealand. At the beginning of June, the bishop presided over a confirmation service at St Matthias, Stoke Newington where there were 160 candidates. Then, towards the end of 1867, on 30 November, there was more news of Mamerto, but this time back in Cornwall. The St Ives branch of the English Church Union had chosen St Andrew's Day as their anniversary. There were choral services morning and afternoon with the business meeting in between. The Revd Upton Richards, a Cornishman himself, was nominated to represent the branch in council and Mamerto Gueritz was among those who proposed the toasts at the dinner that evening. Upton Richards was the incumbent of All Saints, Margaret Street, one of the London churches where Mamerto had been attempting to recover himself. Perhaps they had travelled from London together.

In any event, Gueritz returned to Colyton two weeks later, and the bells were rung to welcome him home. Uncharacteristically the *Western Times* printed a kindly notice on his return which, because it contrasted so markedly with the tone of earlier reports, deserves attention. Quite probably this was from the pen of a different correspondent from the usual one. Having noted that Gueritz had "been away for the benefit of his health—indifferent of late and far from being restored now", the report continued:

> Notwithstanding the pertinacity with which he pushes the extreme views he
> holds, and the busy host of detractors his conduct in this respect has called
> into being, yet no one will deny his unimpeachable self denial, industry
> and kind heartedness on all other points; and it would sometimes be wise
> to take the mote out of the eye that claps on the well-fitting spectacles of
> satire to see the way to throw a stone at him, and remember the golden
> rule of charity at all times.[16]

This report was, in part, a response to Gueritz' intervention in a project intended to improve the living standards of Colytonians. The Feoffees, with the help of other bodies, intended to provide a gas supply to the town. Land was needed for the gasworks. Several landowners had been approached but had set a high, possibly opportunistic, price on the required land. Gueritz, who only had a small glebe holding, nevertheless offered part of it "at a most reasonable price when no other land could be obtained except at a most extravagant figure".

The contrast between Gueritz and the other landowners was not lost on the pragmatic people of Colyton. The selling of glebe land may have raised a cash injection for Gueritz but it also represented a permanent loss of income. Although the reduced level of animosity did not heal all wounds, it must have been with a lighter heart that he, Anne and some of the younger children planned to leave for a further period of restoration. The year 1868 arrived and would prove to be a year of new experiences which would shape Mamerto's future priesthood and extend his vision of the Church's ministry.

Gueritz had been granted leave of absence by Henry Phillpotts, who was now nearing the end of his life. It had been supposed by some that the Gueritz family were going to spend time on the Continent, but Mamerto's passport, issued in 1864, shows no evidence of use until 1871. Such travels, however, would not have been particularly remarkable. Many ritualist clergy travelled in Belgium and France, some never to return. T. A. Pope, the first incumbent of St Matthias, Stoke Newington, was received into the Roman Catholic Church while on holiday in Belgium, less than a year after the consecration of the church. Others took advantage of the opportunity to observe the latest liturgical fashions, the cut of a chasuble and the hang of a cope. There was also a constant, if gentle at this stage, seepage of lay converts from Anglicanism to the Roman Catholic Church: one such is of more than passing interest at this point in the story. In May of 1865, Henry Phillpotts' granddaughter, who had been wintering at Pau, "crossed the Tiber" and converted to Rome. By this stage Phillpotts, although enfeebled in body, was still in command of his incisive intellect. His granddaughter was very much a part of the Exeter establishment, and a daughter of the late sub-dean. Henry Phillpotts was said to be much concerned by her secession.

That concern was, of course, personal to Phillpotts but it also touched on his identity as a bishop of the Church. Newman's secession and the tide of those who followed him had challenged the credibility of those who still argued for the catholicity of the Church of England. Pusey was the focal point for those who remained to sustain the argument. Every secession, lay or priest, was effectively telling those who remained that their departing brothers and sisters no longer believed their claim to be members of the One Holy, Catholic and Apostolic Church. Small wonder, then, that Anglo-Catholics came together whenever they could to sustain one another. So it was that Mamerto Gueritz and, at various times, members of his family passed 1868 and 1869 not on the Continent but for the most part in London, cementing and developing relationships with the clergy and other friends. There seems to have been a considerable amount of movement backwards and forwards between London and Colyton during that period. Of course, the new railway made such journeys relatively easy.

The first visit of the Gueritz family to London early in 1868 coincided with the emigration of the eldest son, Mamerto George. Having completed his education, he was setting off to begin a career in the service of the Brooke Administration of Sarawak on the island of Borneo.

Mamerto Gueritz had long shown an avid interest in Borneo. He had become acquainted with Rajah Sir James Brooke during one of his visits to Oxford University and, with the help of the Brooke family and the loan of their artefacts, had lectured on the history of the country. One such lecture was given in Penzance when George was ten and Edward Peregrine five. Whether or not their father's fascination had any direct effect on them, George began his colonial career at Sarawak in Borneo. He left London early in March to arrive in Perth in June of that year in transit to his new home. The family were in London when he sailed. His brother Edward was later to follow him to North Borneo, ultimately with marked success.

There was a brief return to Colyton, and before Mamerto Gueritz set out again there was a visit from Henry Lascelles Jenner who, although bishop designate of Dunedin, had not been able to take up his episcopal duties in New Zealand. He had been consecrated bishop by royal warrant in Canterbury Cathedral, but opposition to his appointment to the new diocese of Dunedin had been growing and he had not yet sailed. In the meantime, he continued his support for the Anglo-Catholic movement and its clergy in England. Although his presence in Colyton indicates clearly Jenner's personal support for Mamerto Gueritz, it should not be taken as any indication of estrangement between Mamerto and Bishop Phillpotts. By that time, it was commonplace for colonial bishops to carry out episcopal duties on behalf of Bishop Phillpotts, whose health was beginning to fail. The most widely employed in Exeter diocese, as Henry Phillpotts became less able to travel, were Bishops Spencer of Jamaica and Chapman of Colombo. Bishop Henry Jenner came to Colyton to preside at a confirmation service, at which Edward Peregrine Gueritz, aged 13, and Mary Louisa, aged 15, were confirmed. Significantly, so also were two members of the family of Woram the Bellman, late town crier at whose funeral William Proby had caused such outrage.

Ever loyal to his bishop and aware of Phillpotts' aversion to parishes being left without proper provision, Mamerto had taken steps to ensure that this time during his absence there would be a formally licensed curate in charge. The *Pall Mall Gazette* of 10 March 1868 carried an advertisement for "the curacy of Colyton near Axminster; patron the Rev M Gueritz".

There was neither stipend specified nor housing, but possibly that was because a candidate was already in view. The official curate at this stage was still Nettleton Balme Whitby, and he and W. H. B. Proby were equally engaged in looking after the parish for most of 1868. At the end of the year, Whitby left the parish and Proby's appearance in the registers was much reduced by the formal appointment of the curate in charge. There was a Revd J. W. Bennett resident at the vicarage in late 1868. This is known because he received an exercise book in the post, sent on a "Penny Red" stamp, which is not as trivial an event as it might seem. In the first place, it confirms where the curate in charge was living, and secondly, he used the exercise book to continue the kind of proto service register that Whitby had begun. J. W. Bennett was the curate in charge and both he and the Revd D. J. Mackey were present for the episcopal visitation at Honiton the following year, signing in as the clergy of Colyton.[17]

The responsibility for the day-to-day running of the parish lay with John Bennett, the appointed curate in charge, with Donald Mackey taking on such duties as a deacon may with Bennett acting as his mentor. W. H. B. Proby had no authority in the parish; he was, after all, someone else's curate at the time. Incidentally, around this time Proby purchased Colyton House, although he did not live there until 1885.

Donald John Mackey had been ordained deacon in Exeter Cathedral by the Bishop of Jamaica, acting for Henry Phillpotts, in 1868 and was already serving his title at Colyton before Gueritz left.[18] Mackey was an accomplished musician and would later compose mass settings and hymn tunes. He was not ordained priest until 1870. The episcopally authorized absence of Mamerto Gueritz meant that another priest was needed to supervise the new deacon, and that was to be J. W. Bennett. Bennett had been ordained priest in 1867 and immediately was made rector of Markshall in Essex.[19] As we have seen, at this period the incumbent of a benefice was not always tied to his parish and, if he made appropriate provision for the ministry, was free to engage in other activities. Bennett was also thoroughly involved in the development of Gregorian chant and was for many years precentor to the London Gregorian Association. He was later described as a "Broad High Churchman". How he and Gueritz first met is not known, but their paths crossed several times after the Colyton appointment, most significantly at St Matthias, Stoke Newington. While Mamerto was exercising his musical talents in London, John Bennett was doing the same, on his behalf, in Colyton. Further confirmation of Bennett's role in Colyton came from an unlikely source. A year or so later both the *Record* and *Pulman's Weekly News* carried a story about ritual extremists in a "Parish in the West of England". By then, it was stale news, but the description of the curate in charge is illuminating:

> One of the curates in charge during the vicar's absence was not accustomed in his own parish to wear ecclesiastical vestments, but readily accommodated himself to his change of position. . . . This temporising appears to have produced such a result as might have been fairly expected. The questionable practices became pleasant, and the curate in charge, (a rector from another parish) was soon in a "transition" state. Now mark what happens. He too went to London (leave being obtained on the grounds of his wife's ill health) and to the same notorious church whither his friend the vicar had led the way. After some months of such performances what will this rector think of his own quiet services at home? Will he not return to his flock to disseminate the soul destroying teachings of Rome?[20]

This is further confirmation, should it be needed, that before his second period of refreshment in London Gueritz had already established considerable advances in ritual in Colyton, the wearing of Eucharistic vestments being but one of them.

Meanwhile in London Edward Peregrine Gueritz returned to his education in Stoke Newington,[21] and his father took up a role as an honorary assistant priest in the parish of St Matthias. Significantly, in Mamerto's published obituary, given all there was to recall of his history, these relationships—with St Matthias, with C. J. Le Geyt the incumbent and with Robert Brett, a surgeon in that parish—were mentioned first:

> Finding refreshment from time to time in the London churches where in those days the beginnings of "Ritualism" were appearing, he once served at Mr. Le Geyt's place in Stoke Newington and won the valuable acquaintance of Robert Brett.

Although they had only arrived in London in late March, Mamerto and Anne were back in Colyton for Easter, which was 12 April that year. It seems that Mamerto stayed in Colyton until the middle of Easter week and then returned to London. In May, St Matthias, Stoke Newington held its dedication festival, in which once again Mamerto took part and Bishop Henry Jenner lent an episcopal presence, presiding at several of the services.

Although the remaining family had decamped to London as a whole, it seems that this time Anne Gueritz stayed behind in Colyton and began to take a hand in church finances. It was noted in the service register that several church collections were "retained by Mrs. G". Mamerto was in London for Trinity Sunday, which fell on 7 June, and we have Mamerto's notes of the homily for that day. It is just a series of headings and seems to mark a return to the simple and earnest style of preaching of his days in Penzance. At St Matthias, within the Eucharistic rite, the sermon was servant to the sacrament and Mattins and Evensong were the main preaching services. Given the constant battles with the Unitarians of East Devon, Trinity Sunday 1868 may well have seen Gueritz preaching with even more than his customary fervour.

Other friendships made in Stoke Newington were also to shape life in Devon. W. H. Monk, the first compiler of *Hymns Ancient & Modern*, was organist and choirmaster at St Matthias, and he was later to visit Colyton on a number of occasions. Indeed, a photograph of Monk in country attire hung in The Bear Inn until its closure as a public house. Monk's pioneering work on the restoration of plainchant and the development of music and hymnody as a means of expressing the seasonal themes of worship had already shaped Mamerto's own development as a musician and a priest, possibly as early as his curacy in Barrington but certainly in Penzance. Monk had been organist and choirmaster at Stoke Newington for more than a decade before Mamerto Gueritz began his association with the parish.

St Matthias, Stoke Newington was consecrated by Bishop Blomfield of London on 13 June 1853. The fact that Monk was the organist, and T. A. Pope the first incumbent, provoked the bishop to wry humour about the churchmanship which would be promoted. His humour turned out to be prophetic. As we noted earlier, T. A. Pope, as common parlance has it, "poped".

In 1858, Charles James Le Geyt was appointed the third incumbent and served there until 1877, although prolonged periods of ill health made the assistance of a *locum tenens* necessary, a role that Mamerto Gueritz filled over a period of several years. Nevertheless, under Le Geyt and with Monk's assistance, the musical tradition and advances in liturgical practice grew side by side. Even at this stage, there were distinctions to be drawn between the musical traditions which were emerging in different places. Some of these might be summed up as professional versus amateur—in this instance an amateur being one who works to no lower a standard but who works without payment. Monk had a declared aim: to produce a singing congregation. To this end, the choir was never allowed to dominate the worship or to develop a polished concert style. Always the choir at St Matthias was a voluntary one, based on Monk's declared belief that professionals would never work as hard or maintain the same motives. This provided a distinctive tone and style to the worship at St Matthias, which was readily transferred to parish life in Colyton. Mamerto had found a musical tradition at the heart of the Revival which affirmed his own musical methods in rural Devon.

Liturgically and ceremonially, in Stoke Newington, Gueritz was on the bow wave of developments. St Matthias had begun the use of vestments even before All Saints, Margaret Street. By 1868, the various manuals of liturgical practice already mentioned were widely available, but by then Le Geyt himself had become acknowledged as an authority on ceremonial. In 1866, he published a lecture,

Catholic Ritual in the Church of England, which he had delivered at the Oxford branch of the English Church Union. In the lecture, there was a clear link with John Purchas' first edition of the *Directorium Anglicanum*. Purchas wrote of Catholic ritual as echoing the worship of heaven as revealed in the Apocalypse, thus giving scriptural authority to his vision of ceremonial. Le Geyt spoke of the same image in his lecture:

> Is it not wonderful that the Ritual of the holy Oblation, the vestments and the ornaments of the altar and of the priest, should bear resemblance if not precise identity.

Then in 1867, Le Geyt published *On the Symbolism of Ritual; in the Church and in the World*. So it was that when Mamerto Gueritz arrived in Stoke Newington, he found himself at the epicentre of the Ritual Revival.

For Mamerto, there were other discoveries during this time. Liturgical renewal was not (or should not have been) the sole aim of this phase of the Oxford Movement; it was rather a means to an end. Catholic ritual was a visible statement that the Church of England was part of the One Holy Catholic and Apostolic Church, but it was equally a means of mission. The sharing of the faith with the poor and deprived of St Matthias was a high priority. The beauty of holiness expressed in the Sunday mass was to be something which attracted those who had little of beauty or the numinous in their daily lives. Liturgy was to be missional, and this had already led to developments like the Guild of St Alban the Martyr and its many associated brotherhoods. The Guild was formed in 1851 from lay communicants, with clergy being admitted as associates, the intention being the mobilization of lay people in support of the work of the clergy, even to the extent of lay people proclaiming the gospel at simple mission services. The concept of episcopally authorized lay vocation gained credibility, and the order of readers was revived in 1866.

Its detractors have long characterized the Oxford Movement as being excessively sacerdotal. The enthusiasm for lay participation in mission expressed in the journal of the Guild of St Alban the Martyr partly counters that charge. The journal reported that the Brotherhood of St Augustine, Stoke Newington, held a special meeting on 26 June 1868. The Brotherhood had acquired a house for mission services, a youth club and other work. There was a room set aside for a mission oratory, and a club room for social activity: "There was a capital muster of friends including the Rev Associate M Gueritz, Vicar of Colyton, who is at present assisting at S. Matthias."

The report concluded:

> The Rev. M. Gueritz added some practical advice relating to his own experience of a country guild, and of the great assistance it has been to him in many ways; he thought the reluctance shown to use laymen in the conduct of religious services was natural at this time but that by degrees it would melt away. Compline was heartily sung and the meeting dismissed with the benediction pronounced by Rev. M. Gueritz.[22]

The idea that lay ministry, properly authorized, trained and managed, is a valid vocation in itself and not just a sop for failed aspirants to the priesthood has always been difficult for people to grasp, especially the clergy. In Stoke Newington, immersed in the work of lay brotherhoods and sisterhoods, Mamerto Gueritz made the first tentative steps in exploring the concept and then put it into practice in his parish and, as we shall see, in family life.

Later in 1869, on 4 August, there was the annual general meeting of the Brotherhood of St Augustine's Missionary Association, at which the clerical associate, the Revd M. Gueritz, seconded the motion proposing to divide the year's subscriptions in equal proportions between the Orange River and Natal Missions in Central Africa and the diocese of Tennessee. This money was given from one of the poorest and most deprived areas in London.[23] For Mamerto, the championing of mission was no new thing. He was simply continuing a long-held commitment to overseas missions which we witnessed in his sermon on the Indian mutiny given in Penzance and also his longstanding membership of the Church Missionary Society. He first began fundraising for the society as an undergraduate in Oxford. The year 1869 dawned and back in Colyton J. W. Bennett had firmly taken the wheel, or rather the altar, with Proby very much in the background. Liturgical life in Colyton was being continued along the line that Gueritz had set. For example, during Holy Week there was a daily mass, recorded as such, until Friday when the liturgy of the day was celebrated. In Whitsun week, there was again a daily mass. In London, as the months unfolded, the rhythms of St Matthias—the daily office and the daily mass, the burgeoning lay work, the ministry of sisterhoods and brotherhoods—all became part of Mamerto's understanding of the Church at work in the world.

The friendships and alliances made in Stoke Newington were to sustain and shape Mamerto's ministry lifelong and most of that was, of course, in Colyton. Towards the end of September 1869, with his liturgical, ministerial and missional vision broadened and affirmed, Mamerto returned to Devon. Mary Louisa remained at school in London, where her earlier noted "tom-boy" qualities proved something of a trial to the ladies who ran the school. Her brothers, Fortescue and Edward, remained working for a while as clerks to an accountant.

Mamerto had not been completely absent from Colyton and had made visits from time to time to take a wedding or a funeral, but before he finally returned to take up his cure, on 18 September 1869 Henry Phillpotts, bishop of the diocese for 39 years, died. Phillpotts had known Colyton for many years, because well before his appointment as Bishop of Exeter he had become friends with Gueritz' predecessor, Frederick Barnes, in Oxford.[24] Having placed his trust in Mamerto Gueritz over several quite demanding curacies, Phillpotts had preferred him to the living, which is illustrative of their relationship.

When a bishop dies or leaves the diocese, even if their relationship with the bishop was not as cordial as that enjoyed by Gueritz, the clergy await with trepidation the arrival of a stranger to be their father in God. "And there arose a new King up over Egypt which knew not Joseph" (Exodus 1:8). Would their previous service be remembered and their achievements honoured, or would it all be forgotten?

The appointment of Frederick Temple, when it was made known, was initially felt as a blow by Gueritz and the other Tractarian clergy. Temple had contributed to the book *Essays and Reviews*. The first essay in the book, "The Education of the World", was his. The authors of the volume were responsible only for their respective articles, but some of these were deemed so liberal and so destructive that many people banned the whole book. Senior clergy called on Temple to dissociate himself from the other contributors and although Temple initially refused to repudiate his associates, he later decided to withdraw his essay. It was, in one sense, a matter of guilt by association.

The proposed appointment to Exeter provoked George Anthony Denison, Archdeacon of Taunton, together with the Earl of Shaftesbury, to form a protest committee. It will be remembered that Denison was the bishop's examining chaplain at the time of Mamerto's ordination and became archdeacon shortly after the curacy at Shepton Beauchamp ended. Dr Pusey declared that the choice of Temple was the most frightful enormity ever perpetrated by a prime minister. At the confirmation of Temple's election, the committee instructed counsel to object to it, and in the first voting the chapter of Exeter Cathedral was divided. A mass was offered in Colyton for the right guidance of the chapter. Gladstone stood firm, and the cathedral chapter minutes record that they acted "In obedience to the will of Her Majesty". Temple was consecrated on 21 December 1869.

When the consecration of a new bishop is announced, the tradition is that bells are rung in every parish in the diocese. They were rung in Colyton. It was not, as the Unitarian press tried to assert, an attempt on the part of the ringers to demonstrate "their hatred of the priestly despotism to which the Colytonians have long been subjected".[25] However, Gueritz had not been consulted about the peal, and when he sent his son over to the tower to suggest that the bellringers stop, they refused. Mamerto's response was: "They would ring for the devil if they were paid for it!"

The same newspaper report, printed on 28 December, went on to mock the Christmas ceremonies in the church:

> On Christmas Eve midnight mass was performed in the Church when the vicar and his "conjurin borde" were decked out in a style worthy of a pantomime.

This was not the first time that the press had likened the liturgy in Colyton to a conjuring performance, as we saw in 1866, but when an opponent forsakes rational argument and descends to the level of blasphemous mockery, then they have already lost the moral and intellectual high ground. It has been shown that Gueritz did himself little good in his early uncompromising encounters with the Unitarians, but once matters were settled over the Pavey funeral and once the Woram and Sweetland arguments had receded, there seems to have been something of a lessening of hostilities locally. The press, however, were another matter. *Pulman's* and the *Record* carried on attacking Gueritz in this way, well after other individuals, and even the *Western Times*, had begun to temper the tone of their criticism. Stuckey Coles was later to write:

> Those were the days when certain West Country newspapers fell upon manifestations of the Revival with unrestrained violence, and the Vicar of Colyton was not spared.[26]

There were indeed occasional flashpoints in the parish, some quite striking, but in the main these were either the result of injudicious activity by the so-called "worthy coadjutor" William Proby or inflammatory articles in the press. Proby appears only sporadically as "Officiating Priest" in the service records during 1870, and infrequently thereafter until 1872 when in the latter part of the year he was very active. That continued until April 1873, after which he disappears from the liturgical life of the town, the reasons for which will emerge.

In February 1870, Henry Parry Liddon was preferred to a canonry at St Paul's Cathedral. This was a moment of reflected glory for Colyton, whose townsfolk still thought of Liddon as one of their own.

During Lent, the bells, which had not been heard since the consecration of Bishop Temple, were being rung again but not yet as a peal:

> Three measured tolls on the bell are given twice at the celebration of the Holy Communion to signify to the people the exact time of the elevation of the host. I wonder if this is lawful . . . I suppose these things indicate the spread of church buffoonery here.[27]

And then in Holy Week resentful comments about the "incessant clanging of the bells" and the fact that "a few infatuated persons seem to have lived in the church" were made by Gueritz' adversaries, but in so doing they also inadvertently revealed that support for the worship was not lacking. The service registers indicate a healthy attendance rather than just a few infatuated persons.

The first ten years had been a period of hard work and consistent teaching, with some considerable pastoral disasters to look back on. Local relationships were being rebuilt but on a different basis from that previously experienced under

Frederick Barnes. The differences between the various religious bodies in the town were now acknowledged openly, but with the early combative style tempered by time and by the acknowledgement from his more objective detractors that Mamerto Gueritz was a man of "unimpeachable self-denial, industry and kind heartedness on all other points".[28]

This thawing did not immediately extend to all Gueritz' opponents. "J S G" was the Colyton resident who, until 1874, was acting as correspondent for the Unitarian press. In June 1870, he wrote an article which declared that certain Romish doctrines were being taught by the vicar and listed them as:

1. The flesh of Christ is actually eaten in the Lord's Supper.
2. There are seven sacraments.
3. Christians should "repeat the sign of the holy cross upon their bodies to ward off evil spirits".
4. One "office" said in church by the priest, even if alone, is of more benefit to the parish than 12 hours of visiting among the sick and the poor.
5. The Bible is a dangerous book in the hands of the laity.

It is easy to see, especially when the provenance of this report is understood, how Gueritz' teaching could be thus represented, even distorted, in transmission. There were indeed shades of opinion among Tractarians and Ritualists regarding the presence of Christ in the sacrament of the altar. There is nothing to suggest, however, that Mamerto held more "Romish" views than, for example, J. W. E. Bennett of Frome. Bennett's letter to Pusey entitled *A Plea for Toleration in the Church of England* was widely accepted as confirming that the doctrine of the Real Presence of Christ in the Eucharist and Anglican dogma are indeed compatible.

Gueritz, together with most Tractarian clergy, affirmed that there were two Dominical sacraments, namely Baptism and the Eucharist, and five others, not given directly by Christ but as gifts of the Holy Spirit to the Church.

In a later article in the parish magazine, Gueritz replied more fully to the fourth point of his critic. The work of the parish priest is, he asserted, only efficacious as such if it is unvaryingly rooted in prayer, and the daily prayer of the Church is the morning and evening office. It was not, he said, a matter of either prayer or visiting the sick but of both. Pastoral duties must be undergirded by and enfolded in prayer.

Reflecting on the comment that the Bible was a dangerous book in the hands of the laity, Mamerto might well, given the multiplicity of sects in Colyton each with their own distinctive use of the Scriptures, have wanted to warn of the dangers of misinterpretation and distortion.

The same reporter also described a paper that was being circulated among the poor of the town by another clergyman described as "the vicar's most intimate friend". That friendship was becoming increasingly strained. The paper W. H. B. Proby circulated contained instructions to make the sign of the cross on waking and to pray for the living and the dead each day. It also advocated sacramental confession as a means of obtaining immediate forgiveness of sins. In a later tract circulated in the town, Proby attempted to prove that ritualistic practices were scriptural and that Protestantism was unscriptural and a distortion of the true faith. The intemperate Proby might well have learned from Ecclesiastes 3 that there is a time to keep silent and a time to speak.

During 1870, the pattern of services and meetings began to reflect a change in emphasis. The normal liturgical pattern remained, but there were also regular Sunday afternoon services for the children. Often these took the form of the Catechism and the Litany of the Holy Child. A Society of the Holy Childhood was formed which met monthly. The Guild of St Andrew, which had been inaugurated some years earlier, grew in strength, and evening classes for communicants were begun. A branch of the Confraternity of the Blessed Sacrament attracted a considerable membership. Some of these developments had already been explored a year or so beforehand, but the experience of Stoke Newington gave the foundation Gueritz needed to bring them fully into the life of the parish of Colyton.

In November 1870, there was a confirmation service taken by the Bishop of Exeter, indicating perhaps an easing of the relationship between Gueritz and Frederick Temple. Seventy-five candidates were presented from Colyton and four nearby parishes. Advent preparations that year included congregational carol practices on Sunday evenings, which in many places was something of an innovation. However, the work of W. H. Monk had expanded the range of Christmas hymns, and for almost a decade *Hymns Ancient & Modern* had been available with its seasonal hymnody. Additionally, Sabine Baring-Gould's carol collection was more widely available.[29]

At the end of the year, another relationship had apparently been healed in that the bellringers were back in the tower to ring out the old year and ring in the new.

Before we look at the next phase of Gueritz' life and ministry in Colyton, one service in May 1871 is described here in order to illustrate how the ritual in Colyton had evolved from the early surplice and stole in 1860 to something rather more advanced. This was the funeral of George Trevelyan, vicar of Stogumber and resident of Colyton. Trevelyan had been living in Colyton for some time, leaving Stogumber in the care of a curate. That curate, J. R. Vernon, had also taken several services in Colyton the previous autumn. The Trevelyan family were well connected. In fact, not long before Trevelyan's death there were some distinguished guests at their house in Fore Street. The Hon. William Stuart and his wife were staying; Stuart was the Minister Plenipotentiary to the Argentine Republic.

On the day of the funeral, there was a full requiem celebrated in the church and then a procession to the graveyard on the hill. This was an uphill walk of more than half a mile. The newspapers commented in their usual style but for once *Pulman's Weekly News* focussed on recording the event in detail, leaving the provocative comments to the local correspondent for the *Western Times*:

> Disgust devoured me as I heard choristers singing from the church to the cemetery and carrying a large crucifix . . . and Father Gueritz the priest—heaven save the mark of pastor!—with his poor deluded satellites, the Sisters of Mercy, with the corpse.[30]

Pulman's more informative report, having described the event as an "extraordinary exhibition", went on:

> The coffin, which was of a very unusual shape with a large cross on it and with curious red and black handles was borne on a litter of oak underhanded and over it was thrown a grand silk pall of purple with a large yellow cross and fringe. This was supported by six pallbearers—clergymen in white surplices—among whom were Revs Thrupp (Musbury), Selwood

(Shute),[31] Loring (Honiton), Cornish (Ottery), Willesford (Awliscombe) and another. Before the corpse walked the vicar with a long black cloak and a curious three cornered capon (sic—presumably "cap on" meaning a biretta) then the choir boys in black and white surplices, while immediately in front of the corpse was a lad in a white surplice holding aloft on a staff a golden crucifix *with the figure turned towards the coffin*. The bier was borne by twelve communicants selected for that office. In church numerous ceremonies were adopted and lighted candles placed around the body . . . The streets swarmed with people anxious to see the proceedings.[32]

This record unwittingly reveals some of the liturgical distinctions proper to the obsequies of a priest, and it took place in Colyton a mere four years after vestments were first worn in All Saints, Margaret Street. Most of the clergy listed as pallbearers appeared at some point in the Colyton service registers, Selwood of Shute and Loring of Honiton most often, and the unnamed pallbearer was J. R. Vernon, the curate of Stogumber. The presence of supportive clergy was considerable, but even that was surpassed by the lay involvement in the liturgy. This took place on a Monday during the working day, and yet the occasion was attended by a robed choir, acolytes and 12 communicant bearers, especially selected for the purpose. Lay involvement and the conscious fostering of lay ministries was a vision Gueritz had brought home with him from Stoke Newington.

However, before an account of the fostering of local lay ministries is given there was another development which, for a few years, was highly significant for Gueritz' ministry in Colyton and yet . . . "Behold I show unto you a mystery" (1 Corinthians 15:51).

Notes

1   Exeter Cathedral Archives, *Chapter Minute Books.*

2   Or "in case ..."

3   Popeday night was a term that was carried by South and West Country emigres to the American colonies, especially those who settled in New England. In England, Lewes is still famous for its commemoration not only of the Gunpowder Plot but also

of the 17 Protestant martyrs who were burned at the stake under Queen Mary. The commemoration includes a burning of the Pope in effigy. Whoever wrote the article above was evidently aware that this tradition had not entirely departed from East Devon.

[4]   Proby was dressed to act as liturgical deacon in the High Mass. The deacon wears the stole over the left shoulder rather than upon the neck as does the priest.

[5]   This was Mary M. Winter who was organist almost from the beginning of Gueritz' ministry in Colyton.

[6]   An example of the inconsistencies in the use of dialect in this article.

[7]   In the Cornish language nagus has been translated as port wine (cf. F. W. P. Jago, *The Ancient Language and the Dialect of Cornwall* (Truro: Netherton & Worth, 1882)). Here the context indicates wine watered down.

[8]   "Kovetchus". A term of derogation meaning a person held in low esteem. "Go fetch us"—an errand boy, menial or servant.

[9]   Vakshurate?

[10] If the headgear worn in procession was truly mortar boards or canterbury caps and not birettas, then there must have been a choir office of some kind in Colyton that evening. It is entirely possible that the local clergy had gathered in support of Gueritz, to celebrate a Solemn Evensong on a night when the Protestant forces in Colyton would be at their most incendiary. Unfortunately, keeping records of the services did not fully begin until the following year.

[11] Author's papers (Notes on an interview with Admiral Gueritz), Ms. letter from Dorothy Mortimer, aged 92, dated 4 January 1970. This incident cannot be dated from the letter itself. However, the discovery by Jean Robin of a dialect poem on the burning of "Pope Gurtz's" effigy, published in the *Devon Weekly Times* on 23 November 1865, sets it clearly in the context of the demonstrations in Colyton in October and November of that year and gives us a close dating. J. Robin, *The Way We Lived Then* (Aldershot: Ashgate, 2000), p. 27.

[12] *Western Times*, Friday, 7 December 1866.

[13] See Chapter 15, "The next generation".

[14] *Pulman's Weekly News*, 20 January 1867.

[15] *Pulman's Weekly News*, 23 April 1867. When we consider that, at this juncture, any Colytonian who had been baptized in the parish church, whether communicant or not,

considered themselves a member of the church with an inalienable right to comment on its activity, it is surprising that the number of subscribers was so low!

[16]   *Western Times*, Exeter, Friday, 29 December 1867.

[17]   The *Alumni Cantabrigiensis* states that the Revd D. J. Mackey was curate of Colyton from 1868 to 1870. Unfortunately, the *Clergy List* of that period has no record of his appointment to Colyton, but that is not unusual. Later editions of *Crockford's* confirm his history as recorded in the Cambridge list.

[18]   Shortly after his Colyton curacy, Mackey departed for a clerical and teaching career in India and Australia. He returned to England to take a vicariate in 1886 but died only two years later aged just 43.

[19]   John Bennett held two further livings after Markshall, dying in office in 1905. In his obituary, he was described as a "Broad High Churchman", *Pulman's Weekly News*, 28 June 1870.

[20]   *Pulman's Weekly News*, 28 June 1870.

[21]   Several records state that Edward Peregrine Gueritz was educated at St Andrew's School, Stoke Newington. Although the parish of St Andrew's was not formed until 1876 and the new church not consecrated until 1884, there was at the time a St Andrew's Collegiate School in Stoke Newington. The name Gueritz appears in the lists of cricket matches between the Iceni Team and that of Islington Proprietary School in 1872. Two years later, in 1871, Edward, aged 16, and his brother Jose Fortescue, 18, were employed as clerks by an accountant in Hackney and living there as boarders.

[22]   *The Monthly Paper of the Guild of St Alban*, vol. VII, "Church Work", January 1868 to December 1869, pp. 191–2.

[23]   *Monthly Paper of the Guild of St Alban*, p. 215. The next entry in the journal was very close to home in the diocese of Exeter. The Revd John Gilberd Pearse of Exeter "Surplice Riots" fame will appear again in the story, in Colyton. The entry in the journal runs: "The Annual Commemoration of the Brotherhood of S Peter G S A (Guild of St. Alban) was held on the Festival of the Transfiguration of our LORD August 6th. The brethren attended a celebration at St. Sidwell's, Exeter. Besides the Guildsmen and Rev Associate J G Pearse there was present in addition to the ordinary congregation that great champion of the faith Robert, Bishop of Capetown. The brethren were habited as usual in the Guild cassock and badge." Robert Gray, Bishop of Capetown, had, in January 1868, been engaged in a challenging correspondence over the consecration of a new bishop for Natal. During that time Gray was staying in Shepton Beauchamp

where James Coles was incumbent and where Mamerto Gueritz had served his first curacy. At this point V. S. S. (Stuckey) Coles had taken his degree at Oxford and was at Cuddesdon preparing for ordination.

24 G. C. B. Davies, *Henry Phillpotts, Bishop of Exeter 1778–1869* (London: SPCK, 1954), p. 89.

25 *Pulman's Weekly News*, 28 December 1869.

26 V. S. S. Coles, Obituary of Mamerto Gueritz, *Church Times*, 16 February 1912.

27 *Pulman's Weekly News*, 5 April 1870. The tone of this report differs markedly from previous vitriolic outpourings. The correspondent is evidently more familiar with the details of liturgical practice than hitherto, and the article ends on a rather matter-of-fact note.

28 *Western Times*, Friday, 20 December 1867.

29 It would be another five years before R. R. Chope, the vicar of St Augustine's, South Kensington, published *Carols For Use In Church* (London: Metzler & Co, 1875). It was published with a foreword by Sabine Baring-Gould, written while he was still at East Mersea. Few of the carols in that collection would be recognized as such today.

30 *Western Times*, Wednesday, 10 May 1871.

31 The Revd J. Selwood of Shute was the victim of repeated bouts of depression. After the Trevelyan funeral, he travelled in Italy in an attempt to recover his health. On his return, he appeared to be able to manage his parochial duties and, indeed, helped once at Colyton. Tragically, in the middle of October, he took his own life. The kindly verdict of the inquest was that he had done so while a victim of "temporary insanity". Thus, he could not be held culpable and could be given Christian burial.

32 *Taunton Courier*, Wednesday, 10 May 1871 and *Pulman's Weekly News*, 9 May 1871.

8

Sisters of Mercy: The Sisterhood of Our Lady of Compassion

1870–4

Edward Bouverie Pusey was a committed supporter of the revival of the religious life in the Church of England, but his profound understanding of the human condition led him to foresee some of the disasters that might befall and to caution against them. In a letter to the Revd D. S. Govett, dated 1855, he wrote:

> I think the plan of clergy "forming Sisterhoods" an amiable mistake. Of course the clergy can help . . . Many can carry on such a work; few can begin it. Sisters can only be trained in a Sisterhood: and if God gives the increase, future superiors would come best from training in existing Sisterhoods.[1]

It was the idea of parish sisterhoods formed under the direction of the parish priest that concerned him. As H. P. Liddon wrote:

> More than one clergyman thought that he might "start a sisterhood" just as he would institute a coal club . . . and Pusey was asked for counsel and assistance.[2]

One of the dangers attendant upon the proliferation of small parish sisterhoods was highlighted by a number of spurious accusations and, sadly, some real scandals. These were mainly the result of circumstances in which a young, single, unworldly priest tried to direct the lives of a group of women, many of whom, initially at least, would have been equally naïve.

When Arthur Stanton, curate of St Alban's, Holborn, was negotiating with Pusey to become vicar of St Saviour's, Leeds, there were two things that, taken together, worried Pusey enough to induce him to make strict conditions to the appointment. These were Stanton's extreme youth—he was 25 at the time—and his avowed intention to set up a parochial sisterhood. Pusey further argued:

> I think it a wrong ambition of men to wish to have the direction of the work
> of women . . . women ought to understand their own work, the education
> and care of young women, or they would not be fit for it at all.[3]

As we have seen, there were individual Sisters of Mercy exercising a ministry at various times almost from the beginning of Gueritz' incumbency. However, there was an enormously significant development in that there was a formally structured community of Sisters of Mercy at work in Colyton certainly between September 1870 and March 1874. From individual sisters at work under the authority of the incumbent to the establishment of a community is a considerable leap. Did Mamerto Gueritz initiate the establishment of a sisterhood in Colyton or was it the work of another? Such a community could not have had place in the work of the parish without his full support, but other forceful characters were in play: W. H. B. Proby was one and John Gilberd Pearse of Exeter was another. Were Pusey's warnings heeded or was the presence of Sisters of Mercy in Colyton exactly what Pusey feared: the formation of a parochial sisterhood? Parochial ventures of this kind were particularly vulnerable to the cult of personality and the influence of a charismatic parish priest. If a community emerged from and was supported by a mother house, were the parish priest to lose interest or be replaced by an unsympathetic successor, the sisters would have outside support and, in the worst case, a home to go to. In a parochial community there would be no such support and the resulting damage to the sisters, both emotionally and spiritually, quite aside from the destitution some would suffer, can be sufficiently envisaged for Pusey's wisdom to be clear.

Given the lack of a written record of the Colyton community, its story has to be pieced together from fragments. As with so much of this tale, it is like a jigsaw not only without the picture on the lid but lacking some of the pieces as well. The first intimation of the presence of a community of Sisters of Mercy in Colyton is found in the service register, where the entry for 23 September 1870 records a celebration of the Holy Communion at the "Sisterhood". There were, however, previous hints of individual sisters at work in the parish. First there was Frances Glanville, whose presence was noted by H. P. Liddon in 1860; then in the newspaper reports of November 1866, when the burning of effigies of Gueritz and Proby were described, it was again noted that a Sister of Mercy was present.

According to the census of 1871, most of the sisters who were part of the community lived in The Tanyard, while another sister, Isabel Robson, lived separately with a group of children in King Street. The house in King Street was close to Colyton House, owned by W. H. B. Proby, and may have been the cottage he later converted into a chapel.

This information is not, of itself, entirely helpful because there were two possibilities as to which tanyard this was. There was Hamlyn's Tannery, with a building set apart from the main structure, close to the river. That building still has a cross set into the gable end and would have been an ideal base for the sisterhood. However, the evidence is clear that the community was actually based in the former tannery at Chantry Bridge.[4] There is an odd synergy here with the community at East Grinstead which, in 1864, included among its buildings a wooden structure that had been built as a tannery.

The tanyard at Chantry Bridge was owned by John. G. Hann, who was resident there at the time of the 1871 census. He was described at the time as a "Proprietor and Seed Merchant", but he later opened a sawmill and became a considerable presence in the town. He and his family were still living at Chantry Bridge a decade later. He might well have been described as a prominent tradesman, the significance of which will appear shortly.

Before we attempt to discern the size, shape and function of the sisterhood at its first appearing in Colyton, there was an event which illuminates their story in several ways. In 1871, on 1 February, the eve of the Feast of the Purification of the Blessed Virgin Mary, there was a ceremony in Colyton Church which took place after Evensong and behind locked doors. The antipathetic press reported according to form, but in so doing left us a record of the proceedings:

On Wednesday evening a ceremony took place in our parish church which will scarcely find parallel perhaps in all the later doings of ritualistic tomfoolery—namely the admission of a nun. The ceremony took place about eight p.m. the 'altar' being covered with lighted candles and a large crucifix displayed between them. A priest from Exeter—Rev. Mr. Pearse—conducted the ceremony and the poor silly girl was put through an elaborate performance—first arrayed as a bride in white, with a long white veil which had previously, with much ceremony, been presented, placed and "blessed" on the altar. She was then taken back to the vestry, whence, her hair being all cut off, she reappeared in the hideous black garments of the "order", members of which, resembling guys or scarecrows, may be daily seen stalking about the streets. This is the story as related in the town. The whole affair was kept very private, the church being locked up during the ceremony. No males were present, it seems, except the priest, a certain prominent Ritualistic tradesman of the place, and some choir boys. Mr. Gueritz the vicar is said not to have been there, but of course he gave the required permission to use the church.[5]

The service register, in a less inflammatory style, records:

Miss. Daniels (sic) admitted to the Novitiate of the *Sisterhood of Our Lady of Compassion* under the name of sister Mary.

The name of the officiating priest was later crossed through but is still legible as J. G. Pearse. The following morning at 9.15 Pearse celebrated a public mass in the church with the special intention for the sisterhood. The sisters were all present and a collection was taken in their support. John Gilberd Pearse has already appeared in this tale and his place in our understanding of this little community will prove essential. We also have the name of the community. That name, the *Sisterhood of Our Lady of Compassion*, appears nowhere else in the history of Anglican religious orders. The only other communities under that exact title were French Roman Catholic foundations, one of which was defunct by 1870, which helps not at all with the question of the provenance of the Colyton community.

Further illumination, of a kind, came from a letter published the following week in the same newspaper. The writer identified Henrietta Daniell as "the daughter of a deceased clergyman of this neighbourhood who lived at a place called Northleigh", and also noted the existence of "a kind of boarding school for young girls" in King Street. The description given of the sisterhood was as follows:

> There is in Colyton a settlement of Sisters of Mercy, women who wear immense black garments and white tippets, and whose office, it seems, is to minister to the necessities of the poor, although I could not find that they were heard much of in this good work.

The writer of the letter refers to his "informant", so this is clearly a second- or third-hand account. He averred that the sisterhood had been introduced by the vicar, who had them living at the vicarage for some considerable time. This may refer to the individual sisters who had been at work in Colyton at times since 1860. There simply would not have been room at Colyton vicarage for the whole community as it was in 1871, but in any case, they were soon in their own establishment at Chantry Bridge. The responsibility for their introduction into the parish is placed firmly on Gueritz which, even if he were not the principal or even the only mover in the exercise, was reasonable given that he was the incumbent.

The 1871 census gives the baptismal names of the sisters and those living with them. There is a Sister Edith noted in the vestry book as a baptismal sponsor alongside Sister Margaret. Edith does not appear in the census:

Entry	Irene[1] Griffish	Head	Un	Sister of Mercy	40	Oxford
No. 137	Margaret Goodyear	Boarder	"	Sister of Mercy	33	London
Tan Yard 1 inhabited House	Henrietta M Daniell	"	"	Sister of Mercy	23	Wootton Fitzpayne
	Maude T Williams	"	"	Clergyman's daughter	4	Porthleaven
	Alice M Bloomfield	"	"	Servant	11	Dalwood

---

[1]   The handwriting on the census is such that the name has been variously rendered as "Grene", "June" and "Irene".

Entry No. 165 King Street	Isabel Robson	Head	"	Sister of Mercy	33	North'berland
	Isabel A Boyd	Boarder	Un	Scholar	12	Corston Wiltshire
	Mary E Mould	"	"	"	11	Malta Brit Subject
	Eliza P Partenford	"	"	"	11	London
	Edith L Pickwood	"	"	"	16	Australia Brit Subject
	Charles W Thomas	"	"	"	7	Plymouth

Thus, only six or seven months after first appearing in the service registers the Sisterhood of Our Lady of Compassion had at least five members, one a recently professed novice, the care and education of seven children, and was operating as a fully fledged religious house.

The fact that individual sisters had been at work in the parish from Gueritz' earliest days in Colyton, possibly continuously but certainly in 1860 and 1866, means that the ground had been well prepared. However, the apparently sudden appearance of the community of the Sisterhood of Our Lady of Compassion, complete with its teaching work and pupils, makes it unlikely that it could have arisen in entirety as a locally grown community or as a development of the work of an individual sister. It seems rather to have been a "plant", bringing children already in their care with them. But from where and were they from an existing community?

Some indication could be given by tracing where the children had come from. Little Maude Williams was the daughter of the Revd Thomas Lockyer Williams, the vicar of Porthleaven. Thomas Williams had 18 children, and in 1871 several of them were living otherwise than the family home. Williams had known Gueritz in Penzance. Mary Mould was the daughter of a half pay Royal Navy surgeon who had been previously widowed; Mary was one of the children by his second wife. She had 12 siblings and step-siblings. Isabel Boyd's father was also a clergyman who had been curate of Malmesbury[6]

This gives us the beginning of a pattern. These were the children of clergy and other professionals whose family circumstances were such that a period boarding with a sisterhood and receiving an education would be welcomed by the parents if not necessarily by the children.

It is tempting, given Gueritz' past links with Plymouth, to attempt to discern some connection with the formidable Lydia Sellon and the Society of the Most Holy Trinity, especially when it is noted that the Plymouth sisterhood was originally called the Society of the Sisters of Mercy. However, by 1870 the title "Sister of Mercy" was almost as generic a term in the Church of England as in the Roman Catholic Church and could no longer safely be taken to refer to any specific order or community. Lydia Sellon's original scheme for a nationwide system of religious houses under her rule, which would have had Colyton near the centre of the Bristol, Plymouth, Gosport triangle she had envisaged, had never been realized. In any case, by 1870 the society in Devonport was contracting rather than expanding and was unlikely to have had the resources for such a venture as this.

Another possible link might have been with the Devon House of Mercy in Bovey Tracey. The house was founded at Chapple in 1863 by sisters who came from the Community of St John Baptist, at Clewer, Windsor. They were originally named "Sisters of Mercy" before they took the name by which the community has been known ever since, through its time at Clewer, at Begbroke and now (2023) Ripon College, Cuddesdon. Invited to the parish by the Hon. Charles Leslie Courtenay, the incumbent, they established a home for abused women, often unjustly described as "fallen" women. Many of them did not fall; they were pushed. From its small beginnings, the community and the home grew rapidly, moving to purpose-built premises in 1868. The new house was large and allowed the sisters to shelter many more unfortunates. The 1871 census shows eight sisters and 48 inmates being trained for domestic service, the youngest being ten years old. The 1881 census shows that there were ten sisters and 73 inmates ranging from age 16 to a widow of 37. When we consider the specific nature of this work and compare it with that of the sisters in Colyton, where the young girls were scholars rather than inmates, any link seems tenuous. None of the names of the sisters in Colyton appear in the Bovey records either before the Sisterhood of Our

Lady of Compassion appeared or after it vanished. Neither are they to be found among the Clewer sisters.

Around the country other communities took on similar tasks, work among the poor and the care and nurture of children, and prior to this appearance in Colyton almost 30 recorded communities had been formed since the Sisterhood of the Holy Cross in London in 1845. None bore a name even vaguely similar to that of the Sisterhood of Our Lady of Compassion. It was not uncommon for offshoots bearing their own name to be "extruded" from a central body for work in the local community. Although it does not bear exact comparison, for example the Guild of St Alban the Martyr in London worked on exactly that basis, and there was, as we have seen, a Brotherhood of St Peter G.S.A. (Guild of St Alban) in Exeter, at a meeting of which J. G. Pearse was noted as "Priest Associate".[7] These were guilds rather than communities, but there were also a number of affiliated sisterhoods around the London area. This might well have been the process, but it does not answer the question of provenance. There are three factors which, while they do not give a definitive answer to the question, at least give rise to a credible hypothesis. These are first, the presumed absence of Mamerto Gueritz from the profession of Henrietta Daniell as Sister Mary in Colyton Church; second, the presence, at that profession and in a position of authority, of John Gilberd Pearse; third, the story of Henrietta Daniell both before and after the Colyton experience.

As we look at the day-to-day ministry of the sisters in Colyton, it is clear that Mamerto Gueritz understood the workings of the sisterhood. He ministered diligently to their spiritual needs and was able to integrate them into parochial life in a manner acceptable to the people (well some of them) and helpful to the sisters. If he had founded the sisterhood himself or if it had been intended that he should be its guardian, then it would have been he who presided at the profession of a novice. Instead, his absence was specifically noted. Therefore, a sisterhood was being received into Colyton with Gueritz' approval and support and to an extent under his authority, but as the parish priest and not necessarily as the guardian or visitor. In any case, Mamerto's plans had already been laid for a relatively brief absence later in 1871. His passport bears the stamp of the French Consulate in London on 21 June, that of the Belgian Consulate in Lille on 27 June, and then, after spending time in Belgium and Wallonie, he is shown to be back in England on 3 August. If the sisterhood were entirely dependent on him for their priestly

The facing page of Mamerto Gueritz' passport

The reverse of the passport showing the French and Belgian stamps

supervision and direction, it is doubtful that he would have been absent for even as short a time as six weeks during their first year in Colyton.

John Gilberd Pearse had been curate of St David's in Exeter, then of Kenn, a few miles outside the city, where he served under Reginald Porter, who was a friend of H. P. Liddon. Since 1861 and at the time of these events, he was rector of Allhallows-on-the-Wall in Exeter, which had been the scene for the Exeter surplice riots. His name appeared on the list of those who signed the *Remonstrance addressed to the Archbishops and Bishops of the Church of England* on the Judicial Committee report on the case of Herbert v Purchas.[8] His "pedigree" is clear. Pearse had become increasingly concerned for the welfare of the many poor families who lived in the West Quarter of Exeter, and in 1866 he founded the Community of St Wilfred.[9] The St Wilfred sisters visited and nursed the sick and elderly, and set up soup kitchens for the unemployed. They gave practical help to needy families and founded an orphanage. Some of the women who joined the community brought with them substantial inherited property and landholdings which they placed at the disposal of their sisterhood. In 1870, the Education Act was passed, which made education compulsory for all children. There were not enough schools so Pearse proposed that the Community of St Wilfred should open a school offering places to 40 children. There were ten sisters at work in Exeter at the time, looked after by three servants. The first headmistress of the school was Sister Matilda, one of the youngest sisters, and the curriculum included reading, writing, arithmetic, French, art, deportment and dancing. The "forty school" as it was known was an example that other towns and villages wanted to emulate, so ventures were undertaken by the Community of St Wilfred in Torquay and Bideford. There were others but, tantalizingly, the details are lost. The question is raised as to whether Colyton could have been a "pilot" venture. The Bideford and Torquay work started later.

The Colyton sisterhood may possibly have had its origins in the Community of St Wilfred and in the growth precipitated by the Education Act. The presence of J. G. Pearse is a strong indicator that there was a connection but the exact nature of the relationship between the Exeter and Colyton communities is difficult to discern. Later on, the Colyton service registers were to record many celebrations of Holy Communion at the oratory in the sisterhood, and on Easter Day in 1871 Mamerto Gueritz noted having communicated "Rev'd Mother and Sister Mary".

The title "Rev'd Mother" may well have been an honorific, a courtesy afforded by Gueritz to the local superior. A daughter house would normally have a "Sister Superior" in charge rather than a "Mother". However, it is possible that the Sisterhood of Our Lady of Compassion was a quasi-autonomous body, created by drawing sisters from the Community of St Wilfred in Exeter, under the authority of the parish priest, with John Gilberd Pearse as its guardian or visitor.

The Bishop of Exeter was latterly the visitor of the Community of St Wilfred, and Bishop Temple was in Colyton for a confirmation on 9 November 1870. By then, the sisters were high profile in the town, and their presence would not have been hidden, especially as they had been involved in catechizing some of the candidates. There is no indication of any negative reaction from Bishop Temple.

So far this hypothesis raises as many questions as it suggests answers. However, there is one more factor to take into account: the presence of Henrietta Mary Daniell, or Sister Mary as she became.

Henrietta Daniell was the daughter of Henery (the spelling is correct) Daniell, the rector of Northleigh, and she lived in the rectory as a child with her brother, an aunt and five servants. The Daniell family and the Proby family would have been unavoidably acquainted given the nature of small rural communities.[10] A sister, Laura, was born in 1851 but the little family was destined for sorrow. Henery died when Henrietta was 11 and her mother, Mary Jane, when she was 14. There is no trace of her for a decade until she reappears in Colyton as a postulant to the Sisterhood of Our Lady of Compassion. Henrietta, or Sister Mary as she became, served with the Colyton community until it disappeared from view. She then appears as a sister of the Community of St Wilfred in Exeter, where she lived for around 17 years until her death in 1892 aged 45.

Many records that may have helped our understanding were destroyed in the Second World War and we are left with only the knowledge that the Sisterhood of Our Lady of Compassion appeared in Colyton in 1870, and that there was a demonstrable connection with John Gilberd Pearse of Exeter and through him and Henrietta Daniell with the Community of St Wilfred in Exeter.

Although this lack of clarity is unsatisfactory, it does not obscure our vision of the daily work of the sisterhood in Colyton, where they quickly became embedded in the life of the Church and the community.

The spiritual life of the sisters was sustained by the daily offices and celebrations of the Holy Communion during the week. Sundays were an opportunity for them to share in the worshipping life of the local church, but in the main during the week their prayer and worship was conducted at the house in the Tanyard. Reference is often made in the service records to celebrations at their "Oratory" and at "The Sisterhood". During their time in Colyton, the registers were not always assiduously kept, especially when Gueritz was absent, but what there is shows a consistent pattern.

From the autumn of 1870, there were celebrations of the Holy Communion at the "Sisterhood" and sometimes a celebration particularly for the sisters in the church. On several occasions the entire Sunday offering of the 8 o'clock Communion was devoted to their work. Once the oratory was established, Holy Communion at the Tanyard became more frequent, averaging once a week.

The prime purpose of Sisters of Mercy was and is to serve the needs of the people, especially the poor and needy. Therefore, it is indicative that they were fulfilling their calling in Colyton in that they were recorded as being present in the community, notable for "the hideous black garments of the 'order', members of which, resembling guys or scarecrows, may be daily seen stalking about the streets".[11]

The correspondent responsible for this report was a resident of Colyton and was referring to the streets of Colyton. By February 1871, the sisters were an accustomed sight in the town, going about their visits and, to quote H. P. Liddon from a decade before, "doing good all day long". Sectarian prejudice, although not silenced, was disadvantaged against dedicated women who were alongside the common people of the town, in every need and in every circumstance.

The appearance of the sisterhood is noted just after the establishment of one of several parochial guilds or societies, namely the Society of the Holy Childhood. Given the work of the sisters among the children of the parish, the ensuing correlation between their work and that of the society was only to be expected. The registers show that this society grew rapidly during the years 1870 to 1875, with the monthly meetings recorded in the register. This also connected to another part of the work of the sisterhood, that related to the baptism of infants. From March 1871, the names of sponsors or godparents began to be entered in the service registers, there being no place for them in the printed baptismal registers of the time. Among those listed there would frequently be found the name of one or more of the sisters and indeed, on one occasion, the Reverend Mother, Sisters Mary, Edith, Isabel and Margaret all appeared as "Godmothers". Clearly Gueritz was operating a baptismal policy which involved the provision of sponsors who would ensure a continuing contact with the life of the church. The sisters were involved but so were other ladies of the parish, drawn from among the district visitors and members of the Confraternity of the Blessed Sacrament. Anne Gueritz was among them, as was Adelina. This policy is underlined by a slightly disdainful entry against the record of one baptism where the family had declined this arrangement and supplied "their own sponsors".

In 1871, at the beginning of July, there was an incident which involved the sisterhood "riding to the rescue", quite literally. Gueritz had been absent since the beginning of June and the Revd J. G. Dangar of Exeter had been taking care of the parish and officiated at most of the services. He was a priest of considerable note and since 1869 had been the principal of the Exeter Diocesan Training College which later became St Luke's College. He was obviously not in Colyton at the time because:

> On Saturday last there was a hunt up for a clergyman to perform the burial service over the body of Mr. Simon Summers of Streethayne Farm. The body was brought for interment and the bell was tolled and tolled again, and yet no clergyman appeared. The upshot was that a "Sister of Mercy" came to the rescue, hired a fly and posted in express haste to Seaton for a minister to perform the service.[12]

The sisterhood came to public notice again later in the year, this time in the national press. The *London Standard* of 22 December carried a letter purporting to come from "The Sisters" in Colyton, but even their critics had difficulty in believing that they were the originators. The *Western Times* immediately took up the story, but even in that publication the authenticity and provenance of the letter were called into question. It seemed that the reporters balked at too acrimonious an attack on women who were increasingly well regarded in the community.

The letter began by describing the plight of the poor in Colyton, "well nigh starving from cold and hunger", and went on to speak of Colyton as a town with few resident gentry and even those not wealthy. It lamented the lack of support from "County families" and the resulting poverty which was almost as deplorable as that of any East London district. The earnings of the workers were represented as being well below the average for an agricultural community:

> The men earn an average of from 5s.6d to 7s.6d. a week at farm labour. The women are mostly brought up to Honiton lace work, to the destruction of all home comfort and respectability, as to gain even a very small pittance at the hands of the middlemen or agents they must sit from morning to night at the lace pillow, leaving their homes and children to go to ruin in the meantime . . . They are particularly badly off this winter from the half ruin of so many farmers through the drought of last summer and the prevalence of the cattle disease, and many, if we cannot help them, will have neither Christmas dinner nor firing.[13]

The letter concludes with an appeal for money and is signed simply "The Sisters". The *Western Times* oscillated between condemning the sisters with comments like "They may be 'Sisters of Mercy' but they are not Sisters of Truth" and sympathizing with them as the victims of "an impudent fraud which has been palmed off on the poor deluded women who call themselves Sisters of Mercy". Or in a grossly patronizing article:

> The sisters mean well no doubt, but like many other women in this world they are easily humbugged by designing and artful men . . . that is if the letter is really the production of the "Sisters of Colyton".[14]

The *Western Times* kept the story going until late February, but that newspaper's antipathy to "Ritualism and Popery" was only one element in the conflict. The leaders of the community in Colyton, the farmers and businessmen, considered that they and the town had been libelled by the letter. As we have seen, Colytonian pride could be a very powerful force. They pointed to the continuing work of the Feoffees and claimed that no market town in the west was better provided for by the generosity of their ancestors and by those who, in the present day, were custodians of that wealth. They pointed to the actions of Sir John de la Pole of

Shute, who provided a fatted bullock for giving meat to the poor of Colyton at Christmas. This was matched by public subscription and a second beast was given. The Dowager Lady Pole also gave away 45 dozen quartern loaves to the poor, worth hardly less than a lacemaker might earn in a year and enough for almost every person living in Colyton to have a pound of bread; rich and poor alike. The Feoffees gave their usual Christmas dole to those in need, and all taken together over 300 families received a share of this beneficence. And in addition to the generosity received from the head of a "County Family", deemed by the sisters' letter to have been absent from Colyton, it was asserted:

> We have not a labourer out of work, and the lace trade is good. The poor
> rate is reduced from elevenpence in the pound last quarter to seven pence
> in the pound this quarter and although the sisters are made to sneer at the
> "middle men" in the lace trade it would be well for them if they had some
> middle party to step between them and the party who humbugs them into
> putting forth falsehoods about the state of Colyton.[15]

There were those who suspected that the sisters' letter was simply a money-raising ruse and the last shot in this particular battle, fired on 23 February 1872, was an accusation that there had been no accounting for any monies received and that the only visible outcome was a tea for some poor elderly women and broth taken around the houses, which was derided as being inedible. "No sooner were the sisters out of the house than the broth followed them."

The newspaper writers clearly believed that the sisters would not deliberately perpetrate such a misrepresentation, and it seems that they had been given some idea who was behind this ill-informed and ill-advised letter. They did not go so far as to name the suspect.

Among the possible "humbuggers" was, of course, Mamerto Gueritz. This is unlikely on several counts. By 1871 Gueritz was fully aware of the workings of the wider community and of the historic charities at work. Only three years later he was himself appointed a Feoffee. In addition, because of personal experience, he could have been under no illusions as to the capacity of the Devon press to pick up on anything to do with Colyton in the London newspapers, where the sisters' letter had first appeared. On 2 January, Gueritz hosted a New Year's Feast for the aged poor, provided by an anonymous benefactor, which gave a dinner to 26 poor men and a tea to between 40 and 50 poor women. He had become part of the social machinery by which Colyton cared for its underprivileged. The fact that he and the other clergy absented themselves from the annual Tithe Banquet on 16 January was attributed by those present to embarrassment at what had been done in the name of the sisterhood and a reluctance to face the misrepresented farmers, rather than an admission of guilt. Gueritz himself provided the Tithe Banquet as part of the *quid pro quo* of being the recipient of the tithes. All of this, taken together, suggests that Gueritz was not the prime mover in this debacle. He would have to have been stupid or duplicitous. He appears to have been neither.

W. H. B. Proby's connection with the sisterhood has not been established. We know that he would have known Sister Mary (Henrietta Daniell) from her childhood, but that is not evidence of an ongoing involvement. He was, by this stage, re-engaged with the religious life of the parish, albeit briefly. Proby was perfectly capable of stirring up public feeling with the written word, as his distribution of ritualistic tracts in Colyton demonstrated. In later life, he showed a complete disregard for how he was viewed by other Colytonians and a capacity for diplomacy only rivalled by Genghis Khan. Proby was, however, of the landed gentry that the sisters' letter claimed hardly existed in Colyton and, although it was often hidden, he was capable of kindness and great generosity.

J. G. Pearse is the only other obvious candidate. He could not have been as acutely aware of Colyton and its social structures as were Proby and Gueritz; therefore he would be prone to inaccuracies in his representation of the community. He had long experience of fundraising for the work of a sisterhood and had solid connections with such work both in Exeter and in the ritualist parishes in London. If he still had a role in directing the life of the sisterhood he may well have proposed such a course of action.

Of course, the writer of the letter may have been none of them. The reverend mother of a community had, of necessity, to be of independent mind and capable of acting without reference to the priests who happened to be in the vicinity. There would be a particular relationship with whichever priest was the confessor and guardian or mentor of the community, but that would be a relationship between equals. Possibly their critics, who were so anxious not to apportion blame to the sisters, were too generous in their judgement.

Whoever was responsible for the letter, it was widely agreed at the time that the sisters had been the victims of a manipulation of their good intentions and, in spite of the suspicions just noted, their work simply carried on. It would have been satisfying, however, to have been able to throw the shadow of suspicion more firmly where it belonged.

The recording of church life changed markedly at the beginning of 1872 with the commencement of a new vestry journal. This was a combination of a service register and a narrative of church-related activity and should not be confused with the vestry minute book, which was a record of the meetings of ratepayers. It became quite detailed in the noting of events and recording of extra-liturgical activity. Prior to that, as we have seen, the recording of matters in the registers, especially in relation to the sisterhood, was sporadic. However, between 23 September 1870 and 1 November 1871, a total of 20 collections were noted yielding a total of four pounds, nine shillings and fivepence halfpenny for their work. Later collections, if there were any, are not recorded. Such a sum, collected over a year, would not have been sufficient to sustain the life of the community. Their funding was obviously provided from elsewhere.

Between 23 September 1870 and 20 March 1874, there were 63 recorded celebrations of the Holy Communion at the sisterhood or in their oratory. In the main, they were noted not as part of the parochial services, but as entries in the narrative which was kept, if somewhat sporadically, on the facing page of the register. According to the register, Mamerto Gueritz was the president in almost every recorded case; however, when he was absent from the parish, not only did the accurate keeping of the registers falter, so did any public record of Eucharistic worship at the sisterhood. It is unlikely that it ceased in his absence. Loring of Honiton appears once as president and other local clergy were supportive of the work, George Trevelyan, the late incumbent of Stogumber, among them. The collection at his requiem mass in May 1871 was devoted entirely to the work of the sisterhood. Nevertheless, with only occasional appearances of J. G. Pearse, it seems Mamerto Gueritz was the acknowledged source of ongoing priestly ministry and oversight for the sisters.

What happened after March 1874? A search of the vestry journal for the following five years reveals no mention of the sisters, and they disappear from the life of the parish without comment. Indeed, with the exception of Henrietta Daniell, all the other sisters save one vanish from public view altogether.

Sister Isabel, whose given name was Mary Isabel Robson, was the daughter of a Northumbrian millwright. She had left the family home by the time she was 23 and then appeared in Colyton in 1870, living apart from the other sisters in the house in King Street where the children also lived. Ten years later she was living in Chorlton on Medlock, a parish in Manchester, serving there as a "Sister of Mercy" but without companions other than a servant.

Between 1873 and 1875, the local Unitarian newspapers were devoid of comment on the sisters. These papers were still virulently anti-ritualist and would have pounced on any scandal there might have been or at least might have noted a sudden departure. Instead, there was only silence.

Around the same time, W. H. B. Proby opens his Irvingite Chapel in King Street and withdraws (or is ejected) from any ministerial involvement in the life of the parish church.

There is, as yet, no satisfactory resolution of this mystery. The search continues.

Notes

[1]   H. P. Liddon, *Life of Edward Bouverie Pusey* (London: Longmans, 1894 to 1898), vol. III (of IV), p. 32.

[2]   G. W. E. Russell, *Arthur Stanton: A Memoir* (London: Longmans, 1917), pp. 57–8.

[3]   Liddon, *Life of Pusey*, p. 32.

[4]   There were two possibilities for the location of the sisterhood: Hamlyn's Tannery, which was (and is) a fully working tanyard, and the tanyard at the junction of King Street and Vicarage Street. The first is half a mile upstream of Chantry Bridge, so named after a long-vanished medieval chantry. The second was immediately adjacent to the bridge with buildings fronting an inner yard. Hamlyn's Tannery has a detached building within the "tanyard" but closer to the river than the tannery itself. It has several floors and a cross set in the gable end. This would have provided adequate space for housing for the sisters and an oratory for the use of the small sisterhood. However, the Chantry Bridge tanyard had more freedom for alternative occupancy, having been purchased with, as it turned out, a change of use in view by John G. Hann. We know that closely

involved with the development and support of the sisterhood was a "Prominent Ritualistic tradesman of the place". This might possibly have been Hann, who was also residing without his family at the "Tanyard" when the presence of the sisterhood was first noted and was then described as a "Proprietor and Seed Merchant". Hann later opened a sawmill a little further east along the Coly and set up as a timber merchant, and by the time of the 1881 census he and his family were living in the disused tannery. However, Hann was not always to show himself an unequivocal supporter of Mamerto Gueritz, so perhaps "we look for another". The final confirmation that the sisters were based at the Chantry Bridge site comes from the 1871 census. The order in which the streets were recorded, and the way in which the town was divided up for the purpose, leaves no doubt that the "Tanyard" in question was at Chantry Bridge, accessed from Vicarage Street. It is still a possibility that the building at Hamlyn's Tannery, with the cross in the gable end, was used as a schoolroom by Sister Isabel and her King Street charges.

[5] *Pulman's Weekly News*, 7 February 1871.

[6] The history of these children is fascinating but not really germane to the chapter. Maude Williams died aged only 17. Isabel Boyd married Wallace Mackie in St Paul's, Ranchi, Jharkand when she was 26. They made their home in Rome, and she outlived her husband by 15 years, dying in the South Kensington Hotel in 1940. She was buried with her husband in Rome. Sadly, all we know of Charles Thomas is that ten years later he was a "juvenile offender under detention" in Redhill Reformatory.

[7] See note 22 to Chapter 7 above.

[8] John Purchas was the compiler of the first edition of the *Directorium Anglicanum*, published in 1858, which attempted to bring some uniformity and authenticity to the ritual of the Church of England. He was prosecuted for ritual practices at the instigation of the Church Association. A. H. Mackonochie of St Alban's, Holborn and J. M. Neale had already been attacked. Purchas refused to appear before the court. When the judgement was not as punitive as it had wished, the Church Association took the case to the Judicial Committee of the Privy Council which, in 1871, overturned the perceived leniency of the previous ruling. Some 4,700 clergy signed a petition in protest at the action of the Judicial Committee and in support of John Purchas. It failed to gain a new hearing. Purchas died in 1872.

9   It was almost certainly a coincidence, but this was also the name of the community formed by John Henry Newman after his secession to Rome; a community which later issued in the establishment of the London and Birmingham Oratories.

10   W. H. B. Proby, as lord of the manor of Northleigh himself and previously while his mother held that role, would have been well acquainted with the Daniell family. His involvement with the Colyton sisterhood, and specifically with Henrietta Daniell, is less clear, but in any case his disillusionment with the Church of England had taken hold and his journey into the Catholic Apostolic Church had already begun by 1870 or 1871.

11   *Pulman's Weekly News*, 7 February 1871.

12   *Pulman's Weekly News*, 4 July 1871.

13   *London Standard*, Friday, 22 December 1871.

14   *Western Times*, Tuesday, 26 December 1871.

15   *Western Times*, Tuesday, 26 December 1871.

In the following chapters, 9, 10 and 11, we set aside, for a moment, the chronological approach adopted so far and look at several aspects of Gueritz' ministry thematically. In order fully to understand these elements it is necessary to view them over a span of decades.

9

"In quires and places where they sing": Mamerto and music

One of the first reports announcing the arrival of Gueritz in Colyton commented on his musical talents:

> our new vicar, The Rev. Mamerto Gueritz, (who we hope soon to have residing among us) is a man of considerable attainments in this beautiful branch of a beautiful art, and which we think augurs well for the future of our church choir.

Gueritz had been noted for improving the singing in his first curacy, and from childhood days Stuckey Coles remembered very clearly Mamerto's "beautiful tenor voice". However, it was from his time in Penzance that Gueritz' reputation began to grow both for sacred music and for music as a means of mission—or just enjoyment. He was ever content to be putting together parish evenings of music and readings which would attract those who might not otherwise have found themselves in conversation with their parish priest. However, liturgical music had become his passion, and during his time in Penzance Gueritz was not only concerned with raising the standard of music at St Mary's, he was also influential in the establishment of the Cornish Church Choral Association and bringing choir festivals into being. He was there at the very beginning and, in April 1860, before the family moved to Colyton, the Association of Church Choirs in Cornwall met at St Ives. This was its fourth annual meeting, and Mamerto was among those praised for their part in bringing the choirs together and training them in plainsong. The fact that there were at least 90 surpliced singers at the

Festival Eucharist, not counting the large number of unrobed choristers, speaks volumes for how effective that training had been.

Gueritz might reasonably have hoped that the musical aspect of his proposed "innovations" in Colyton would be considered uncontentious, but that was not to be, at least not so far as the Unitarian press was concerned. Before long choral services in Colyton were commonplace. As early as January 1861, there were negative comments in the press about the "monotonous Gregorian chants". Later the same year Gueritz organized a concert of sacred music in the church. The church choir took part in the affair which gave rise to criticism from a different direction. There were those who felt that Gueritz had compromised his "High Church Principles" by holding a concert in church and that it was inappropriate in a sacred space. Nevertheless, shortly afterwards he was able to form a choral society in Colyton, so not everyone could have disapproved. The new organ was installed on 12 September in the same year and, it seems, was in use for the concert. However glad Gueritz might have been at this musical development, the design of the organ and fundraising for its purchase and installation was not his initiative; it was almost ready before he appeared on the scene and completed just as he arrived. The report of the service of dedication and the celebration of the organ's first use in a service perhaps reflects something of this in that, while a number of the other attending clergy are mentioned, he is simply called "The Vicar". Preaching at that occasion was Prebendary Mackarness, who we already know was to become a friend and supporter of Mamerto Gueritz.

In the late 1860s and early 1870s, the Choral Eucharist on major feasts was at 7.30 in the morning, and although the early enthusiasm for daily sung Mattins waned once the novelty wore off, the discipline of the offices was maintained but spoken rather than sung. The modern mind might well balk at the thought of persuading even a paid choir to turn out at such an hour, but Gueritz had taken a leaf out of W. H. Monk's book. A "professional" choir would never sing with the same commitment to the real purpose of the music, which was the worship of Almighty God, as would faithful amateurs. The time Gueritz spent at St Matthias, Stoke Newington, where Monk was organist, had demonstrated for him how choral music could be developed to a high standard with a volunteer choir and an ordinary congregation. We have already noted Gueritz' friendship around that time with other scholars of church music such as J. W. Bennett and D. J. Mackey, who served as curates in Colyton while Mamerto was in London. For many priests who were working to enhance Anglican liturgy and to reveal its Catholic heart, music was indeed "the food of love", love of God, love of the Church, love of beauty in worship.

Once in Colyton, the place of music in Gueritz' ministry was not limited to the liturgy. He brought with him from Penzance and earlier experience the conviction that one way of reaching hearts and minds was to offer moments of enjoyment to the community. Penny readings were begun, at which there would also be musical entertainment. With Gueritz leading the way, other musicians and singers joined in, and soon there were evenings of musical entertainment several times each year. This grew as time passed, involving most members of the Gueritz family when they were available, but just as importantly, drawing others to the work of giving pleasure to the community in a way which would enhance relationships. Gueritz seems to have understood that when people have laughed together and enjoyed themselves in each other's company, they will respond to each other differently, be that in the street or in the church. A vicar who stands up and sings an old ballad rather beautifully, or a comic song with evident glee, can never again be quite the ogre that some would paint him.

Over the years following Gueritz' arrival, choral festivals were increasingly held around the churches of East Devon, with more and more parishes training their choirs in plainchant and in mass settings. Even parishes with only three or four singers joined in the gatherings. Soon the East Devon Choral Association was formed. It grew rapidly in strength and numbers and later became known as the East Devon Choral Union (EDCU), and from the outset Mamerto Gueritz was there leading and guiding. For many years, he served as the precentor for their gatherings.

By 1870, the Choral Association, as it still then was, had been holding an annual festival for several years. On 25 May at Ottery St Mary, the festival, which lasted all day, had 358 choristers, of whom the *Exeter Flying Post* reported:

> surpliced males 163; unsurpliced males 100; females 105. In the morning
> Anglican chant was used and in the afternoon Gregorian chant.[1]

It is often assumed that from the outset choirs were a male province and that the advent of female choristers was something that happened much later and only as necessity demanded. From this and other reports, it is clear that this was not so. It is true that, at this stage, the "surpliced singers" were boys and men, but many of the East Devon parishes were small and would be able to field only three or four choristers for a festival. They almost certainly would not be able to sustain a robed choir, and given the small number of parishioners, they would have both male and female singers as a matter of course. The important thing is that they were present, women, boys and men, singing with the Choral Union and taking new music and new possibilities back to some of the most out-of-the-way parishes. Some East Devon parishes were very "out of the way".

Of the surpliced choristers present at the 1870 festival, Colyton supplied 35 voices (only Honiton sent as many), but the training and equipping of a robed church choir requires resources. The Colyton church accounts for 1872 show that five pounds and threepence ha'penny was spent on music books and carriage, 18 shillings and seven pence on Russell cord for cassocks and seven shillings and sixpence on washing the surplices; a total of six pounds, seven shillings and fourpence ha'penny, a considerable sum. This alone demonstrates how highly valued the work of the choir had become by those concerned, especially the churchwardens and, of course, the congregation.

The 1872 festival was held at Colyton, where, once again, Bishop Henry Jenner was a welcome presence, supporting and encouraging the local clergy. The event, as had become inevitable, attracted the attention of the local correspondent for the Unitarian press. The report is an odd mixture of facts—the numbers attending, the parishes represented—combined with a rather desperate attempt to mock the proceedings. Having noted the attendance of more than 300 members of the association, the decorations in the church and the ringing of the bells:

> The whole proceeding was something like what you read of in the religious festivals of the Hindoos, and is one of the ways by which what is called "The church" is being seduced to Popery. The whole proceeding was of the ritualistic pattern . . . The Rev. M. Gueritz was the choirmaster. There was the usual sacerdotal display of pomp and vanity in the procession to the church and through it the incumbent of each parish church marching at the head of his choir by this covered way to Rome.[2]

After noting the number of choristers, the parishes represented and some of the clergy present, and after remarking in surprisingly positive terms on Bishop Jenner's sermon, the writer continued:

> The priest was in his glory, with three hundred country yokels shouting at the top of their voices, not one half of whom could read a verse with propriety, much more sing the service. We opine this to be the last appearance nearly of this jubilee of noise, yclept worship. The afternoon performance was much after the fashion of the morning, the style being "Gregroanian".[3]

The reporter could "opine" all he liked. The EDCU was still going strong well into the twentieth century and his opinion of the standard achieved in 1872 was not widely shared.

By 1878, the union, for such it had become by then, had grown to such an extent that it had been split into three districts, each of which had its own festival. However, the parishes from one district still took part in the festivals of the others. In October 1878, the third festival of the year was held at St Andrew's, Exmouth, the two earlier ones having been at Colyton and Ottery St Mary. One account of the event included the comment:

> To the Rev. M. Gueritz, the rector (sic) of Colyton is to be attributed in a great measure the position to which the Union has now attained.[4]

At several of the East Devon festivals, it was noted that elements of the music had been composed by Mamerto Gueritz. In addition to his "fine tenor voice" and his ability to teach both individuals and choirs to sing, Gueritz was a composer. His aim from the days of his first curacy had been to make music accessible to everyone, either as a listener or as a performer. His reputation for composition may not have rivalled that of his friend W. H. Monk, but it spread abroad nearly as far. When Mamerto's daughter Mary Louisa and her husband Reginald Mortimer set sail for New Zealand in early June 1878, they took with them, among other things, some of her father's music. When Reginald was ordained in New Zealand, that music began to be used in services in Christchurch and in churches elsewhere in the diocese. When, in 1885, the report of the Christmas celebration at the Church of the Good Shepherd, Phillipstown appeared, it was noted:

> The service was full choral and it was the composition of the Rev. M. Gueritz of Colyton, Devon, the Honorary Secretary to the Devon Choral Association.[5]

As the report implies, by that time Gueritz had been recognized as a musical resource throughout the diocese of Exeter and not just East Devon.

The setting continued in use in New Zealand long after Reginald and Mary Mortimer returned to England in 1884. In 1889, it was still in use in the Church of St Matthew, St Albans, New Zealand, where Reginald had been the first incumbent. Forty years later, in 1929, it was the setting for an episcopal service at St Andrew's, Tinwald. Closer to home, at Eastertide in St Martin's, Colchester in 1888, there was a choral celebration of the Holy Communion and the music used included "Gueritz in E".[6]

In 1889, the East Devon Choral Union annual report noted that Viscount Sidmouth had become the president, Sir John Kennaway the vice-president, Mamerto Gueritz the precentor and Henry "Frank" Gueritz the choirmaster. Frank Gueritz, who was Mamerto and Anne's youngest son, had already made a substantial contribution to the work of the EDCU and, when the festival was held in Colyton in that year, it was he who held the baton. Frank was also very active in the world of music outside the confines of the Church, and there is much more of his part in the story to tell. Suffice it for now to note that, in 1889, he too was becoming a musical force to be reckoned with.

The United Magazine for the parishes of East Devon carried accounts of the two festivals which were held that year. The first, in Colyton, began with a choral celebration of the Holy Communion:

> The Vicar of the parish, the Rev. M. Gueritz, was the celebrant, and as Precentor of the East Devon Choral Union he also composed and arranged the musical portions of the office.

The following year there were again two festivals, and in June, at the festival held in Honiton,

> the Rev. M Gueritz, vicar of Colyton said that he had now held the office of Precentor to the E.D.C.U. for twenty years, and that he felt it was time for him to ask to be relieved. It was consoling to him that the Union could muster over 20 choirs, which, with hardly an exception, had attended one or other of the two festivals held by the Union for this year.

Gueritz would play a considerable part in the diocesan as well as the local choral associations for some years yet, but the time had come to ensure that the next generation would have adequate leadership. Having first "primed" him, Gueritz suggested, perhaps named would be more accurate, his successor, the Revd T. Lowe of West Hill. The suggestion was unanimously acclaimed.

Notes

[1] *Exeter Flying Post*, Wednesday, 25 May 1870.

[2] *Western Times*, Friday, 28 June 1872.

[3] *Western Times*, Friday, 28 June 1872. There were 311 choristers in all: 150 surpliced, 67 unsurpliced and 94 females; 100 trebles, 19 altos, 42 tenors, 56 basses, 81 sopranos and 13 contraltos. The parishes were: Axminster, Axmouth, Churchstanton, Colyton, Cotleigh, Farringdon, Gittisham, Honiton, Musbury, Offwell, Ottery St Mary, Seaton, Shute, Sidbury, Talaton, Whimple, Widworthy and Withycombe Raleigh. Some parishes sent both the incumbent and the curate, and there were 22 clergy present. The reporter took all this to be an indication of how far the "Romanizing conspiracy" had spread.

[4] *Express and Echo*, Friday, 4 October 1878.

[5] *The Phillipstown Star*, Issue 5501, 26 December 1885.

[6] *Essex Standard* and *West Suffolk Gazette* and *Eastern Counties Advertiser*, 7 April 1888. See Appendix 2: Gueritz in "E": A musical setting for the Holy Communion.

Belonging and believing: Guilds, associations and societies

Parochial societies

The disappearance of the Sisterhood of Our Lady of Compassion would have left a noticeable gap in the pastoral care offered by the church in Colyton had not Gueritz already thoroughly embraced one of the central tenets of mission in Stoke Newington and the Anglo-Catholic parishes of London. This was the importance of giving ordinary people a sense of self-worth in their membership of the Church, something which they could own and be owned by. With a sense of belonging comes a greater capacity to own the faith being proclaimed. Some people joined a guild because of their faith. Others found the fullness of faith through their membership of a guild.

As we have seen from Gueritz' time in London, the work of guilds and societies enabled many aspects of the Church's outreach into the local community and into the mission field abroad. They also offered a means of showing solidarity with other, oft beleaguered, "Revival" parishes, not only in London but much further afield. The journal of the Guild of St Alban included reports from London parishes like Stoke Newington, but also from Exeter, where John Gilberd Pearse was the "Priest Associate" of the essentially lay guild.

Gueritz wasted little time in transplanting these ideas into what proved to be the fertile soil of Colyton. Within a few months of his return and no more than a year later, a wide network of "belonging" had been established in the parish. There were already the temporary catechetical groups formed before each confirmation, which then transmuted into groups to help new communicants prepare for Sundays or festivals, but in addition to these there were other significant bodies.

Some, like the Guild of St Andrew, had already been formed before Gueritz went to London, but it was in the period from 1870 onwards that these groups and societies began fully to flourish in the life of the parish.

The Guild of St Andrew

The Guild of St Andrew was one of the first groups to be formed. It was for communicant members of the parish and provided teaching, fellowship, and regular monthly meetings. Following the pattern established by the Guild of St Alban in London, it also provided a milieu in which lay people could find a place in the work of the church. Such was the initial uptake that to the First Order was soon added the Second Order and later a Third. At this point, several names begin to emerge, people who would turn out to be longstanding champions of the work.

In addition to the members' meetings, special services were held for the guild, but these latter were not private affairs. Members were encouraged to bring their friends and to share the vision with them. Thus, the work of the guild, like most of the other parochial groups, was both inward- and outward-looking. It was for the strengthening of the spiritual life of the members and also a means of drawing others into the experience. Belonging before, perhaps, believing. Of course, like any such organization, after the initial surge of enthusiasm the guild would have its ups and downs, with Gueritz frequently needing to point out that membership carried with it responsibilities:

> The members of the Guild are earnestly requested to make a point of attending the monthly meetings and also the Holy Communion on the second Sunday ... our great object of the Guild is to set a good example and to strengthen the hand of the clergy in these matters, and that the members while being thereby a blessing to others, should also gain an increased blessing in their own souls.[1]

At other times, the suggestion that others should be invited to the meetings was so enthusiastically heeded that numbers of guests exceeded the number of members. On one memorable occasion the officer in charge of the local company of the Volunteer Battalion of the Devon Regiment, himself a member of the guild, instructed the entire contingent to accompany him to a guild service. This may not have been quite what Gueritz had in mind.

Predictably, another such outburst of enthusiasm was the guild summer treat in 1889, with a train ride from Colyton to Seaton and a walk to the Axmouth undercliff where kettles were boiling and the sumptuous picnic, arranged by Mrs Gueritz and her "kind auxiliaries", was laid. Almost the whole membership turned out, together with many of their children. Among the participants were local gentry such as Mrs A. De la Pole but also a goodly number of people who had been members for most of their adult lives. Significantly, Mrs Proby was there and helping. A picture begins to emerge of the senior women of the parish acting as a gentle restraint upon the naturally combative nature of their husbands.

The Society of the Holy Childhood

At around the same time, the Society of the Holy Childhood was instituted, with monthly meetings. This was a group for children who were not yet communicants and for whom there had previously been little provision. This was reinforced by the appearance of children's services on a Sunday afternoon which on alternate weeks would take the form of the Litany of the Holy Child. These services were followed by the catechism. The society was up and running before August 1870, by which time the monthly meeting was well established. That month it was noted in the registers that three boys and 12 girls were admitted to membership. At the monthly meeting on 23 September, there were 12 boys and 17 girls present. A further five members were added in November, and so it grew.

This continued until the work of Sunday schools changed. Originally designed to provide basic education for those who would otherwise have none, as the requirements of the Education Act of 1870 began to be met and the provision for schools became a legal obligation for secular authorities, so the Sunday schools began to offer a specifically religious curriculum. In Colyton, this overlapped with and ultimately absorbed the work of the Society of the Holy Childhood. Twenty years later there would be a highly developed diocesan system of training for Sunday school teachers and a syllabus with examinations and awards. In 1889, the bishop of the diocese would host a day at the palace for over a thousand Sunday school teachers and entertain them royally. In 1870, however, the children of Colyton had their own provision designed to strengthen their faith, not just in classes or in the worshipping life of the church but also in that by which children set such store—parties!

Here again was the quiet influence of Anne Gueritz. The children's parties at the vicarage became the stuff of legend. It is difficult now to envisage a world in which the concept of childhood, as currently understood, had not yet fully emerged and in which precious little attention was paid to the younger children outside the home. The excitement among the children of having teaching and services specially for them, and of being afforded their own place in the life of the church, can hardly be overestimated. The welcome and affirmation of them offered by Anne Gueritz was but a part of her continuing influence on their lives. In all that her husband initiated, she was there cementing relationships and leading the ladies of the parish in their work, which was anything but passive!

The Confraternity of the Blessed Sacrament

The full name of the society is "The Confraternity of the Blessed Sacrament of the Body and Blood of Christ", and its motto is "*Adoremus in aeternum sanctissimum sacramentum*", which in translation is "Let us forever adore the Most Holy Sacrament". It expressed, most succinctly, the sacramental heart of the later Oxford Movement. The CBS was and still is a society dedicated to venerating the Real Presence of Christ in the Eucharist and is the longest standing Anglican devotional society. By 1870, its predecessors, the Society of the Blessed Sacrament, founded in 1860, and the Confraternity of the Blessed Sacrament, founded in 1862 by T. T. Carter, had come together in the body which continues to this day.

All members of the confraternity are called "Associates"; Mamerto Gueritz was a "Priest Associate". The requirements of both priest and lay members were and are the same. They must strive to promote reverence for Jesus in the Holy Eucharist through the witness of their lives, words, prayers and teaching. They must pray for one another at mass and before the Blessed Sacrament and make use of the sacrament of confession.

This gives an insight into the devotional and liturgical life in Colyton in 1870. The service registers contain no detail of the nature of the liturgy when the confraternity met for worship. It would have been highly inadvisable for there to be a specific record of a practice which was considered to be illegal, that of the Benediction of the Blessed Sacrament: the consecrated host placed on the altar

Anne Derby Gueritz c 1860.

to be venerated and then raised over the congregation in blessing. Possibly, in Colyton, the members simply gathered for prayer before the sacrament reserved in the "Morning Chapel", which would have satisfied the requirement to pray for one another before the Blessed Sacrament.

Gueritz seemed to have been content to make it known that confession was available to all and perhaps even required of confirmands, but he needed to keep a balance over this particular teaching. The CBS was coming into being in Colyton at exactly the time when W. H. B. Proby was circulating tracts claiming that sacramental confession was essential for salvation.

In the autumn of 1869, Anne Derby Gueritz, Mary M. Winter and Elizabeth Shellswick were admitted as Associates, and between 9 November and 3 March the following year another seven parishioners had joined them.[2] On 16 June 1870, there was a celebration of the Holy Communion for the intention of the Confraternity of the Blessed Sacrament and a total of £3.6.9 was donated to the national body. This pattern was repeated through the years that followed.

Becoming an Associate of the Colyton branch of the CBS was not to be undertaken "unadvisedly, lightly or wantonly", but after serious thought. The "postulants", as they are described in notes in the back of the 1870 vestry book, were examined and the impression gained noted:

> Has been to Unitarian Chapel until last few Sundays.
> Promises to be regular at Church.
> Understands pretty well. Inclined to be giddy.
> Unrepentant and inclined to think too well of herself.
> Has been a dissenter.

Comments in a record which seemed perfectly acceptable in 1870 would today be thought outrageous and probably illegal! *Aut temps, aut mores.* At the same time, the admission of 11 males was also noted, but no further details provided.

One other role that some of the Associates of the CBS took on was that of baptismal sponsors. Anne Gueritz was among them. Lucy Street and Elizabeth Simmons, who had been admitted on 9 November 1869, were also frequently noted, alongside several of the Sisters of Mercy and others who appear elsewhere as district visitors.

The Dorcas Society

It was probably around 1874 that the Colyton Dorcas Society was formed. The name of the society was taken from Dorcas, also called Tabitha, whose story is found in Acts 9. St Peter was called when Dorcas, a leading woman of the church in Joppa, died: "And all the widows stood by him weeping, and showing the coats and garments which Dorcas made while she was with them."[3] The first of the Dorcas Societies was probably established in 1834, following an outbreak of cholera on the Isle of Man. The poor people of the island had all their bedding and clothing destroyed in order to halt the spread of the disease. The women of the local churches banded together to make or buy replacements. By 1870, the movement had spread far and wide.

The Colyton Society was both effective and long-lasting, and it filled a need that in other places was an element of the work of Sisters of Mercy. Its formation may well have been a response to an increased awareness of need which was revealed by the work of the district visitors. A report in the February parish magazine of 1890, almost 20 years after the society was first formed, summarizes the work undertaken:

> This Society, in a very quiet and unobtrusive way, does an immense amount of good in the parish. Its maternity bags provide necessities for many a poor mother and infant. Its store of blankets gives warmth and comfort to many of the aged poor through the dreary winter, and many a poor girl is helped with clothing to enable her to go out decently into good service.

The provision of those necessities and decent clothing also meant that a wide range of people could be involved. There would be those who offered financial help, buying the raw materials and the fabrics. There would also be those whose physical ability to contribute to the work of the parish was limited but who could still weave, sew and knit. They were able to offer their skills as a ministry and have that offering acknowledged as such. Even the housebound could still be involved. In Colyton, the Dorcas Society lived out its motto, "Love in Deed", ministering both to the needy and to those who helped meet the need. The same report in 1890 listed 30 donors supporting the work, among them the Elton sisters, formerly of Colyton House, and W. H. B. Proby and his wife. It seems that Proby's estrangement from the Church of England was not entirely shared by Mrs Proby and had affected their involvement in parochial affairs not a whit.

District visitors

From the earliest days the work of the Dorcas Society and that of the district visitors was complementary but distinct. The talents required for the work of each were quite different.

District visitors were women workers in a Church of England parish who gave voluntary assistance to the parish priest by visiting and reporting cases of sickness or need. Canon law requires that the priest of a parish shall be diligent in visiting the parishioners, but it was recognized that, in various circumstances, the task could not be carried out alone. In cities the sheer density of the population made it impossible. In country areas, the distances involved, especially with more than one benefice to care for, were a challenge. We have noted how long it would have taken to get to Monckton from Colyton. Even after that parish had been detached and reassigned elsewhere, Gueritz would have to spend a whole morning walking to reach the people of Borcombe or of Pottlelake. Even when there was a curate to share the load, there was still always the need for good intelligence: who was ill? Who was in financial difficulty? Who was untimely pregnant and likely to be thrown out of home? Things folk might not have the courage to tell a clergyman they would share with a sympathetic female ear, and yet the task could still be unrewarding. Parishioners then, as now, had the conviction that unless the vicar called, they had not been properly visited by the "Church".

The first intimation of the existence of the visitors comes in notes in the early, rather scant, service records. They seem to have been in existence before the departure of the sisterhood, but it was around 1874, when the sisterhood had gone and their work among the poor had ceased, that the visitors began to appear in notes and accounts more frequently. They seem initially to have been recruited from the Guild of St Andrew and the Confraternity of the Blessed Sacrament, with one or two other volunteers being included. The visitors were still fully active 30 years later.

The parochial accounts for 1888 show an expenditure of £30.2.10 on this work alone; this at a time when the average wage was still under £1 a week.

After the opening of the chapel of ease in Colyford in 1889, there were visitors designated specifically for work there. By 1896, there were nine visitors in Colyton and four in Colyford, each with clearly defined areas of the parish as their responsibility. The Gueritz' youngest son, Henry Francis (Frank), then serving as the licensed lay reader, was the only male among them. Anne Gueritz, still active at age 76, was looking after Vicarage Street and the various courts that led off it. In Colyford, the wife of the curate, Mrs Rosser, was following her example.

National associations

From 1850 onwards, various guilds, societies and associations began to appear among the national activities of the Oxford Movement. Those noted here illustrate how thoroughly the national development of the Church Revival was reflected in the parochial life of Colyton. In one sense, these groups represented a drawing together and a standardization of individual efforts; an "easing out of idiosyncrasies". Some of these societies, as we have seen with the Confraternity of the Blessed Sacrament, spread through smaller local units, or "wards", which were essentially parochial and set within the local worshipping community but which also gave that community a sense of identification with the wider work within the Oxford Movement. In fostering Catholic devotion in their parishes, they became aware that they were part of something much bigger. Other groups remained essentially national bodies relying on support, financial and moral, from sympathetic priests and parishes up and down the country in order to address their own wider agenda. It depended on the remit of the society. One such was created to address a national need but ultimately gained support in a huge number of local branches.

The English Church Union
In 1844, the Bristol Church Union was formed to combat state intervention in religious education in Church schools. Archdeacon Denison, champion of the doctrine of the Real Presence and known to Gueritz since his ordination, was its first secretary. More such unions were formed around the country, and as early as 1850 attempts were made to draw them together. In 1859, a gathering of five such bodies, including the Church of England Protection Society, gave assent to

the formation of a new association which was to give cohesion, and consequently more effective influence, to the diverse groups. In May 1860, the English Church Union came into being with three objects: the maintenance of the doctrine and discipline of the Church of England, the protection of those who were threatened with prosecution because of their stand over such matters and, quite simply, to promote the interests of religion and the good of the Church. In 1860, there were 205 members. Three years later there were more than 1,000. Thirty years later the membership exceeded 35,000 laymen and priests.

In 1867, as we noted earlier, Mamerto Gueritz journeyed from London to Penzance for the meeting of the St Ives branch of the ECU, which illustrates its strength and the priority its members gave it. In Colyton, members of the Guild of St Andrew joined the ranks, several within the first few years of the union's existence. Among them were Edmund Drower and Henry Deane, whose names appear in Colyton affairs for decades afterwards. Deane was the long-serving treasurer of the Dorcas Society, indeed of most societies linked with the church. In 1877, Deane and Drower sponsored Henry "Frank" Gueritz to membership of the ECU. His was one of over 300 names submitted on that occasion.[4]

Earlier that year, in February, the Honiton deanery branch had met in Colyton with Mamerto in the chair. Among other resolutions passed, there was one which unmistakeably linked East Devon with the battles fought elsewhere. Arthur Tooth, incumbent of Hatcham, had been imprisoned on 22 January following a protracted prosecution under the Public Worship Regulation Act of 1874.[5] His Devon supporters declared:

> This branch desires to express its sympathy with Rev. Arthur Tooth in his
> present suffering for Conscience sake . . .[6]

In the years that followed, the union burgeoned rapidly in East Devon, in line with the growth in the rest of the country. There are many reports in local papers and magazines of deanery and parochial gatherings.

Later still, in 1894, the *Church Union Gazette* noted that the Devon (South East) District Union had elected officers for the year commencing 1 August. They were the Revd W. P. S. Bingham as president, with vice-presidents the Revd John Gilberd Pearse, the Revd Mamerto Gueritz and the Revd Sabine Baring-Gould.

The members of the East Devon branch supported the national ECU financially until well into the twentieth century. The Colyton congregation did the same. Each year the parish accounts show a donation.

The Confraternity of the Blessed Sacrament

We have seen how the CBS took root and flourished in Colyton. Again, the parish accounts show financial support for the national body for many years, quite aside from special collections which were not infrequent. However, in 1873, the activities of the national confraternity provoked another virulent attack on West Country clergy by the *Western Times*:

> First of all we became possessed of a copy of the "Constitutions of the Society for the Maintenance of the Faith" which was found to be placed under the protection of our Lady and Saint Augustine and the clerical members of which (including Archdeacon Denison) were required at certain seasons to say "Mass" ... it soon became evident that the most intimate relations existed between the "Society for the Maintenance of the (Romish) Faith" and another secret society called the "C.B.S." (i.e., "Confraternity of the Blessed Sacrament") of which little or nothing was known beyond the fact that it had been secretly working for some years.[7]

Having raised the spectre of secret societies and subversive activities, the writer went on to claim possession of a full list of the members of these societies, together with the assertion that many of them were also members of "another mischievous body, the E.C.U. (English Church Union)".

The matter which sparked the attack was a petition to Convocation, which asked for the selection and licensing of duly qualified confessors and also sought, among other doctrinal points, the promotion of the doctrine of the Real Presence of Christ in the sacrament of the altar and the adoration of Christ thus made present. Provision for "the decent and reverent reservation of the blessed Eucharist" and the reinstatement of the use of unction were also requested in the petition. It had been signed by 480 clergy.

The anti-ritualist correspondents of the *Western Times* were incandescent! A list of all the West Country clergy who had signed the petition was published and a note of what role they held in all or any of these "secret societies". Some of the names listed have already appeared in the story, namely the Hon. and Revd C. L. Courtenay of Bovey Tracey together with all his curates; M. Gueritz of Colyton; J. G. Pearse of Exeter; R. Porter of Kenn and his curate; W. H. B. Proby also of Colyton; and C. Woodstock of Chard, who was frequently in Colyton supporting Gueritz. There were many others; 63 in all.

This rather sad effort to "out" the ritualist clergy was unnecessary and ineffective. Many of them had already been the subject of the "scurrilities" of the Unitarian press. By this stage, such attacks had become wearisome rather than damaging. When the list published in this article is compared with a table of clearly identified Tractarian clergy in the West Country, it is evident that the *Western Times* seriously underestimated their numbers and strength.[8]

The Association for the Promotion of the Unity of Christendom

The Association for the Promotion of the Unity of Christendom (APUC) differed from the other groups in that it was a society with a global agenda, which sought the membership of individuals rather than the proliferation of local cells. The desire for the reunion of Christendom, the coming together of those churches which had preserved a sense of their catholic heritage, was its motive force. It was a desire that ran deep in Tractarians and in ritualists alike. Bernard Walke, writing in 1936, said:

> I had been brought up in the Catholic tradition, my Grandfather and father being among the first of the Tractarians to adopt a Catholic form of worship, and was convinced that the Catholic Movement in the Church of England … could have no other end but a corporate union with the Apostolic See of Rome.[9]

The hope was that the Church of England, or at least a substantial portion of it, should be made acceptable to the see of Rome and to the Orthodox churches of the East. The result would be a "corporate reunion". The APUC was founded on 8 September 1857 with the stated desire of ultimately bringing about such a reunion but with the immediate intention of drawing its members together in prayer for that unity. The declaration of members simply stated:

I willingly join the Association for the Promotion of the Unity of Christendom, and undertake [to offer the Holy Sacrifice once in three months and] to recite daily the above prayer for the intention of the same.

There was to be no compromise of any principle of doctrine or discipline. Each was to be free to occupy their place as a member of their own denomination without challenge. All that was required was that they should pray the same prayer for unity and that priests should offer the mass for the same intention. One of the main modes of disseminating the work of the association was its periodical, *The Union*.

Two of the leading proponents were Frederick George Lee and Ambrose Phillipps de Lisle. Lee and his earlier connections with Gueritz we have already noted. A. P. de Lisle was a prominent Roman Catholic layman who had earlier written to Lee warmly commending *The Union* paper and asking to become a subscriber. He writes:

As a member of the Catholic church I need not say that I look to the ultimate restoration of catholic unity as the only possible solution of the religious problems of the present day... Now to a man holding such views as those I have just expressed, and actually desiring to see them realised it is obvious that he is bound to sympathise and cooperate, as far as possible, with whatever may tend to their realization and advancement.[10]

The letter was dated 17 February 1857 and was sent from de Lisle's home, Grace Dieu Manor. This was when he was still signing himself Ambrose Lisle Phillipps, and it was a very long letter indeed. Further correspondence ensued, and de Lisle became an ardent supporter of the APUC and its work, recruiting tirelessly among his Roman Catholic contacts.

A multi-national mailing was sent out by the association in English, Latin, French and Greek, the result of which, or so it was claimed, was that

between nine and ten thousand clergymen and laymen of the Latin, Greek and Anglican Churches have been led to enrol themselves members.[11]

Given Lee's tendency to extrapolate from self-evident sources,[12] demonstrated amply in his amplification of the *Directorium Anglicanum*, we might be forgiven for not taking these numbers at face value. However, there was a substantial and positive response to the letter from clergy and lay people in the countries to which the letter had been sent. In Great Britain, the Roman Catholic members included, apart from de Lisle, Fr Lockhart, who was one of the Oxford converts, and the Roman Catholic Bishop of Kerry, Dr Moriarty.

In 1864, Lee published a list of 22 people, in various countries, who he claimed were prepared to receive applications for membership on his behalf. Among them were the Very Revd Thomas Sing of the Roman Catholic Cathedral of Nottingham, Prince Emanuel Charles Gody of Bassano at the Spanish Legation in Paris, and the Very Revd Dr Sceberras, of Valetta in Malta.[13] Dr Sceberras, at least, appears not to have been consulted regarding the use of his name because he wrote to Lee, in no uncertain terms. He had received an APUC programme which listed him as the association's secretary in the Roman Catholic diocese of Malta and he responded:

> I beg to say that I have never given my consent to be the secretary of the A.P.U.C. Association. On the contrary, having seen the Holy See's formal disapproval ... I request you to withdraw immediately my name from the Association.[14]

In spite of Lee's earlier assertion that the Holy Father had looked kindly on the venture, in 1864 the association was denounced by the Holy Office. The reasons for this are clear.

In the first place, although it was to be another 30 years before the Pope would declare Anglican orders "Absolutely null and utterly void", the question of the validity of those orders was a factor in the denunciation of 1864. Some have detected the influence of Cardinal, formerly Archdeacon, Manning in the process of condemnation. Manning would be created Archbishop of Westminster the following year and was already absolutely clear that the Church of England, which he had left because he believed it to be Erastian and apostate, had no valid orders or sacraments. How then could its ministers offer the Holy Sacrifice? For a Roman Catholic priest to offer a mass for the intention of the APUC would imply an acceptance that Anglican sacraments actually existed. The intention that each was to be free to occupy their place as a member of their own denomination without challenge was not sufficient to withstand the Inquisition.

Another element was inherent in the letters sent when the association was first launched. Paradoxically, it was the French translation of the letter which attracted the attention of the Roman Catholic bishops in England. There was one paragraph which, in the English edition, referred to "three great bodies which claim for themselves the inheritance of the priesthood and the name of Catholic", whereas the French translation had "trois grand corps qui ont conservé l'eritage du sacerdote, et le nom de Catholique".[15] The French is clear that the three great bodies had actually preserved Catholic identity, which is an assertion not made in the English version. The difference was important to the Roman Catholic hierarchy and the matter was referred to the Holy Office, which required "that the faithful be instructed not to join, under the guidance of heretics, this society".[16]

De Lisle was particularly devastated by this judgement. He had believed, not unreasonably, that conversations and shared prayer with other Christians who claimed the name of Catholic were valid even if their claim was in doubt. The Holy Office thought otherwise.

The Roman Catholic members of the APUC were obliged to withdraw. Moriarty, Lockhart and de Lisle, who had helped lead them together, were now constrained to lead them apart.

The initial vision which inspired its members was that the APUC could be the means whereby a large body of Anglicans could be made acceptable to Rome while retaining their Anglican identity. The deleterious effect of the persistent trickle of secessions would be eased if those who were intent on going could be persuaded to wait for the rest. Spencer Jones reflected something of this when he wrote:

> if we can only acknowledge plainly ... the primacy of the Holy See and regard our own separation as temporary and provisional, we shall be encouraged to work for a unity which will bear looking into.[17]

The departure of the Roman Catholic members was a body blow to the association but not a mortal wound. The work continued and the vision continued to draw support. The leadership of the English Church Union had already indicated a willingness to work with the association. Following a council meeting of the ECU, the secretary wrote to F. G. Lee offering personal and ECU support to distribute the prospectus of the APUC, and for a while the two bodies were closely identified in the promotion of the Catholic Revival and in the desire for some form of continuing dialogue with Rome.[18]

The history of the APUC and F. G. Lee had a direct bearing on the story of Mamerto Gueritz. Gueritz had several links with Lee over the years, but the two were not on particularly intimate terms. Thus, the connection was not based on personal loyalty but rather shared aims, at least at the beginning. Lee's hopes and aspiration later took a different direction altogether. Given his family history, it is not surprising that Gueritz evinced no desire to make or encourage submission to Rome, but "submission" was never part of the APUC agenda; the hope was for incorporation.

Gueritz' liturgical reforms at Colyton, although they resembled in some measure contemporary Roman practice, were also distinctively English. The "Sarum" influence was evident. The uses of the old Salisbury rite and ceremonial, as the development of liturgical scholarship revealed them, were increasingly adopted by those who desired to affirm both the Catholic identity of the Anglican Church and its distinctively English character. This was very much the declared stance of, for example, Robert Brett in St Matthias, Stoke Newington. It is therefore unsurprising that the same tradition became increasingly evident in Colyton, especially in the latter decades of Gueritz' ministry there.[19]

Support for the APUC from Colyton was generous and sustained. The first recorded indication that the association had its place in local church life appeared on 8 September 1871, the Feast of the Nativity of the Blessed Virgin and the fifteenth anniversary of the foundation of the association. The vestry journal records Mattins at 8 o'clock and Holy Communion at 20 minutes past the hour. There were eight communicants, and the marginal note reads: "Celebration for the intention of APUC".[20] Of course, as a member of the association, Gueritz was bound to offer the Holy Communion with special intention at least once every three months. According to the registers, he more than kept his promise. There were numerous collections and donations during the 1870s and 1880s. The early Communion on 16 May 1882 was kept as a votive for the Unity of Christendom, with the APUC as the special intention.

Having looked at these three organizations in sufficient detail to allow an understanding of the relationship between the local and the national, between Gueritz in Colyton and the wider work of the Church Revival, it will suffice to note other links in passing.

The Additional Curates Society (ACS) was supported by the people of Colyton for many years, with interest being sustained by visits from H. A. Cartwright and C. Carter. They were organizing secretaries for the ACS, Cartwright from 1872 to 1881 and Carter from 1878 to 1886. Carter had been curate of St David's in Exeter while Henry Cartwright had served at St John's, Hammersmith and St Augustine's, Stepney. Cartwright preached no fewer than five times at Colyton between December 1880 and January 1883. There was a period when it became necessary to direct funds into the parochial Curate's Stipend Fund, the benefice income having reduced markedly, but support for the ACS was later resumed. Two marginal notes in the vestry journal illustrate the relationship:

> Additional Curates Society collection and boxes remitted by cheque to Mr. Cutts, Sep. 13.71 MG.

> 30. May Tues (1872) collection for Rev, C. Carter's new church remitted to Rev. E.D. Cleaver. 14/6d.

A selection of entries from the church accounts for 1889 illustrates the outward-looking nature of the congregation. By this stage, donations to the APUC were being made by special collections and did not appear every year, but the following donations are significant:

English Church Union	10/-
Confraternity of the Blessed Sacrament	17/9
Devon Home of Mercy	11/8
Curate's Stipend Fund	£5/10/7
East Devon Choral Union	£5/12/9
S.P.C.K.	£4/ 1/ -
Additional Curates Society	£1/ 5/8

The connection with the Society for Promoting Christian Knowledge (SPCK) was equally strong. Colyton began distributing the society's magazine, *The Dawn of Day*, from its first appearance. Later the parish magazine was produced in the same size and format, so that they could be bound together, and an SPCK depot was established to serve the surrounding area of East Devon.

*   *   *

For the present purpose, just two more societies remain to note. The Society of the Holy Cross was founded by Fr Charles Lowder in 1855:

> His new society was to give support and encouragement to priests . . .
> he recognised then, as we do now, that it all began with holiness of life.[21]

There was also the Guild of All Souls which was begun in 1873 at St James', Hatcham with Arthur Tooth as its first president. It was originally called the Guild Burial Society and its purpose was then stated as

> To provide furniture for Burial according to the use of the Catholic Church
> so as to set forth the two great doctrines of the Communion of Saints and
> the Resurrection of the Body; and Intercessory prayer for the Dying and
> for the repose of the souls of the deceased members and all the faithful
> departed.

Today the guild describes itself as a

> devotional society praying for the souls of the Faithful Departed, and
> teaching the Catholic doctrine of the Communion of Saints.

The funeral at Colyton of George Trevelyan in 1871 predated the formation of the Guild of All Souls by two years. However, the rites and ceremonies there employed reflected exactly that which the Guild of All Souls would be formed to promote. For a number of Catholic Anglicans, the formation of the guild consolidated support for a position they had already taken, a position thoroughly embraced by Mamerto Gueritz, as evidenced by numerous entries for a "Missa de Requiem" in the records of Colyton Church.

These two societies and the Confraternity of the Blessed Sacrament were primarily devotional in intent. The offering of devotion and the pursuit of holiness, as was stated at the outset of this study, is that which binds the whole together, providing continuity to the Oxford Movement in its many and varied aspects. It holds the pre-Tractarian High Churchmen together with the Oxford men and them, in turn, with the Ritualists and today with those who may differ in their stand on many things but still hold themselves to be Catholic Anglicans.

Notes

[1]   *Colyton Parish Magazine*, July 1889.

[2]   The membership at this time was: Anne Derby Gueritz—wife of the incumbent; Elizabeth Shellswick; Mary M. Winter—organist almost from the first placing of the organ in the church; Frances Ann Trevelyan—wife, soon to be widow, of the Revd George Trevelyan of Stogumber; Lucy Street; Elizabeth Simmons; Claire Biddle; Emma Dart; Mary Collins; Lucy Street junior.

[3]   Acts 9:36–40: "Now there was at Joppa a certain disciple named Tabitha, which by interpretation is called Dorcas: this woman was full of good works and almsdeeds which she did. And it came to pass in those days, that she was sick, and died: ... Then Peter arose and went with them. When he was come, they brought him into the upper chamber: and all the widows stood by him weeping, and shewing the coats and garments which Dorcas made, while she was with them. But Peter put them all forth, and kneeled down, and prayed; and turning him to the body said, Tabitha, arise. And she opened her eyes: and when she saw Peter, she sat up."

[4]   *Church Union Gazette* 8:83 (1877), p. 87.

[5]   Bernard Palmer, *Reverend Rebels* (London: Darton, Longman & Todd, 1993), pp. 117ff.

[6]   *Church Union Gazette* 8:83 (1877), p. 80.

[7]   *Western Times*, Friday, 13 June 1873.

[8]   G. Herring, *The Oxford Movement in Practice* (Oxford: Oxford University Press, 2016), pp. 251.

[9]   B. Walke, *Twenty Years at St Hilary* (London: Methuen, 1936), p. 30.

10 Pusey House Library Archives, APUC Papers, Box 1, Letters De Lisle to Lee.

11 F. G. Lee (ed.), *Essays on Reunion* (London: Hayes, 1867), p. 297.

12 In his Discworld series, the author Terry Pratchett coined this phrase as a euphemism for "making stuff up".

13 F. G. Lee (ed.), *Sermons on the Reunion of Christendom* (London: Masters & Son, 1864), p. 325.

14 Pusey House Library Archives, APUC Papers, Box 1, File 4, Letter to Lee from Sceberras.

15 Lee, *Essays on Reunion*, pp. 298 and 303.

16 S. Jones, *England and the Holy See* (London: Longmans, 1902), p. 417.

17 Jones, *England and the Holy See*, p. 429.

18 W. H. B. Proby, *Annals of the Low Church Party in England: Down to the Death of Archbishop Tait* (London: Hayes, 1888), p. v. Proby names the ECU and the APUC as the two main targets of Low Church vilification.

19 The two strands of tradition in Anglo-Catholicism were evident from the beginnings of the Ritual Revival. In the 1901 revision of *The Ritual "Reason Why"* (first edition London: Mowbray, 1886), the reviser's preface speaks of those who wish to conform to "Old English usage" and those who would follow "European (Roman) usage", pointing out that the original author "sought to exhibit the two sets of observances, side by side, as two legitimate ways of doing the same thing". As late as the 1980s, when comparing theological colleges, it was common, for example, to call St Stephen's House, Oxford "Modern Roman" and the College of the Resurrection, Mirfield "Sarum", Salisbury being the main source for "Old English" liturgical scholarship.

20 South West Heritage Centre, Devon Archives. Ref. Colyton 3483A/PR14.

21 W. Davage SSC (ed.), *In This Sign Conquer* (London: Continuum, 2006), p. ix.

Reordering and resistance:
Of "pues" and pulpits

To the goodly house of worship, where, in order due and fit,
As by public vote directed, classed and ranked the people sit.

"Mary Garvin" by John Greenleaf Whittier

The members and supporters of the Ecclesiological Society, and the Cambridge Camden Society before it, had always before them the words of one of their founders, John Mason Neale:

For what is the HISTORY OF PUES, but the history of the intrusion of human pride and selfishness and indolence into the worship of God.[1]

The builders of new churches in the mid-nineteenth century created spaces which were specifically tailored not only to the flowering of ritual in the Church of England but also to the needs of the worshippers. No one was to own a seat in the house of God. New churches were built which, apart from clergy and choir stalls, never saw a pew. Rush seated chairs, sometimes fixed together in rows, took their place.

Those who inherited churches in need of repair were also able to put these principles into practice. Faced with a dilapidated vicarage and a run-down church at St James', Hatcham, Arthur Tooth seized the opportunity. The pews were torn out and carted away and the church reordered to fit the liturgy.

The ancient church of Colyton, however, was neither run down nor in need of radical rebuilding. Gueritz, who had made the aspirations of J. M. Neale his own, had a difficult task ahead, for not only was the building full of pews, with galleries all around, but the best pews were nearly all privately owned. This was the unlooked-for result of an earlier attempt to provide more "free" seats. Gueritz' predecessor, Barnes, had attempted this as part of the enlargement of the church in 1817, but the money ran out. His solution was to sell "by faculty" pew rights in the centre of the nave and under the central tower. The money raised was to be used to finish the project and provide seats for the poor parishioners. The project was successful but only at the expense of privatizing prime seating. It also created a seating arrangement which, while suitable for a service focussed on the pulpit, provided a space completely unfitted for sacramental worship with the altar at its heart.

The minutes book of the ratepayers' meetings traces the progress, or otherwise, of Mamerto Gueritz' attempts, if not to abolish the pews entirely, at least to make it possible for sacramental worship to take place and for ordinary folk to be able to sit where they could see and hear the services.

The notification of the meeting of 3 May 1866 disclosed that the purpose of the gathering was "to take into consideration the lowering of the pews in Colyton Church".[2]

Most of the private pews had such high sides, the owners having had them built to their own specification, that the occupants were invisible from anywhere except the pulpit. The notice was sent out on 28 April. By the date of the meeting, however, Gueritz had gained an awareness of the opposition he was going to encounter so, wisely, he withdrew for the time being, "and as he had ascertained that the general feeling of the meeting was opposed to the lowering of the pews, no motion would be made by him on the subject".[3]

The idealist could also be a pragmatist. The matter lay dormant until November 1869, a point at which three convergent factors induced Gueritz to make another attempt. The first was that he had just spent 18 months in London, mainly at St Matthias, Stoke Newington. There he had not only been immersed in ritualist liturgy but had also seen what could be achieved in churches built or adapted for the purpose. The second factor was that of the Church Rate which, ever since nonconformity had begun to proliferate, had been a vexed question. It was levied on householders and landowners in a parish to support the parish church and the churchwardens were responsible for its collection. The very first page in the vestry minute book illustrates the practice:

June 27th 1861. At a Vestry Meeting held this day pursuant to the above
notice It is ordered that the Churchwardens do make and collect a rate of
one penny in the pound.

  M. Gueritz, Chairman.

However, more and more resistance was being experienced from those who
had a conscientious objection to supporting the Church of England, the local
Unitarians especially. In 1868, an Act of Parliament removed the right to take any
legal proceedings against non-payers of the rate; in other words, it was no longer
compulsory. It was, however, open to ratepayers to make a voluntary commitment
to the rate. There was a vestry meeting of ratepayers held on 17 February 1869
when Gueritz was still in London. The curate in charge, J. W. Bennett, was in
the chair. The meeting was to deal with the question of the future provision for
the financial needs of the parish church. At the meeting John White proposed,
seconded by Captain Dick, that "[t]he money necessary . . . should be collected
by a Monthly Offertory and not by a Church Rate as heretofore".

  Strangely, the minutes book does not record whether the motion was put to
the vote, or whether it was won or lost, but no Church Rate was subsequently
levied. Hitherto, in theory at least and when the churchwardens had actually
collected their dues, all the ratepayers of the town had paid towards the upkeep
of the church and its services. They therefore maintained their right to take part
in any decision-making which affected the church and its fabric. While the Act
abolishing the Church Rate did not specifically remove that right, it did erode
the moral basis for it. Gueritz' argument was that if the dissenters no longer paid,
they no longer had any right to interfere in church affairs. However, their answer
to this argument was that the business of the Established Church was still the
business of every citizen. It was, for Gueritz and countless other priests like him,
the tension between what was legal and what was just.

  The third factor was W. H. B. Proby. Despite Proby's pastoral disasters Gueritz
was still accepting his support and did so specifically over the question of the
pews. There was a meeting called for 4 November 1869 to reopen the debate.
There were two main proposals before the meeting. The first was to completely
re-pew some areas of the church and to make all the new pews free seats, open
to all. The second was to draughtproof the church doors so that the doors of the

existing enclosed pews could be removed. At the meeting, Proby offered £100 towards the cost of re-pewing, hoping to gain the consent of those who held pews in the proposed area, or at least hoping to persuade them to exchange pews with others who approved the scheme.

The meeting was adjourned with the offer conditionally accepted subject to final approval of the detailed plans. A month later the meeting was reconvened. The minutes are written in a hand heavy and angry when compared with the graceful style of a month earlier. Captain Dick moved that the scheme go forward with certain limitations as to financial liability. Before the motion was put, Mr Mountstephen and Mr Samuel White proposed an amendment: "That the parish Church Pews remain in their present state".[4]

The amendment was carried by 13 votes to five. Again, the proposal was allowed to rest, this time for just over six years.

In the time between the meetings of December 1869 and April 1876, matters had not been allowed to lie entirely dormant. Other changes which did not relate to the pews included the establishment of the "Morning Chapel", now known as the Lady Chapel. This and several other changes which came later were not carried out with the authority of a faculty. They were legalized almost three decades later by being included in the successful faculty application of 1897, as the correspondence of the time reveals:

> The second Holy Table is not now proposed but has been in existence for about 30 years. When a new roof was put on the chancel and a Reredos and East Window (the gifts of the Barnes and Liddon families) the old Holy Table was moved to the North Chancel aisle.[5]

Note the avoidance of contentious language. "Holy Table" was acceptable to all; "Altar" was still a sticking point for some. That letter puts the establishment of what is now called the Lady Chapel at between 1869 and 1870. Incidentally it also reveals when the new high altar was installed, complete with a solid stone top.

A scrap of notepaper, folded into some old accounts, has, in Gueritz' hand, a note of work undertaken in 1872 and 1873. It included new altar rails at a cost of £7.15.6, choir seats, tiles for the sanctuary floor and a remodelling of the altar steps. This comment follows:

The above are some items of what was done later on when the new window, reredos, altar and choir seats etc. were done, and then I appear to have paid Mr. Street for his visit and his advice.

Also, in 1873 the Norman font was removed from the south transept. It later reappeared in Templeton Church when Mamerto's second son, Jose Fortescue, was made incumbent in 1879, but its whereabouts in the interval remain to be discovered. The new font was a gift of the Snook family. It was of carved stone and polished pink marble and harmonized with the kind of Italianate fittings that were appearing in the "Revival" churches in London. Supported on a marble stem, with marble pillars at each corner, it stood high above the surrounding congregation just inside the west door. The service register entry dated 22 April 1873 reads:

> The above were the first Baptisms in the font presented by the widow and family of the late J. S. Snook.

The Snook and Gueritz families were later to be united in marriage, but that is another part of the story.

There was the removal of the organ from the south tower arch to the north transept. It was first used in the new location on Whitsunday 1874, and the narrative in the vestry journal tells that the instrument

> was enlarged by the addition of a Swell (and) was used for the first time at service since such alteration, by Miss Mary M. Winter who has so zealously and ably given of her services almost from the first placing of the organ in the church.

The year 1876 was another in which the seamstresses, stonemasons and carpenters were kept busy. The previous December a new white altar frontal had been presented and blessed in time for use at Christmas. Then again, the register shows:

> 23rd January. The new stalls for the priests completed and used for the first time this Sunday.

The annual visit of the rural dean took place in April. His report was both complimentary and revealing:

> It is very pleasant to see the great improvements as funds can be got in this church: and I have no doubt that the renewing of the seats and the removal of the Galleries will soon be effected by the combined exertions of the Vicar and the Wardens.
>
> J. G. Coplestone RD[6]

In fact, "soon" would be another 20 years. On 21 April 1876, a meeting was held and again a motion was put:

> That a Faculty be applied for to lower the seats in the Parish Church and remove the galleries.

John White and H. D. Kingdon moved "That such a Faculty be not applied for". Again, the amendment won. Harry De Spencer Kingdon, who moved the amendment, was, to put it mildly, an eccentric. In earlier life he had been a staunch Unitarian and although that commitment faded with the passing of time, he was always ready to take their side against the vicar and his "Church Principles". His role as antagonist in the story of Mamerto Gueritz was such that he warrants a place of his own among the "supporting cast", and by the time the last battle of the "pues" was fought, H. D. Kingdon was the last opponent to be faced. However, the final outcome of the reordering of Colyton Church came 24 years later in 1900 and belongs to the closing years of the story of Mamerto Gueritz as parish priest of Colyton. In the interval, we shall chart the method and process by which numerous other changes had been quietly put in place with, it appears, scant attention to the need for faculties. It was important, given the question of ownership, that the legal process of re-pewing the church should be above reproach, but other matters, especially where they were related to the liturgy, were dealt with differently.

Apart from the matter of the ownership of pews, another aspect of the question which was anathema to Gueritz was that several pews were placed with their backs to the altar and with a view only of the elevated pulpit which was halfway down the north side of the nave against a pillar. This was what was called a "three-decker" with desks either side of the pulpit itself for the clerk and the minister. A radical solution presented itself. Later, H. D. Kingdon accused Gueritz of "tearing down the desks",[7] which he had undoubtedly done, but the old pulpit also disappeared from Colyton and, legend has it, appeared in another church. It is asserted that the recipient was Branscombe, just to the west of Beer. This is heartily denied by Branscombe folk.

In 1876, a new pulpit, matching the new font in style and materials, was placed on the north side of the outer chancel arch. Those who clung to their ownership of pews which had their backs to the altar could now hear little and see even less:

> Advent IV, 24th December. The pulpit of Caen stone presented by the Misses Winter and Mrs. K.H. Smith completed and preached from for the first time this day.[8]

The donors were three sisters, two of whom, Mary and Catharine, were still living at The Grove in Colyton. The other sister, Frances, had married a former curate of the parish, Kenelm Smith, and was by this time living in Ely.

The pulpit was richly carved and decorated with a sculpture of St Andrew set in the front panel, holding his cross saltire, painted in lifelike colours and with the decorations highlighted in gold leaf. Mary M. Winter was a longstanding supporter, had been organist almost from the installation of the organ and was active in the work of the district visitors.

The defeat of 21 April 1876 regarding the pews and galleries notwithstanding, the vestry journal of 1878 records the rural dean's inspection in Lent and his suggestion that action be taken to "convert some old pews into open seats for children".

Then at Easter it was noted in the same journal: "The Chancel Iron Gates (were) placed about this time." On Sunday 8 July, the new brass lectern was in use and, on 3 November, the choir vestry in the south transept had been completed in time for use that day. Two weeks later, two radiating stoves, used to warm the church, were placed at the west wall and in the north transept.

After that flurry of activity, it was not until May of 1879 that it was recorded that the pews in the north aisle had been cut down and made seats open to all.

A bald statement for a bold move. The north aisle seating had been part of the original plan, supported by Proby, where it was felt pew owners might be more amenable to change. This might have meant that the owners had simply agreed to have the doors removed, but in the vocabulary of the Church Revival, "open seats" meant seats available to anyone. This was a step unlikely to have been taken in the absence of a consensus, but there seems to be no evidence of a faculty. Also, by this time Gueritz had closed off one of the galleries as being unsafe. Another reason for closing it off was the unseemly behaviour of some young couples who were in the habit of sitting there!

By this time, most of the changes to the liturgical use of the building that could be made, without finally removing the high pews in the nave and under the tower, had been achieved. Between 1880 and 1881, a protracted period of ill health induced Mamerto to withdraw from any major activity in Colyton, and he and Jose Fortescue, his son, arranged an informal exchange of livings. Given all else that supervened, it is not surprising that the next and final assault on the question of "pues" did not take place until 1892.

In November 1892, Gueritz called a meeting of all interested parishioners, not just the ratepayers. The parish magazine carried an article setting out the purpose and limits of the meeting very clearly. Equally clear was the intention that this should be a gathering for everyone without any distinction of class. They met in the church, where the plans for reordering were openly discussed and comment invited. W. H. B. Proby was present at the meeting in spite of the fact that he had transferred his ecclesiastical loyalties to lie primarily with the Irvingites or the Catholic Apostolic Church. He declared that Gueritz was wrong to have involved all the parishioners and that the matter should have been left to the worshipping congregation to decide. He then left the meeting.

This incident illustrates the division that had opened between the two men. Proby was still defensive and confrontational in his attitude to church affairs, seeing everything as a matter of principle which had to be defended. Gueritz, on the other hand, reveals in this encounter an openness and confidence in dealing with his parishioners that had obviously grown over time. When Harry De Spencer Kingdon set up a loud complaint at the meeting that his pew was owned "by faculty", the meeting was not much disturbed. Indeed, it seems to have been conducted for the most part in high good humour and much laughter was recorded.

Gueritz' wisdom in first gaining the support of the general population was demonstrated the following month when the vestry meeting was again asked to debate the matter of the pews and galleries after a break of 16 years:

> December 17th 1892
>
> ... this Vestry Meeting approves of an application being made for a Faculty to make the proposed alterations to the Church namely, new floors, seats, heating apparatus, repairs of windows, raising floor under tower, removing chancel screen to outer arch, taking down galleries, building a new vestry.[9]

The proposal was carried unanimously; however, the vote was taken in the absence of H. D. Kingdon, who immediately launched a protracted correspondence with the Bishop of Exeter. He could not claim, as he had earlier, that Gueritz had acted in a high-handed manner; the public meeting demonstrated that he had not done so. The correspondence itself was evidence of Kingdon's growing eccentricity. In the first of his letters to the bishop, he describes himself as an invalid and asks for the bishop's sympathy; he also complains bitterly about the incumbent of Colyton. A further letter to the bishop, written on double foolscap-sized paper, goes into considerable detail about life in the parish church, or at least Kingdon's view of it.[10] It also confirms some of the changes that had been made over the previous 30 years.

That part of the faculty application of 1892 which dealt with the reordering of the pews was challenged by Kingdon on a legal basis. When the church had been enlarged in 1817, there had been insufficient funds to complete the work. In order to make up the shortfall, 118 pew plots were sold by a process already described. Kingdon refers to his father, who was "an eminent lawyer and was a purchaser and a pew builder", in order to illustrate the validity of his claim.

As the application was proceeding, in January 1893 Gueritz was in correspondence with Arthur Burch, the diocesan registrar. Gueritz doubted the existence of the particular faculty for the sale of 118 seats but not that for the reordering of 1817:

I am very doubtful that these faculties can be produced but there was
certainly a general faculty for the enlargement of the church about 1818.[11]

In fact, the list of 118 names appended to that faculty did, and still does, exist,
but it was not in the parish records at that time and either by design or oversight
the registrar's office failed to produce it.

Kingdon's letter, although convoluted and repetitive, reveals much of interest
about the fabric of the church, but even more about Kingdon's understanding of
Gueritz. One of the charges he laid against the vicar was really quite justified, up
to a point: "he had long wished and still desires to destroy all pews and substitute
chairs as free sittings".

Of course, this was partially true and, indeed, at the public meeting Gueritz had
raised the idea that chairs would be less expense and less likely to be appropriated
than pews. However, he recognized, as the discussions progressed, that doing
away with pews in Colyton altogether was not a possibility. Making the seating
all free and open was the aim. Kingdon wrote, quoting Gueritz:

> no one had any right to a private pew; pew owners were robbers of the
> poor . . . no social distinctions are to exist in church, except between priest
> and people—though by God's will distinctions exist in his own great
> Temple—Creation.

Kingdon complained that he had only found out about the public meeting by
accident and had not been personally invited. He obviously did not take or read
the parish magazine. He objected to the fact that the meeting was packed with
newcomers to the parish who had everything to gain and nothing to lose, and that
it was held at an hour inconvenient to those who lived at a distance. The meeting
was held at 7 o'clock in the evening. He made similar complaints at the calling of
the vestry meeting of 17 December. That was held at 7.30 in the evening, and at
a time when, according to Kingdon, the ordinary ratepayers would have wished
to be about their customary preparations for Christmas. And of the meeting itself
he claimed that the attendees were:

chiefly small mechanics who had just left work and had probably never attended a Vestry Meeting before; and a few High Church gentry, personal friends of the Vicar . . . and who were relied on to help his views, without perhaps any strong views of their own.

In commenting on the liturgical changes:

Yet he has abolished the good old afternoon services the farmers and work people could attend and substituted night services they can not attend, to say nothing of offensive innovations; processions in the church, with banners; or the use of wafers instead of bread as ordered, in the respect of which I hear complaints.

The "good old afternoon services" instituted by Frederick Barnes, and with little content that might have offended Unitarian sensibilities, had been replaced by services for the children more than 20 years earlier.

Because of all the objections the faculty application of 1893 was considerably delayed and revised. A new citation dated 30 April 1897 was published on 9 May on the church door. The registrar's note on the foot of the faculty document reads:

No appliance in opposition having been entered, faculty granted 29 June 1898 subject and without prejudice to any private rights existing in any of the seats by faculty or otherwise.

Arthur Burch. Registrar.

This part of Gueritz' story had taken 35 years to reach a conclusion. In the event, no evidence to confirm any private right was forthcoming and the work proceeded. The report of its completion and celebration will come as we look at Gueritz' closing years in Colyton.

Notes

1 John Mason Neale, *The History of Pues*, a paper read before the Cambridge Camden Society on 22 November 1841, p. 3.

2 Minute Book of the Parish of Colyton 1861 to 1964, 3 May 1866.

3 Minute Book 1861 to 1964, 3 May 1866.

4 Minute Book 1861 to 1864, 5 December 1869.

5 South West Heritage Centre, Exeter. Colyton Faculty File. Correspondence with the registrar.

6 Rural Dean's Report Book. Colyton Parish Records.

7 South West Heritage Centre, Exeter. Colyton Faculty File. H. D. Kingdon's letter to the bishop 1897.

8 South West Heritage Centre, Exeter. Colyton File 3483A/Pr14 ff.

9 Minute Book 1861 to 1964, 17 December 1892.

10 South West Heritage Centre, Exeter. Colyton Faculty File. H. D. Kingdon's letter to the bishop 1897.

11 South West Heritage Centre, Exeter. Colyton Faculty File.

1 2

Filling in the gaps

1870–80

Having looked at some of the major themes of Gueritz' work in Colyton and their relation to and implications for the wider Church, there are a number of events to be remarked as his second decade in the parish unfolded. We noted the liturgical developments of 1866 and the funeral of George Trevelyan of Stogumber in 1871; there was the arrival and disappearance of the sisterhood; we have seen the establishment of lay groups for the strengthening of individual spirituality, mission and pastoral ministry; we have shared, in some measure, the long battle of the "pues". Early in January 1873, the news came that Prebendary James Coles, the incumbent of Shepton Beauchamp, the father of Stuckey Coles and the priest with whom Mamerto Gueritz had served his title, had died suddenly. He collapsed on the road between the church and his house; death was immediate. This bereavement was felt keenly by the Gueritz family and also, if vicariously, by the people of Colyton. Stuckey's engaging personality meant that he was already a firm favourite with the community.

So much besides remains that "filling in the gaps" seems an unworthy title for this chapter.

The Elementary Education Act of 1870 meant that change was inevitable in the way in which education was provided and by whom it was controlled, and Colyton could not escape the consequences. Almost immediately the opening shots were fired. *Pulman's Weekly* of 27 June 1870 carried an anonymous letter, the writer of which hoped that a school board would be formed "on fair principles and not placed under the sole control of the vicar, whose very ultra views in the pulpit . . . make him a most undesirable man".

Mamerto Gueritz had inherited the Tractarian ideal of education which was exemplified by Nathaniel Woodard both in the schools he founded and the unequivocal relationship those schools had with the teaching of Anglican Catholicity. In setting out his programme of education, Woodard had incurred the displeasure of Bishop Blomfield of London, who not only objected to his doctrinal stance but even more to his criticism of some of the clergy who were currently engaged in the education of the young. Woodard condemned them as inefficient and godless. Given the amply demonstrated will of a secular government to intrude into the affairs of the Church according to a secular agenda, any intervention of politicians was regarded with suspicion if not outright rejection. Woodard's reaction to political plans for the education of the young was characteristically straightforward:

> Some look to the Government for everything. For my part, in the present
> state of the parties in the Kingdom, I heartily trust that the Government
> will not interfere. It would be unjust.[1]

The Act of 1870 and that of 1873 which amended it were not primarily designed to remove ecclesiastical provision of education, but the clergy who were involved in the work of schools had a choice to make. They could either withdraw from the public arena and continue their labours in the world of private education, as did John Gilberd Pearse in Exeter, or they could get involved with the new initiatives and the implementation of the new laws. Many did both.

There was a "Requisition in writing signed by fifty Ratepayers of the Parish of Colyton" by which the Clerk to the Guardians of the Axminster Law Union was required to call a meeting to discuss the formation of a school board for Colyton. On 31 March 1874, the vestry meeting unanimously agreed that "it is expedient that a School Board should be formed for the parish of Colyton".[2]

Gueritz was in the chair for that meeting and was evidently hoping that the board formed would seek to provide what was later called a "voluntary" school, a school operated under the aegis of the Church of England but receiving public funds. However, the Act provided that, in a new school not provided by the Church, religious education should be non-denominational. The new board was elected, which was hailed as a triumph for the Unitarian "Protestants" of the town. The newspaper headline was "School Board Election and the Defeat of the Sectarians", which was followed by the claim that

> The friends of Protestant education have triumphed in the School Board
> election on Saturday. The parish has long been plagued with the taint
> of Ritualism through the minister with a Spanish name . . . and he did
> his best to get a School Board of the same pattern. The candidates were
> Messrs. Hawkings, Kingdon and Kittle who were advocates of fair play for
> all undenominational teaching for the School Board. The Ritualists put
> forward their precious parson . . . Mr. Dommett and Mr. Stokes. Their
> pious women were in and out trying to cajole the poorer ratepayers to
> vote for the priest.[3]

The Unitarian candidates took 920 votes between them, Gueritz and his party 665. This was in the latter part of May. At the end of the month, at a social gathering which was nothing to do with the school, Gueritz took the opportunity to comment on the recent election:

> [I]n the hope that anything which in the heat of the moment had been
> unfriendly or unpleasant might be forgotten by all others as he himself
> was anxious to forget it and he desired to bear the defeat of his side with
> good humour and hoped that all would now be friendly again and work
> well together for the future.[4]

In September 1874, the vestry meeting made a rate to fund the school board in the sum of £100, the second largest allocation in the accounts that year. The members of the board busied themselves with the work of finding a site and building or converting an existing building into a school. The first intimation that all was not well came in the ratepayers' meeting of 9 July the next year, 1875, when Gueritz' hopes for an eirenic future were seriously dampened.

The reason given for calling the meeting was to discuss the viability of the site for the new school proposed by the board. At the meeting, the motion was put:

That this meeting desires to protest against the purchase of the property
recently made by the School Board at a price of £780 for the following
reasons;

    1. That the price is excessive.

    2. That it will be attended by considerable expense in adapting the same
for the purpose it is required.

    3. That the situation is unhealthy.

An amendment was moved by Mr F. W. Kingdon and seconded by Mr J. B. Kettle
to the effect that the site was a desirable one. (F. W. Kingdon was H. D. Kingdon's
nephew.) Neither resolution nor amendment was put to the meeting by the
chairman and the meeting broke up in "the greatest tumult and disorder".[5] The
customary neatness in recording the minutes was also abandoned and the writing
is heavy and angry. The matter was not discussed at a ratepayers' meeting again,
it being the business of the school board which was a publicly elected body. The
next skirmishes in the battle came five years later when the elections were held
once more, but as this argument unfolded and in the interval before 1879, there
were several other matters of more than passing interest.

Throughout 1873, there were even more vituperative attacks than usual on
"Ritualist excesses" from the Colyton correspondent for *Pulman's Weekly*. The
attacks, in the correspondence column, focussed on the usual targets and although
Gueritz was seldom named it was obvious that he was the subject. The doctrines
of the Real Presence and Eucharistic adoration were repeatedly scorned, before
the writers settled on the dangers of the "Romish" practice of confession heard by
the priest. One letter-writer asserted that there was great danger in young women
being closeted for hours at a time with their priest and spoke of "ladies led astray".
The letters became so extreme and obsessional that even the editor of *Pulman's*
was disturbed. He refused to take any more such letters from that source, which
is probably why, the following year, *Pulman's Weekly* was advertising for a paid
correspondent in Colyton. There is no indication that anyone wanted the job.

As ever, there were highs and lows for the community, and 1874 was no
exception. On one occasion, the joy and the sorrow were all bound up in the same
person. On 13 August, aged just 19, William Ernest Snook passed the examination
in the science and practice of medicine at the Apothecaries Hall in London, which

caused much rejoicing back in Colyton. He was following in the footsteps of his father, J. S. Snook, who had died in 1871.

In December, just four months later, the local papers carried news of William's death and the report of his funeral. Gueritz had known him since he became parish priest of Colyton, at which point William was five years old, and, when he was of age, welcomed him into the Guild of St Andrew.

The funeral was everything St Andrew's Church and the community could offer. There was a fully choral requiem in the church. The coffin was covered in a silk pall. The 12 bearers had all been friends and colleagues in the work of the church and the Guild of St Andrew. As we know, the Snook family were staunch supporters of Gueritz' attempts to bring Tractarian teaching and practice to Colyton. The two families were already "heart to heart" and would soon become even more closely tied.

Also during 1874 there were several clergy who, officially and unofficially, were supporting Mamerto in the work, allowing him time for rest and ministry elsewhere. One such was the Revd John Riley, who was the curate of Sarawak in Borneo. That should strike a chord because Mamerto George Gueritz was, by then, Acting British Resident at Sarawak.

We have seen that W. H. B. Proby no longer exercised a public ministry as an Anglican priest after April 1873 and that around that time he opened a small Catholic Apostolic chapel in King Street. Early in 1875, there was a report of a fire in King Street which started in the Irvingite Chapel. It was extinguished, and the chapel returned to use as a place of worship.

Later in 1875, a fire of a different kind was set in Colyton, that of missionary zeal. The work of reaching out into the community by acts of practical care and the establishment of guilds and societies was to be supplemented by the direct and public proclamation of the gospel in a way that had, up to that point, been the province of the itinerant "Tent Evangelists". Such roving preachers often claimed to preach the "Pure Bible Gospel" as opposed to the tainted version offered by the Established Church. *The Dawn of Day* monthly magazine ran a whole series of articles under the heading "Church teaching is Bible teaching" with the specific intention of countering the accusation of offering anything less than the true gospel message. This was done by teaching the difference between the subjective and emotional experience offered by the Evangelists and the objective biblical exposition to be heard in church. How much better, though, to have a demonstration of a proper Tractarian mission. The mission was to be preached from 6 November to 15 November and, according to the handbills, would be led by the Revd V. S. S. Coles. In the event, he was assisted by another missioner, the Revd A. H. Drummond.

The two of them, together with Mamerto Gueritz, maintained a full programme of services. On the two Sundays the day began at seven in the morning with Holy Communion, followed by a meditation. Another Holy Communion followed at eight, then Mattins and sermon at 10.30. There was a service for men only at 2 o'clock, followed by a children's service at three. Evensong was said at six, and the day finished with a mission service, essentially a call to repentance and holiness. Weekdays followed the same sort of pattern but with a special address for women to which domestic servants were specifically invited. The effect was marked by increased congregations at the special Advent services which followed in December.

Having had Stuckey Coles demonstrate what might be done, the following Advent in 1876 Gueritz took the leadership himself, with Coles preaching at one of the special services and J. Izod, curate of Honiton, and H. A. Cartwright, by this time incumbent of Whitestaunton, preaching at others. There was not such an intensive programme, and the tone of the handbills had also changed, perhaps reflecting more of the spirituality of Gueritz himself at that stage than the previous year. Perhaps that is why he took the reins:

> Attend the SPECIAL SERVICES, that you may learn of the love of JESUS CHRIST for sinners, and how you may prepare to meet him at the Judgement Day.
>   Your loving Friend & Pastor, M. Gueritz.

There was an opportunity to make special preparation for Christmas Communion, and Gueritz himself led the work with the children. With a style and vocabulary of preaching almost evangelical in tone, Gueritz was at one with others in the Oxford Movement, men like Stanton and Mackonochie of St Alban's, Holborn and Charles Lowder of St Peter's, London Docks. They too combined advanced ritual with fervent and challenging preaching. This was another element of Gueritz'

COLYTON MISSION, 1875.

A Mission will be preached in this Parish (D.V.) from SATURDAY, NOV. 6, to MONDAY, NOV. 15, by the

REV. V. S. S. COLES,

RECTOR OF SHEPTON BEAUCHAMP.

List of Services:

SATURDAY, 6th Nov.	7:30 p.m.	Reception of the Missioners.
SUNDAYS, 7th. & 14th.	7.0 a.m.	Celebration.
,, ,,	7.45 ,,	Meditation.
,, ,,	8. 0 ,,	Celebration.
,, ,,	10.30 ,,	Mattins and Sermon.
,, ,,	2. 0 p.m.	Service for Men only.
,, ,,	3. 0 ,,	Children's Service.
,, ,,	6. 0 ,,	Evensong.
,, ,,	6.45 ,,	Mission Service.
WEEK DAYS.	7.30 a.m.	Meditation.
,, ,,	7.45 ,,	Celebration.
,, ,,	10. 0 ,,	Mattins.
,, ,,	12. 0 ,,	Children's Service.
,, ,,	3. 0 p.m.	Address to Women, (domestic Servants especially invited.)
,, ,,	5. 0 ,,	Evensong.
,, ,,	7.30 ,,	Mission Service, followed by an Instruction.

Those who desire to speak to the Mission Priest will find him in Church after any Service, and also from 11 to 12, and from 4 to 5.

J. B. KETTLE, PRINTER, COLYTON.

Colyton mission pamphlet 1875

ministry which had been first manifested in Penzance, then further developed during his time in London and finally brought to fruition in the Colyton missions.

With such events, especially when repeatedly held in the same community, there is a law of diminishing returns, and if they are to be repeated, they must necessarily change from straightforward challenge to a mixture of challenge and nurture, repentance and renewal. There were several more such missions. They were held in Lent and Advent in 1877 and again in Lent 1878. Stuckey Coles appeared at most of them, having become something of a favourite in the parish, but as time passed the missions metamorphosed into an Advent or Lent programme of special services and teaching; a call to repentance and holiness, with a cast of visiting clergy from near and far, some of whom came back year after year. They did so even when, perhaps especially when, Mamerto Gueritz himself was unwell and unable to take part, as in 1881, when he was in Templeton. The handbill for Advent of that year (see below) demonstrates such support.

It is interesting to compare the handbills for these missions and seasonal programmes with those put out by W. H. B. Proby almost a decade previously. Then the emphasis had all been on Catholic doctrine and practice. These mission handbills focussed on a right relationship with God and the need for reconciliation with Him and with other Christians. The doctrine and the ritual had become the context in which that experience could be found.

When he wrote the Advent challenge of this handbill, Jose Fortescue Lawrence Gueritz had been in holy orders for five years. He was ordained to the diaconate in 1876. Fortescue, as he was normally known to the family, was ordained as a *literatus*. That meant he had not been to a university but was deemed through a programme of preparation and examination to be a suitable candidate. His ordination had taken place on Trinity Sunday 1876, and Gueritz recorded in the vestry journal for Trinity III, 2 July: "Fortescue said the service for the first time and preached in the evening his first sermon."

On 2 May 1878, Reginald Snook and his youngest brother, Lionel Henry Mortimer Snook, who was an articled clerk in Long Sutton, Lincolnshire, legally adopted their mother's family name of Mortimer.[6] In the deed of name change, Reginald described himself as a "Student for holy orders". The brothers were the sons of John Snook, who died in 1871 and in whose memory the new font had been given. Of the surviving children of Elizabeth and John Snook, only

ADVENT, 1881.

Dear Friends,

The Season of Advent is once more at hand. In the Epistle for the first Sunday we are bidden with words of solemn warning to think of our Saviour coming at the Last Day with power and great glory to judge the Living and the Dead.

The Night of this World is far spent. The Day of Eternity is at hand.

On the Sunday before Christmas Day we are bidden to rejoice. The Lord is at hand. Coming to us as He came one cold winter night, nearly 1900 years ago to gladden the world with His Presence.

How can we look forward to meet Him at the last Day, or Rejoice with Him on Christmas Day, unless we are prepared !

The Season of Advent often loses much of its force and meaning because we look upon it as only reminding us of a solemn Truth about the *Future*. This is only half its object. It is also meant as a time of Preparation for *Christmas Day*—for our Christmas Communion.

Our Blessed Saviour wants us to think about Him as being amongst us *now*. He is ready, if we will only let Him, to enter into our life *here*, to share in our Joys and Sorrows, and to fit us for His Second Coming in Glory.

If you want to make the Blessed Truth of "Emmanuel"—God with us—a *Reality* to you, come on Christmas Day to the Holy Communion and make this Season of Advent a time of Preparation for *that*.

Come to the Special Services.

Be more frequent, more earnest in your Prayers.

Make a sincere and thorough examination of your past life.

"Now is our Salvation nearer than when we believed." *Very* near in his loving desire to be *one* with us. Verily how shall we escape hereafter, if we neglect to make Him our own now.

Your faithful Servant in Christ,

J. FORTESCUE L. GUERITZ.

SPECIAL SERVICE AND SERMON EVERY WEDNESDAY EVENING AT 8.0 P.M.

Nov. 30th. F. of S. Andrew.	Christ, The Messiah.	Rev. Canon Woodcock, Vicar of All Saints.
Dec. 7th.	Christ, The Judge.	Rev. H. A. Cartwright, Rector of Whitestaunton.
Dec. 14th.	Christ, The Teacher.	Rev. J. Smith, Vicar of Lyme.
Dec. 21st. F. of S. Thomas.	Christ, The Indweller.	Rev. Preb. Sadler, Rector of Honiton.

J. B. KETTLE, PRINTER, COMYTON.

Advent sermon series flyer 1881

Reginald and Lionel took this step and then not until seven years after their father's death. Their sister Cora had married Samuel Mossop, who was a solicitor with a practice in Long Sutton where Lionel was an articled clerk. The legal process of the change began in Long Sutton, where Samuel Mossop witnessed Lionel's signature, and then it was possible for him to take the document with him to Colyton for Reginald and his witnesses, the O'Mearas, father and son, to sign. Lionel needed to be in Colyton for the end of the month for other reasons; he was to be his brother's best man. Given the seven years' delay between his father's death and the change of name, the fact that it immediately preceded the next great event in Reginald's life may not be a coincidence.

The last weeks of May saw great excitement in the Gueritz and Mortimer-Snook families and indeed the whole community. On 21 May, Mary Louisa Gueritz and Reginald Arthur Mortimer were married. The intervening 19 days between the change of name and the issue of the marriage certificate, and indeed the issue of passports, must have been busy indeed!

Just before 9 o'clock in the morning Mary Louisa, "Min", left the vicarage to walk to the church. As she did so, it was noted that the legendary pomegranate tree was once more in bloom. It had last blossomed when Adelina was married in 1865 and would flower once more for a Gueritz wedding, but not for another seven decades.

The bride entered the church on her father's arm, and her brother Edward Gueritz, who was the one who had commented on the flowering pomegranate tree, was among the groomsmen; Antonia Anne Gueritz was among the bridesmaids, and they were met at the church by Stuckey Coles, who was to conduct the service. Stuckey had known Mamerto since boyhood; Adelina had been his tutor, and he was very much part of the family. He was specifically noted in the newspaper report as "so well known and loved in this parish". Fortescue was also taking part as precentor, organizing the music and the choir. W. H. Monk gave special permission for his setting of the wedding hymn "Heart to Heart and Side by Side" to be used, and there was, of course, a nuptial mass, fully choral and celebrated by Mamerto himself.

The celebrations afterwards at the vicarage were such as might have been expected, with toasts being made and answered by just about everyone who had taken part. Mamerto expressed his gratitude at the way in which people had expressed their affection for Mary and indeed for the whole family, after which farewells had to be said:

> In the afternoon, after paying for their felicity by being pelted with rice—a custom in these parts either descending from barbaric times or imported from barbaric climes—Mr and Mrs R. A. Mortimer drove away *en route* to the North Devon Coast, preparatory to their forthcoming voyage to New Zealand where Mr Mortimer will enter the church of that colony.[7]

It was a joyful celebration but tinged with sadness. The Antipodes was a very long way away in 1878, and most people who left these shores for New Zealand at that time were unlikely to see their families again. Reginald left England with the necessary letters dimissory from the Bishop of Exeter which would allow him to be ordained in New Zealand.

On 8 June, Trinity Sunday 1879, the vestry journal again records:

> F.L. Gueritz, curate of this parish, ordained priest by the Bishop of Exeter, Dr. Temple, at the Church of Ottery St. Mary.

Fortescue had served his title as a deacon for three years, not only assisting his father in the parish but also undergoing the additional training necessary for him as a *literate*. A mere three months later he was presented to the living of Templeton, near Tiverton, which was in the gift of a branch of the Pole family who lived at Shute. He moved there in September 1879. Just as he was able to share in the priestly ministry and take more of a load from Mamerto, he was "preferred", as it is called, but he returned quite often and was back in Colyton for the harvest festival the following month.

Another milestone in the life of the Gueritz family was passed on 21 October when Antonia Josepha Hermogenes Moxica Iparagheri died, aged 85, at Colyton vicarage. The survivor of civil war and of being made a refugee, of being forced into exile with her infant son, not knowing whether she and her husband would be reunited, and then widowed with children still to care for, this indomitable Spanish lady was finally at rest. Once more, Stuckey Coles was there to preside at the funeral and to comfort his friends.

This provides us with a pause in which to take stock of the family as they were in 1879. Mamerto and Anne were in Colyton, with Anne taking an increasing role in supporting her husband's ministry. Adelina was married in 1865 to Samuel Bartlett, a man some 18 years her senior. They lived a short distance from the vicarage in Queen's Square and, for a while, Adelina and Mamerto's mother had lived with them. Mamerto George, the eldest son, was serving under Rajah Brooke in the Sarawak Civil Service. Edward Peregrine had joined him in Sarawak in 1874 but had resigned in 1877 and at the time of his sister's wedding had not yet taken up his employment in the Bank of New Zealand. This left him free to be in Colyton for a period. Jose Fortescue was already in his first incumbency and, as we have just seen, Mary Louisa and Reginald were in New Zealand. Henry Frank Gueritz was in his early twenties at the time of the wedding and appeared frequently in the reports of local cricket matches, but lest that should seem frivolous by comparison with his siblings, we shall hear much more of his praiseworthy part in the story in due course. He followed his sister to New Zealand, arriving at the port of Lyttleton in December 1879. That leaves Antonia Anne, 19 years old when her sister married and much involved in the work with young people and with the poor in Colyton. She was then and for the rest of her short life much beloved of the children of the parish.

In 1880, the end of the decade, it was time once more for the elections to the school board. The whole matter was set out on posters and placards around the town.

On 7 May, the vicar and churchwardens put up a poster offering a reward for information leading to the conviction of anyone who had attempted to coerce voters by threatening to evict them. There was an immediate riposte, couched in idiosyncratic English, attempting to divert attention from this "scurrilous and unfaithful charge against cottage owners" by blaming Gueritz for all the divisions in the town. The same poster attempted to blame him for the waste of money on the new school by suggesting that had he not been so unpopular he and others might have been elected to the school board in the first place. The hilariously unintended implication of those statements was that money had indeed been wasted and that Gueritz and his party would have done a better job!

The charge of wasting money hid a much uglier suspicion that the land for the school had been purchased at a deliberately inflated price in order to line certain dissenting pockets in the town. The memory of the purchase of land needed for

COLYTON

SCHOOL BOARD ELECTION.

£2. REWARD

will be given to any one giving evidence
(leading to conviction) of any

UNDUE INFLUENCE

being used in this Election, such as
**THREATENING TO RAISE THE RENT
OF A VOTER, OR TO TURN HIM OUT
OF HIS HOUSE.**

M. GUERITZ,
THOMAS WHITE,
FRANCIS STOKES.

Colyton, 7th May, 1880.

School Board election poster: The Church party offers a £2 reward

COLYTON

SCHOOL BOARD ELECTION!!

TWO GUINEAS

REWARD,

Will be Paid to anyone giving such information as shall lead to the CONVICTION of any Rational Man who will SAY, to the

CONTRARY,

1st. That the Vicar of Colyton has not been at the bottom of all the mischief, and division sectarian and social, that has infested the Town, ever since he came to reside in it.

2nd. That it was not owing to the distrust and disfavour the PARISHONERS GENERALLY and not the Dissenters who are only a small body viewed him with, that caused them in opposition to elect the first Board, which he now accuses of having wasted SEVENTEEN HUNDRED POUNDS, & of which waste HE is THEREFORE SOLELY RESPONSIBLE FOR and they have to thank HIM entirely for it.

3rd. That it is not as a consequence of his unpopularity, and thus adding so largely to the rates, few respectable people will come into the Town to reside, and owners of House Property here, have set their faces against him, as an enemy to Peace, Comfort, & Welfare of the Town, of which his scurrilious and unfaithful charge against Cottage Owners, is the most recent example.

School Board election poster: The Unitarians offer 2 guineas reward

COLYTON
SCHOOL BOARD
ELECTION.

14th MAY 1880.

The Ratepayers are reminded of the following facts :--

The Church provided a School for 140 Children without any expense to the Ratepayers until 1874.

The Church would have provided Schools for all the Children at the following cost to the Ratepayers :---

	£	s.	d.	£	s.	d.
Site and Conveyance	80	0	0			
Building as per Estimate	1700	0	0			
Add for Extras	100	0	0			
				1880	0	0
Less Subscriptions and Government Grant				800	0	0
			Total, £1080	0	0	

The above Scheme was rejected by the Dissenters, who gained a majority on the first Board, on the cry of " Economy," with the following result :---

	£	s.	d.	£	s.	d.
Cost of Buildings—						
Drewer,	1873	9	10			
White,	18	17	11			
Anning,	24	0	0			
Pinney (Architect)	96	7	0			
				2012	14	9
Cost of Site—						
R. Kittle's expenses,	3	13	0			
Purchase money,	785	0	0			
Interest on ditto,	39	5	0			
Other expenses,		10	0			
Mortgage—Barnes and Barnard,	12	11	8			
Cox and Every—Conveyance and Costs in Chancery,	144	17	6			
Surveyors,	21	1	0			
				1006	18	2
			Total, £3019	12	11	
Allow for Land sold, and worth of Cottage				239	12	11
				£2780	0	0

MONEY THROWN AWAY £1700 0 0.

School Board election poster: money thrown away

the gasworks in 1867 was still in the mind of some parishioners. Gueritz had sold the town some of his glebe land at a much lower price than others were demanding. The suspicion then had been that the landowners had deliberately inflated the price so as to reap an opportunistic benefit from the public need.

The cost comparisons were set out in yet another poster where the total waste of money was asserted to be £1,700, a staggering sum in 1880. In the figures set out, the cost of the land provoked a great deal of anger. Gueritz asserted that the Church would have provided the land for £80, while the board spent £785 to the same purpose. The whole matter had been reduced to a dispute between the Church party and those who called themselves Protestants but were in fact the post-Unitarians headed by Harry De Spencer Kingdon; those who still wore the badge but, like him, seldom attended the meeting house.

It is not known whether there was any direct consequence from the accusations and counter-accusations, with the suspicion of fraud hanging over the whole affair. What is known is that the current members of the board were ousted, a new school board elected and the school, which had been built in The Butts, was filled with pupils.

Notes

[1] L. and E. Cowie, *That One Idea: Nathaniel Woodard and His Schools* (London: Woodard Corporation, 1991), p. 7.

[2] Minute Book of the Parish of Colyton 1861 to 1964.

[3] *Western Times*, Monday, 25 May 1874.

[4] *Colyton Parish Magazine*, June 1874

[5] Minute Book 1861 to 1964.

[6] Reported in the *Stamford Mercury*, Friday, 10 May 1878: "(We) ... do hereby give Notice that we have assumed the maternal name of Mortimer and henceforth intend on all occasions and for all purposes whatsoever to use and employ, sign and subscribe and be known by the names of Reginald Arthur Mortimer and Lionel Henry Mortimer respectively."

[7] *Western Times*, Friday, 24 May 1878.

1 3

An Indian summer turns to autumn

1880–95

Ever since his collapse before finals in St Edmund Hall, Mamerto Gueritz' health evinced a recurring fragility. At intervals over the years these episodes were repeated and appeared to follow periods of great stress and conflict. More than once we hear of absence for health reasons and the need to recuperate. When he returned to the parish after an interval in 1867, the unexpectedly kind comment in the newspapers was that he had "been away for the benefit of his health— indifferent of late and far from being restored now". The nature of the illness was never made explicit but as the years passed the frequency of his struggles with ill health increased.

In 1880, the national outlook for priests of the Catholic Revival like Gueritz seemed sombre. This was the period when priests such as Thomas Pelham Dale and Richard William Enraght were imprisoned under the Public Worship Regulation Act. Green of Miles Platting would be similarly incarcerated the following year. Their offences were simply to conduct worship and to teach doctrine in exactly the same way that Mamerto Gueritz had done since 1866 and earlier.

In Colyton, the future seemed more tranquil. From several external reports of the meetings of the school board, Gueritz was now chairman, and there were no major upsets at the school until the following spring. Mamerto was taking most of the services and occasional offices during the year, with visits from Fortescue and other assisting clergy, Thrupp of Musbury and Henry Cartwright among them. The guild and other church societies continued to meet and earlier in the year the Bishop of Exeter had visited for a confirmation service at which Colyton presented a healthy 38 candidates.

Then on 17 September 1880 the *Western Times* ran an article attacking "Father Gritz" as they called him. It was, following the usual practice of that publication, riddled with blatant untruths but with just enough at the heart of it to provoke Gueritz to angry response. The excuse for writing the article at all was that the paper claimed to have discovered the use of *The Servers' Mass Book* in Colyton, a copy being in the possession of a "chorister". A manual of instruction to servers—not choristers—as to their duties and deportment in church, it was held up as an example of the attempt by the "Rits" to Romanize the "Protestant Church as by law established". An objective reading of the article reveals not only the absurdities of some of the statements, but also the ignorance of the writer concerning the Church of England. Equally obvious is a deliberate blurring between the instructions of the author of the book and Gueritz' own practice in Colyton. In spite of all the absurdities, there were two barbs which may well have stuck. Gueritz was accused of betraying the Protestant supporters in Plymouth who made his ordination possible, and also it was pointed out at length that a Roman Catholic priest in Exeter had made it clear that his church regarded Gueritz and his fellow "Rits" as no more Catholic than the Congregationalist minister. The article concluded with the assertion that Colyton "is supplied with Ritualistic Monks and Nuns, we are told, who are sent down from Clewer in Oxford diocese".

Gueritz made a typically strident response. Although it was undeniable that he had been sent to university with the support of an Evangelical society, the connections asserted in the article with certain Plymouth clergy were simply not true. He denied that *The Servers' Mass Book* was in use in Colyton, and as to the assertion about monks and nuns from Clewer, it was patently evident that this was a deliberate fabrication. Apart from the fact that there never were monks at Clewer, Gueritz' own response makes the situation clear:

> There are no such persons from Clewer or anywhere else in the parish. There is not the slightest ground for your statement. My only helpers are ordinary residents in the parish, who kindly give their services as district visitors, Sunday school teachers &c.[1]

Whether or not that exchange was a contributing factor, at the beginning of December again came signs of ill health. Several services were cancelled, Fortescue came back for ten days in the middle of the month, but Gueritz recovered enough to take the Christmas Day services with the help of a Revd Walter Fell.

It does seem as if Gueritz was someone to whom ritualist clergy, unsure of their future in the Church of England, could come for space to reflect away from their official duties. In return, they would help in the parish. Walter Fell was one of a number who appeared briefly in Colyton before either moving on to a new ministry or ceasing to hold office altogether. Fell was made deacon in 1879 to serve in Sutton on Plym and held that curacy, at least on paper, until 1881. After that, he lived at a private address in Bayswater and held no further appointments in the Church of England. His brief time assisting in Colyton over Christmas 1880 was possibly the turning point.

Gueritz was still in the parish in January 1881 and took a service. He was able to attend a meeting of the school board on 18 February, but clearly all was not well. A solution was found which needed the approval of the bishop and the appropriate churchwardens but which would provide the needed respite. Soon after the meeting of the school board, Mamerto and Anne Gueritz decamped to Templeton, leaving Fortescue to manage Colyton and fill in for his father in various ways. Templeton was a much quieter parish, with few occasional offices, moderate involvement in the secular life of the parish and none of the guilds and societies which took so much time and energy. The 1881 census shows Mamerto and Anne living in the Templeton Rectory with two domestics, a gardener and a housekeeper. In Colyton, Jose Fortescue was living at the vicarage with his younger sister Antonia, while Adelina and her husband were close by in Queen's Square.

During 1881, Mamerto's absence began to be felt although Fortescue was proving to be an able deputy notwithstanding his relative inexperience in running a parish. He had, after all, a lifetime of observing his father to work from. Early in June, the Mutual Friendly Societies of Colyton held their anniversary celebrations. Fortescue preached what was described as an impressive sermon and then at the dinner afterwards

> Mr. F. Stokes proposed the toast to the "Bishop and Clergy of the Diocese", coupling with the toast the name of the Rev. F. L. Gueritz whom they all

loved and respected. (Fortescue) . . . in reply regretted the absence of his
father, the Rev. M. Gueritz who would have been present but for ill health.[2]

A week later, there was a meeting of the school board, with the same Mr Stokes
in the chair. He, with Gueritz and Dommett, had been defeated in the election
five years previously. It was a meeting which appears to have been remarkably
good-natured when compared with earlier performances. However, the mistress
of the girls' school had tendered her resignation, having been discovered by the
schools inspectors to have inflated the numbers in the attendance registers so as to
raise the level of government financial support. When this matter had been fully
explored Mr Hann, formerly of the Chantry Bridge Tanyard, expressed the feeling
that the absence of the vicar for 12 months, with non-attendance at meetings
and non-residence in the parish, might preclude him from the chairmanship,
even from membership of the board. The fact that this was June and Mamerto
had been absent since January reveals that the parish exchange was generally
understood to be for at least a year. Hann was not particularly an opponent of
Gueritz, but neither was he always an active supporter. He had allowed the use of
the Tanyard for the Sisters of Mercy but was later quite strident in his opposition
to Mamerto using the school board room for his own activities without prior
permission from the board. At this point, however, he seems simply to have been
seeking to explore the effects of Gueritz' absence and to ensure that the board
could function properly.

Towards the end of January 1882, Gueritz began to take up the reins in Colyton
again, still with the assistance of Fortescue. In fact, Fortescue was there for all of
March, but from mid-April Gueritz was back and fully functional. In July and
August, he had the assistance of J. S. Chope, the curate of Sidbury, which would
have helped, but the event which really cheered Gueritz and indeed the entire
parish took place in June. During the time standing in for his father, Fortescue
had wooed himself a bride. Jose Fortescue Lawrence Gueritz and Lucy Octavia
Elton married in Colyton Church on 20 June. Lucy, with her mother, sisters and
invalid brother, had been resident for some years at Colyton House, following
the death of her father, the rector of Whitestaunton. The Elton sisters and their
mother had been staunch supporters of Gueritz since their arrival at Colyton

House and gave their considerable energies to the social and pastoral life of the parish in a variety of ways.

Further support was in the offing. In November, the new curate, the Revd Charles James Parsons, arrived, another Oxford man who had already been ordained priest and was able to be of considerable support. The January parish magazine of 1883 was effusive in its welcome.

The year 1883 was comparatively quiet. Parsons the curate and Gueritz between them shared the load of baptisms, weddings and funerals, as well as the Sunday and daily services. The district visitors' work continued, together with that of the Dorcas Society. W. H. B. Proby was still, despite his assumed alienation from the incumbent, making annual donations to the society. An interesting addition to the parish magazine was the publication of the railway timetable. It was now possible to depart from Colyton at 7.29 in the morning and arrive in time for luncheon in London at 1.15! In April, William Smith, the bookseller, opened a sub-office for the SPCK which made it much easier to access theological and liturgical material, such as *The Servers' Mass Book*.

Also by 1883, Henry Frank Gueritz, Mamerto and Anne's youngest son, was back from New Zealand, where he had been since 1879. He soon began to feature in the social life of the parish, especially in those entertainments organized by church members. He was already quite a skilful cricketer and tennis player and evidently popular with the young people of his generation. His first appearance of the year was in the Easter Entertainment, which had "a rich and varied finale scene from H.M.S. Pinafore in which Mr H. F. Gueritz personated the First Lord and sang, "I'm the Monarch of the Sea" to much acclaim".[3]

Frank was evidently coming into his own. The entertainment in June saw him with a higher profile, and it was presented "under the management of Mr. H. F. Gueritz to whose care and energy the success is mainly due. An old ballad, sung by Mr. G. Gueritz, was as popular as ever."

Mamerto George was home from his work in Sarawak for a period of leave. He sang in the entertainment and took part in a tableau with his sister Antonia, but by June 1883 his period of leave on full pay had expired and he had only three months left on half pay in which to journey back to Borneo. He would not be able to stay much longer. His brother Frank also took ship to return to New Zealand and sailed from Plymouth on 15 December, bound for Christchurch. Their sister and brother-in-law, Mary and Reginald, had been in New Zealand since 1879 and there they had four children. The youngest, a son, had been born on 25 October, Reginald Mamerto Mortimer.

After Frank first arrived in Christchurch, also in 1879 but later than his sister, he had taken up the mastership of a school and had matriculated to the University of New Zealand. In 1883, he returned to resume a career in Christchurch, although there was a thought that he might travel to join his brother George. He would only have been in Christchurch a few months before there was devastating news from Devon which would affect them all.

As Advent 1883 began, Mamerto addressed his parishioners with a plea that makes clear his continuing priorities. The battles over ritual and Catholic teaching were largely won, at least among Colyton churchgoers. The focus now was on holiness and devotion, which he expressed in his Advent challenge:

> O dear souls, for whom Christ died, still precious in his sight, to who he is now calling by these words of mine, I pray you in His Name, come to Him now.

Did ever an itinerant Evangelist make a more fervent plea?

The first quarter of 1884 saw Mamerto Gueritz back on fine combative form. The Salvation Army were active in the parish, having established themselves in the old Wesleyan chapel in Rosemary Lane, and Gueritz was highly critical. In the April magazine he was clearly not in a diplomatic frame of mind. He wrote of

> the evil results of their presence . . . the wicked and disgusting profanity with which ignorant people—roaring out sacred words to rowdy tunes— shouting out Hallelujah! In every kind of profane manner.

Before that battle had time to escalate the first of the year's tragedies struck. Antonia Gueritz had been ill, and on 26 May she died aged only 25. Antonia's quiet life had been spent in the service of others. She was a district visitor and a member of the Dorcas Society, but her real joy was working with the children, both in the Children's Guild and in the Sunday school where she was superintendent, and, quite obviously, the children loved her in return. The family was devastated. So were the children of the parish.

Friends gathered from near and far to support them and share in their grief. Edward Peregrine was home from the far east. Stuckey Coles celebrated the requiem and took the funeral, and 50 of the children processed with the coffin, all carrying white blossoms to lay on it for the burial.

As so often happens in a family, death was followed by birth. On 17 July, at Templeton Rectory, Lucy Octavia gave birth to a son, Elton Lawrence Gueritz.

Later in July, the Sunday School Festival was held as usual, but this year it was a solemn occasion, quite unlike the usual party atmosphere. Edward, having left the Bank of New Zealand and joined the British North Borneo Company, was made redundant early in 1884, which is how he came to be in Colyton at the time of his sister's death. He was at the festival, supporting and assisting Mamerto, as he gave each child a small gift as a token of Antonia's touch upon their lives. At the same festival, it was announced that Stuckey Coles was about to resign the rectory of Shepton Beauchamp, having accepted an appointment which was to become of national importance. He was to be the chaplain of the Pusey Memorial at Oxford, now known as Pusey House.

Whether called home by Antonia's death, concern for their infant son or, according to one account, Reginald's own ill health, Mary Louisa and Reginald Mortimer returned to Colyton in late July or early August. Once the bellringers got to hear of their arrival, there was a peal of bells to welcome them home, but then tragedy struck a second time. Their infant son Reginald Mamerto died; he was just ten months old. Fortescue Gueritz officiated at the funeral, and little Reginald was buried on 27 August. Grief upon grief.[4]

Time rolls on and so does parish life. The round of festivals must be celebrated, even though it be with a broken heart. Harvest time came and Mamerto, Fortescue and Reginald supported each other in the work to be done. The harvest party had to be organized, as did the service in church, so they set to. It might have been hoped that the critical press would take note of the sorrows of the year and refrain from any comment, but that was not to be. However, as attacks go, this one was rather muted. Focussing rather on the different methods employed by the Salvation Army and the parish priest to draw people into their services, an attempt at a derisory account of the ritual simply served once more to leave a detailed account of the service. A comment on Reginald Mortimer which began with a sneer at his change of name from Snook ended with the assertion:

> and the appearance in Colyton pulpit of the son of Mr. Snook, improved in both name and position, was a matter of considerable interest, especially as in respect of style he shines as a preacher.[5]

An account of the concert and dance which Mamerto Gueritz had arranged began with a faint air of disdain but reached a point of approval:

> The rector (sic) was master of ceremonies, his son assisting. The choir sang two or three pretty glees and the song by the Rev. J. F. L. Gueritz was—"I go a maid to woo, quoth he" . . . Miss Gillingham sang "The Three Fishers" in excellent style . . . the room was crowded.

It seems the correspondent for the *Western Times* could not decide whether he was being nasty or nice. What a dilemma!

On 9 October, there was a note in the vestry journal which simply read "Pusey Memorial". On that day in 1884, the Pusey Memorial Library was opened by the Bishop of Oxford, John Mackarness, who, while he was incumbent of Honiton and prebendary of Exeter Cathedral, had been a friend and supporter of Gueritz. The first principal of Pusey House was Charles Gore, who founded the Community of the Resurrection, Frank Brightman was the librarian and V. S. S. Coles the chaplain. There were other champions of the Oxford Movement in attendance, among them Henry Parry Liddon and Edward King. Aside from those named there were, as Coles later wrote, "about sixty of our friends".[6] The list of attendees has not survived. If Gueritz was not among them in body, as the vestry journal attests, he was there in spirit.

As 1884 drew to a close, Christmas was celebrated with the customary round of services and carol singing. Little did the Gueritz family know that the year had not yet exhausted its store of grief. On 23 December, on board the river launch *Bujang Baram*, Mamerto George Gueritz died. The news would not reach Colyton immediately, but 1884 has to be, in the story of the Gueritz family, a true *annus horribilis*.

The next few years, apart from periods of ill health, became something of an "Indian summer" for Mamerto and Anne. During 1885, there was family pride when Jose Fortescue was elected rural dean of the Tiverton deanery. In Exeter diocese, this was a sign not only of the bishop's confidence but primarily of the respect of the clergy of the deanery chapter. This was not, as in other dioceses, a bishop's appointment. The clergy elected and nominated, and the bishop was free to accept or refuse. Bishop Bickersteth was happy to accept. Indeed, the following year after visiting Templeton for a confirmation, Bickersteth stayed the night with Fortescue and Lucy at the parsonage. The impression they made must have been favourable because later the same month Fortescue was offered the living of Swymbridge in North Devon and shortly afterwards moved to take up post. The appointment was generally celebrated, apart of course from the sectarian press which lost no opportunity to attack anyone bearing the name of Gueritz. However, this preferment meant that it would be more difficult for Fortescue to spend time at Colyton. It could take most of a day to travel to Colyton from Swymbridge.

Reginald Mortimer remained in Colyton and was licensed by the bishop as assistant curate, an appointment he held for five years until 1889. There is no doubt that his ministry in Colyton provided a supportive and stabilizing presence, not only for Gueritz but for the parish community as a whole.

Reginald's presence, however, did not lessen the flow of supportive clergy from other places, who would come for a weekend or longer and "preach for their keep". Stuckey Coles' visits required less of the Gueritz household than some others because Coles had his own residence in Seaton, just three miles away. In 1886, there was a gloriously confusing entry in the vestry journal to the effect that the Revd C. Le Geyt had preached. Charles James Le Geyt of Stoke Newington, who became a close friend of Mamerto, died at the end of 1877, worn out by years of conflict and hard work. This visitor was C. A. Le Geyt of Beer, just along the coast from Seaton, and not visibly related to the famous Charles James. Also among the visitors in 1887 was J. W. Bennett, who had so ably cared for the parish in 1869 and 1870 and had steered the Revd D. J. Mackey from the diaconate to the priesthood.

Others were local clergy from all over East Devon, and it is clear from the deanery chapter minutes and the records of the Choral Union that the younger Tractarians and Ritualists regarded Mamerto as something of a figurehead and a veteran of the conflicts of earlier years.

The year 1888 was a demanding one. An outbreak of typhoid fever in Colyton meant that the district visitors were needed more than ever. There are always those who respond to such crises by seeking to apportion blame. The Chamber of Feoffees had provided water for the town and therefore, in the minds of some, they were somehow at fault. Gueritz, himself having been a Feoffee for 13 years, was very quick to come to their defence, writing a very firm rebuttal in the parish magazine and pointing out that the Feoffees had only ever provided a water supply for domestic cleaning and sewage purposes and not for drinking water. The outbreak was caused by wells being too near to cesspits, which was the responsibility of the householders and not any public body.

On the national scene, during 1888 the Church Association presented a petition to the Archbishop of Canterbury demanding that Edward King, Bishop of Lincoln, be tried for illegal liturgical acts, such as the placing of lighted candles on the altar, facing east during the prayer of consecration, mixing water with the wine in the chalice and making the sign of the cross at the absolution and the blessing. King had been among those present at the opening of Pusey House in Oxford. The Church Association's part in the trial and imprisonment of ritualist clergy and some of the less savoury methods they used both then and in the case of Bishop King should have prepared the Tractarian clergy and their more ritualist brethren for just such an event. When the archbishop decided to proceed to trial there was an immediate wave of sympathy and support for the saintly Bishop King, who in his spiritual and devotional life exemplified the real heart of the Oxford Movement. Support flooded in from brother bishops and from working-class people whose lives had been touched by him. There were special services held all around the country, indeed all around the world, and Colyton would not be left out. In March 1889, Mamerto Gueritz wrote of the trial in the parish magazine, and what he wrote revealed how he had himself grown and changed over the years of persecution. After all, Bishop King was accused of nothing more than Gueritz and most of the clergy of East Devon had practised at every celebration of the Holy Communion for the previous two decades. Gueritz warmly encouraged his people to pray for Bishop King, but then, in referring to the Church Association, instead of the angry condemnation we might have expected, Gueritz wrote:

This portrait of the family was taken in 1887 in the vicarage garden in Colyton. From left to right are Anne Derby Gueritz next to her grandson John Lawrence Mortimer, then the unmistakable figure of Mamerto Gueritz and below him in the little handcart are Dorothy Antonia and Aimee Winifred. Reginald Mortimer stands next to Mary Louisa, always called "Min", and on her lap George, who was not yet one. Finally, on the right of the picture there is Edith Mary, firstborn of the nine Mortimer children.

We must not try to vanquish but rather to win on all sides. "Pray for the peace of Jerusalem, they shall prosper that love thee".

It seems that the old warrior had become something of a conciliator, although not in every circumstance.

Also in 1888, a chapel of ease was built in Colyford. This was the gift of the Scarborough family, who continued to support the work there for many years. Although initially a private chapel, it was used as a chapel of ease for the residents of Colyford and was declared open by the Bishop of Exeter, Edward Bickersteth, during a ceremony on 17 January 1889.

John Impey Scarborough also had a house built close to the chapel to provide a residence for a curate, but that was not ready until 1891.

April of 1889 saw the passing of another legendary figure and personal friend. W. H. Monk, organist at Stoke Newington, champion of congregational church music and supporter of the revival of Gregorian chant, was laid to rest. Sadly, the Bear Inn at Colyton would see him no more.

May brought the news of the impending departure of Reginald Mortimer. He was to become rector of Roborough in North Devon, which was not very distant from Swymbridge where his brother-in-law, Fortescue, was incumbent. There was an emotional farewell ceremony in Colyton, in which the people of the parish gave thanks for his ministry of more than four years in the parish. Reginald was presented with a purse of 57 sovereigns, which in itself was a mark of the affection in which he, "Minnie" and their children were held.

Mamerto Gueritz was not to be left to bear the ministerial burden alone, and June saw the arrival of a new assistant curate, the Revd George Ellis of St John's College, Cambridge. Ellis had been ordained priest on Trinity Sunday and already had considerable experience as both layman and deacon in town missions and parish work.

The Sunday School Festival in August 1889 was held with customary exuberance, but the day was given an added excitement by a visit from Canon H. P. Liddon. It was to be his last appearance in the parish for he died almost a year later, but there was no shadow of that on the time he spent with Gueritz. They walked around the parish together, visiting the scenes of Liddon's youth and especially taking in the clear signs of the Church Revival which were to be seen in

St Andrew's Church. There had been many developments since Liddon had first commented on Gueritz' activities 30 years previously. After seeing the church, Gueritz took him to meet the present owners of The Grove where he had lived as a child. To Liddon's delight, they allowed him to roam the house, which was little changed, and childhood memories filled the visit until it was time for him to leave. The affection that Liddon always expressed for Colyton and its people was amply returned.

The work of the parish continued, and Gueritz' own commitment to mission, complemented by that of Ellis his new curate, was affirmed at St Andrew's tide by a visit from the diocesan missioner, Canon Atherton, whose eloquence as a preacher drew large congregations to the special services arranged to prepare for Advent. Then, of course, there were the Christmas celebrations and various parties and treats. One such, attended by Mamerto and for which he gave the use of St Andrew's Hall, was given by a Mrs Masters who invited all the poor parishioners over 60 years of age to a so-called tea party. Around 60 of the older people came and were entertained with songs and recitations. One element of the donor's generosity might give rise to comment were it to be offered today:

> There was a plentiful supply of pipes, tobacco and snuff for the delectation
> of the old folks, and refreshments in the way of cake, apples and oranges
> were supplied . . . to those who were not occupied by the fragrant weed.[7]

From the middle of 1890, with Mamerto's health again giving concern, much of the work fell on the shoulders of Ellis, the curate. The Annual Club Day in June was a major event, for which Reginald Mortimer had returned to the parish. He and Ellis led the day, but Mamerto and Anne could not attend. Great concern was expressed that Gueritz had not yet made a better recovery from his ill health. It was around this time that the same bout of illness induced Gueritz to relinquish his role as precentor of the East Devon Choral Union. In August, Mamerto was prevented from taking as much of a part in the Sunday School Festival as was his custom for the same reason. Although he and Anne Gueritz welcomed everyone to the vicarage at the end of the day, they could not take part in the perambulation of the parish.

Towards the end of the year, George Ellis left for his own parish, and in October Frank Gueritz also departed for a new challenge. During 1883, while he was home from New Zealand, Frank had begun to take his place in the story and to establish himself as a character in his own right. This was interrupted by a return to his work in New Zealand, but it was resumed on his return to Colyton in 1887. Frank did not attempt to emulate his brothers, nor did he follow his father into the priesthood. He found his own way; a way which allowed him to offer his exuberant talents to the community and still develop a lay pastoral ministry. Without doubt this had its roots in the revelation of the place of the laity in ministry that Mamerto had experienced in Stoke Newington and the role lay readers might play in that. It was during his time at Stoke Newington that it was reported that:

> The Rev. M. Gueritz added some practical advice . . . (and) he thought the reluctance shown to use laymen in the conduct of religious services was natural at this time but that by degrees it would melt away.

On 3 October 1890, Frank Gueritz left Colyton to take up duties as a lay reader at the parish of Shermanbury in Sussex. As he left Colyton, there was a call in the *United Parishes Magazine* for added support for Mamerto, especially bearing in mind the work Frank had undertaken both with the choir and in the wider parish.

That support was forthcoming and Gueritz carried on with frequent visits also from Fortescue Gueritz and Reginald Mortimer. This, with the aid of a number of clergy from East Devon and beyond, allowed Gueritz to carry on through Advent and Christmas. In the new year, plans began to be laid for Lent and Easter, but Gueritz' health was still poor and it was thought that a change of climate would assist his restoration. In March 1891, the parish magazine carried the notice:

> The Vicar will probably be absent for some weeks in the course of this month and the next month. He hopes to make a satisfactory arrangement for the care of the parish and the services of the church in his absence . . . Wherever he may be he will be thinking of you all at Easter and begs you will not forget him in your prayers.

The newspapers reported the proposed journey, and it is worth quoting the account in full simply because of the profound contrast with the tone of earlier journalistic commentary:

> The esteemed Vicar of Colyton (The Rev. M. Gueritz) has left his parishioners for a short period for the purpose of taking a trip to Spain. The Rev. gentleman was, I understand, born in Spain, but left the country at a very tender age. He is now travelling to the land of his birth and doubtless on coming back to "dear old England" he will have many pleasant experiences to relate. Colytonians to whatever sect they belong, join in wishing that the Vicar may return much benefited in health.[8]

When the newspaper slurs that Gueritz had endured during the period from 1860 and into the 1880s are recalled, the contrast could hardly be more profound. It must be acknowledged that the *Daily Gazette* where this article appeared was neither owned nor controlled by sectarian interests, which were the *fons et origo* of many of the attacks, and the *Gazette* had, in the past, given favourable reviews of the work of Gueritz with the East Devon Choral Association. However, the kind of appreciation expressed in this article must have been refreshing to say the least.

Before Gueritz left, it was announced that the Revd A. A. Brockway would officiate as Gueritz' *locum tenens*, being formally appointed curate in charge. Brockway was a priest of the Episcopal Church in America and was staying with Albert Edwards and his wife at The Fennery in Queen Street. Edwards was the organist at the parish church and also assistant overseer and bailiff to the Feoffees. Brockway seems to have been both popular and effective, and when he spoke at a meeting of the Guild of St Andrew, there was a large attendance to hear him discourse on the Church in the United States and on its own large and influential "Brotherhood of St Andrew".

Brockway did not have to manage Lent unsupported. Before his departure, Gueritz had already arranged for the Revd Richard Turner to give a course of sermons on Thursday evenings on behalf of the Diocesan Mission. Ultimately Turner would return to Colyton as incumbent but that belongs to a later part of the story.

Early in May news came of Gueritz' progress, but by this time he was already on his way home:

> Our Vicar is finding much interest and gaining improvement in health from his present tour in Spain, the land of his birth.

On 17 May, there was a public show of affection and welcome when Gueritz arrived back in Colyton, and there was a peal of bells to mark his return. The same notice in the parish magazine recorded:

> The parish has been well cared for in every way by the Priest-in-charge, the Rev A. A. Brockway, whose zealous and able work has been greatly appreciated.

On 20 May, having preached an "eloquent sermon" at the Club Day service, Albert Brockway took his leave of the people of Colyton.

It seems that Gueritz had become a competent photographer. This is remarkable when it is considered that it was only in 1888 that the first Kodak camera for amateurs was available. Each camera could take a hundred pictures, and then had to be returned to the factory in Rochester for the images to be processed. That probably explains why it was not until February the following year that Gueritz gave two evenings of entertainment, sharing with his parishioners the tour he had made in Spain. His talk "was made very interesting by a large number of Magic Lantern Illustrations of views of the principal places, scenery and people".

While his father was away touring Spain and France, Frank had returned for at least one visit and joined in the choir outing of 18 June to Lyme Regis. It may seem strange to us but some of the junior choristers, living only three miles inland, had never seen the sea! The service was held in Lyme Church at 4 o'clock and "[t]he choirs sang, the musicians played their best. Mr F. Gueritz, the conductor, kept all well together and the archdeacon preached an excellent sermon."

The next month brought the annual Sunday school treat. The previous year Mamerto had been too ill to take much part, but in 1891 he was very much his old self. Ministry to the children had always been a priority with Gueritz and his empathy with the young was demonstrated in various ways during the day, from

the "bright little service taken by the vicar", to the short address to the children
which was a perfect model in its clear, affectionate, but telling simplicity. The
usual perambulation of the town took place, and Mamerto was accompanied by
"Mr H.F. Gueritz, who was on a visit to his old home and who added much to the
hilarity". Wherever he went, Frank Gueritz brought the gift of laughter.

The rest of 1891 brought several things of particular note. In October, there
was another visit from Canon Atherton, one of the diocesan missioners. There
were services for everyone, including the children, and all were, apparently, well
and enthusiastically attended. These missions had become a part of the parish
calendar but even more significantly had become part of the diocesan agenda.
All that Gueritz in the later 1870s had set out to establish with the help of Stuckey
Coles and others, 20 years later had become mainstream in the diocese of Exeter.
The second thing was the Advent sermon series. This, which had been such an
innovation two decades previously, was now considered to be an immutable part
of the life of the church in Colyton. Clergy from across the diocese were willing
to take part.

As 1892 dawned, Colyton was visited with another contagion. Gueritz
commented:

> During the last two months our parish has suffered greatly from Influenza.
> We never remember during the last thirty years anything like so great an
> amount of sickness. It has carried off many of our aged and infirm, and
> it seems to have caused a general feeling of nervousness and depression.[9]

Gradually as the year passed the depression lifted, and in June 1892 new curates
were welcomed to the parish. Arthur Sandbach was a newly ordained deacon and
would stay with Gueritz until 1895. I. J. Rosser was licensed to the parish at the
same time but had evidently been ministering at St Michael's, Colyford, at the
instigation of the Scarborough family, for some time beforehand. Rosser's ministry
focussed mainly on Colyford and the congregation of St Michael's. The mood in
Colyton may have lightened as the year passed, but there was another sadness in
store for the Gueritz family. Charles Mamerto, the five-year-old son of Fortescue
and Lucy, died of diphtheria. The loss affected Lucy and Fortescue very deeply,
and they were given compassionate leave by the bishop. Elton Lawrence, their

elder son, was being educated at the Devon County School at West Buckland, where he was already a promising pupil. Quite possibly the family only stayed in Swymbridge until Elton was ready to move schools and then departed the scene of their sadness.

Two events in November 1892 had an effect on life in Colyton but in quite different ways. First there was the public meeting to raise support for the restoration and reordering of the church, which we have already noted, but November also brought Frank Gueritz back to Colyton. He had served as a licenced lay reader for two years, gaining credibility and skill as a minister away from his hometown, and now returned ready to fill that role alongside his father. He instituted and led a bible class for men that was to meet on Monday evenings at 7.30. Given Gueritz' earlier condemnation of sectarian misuse of the Bible, Frank would have needed to be skilled in biblical exegesis in order to meet his father's standards!

This was followed in January 1893 by the institution of short weekday services for men, at which Frank was normally the one to give the address. He was also the prime mover in founding the working men's club, which was to prove a great success especially with those on the margins of church life. However, other aspects of the exuberant talent of Henry Frank Gueritz have already been remarked and could not long be kept unexpressed. It was to be exercised in ways that perhaps might not then have been deemed appropriate for a priest but were acceptable in a lay reader. This was after all an age in which a bishop, advertising for a chaplain, specified that he must abstain from dancing!

January was to be a very busy month. First there was a "Juveniles Party" at which Frank, with Miss K. White and Mrs Edwards, "afforded a great deal of entertainment to a large company". Then, less than a week later, on 5 January, he organized a party at the vicarage for unmarried ladies and gentlemen. There were impromptu charades in which "Mr F. Gueritz, with his ever-ready tact and merriment, was a leading spirit". And finally, for that month at least, Frank and seven of his friends organized and hosted the Bachelors' Ball, with the stated aim of reducing the number of bachelors.

Another excitement of 1893 centred once more around the activities of W. H. B. Proby. He already owned the Catholic Apostolic or Irvingite Chapel in King Street, Colyton. On 29 July, the newspapers brought news of another chapel, this time at Pottlelake, referred to locally as "Potlake". This was the chapel of St John the

Baptist and Proby was described as the proprietor. Some of the materials for the rood beam, the altar and altar rails had been brought from Northleigh, taken from the church and from one of Proby's manorial cottages. The bell was given by the Revd William Bramley-Moore of Russell Square in London, there was stained glass made by Drake of Exeter and the whole was built by Asa Richards of Colyton. The Sunday before, after teaching a class of children, Proby had led the afternoon service from the Prayer Book and then explained that he would not be preaching, as such, nor celebrating the Holy Communion, because he was not authorized to do so. It seems that he did not keep entirely to this discipline.

Naturally, Gueritz could not let this rest, so the parish magazine carried a warning to parishioners:

> The Rev. W. H. B. Proby has built a Chapel at Potlake in which he intends to hold services. He has also been inviting people to attend them as connected with the Church. I am therefore compelled to give public notice to my parishioners that he is acting without my consent, and that the Bishop entirely refuses to authorize him to officiate as a clergyman of the Church of England.

Proby claimed that he had not invited local people to the services and did not intend to do so. He pointed out that as the services were of an entirely private character, he needed sanction from neither vicar nor bishop. One is forced to wonder where the class of children and the congregation for the opening service had come from if they had not been invited in some way. Gueritz' reply was simply to repeat his warning to parishioners against "the so called Chapel of St John and its services, which will be neither Church nor Irvingite, but private, that is, Probyite".

Pottlelake stayed on Gueritz' mind for the rest of the year, and in January 1894 he wrote of a sense of "age and decay" and his sadness that with the passing of the years what was once an easy and pleasant walk to visit the people of that part of the parish had now become toilsome. He was just over 70 at this point, was becoming unwell again and evidently feeling the years.

The same could not be said of his youngest son who, although in his late thirties, showed signs neither of age nor of any inclination to be sedate. Once more Frank's dramatic flair was in demand. At the entertainment the previous Christmas he and a friend from Exeter, G. H. Kingdon, reprised their lauded double act "Cox and Box", which from all accounts was a distant relation of "Hinge and Bracket". They raised quite a sum for the restoration fund. Then in February there was the Grand Christmas Pantomime, which Frank devised and directed.

As Easter drew near, Mamerto Gueritz was clearly unwell and others stepped in to help with the services and the series of addresses. Reginald Mortimer came, as did Fortescue, who led the Holy Week observances and the Three Hours Devotion on Good Friday. Frank was called into service, giving devotional addresses. Other clergy from the area helped and all carried on just as planned. Soon Mamerto was well enough to send a message of gratitude for their help and "the kind sympathy during a long illness". Then at Trinity tide the curate, Arthur Sandbach, was ordained priest, and the parish was fully supported once more. Mamerto gave public thanks for his curate's "faithful and diligent" ministry as a deacon.

After 35 years of ministry in Colyton, Mamerto Gueritz began to experience what it was to have a younger generation of priests taking for granted those things for which he and his contemporaries had fought hard battles. His faithfulness to Church principles and his championing of the right to use the Church's liturgy according to ancient tradition were beginning to be seen by a succeeding generation as "echoes of battles long ago". Given that East Devon was beginning to be something of a late Tractarian if not fully Ritualist enclave, the newcomers assumed the battles to have been won. This assumption was shaken briefly in 1895. Ritualism was still at this stage, in some of its manifestations, the target of legal action. Bishop Bickersteth in his visitation address of that year attempted to bring some order to the situation regarding vestments and ceremonial, which provoked Gueritz to a rather intemperate response. He called the actions of his bishop "despotic" and quite unwisely suggested that the Bishop of Rome might be a better pastor of the clergy. The delighted response of the opponents of Ritualism was expressed in suggestions that Gueritz should go to Rome if that was where his heart lay, but as we have seen that is not at all where his heart was. His identity as a priest was rooted in the belief that the Church of England had retained its catholicity and was as true a part of the One Holy Catholic and Apostolic Church as was the Church of Rome.[10]

Be that as it may, when the deanery chapter met, Gueritz had to endure fresh new curates excitedly proffering ideas as innovations that he had long ago espoused and even pioneered. It must have been rather like what Hurrell Froude's Zs had felt about the first Tractarians. Or perhaps more like what the twenty-first-century training incumbent feels when the new curate proffers as a "Fresh Expression of Ministry" something which he or she had developed 20 years earlier.

At a deanery chapter meeting in June 1895, a suggestion was made regarding a mission conference for the deanery and the involvement of the major societies, the Society for the Propagation of the Gospel, the Church Missionary Society, and the Society for Promoting Christian Knowledge. The outcome was that "such a meeting was left to private venture though many encouraging remarks were made".[11]

Gueritz had been supporting these societies and holding local missions for decades and not a few of the deanery clergy had taken part. Another of the younger clergy was keen to emphasize the need to include children in the life of the Church and to allow non-communicating attendance at special services. This was 20 years after Gueritz had introduced the Society of the Holy Childhood. Yet another member spoke zealously on the need for a "personal experience of the presence of the Holy Spirit" perhaps evidencing a proto-charismatic approach. The minutes record that Gueritz responded:

> [S]piritual religion is the work of the Holy Spirit but he was very jealous of the Church's function as the chief channel for the working of that Holy Spirit. For the present necessity he advocated "non-communicating attendance" as likely to lead up to more general communicating. He touched on "The Real Presence".[12]

In other words, Gueritz rejected the individualistic and subjective for that which had been proven in the shared and sacramental life of the Church. This battle-scarred Anglo-Catholic, a champion of the mass as the centre of spiritual life and one who had endured vilification, prosecution and slander for the sake of Catholic teaching, appears to have received with grace the enthusiasms of clergy who were scarcely born when he was first defending the faith in Penzance.

Notes

1. *Western Times*, Friday, 17 September 1880 and 24 September 1880.

2. *Exeter and Plymouth Gazette*, Friday, 10 June 1881.

3. *Colyton Parish Magazine*, May 1883.

4. Colyton service registers, 25 August 1884, South West Heritage Centre ref. 3483A/PR14.

5. *Western Times*, Saturday, 27 September 1884.

6. J. F. Briscoe (ed.), *V.S.S. Coles* (London: Mowbray, 1930), p. 200.

7. *Colyton Parish Magazine*, January 1890. As an aside, as late as 1988, the landlady of the Gerrard Arms in Colyton was still taking orders for snuff. Notable among her customers was Mr George Solway, who remembered Mamerto Gueritz and the great occasion of his funeral. It may also be appropriate to compare the lot of the over-sixties poor in Colyton with the national mean. In a report for the proposed National Provident Society for the Poor, Canon Blackley wrote, "Of all the people in this country who are over sixty years of age and who have passed the power of earning, forty five per cent are paupers when they die."

8. *Devon and Exeter Daily Gazette*, Thursday, 26 March 1891.

9. *Colyton Parish Magazine*, February 1892.

10. The Book of Common Prayer omits the "Holy" and instead has "One Catholick and Apostolick Church". In several copies of the Prayer Book used by Gueritz the word "Holy" has been carefully inserted.

11. *Honiton Deanery Chapter Minute Books*, South West Heritage Centre, Colyton 3483A acc 7774.

12. *Honiton Deanery Chapter Minutes*.

1 4

"The Long Day Closes":
Final years, retirement and death

The year 1896 brought a number of changes. One such, while seemingly insignificant, was indicative of a wider shift in the way the deanery parishes communicated. Hitherto the *Colyton Parish Magazine* had been published as part of the *United Parish Magazine* which included Axminster, Awliscombe, Colyton, Dalwood, Hawkchurch, Honiton, Kilmington, Membury, Musbury, Seeton and Beer, and Shute. Bound in with every copy was the current edition of *The Dawn of Day*, the SPCK monthly magazine. The importance of that publication in promoting Tractarian ideals, Anglo-Catholic theology and the search for personal holiness can hardly be overstated. Week after week stories were told of people in every walk of life triumphing over their own sinfulness or that of others. Alongside that was the careful exposition of the relationship between Church teaching and personal experience. The list of parishes which shared in this *United Magazine* gives an indication of those places and clergy which were overtly Tractarian in their theology and, in varying degrees, ritualist in their liturgy.

Various pressures, both financial and administrative, resulted in Colyton, Seaton and Beer producing their own edition and the other parishes either printing individual magazines or, like Colyton, making smaller, more manageable units. They all still had *The Dawn of Day* included. The advantage of the reduced participation and circulation is that more details of parish structures and activities, both secular and ecclesiastical, were recorded. The staff of the parishes were listed and their responsibilities shown clearly. The parish of Colyton now had two licenced clergy, Mamerto Gueritz and I. J. Rosser, and also a lay reader in the person of H. F. Gueritz. The ancient office of sidesman had been revived to assist the work of the churchwardens, and there were six of them in office. There were

20 Sunday school teachers, with Frank Gueritz superintending the boys, Miss Agnes Elton the girls and Miss Kate White the infants. There were nine district visitors in Colyton and four at work in Colyford. The ringers were all named in the magazine and the Colyton Company of the Church Lads' Brigade, which had been launched by Mamerto Gueritz in 1895, had 34 rank and file members and was led by Major de la Pole, assisted by Frank Gueritz.

The beginning of the year passed much as usual. The annual pantomime was a great success and as the months passed Frank Gueritz took on more duties. However, there was a shooting accident on 15 May in which Frank's hand was so seriously damaged that his thumb had to be amputated. This gave a necessary pause to his normally irrepressible enthusiasm and a month or so was needed for recovery. This was felt even more in the parish because the curate, I. J. Rosser, had moved on. The gap was not to last too long because in August a new curate came to Colyton. The parish magazine reported:

> The Vicar is happy to inform the parishioners that he has secured the assistance of The Rev H. F. G. James, formerly Assistant Curate with the Rev F. Gueritz at Swymbridge.

Having already served his title with Fortescue and thus being a known quantity even if at one remove, James was well placed to be a great deal more help to Gueritz than a newly ordained deacon and a stranger would have been.

Although at times precarious, Gueritz' health held up quite well for the rest of the year. He was able to take a full part in the St Andrew's tide round of celebrations and services and when addressing the Guild of St Andrew made it clear how much he relied on its members as "a great power for good in the Parish". At the same event, he shared the news that Reginald Mortimer had been appointed to the living of St Mary Major in Exeter. When a new incumbent was appointed and before the appointment was legalized, there was a process called "reading in" at which his letters of appointment and licence were read in the church before witnesses, normally the churchwardens. This Reginald did on 20 December 1896.

In January 1897, Gueritz was seriously ill, but in February was reported to be recovering:

Our dear Vicar is now convalescent, and we may soon see him about again. He has been seriously ill, but it has pleased God to restore him once more to those among whom he has worked so long . . . Mrs. Gueritz has also been very ill but we are glad to say is now recovering as rapidly as may be expected.

For both Anne and Mamerto, recovery took rather longer than hoped, and they went to stay with Reginald and Mary Louisa at the rectory of St Mary Major in Exeter. The people of Colyton and especially the members of the Guild of St Andrew wrote to express their sadness both at Mamerto and Anne's illness and also at their own inability to greet their vicar on his birthday. His letter to them, written from Exeter, spoke of his frustration at being unable to minister to them as he would wish and thanked them for their much-appreciated birthday gift, but he mostly dwelt on the "forbearance, sympathy and affection" he had received.

The hope that Mamerto and Anne had of returning soon to Colyton vicarage was dashed by another turn of events. In the great storm of Ash Wednesday 1897, the roof of the vicarage was almost completely destroyed. It was no place to convalesce. Still unwell, Mamerto set about trying to remedy the situation. He wrote to the Ecclesiastical Commissioners for help with the repairs, but they declined, so he was obliged to borrow the large sum needed from Queen Anne's Bounty, which would take years to pay back. This came at a time when Gueritz' income was already falling:

The value of the living has gone down by at least one half, and this fresh expense will fall very heavily on the vicar's reduced income, and in consequence he will be unable to assist many of the poor parishioners in the way he wish (sic) and hitherto has done.[1]

Gueritz was unable to take part in the services for Holy Week and Easter, but it was reported that he and Anne were improving in health day by day. That report too was optimistic, and once more they had to miss the Sunday School Festival in July:

One who was very much missed all day was our good old Vicar, who has always been a true friend to the children, and cared so much for their spiritual welfare, as well as for their enjoyment.[2]

In August, however, Gueritz was back in Colyton and taking part in the parish bazaar. The proceeds were to go towards the repair of the vicarage roof, and almost £100 was raised, which was quite astounding at the time.

This was also the time of the long-delayed faculty application for the restoration and reordering of the church, and happily Gueritz seemed in better health for the rest of the year and able to deal with all the detail and complications. Because of the objections and delaying tactics final approval was not given until 20 June 1898 when the final stage of planning and resourcing could begin. In December, Mamerto was singing in the Christmas concert once again.

On 29 May 1899, Anne and Mamerto celebrated their golden wedding anniversary. The photograph taken at the time shows Anne Gueritz in a Bath chair, obviously frail but still looking very determined. A goodly number of presentations were made, some verging on the munificent, especially considering the resources of those who gave. The "Ringers of the Parish Church" between them gave a handsome reading lamp. An illuminated scroll, still in the possession of the family, carries the well wishes of dozens of friends and parishioners. The scroll accompanied a purse of sovereigns which would have been doubly welcome in their reduced circumstances.

Over the two years between June 1898 and March 1900, work on the church progressed by stages which allowed it to be kept open and in use. It was not until the last eight months before completion that the doors had to be closed and worship moved to the parish room. On 21 March 1900, the Lord Bishop of Exeter led the opening ceremony, which was recorded in great detail in the county newspapers.[3] Before recounting that event more fully we should note just two lines at the end of one report:

Considerable assistance in the arranging of the service was rendered by Mr. H. F. Gueritz.[4]

Mamerto and Anne Gueritz: Golden Wedding 1899

Between the granting of the faculty and the completion of the work, the Revd
H. F. G. James had been preferred to Alphington, and a new curate, Ettrick
Havelock Creak, had arrived. Creak did not plan to stay long in Colyton but
needed a brief ministry before his next appointment. While in Colyton he offered
such support as he could, but he was already commissioned as a chaplain in the
Indian Army and was intending to exercise a ministry in the diocese of Madras,
which he began in November 1900. Mamerto was still weakened by recent illness,
and Creak had very little time to settle into the parish before the reopening of
the church. Therefore, a considerable part of the liturgical burden fell on Frank
Gueritz. His experience made him unique among lay readers: he had led the choir
for a number of years and was acknowledged throughout Devon to be a talented
choirmaster and conductor; he had been weaned on the Ritual Revival and was
therefore able to train the servers and acolytes and organize clergy into an orderly
procession.[5] The parishioners and members of St Andrew's were more aware of
the part he had played than was the reporter, and they ensured that Frank knew
that he had their admiration and gratitude.

The day of the reopening began with a choral celebration of the Holy
Communion at 8 o'clock at which Gueritz presided, then at a quarter to noon
the episcopal service began. Among the visiting clergy were H. F. G. James and
Reginald Mortimer. Fortescue Gueritz's absence was inevitable; he had moved to
a new ministry at Dunoon in the Episcopal Church in Scotland. The rural dean,
J. H. Coplestone, was there from Offwell and clergy from eight of the surrounding
parishes. Mamerto took the first part of the service and Creak the second; the rural
dean and Reginald Mortimer read the lessons; and of course the bishop preached.
It was a kind, even loving, sermon. Edward Bickersteth was almost at the end of
his ministry in Exeter, and although he and Gueritz had not always agreed, he
spoke warmly of the "beloved Vicar" who had been 40 years in the parish and he
rejoiced with the parishioners that Gueritz had "the joy of seeing that beautiful
house of prayer so charmingly renovated".

The renovations included a new roof and renewal of almost the entire exterior
with the exception of the windows. Inside, the stone floor had been replaced by
wooden blocks, the walls and pillars cleaned and decorated, the gallery removed
and vestries built for the choir and clergy in the transepts. The reporter, failing
to realize that some of the work had been in place for years, noted the attention

paid to the pulpit, the font and the removal of the reading desk. Gueritz had done away with the reading desk within months of his arrival in 1860!

These were all splendid improvements, but for Gueritz the greatest achievement was the "Pues":

> The old pews have been removed and entirely new and more comfortable seats substituted, capable of accommodating a congregation of 500 . . . the appropriated pews which existed before the carrying out of the work have been done away with, and the whole of the seats in the church are now free.[6]

What Mamerto had set out to achieve with that first abortive meeting in May 1866 was finally complete in March 1900, 34 years later. The festivities during the rest of the day were redolent with expressions of respect and affection for the vicar, and it was noted that of the total cost of £1,300 only £130 remained to be found.

Bishop and vicar were both in failing health and soon after the reopening of Colyton Church Bishop Edward Bickersteth resigned his see. Bickersteth had been an Evangelical of the old school and when he was appointed his predecessor, Temple, prophetically said of him: "That man will do. He is so transparently good."[7] The prophecy was fulfilled.

Without compromise, Bickersteth was on easy terms with clergy of every shade of opinion. For example, around the time of the Colyton visit he also went to the recently reopened Chapel of the Good Shepherd in Seaton where vestments, lights on the altar, the use of the sign of the cross and other signs of the Ritual Revival were in evidence. When the officer of the Royal Commission on Ecclesiastical Discipline inspected the chapel and invited the incumbent to reply to "the charges" he was told:

> Our late diocesan, Dr. Bickersteth, when he was present at Holy Communion, and the church and the ritual were exactly as they are now, expressed his warm approbation of the service.[8]

In December 1900, it was announced that the next Bishop of Exeter would be Herbert Edward Ryle. Ryle described himself as "a Protestant who understands clearly what he means and what he does not mean by that much-discussed word", and it was said of him that "he will probably take firm and consistent methods of grappling with the ritual difficulties that prevail here and there in Devonshire".[9]

Small wonder then that the following year Gueritz announced that he would retire. Assuredly he would not have failed to lock horns with the new "Protestant" bishop if that became necessary, but he had been fighting these battles since he first went to Penzance. He was tired and in ill health; he was almost 80, and it was time to let others take up arms.

A later assessment of Ryle's work in relation to Ritualism, and indeed that of his successors, gives a valuable perspective:

> Bishops Ryle, Robertson and Cecil all tried to put a stop to Ritualism,
> especially in Plymouth where it was strong but they were not successful.
> Incense, confession and reservation of the Sacrament became established
> in a minority of *high* or Anglo-Catholic churches.[10]

As Mamerto's intended retirement became known his fellow clergy as well as his parishioners began to express their feelings. His plans were noted at a meeting of the deanery chapter and "[f]eeling reference was made to Mr. Gueritz' long work at Colyton over 40 years, and the Chairman was unanimously authorised to write to him in terms of compliment, respect and sympathy".[11]

On 21 December 1901, the feast of St Thomas, Mamerto Gueritz formally resigned the incumbency of Colyton. He had been offered the living in January 1860, and to the people of Colyton he had been their vicar for just short of 42 years. He had been living with his daughter and son-in-law in Exeter for some time, as his letter to "friends and parishioners" dated 15 November 1901 reveals. It also indicates that the illness which precipitated the retirement had been so severe as to prevent Gueritz even from being able to go to church for a final farewell. A deputation from Colyton visited Mamerto and Anne at St Mary Major rectory in order to present them with a gift of £102, an album of photographs and a testimonial which included the statement:

> It has given us much pleasure to note the good feeling towards you that
> exists amongst the parishioners of all classes and persuasions.

The truth of this was demonstrated by the list of signatories, more than 120 of them, which included the local gentry, the de la Pole family and the Scarboroughs, and also the names of tannerymen and farm workers. Among them was the signature of Ravenor E. Rose, for 12 years the Congregationalist minister in Colyton. At the time of the visit, Gueritz was not well enough to respond as he wished and he explained this in a letter dated 23 November:

> It was impossible then for me to say what I felt or to express how very greatly I value this token of your affectionate regret, at the close of my long ministry among you.

In retirement in Exeter, physical incapacity did not prevent Gueritz from working at one of his lifelong passions, church music. In 1904, the third edition of *The Office of Holy Communion set to Simple and Easy Music* was published.[12] This was a choral setting suitable for country choirs, being only moderately demanding but still perfectly acceptable as a piece of church music. It reflected the policy which Gueritz had inherited from W. H. Monk in Stoke Newington and then transplanted to Colyton, that of choral and congregational involvement at a level suitable for both. That Gueritz' settings were used around the United Kingdom and in New Zealand is a measure of their worth.

A year had not passed when a final illness took Anne Derby Gueritz, and she died at St Mary Major rectory on 14 August 1902. Four days later she was buried in Colyton, the coffin arriving by train. In her quiet ministry, leading the ladies of the parish, encouraging them to make peace between their husbands when conflict threatened, and supporting Mamerto, Anne had captured the hearts of the people. They came in large numbers to make their farewells. When the service in church was over, they trudged up the hill in the pouring rain to stand at the graveside.

Reginald Mortimer continued his work in what was then one of the most deprived areas of Exeter with his family and father-in-law around him. After years of overwork, Reginald's health too was beginning to fail. He was much in demand outside the parish as a preacher and speaker and went to Manchester for a speaking engagement. He had already caught influenza earlier in the year, and that was followed by bronchitis, but still he kept to his commitments. Following his visit to Manchester, he went to Long Sutton to see his sister and his daughter

Edith, and there he died. On 6 July 1904, Reginald Mortimer, aged 54, was laid to rest in Colyton. An Exeter parishioner said of him that he had worked himself to death. Mary Louisa was left with seven sons and daughters at home, the youngest, William Lionel, being nine years old. Edith Mary had gone to live with her aunt and uncle in Long Sutton more than a decade earlier.

Various members of the family had made their home at Colyton vicarage over the years, and for those who remained Mamerto's retirement had provoked something of a diaspora. Then Reginald's death and the need to vacate the parsonage in Exeter did the same there.

Both Mamerto and Mary Louisa returned to Colyton and lived at Richmond House in King Street. It was a large house, and there was room for those of the children who were still at home. Ernest Mortimer's letter from St Edmund Hall, which told us much about Mamerto's undergraduate days, also revealed something of the rather chaotic domestic scene!

Later, Mary moved in with a friend of many years, Sara "Kate" White, who also lived in King Street with her niece. Kate had been one of the prime movers, with Mary's brother Frank, in all kinds of entertainments and social activities as well as being a longstanding district visitor.

Adelina eventually set up home with her brother in lodgings with the Matthews family in Alexandra Terrace, Colyton and Frank Gueritz left the town to continue his ministry as a lay reader at Calstock, near Tavistock.

Mamerto lived quietly for another eight years, spending the last of them being cared for by Adelina and Mary Louisa, until he too, as he often put it, "passed from this life to a greater light" on 8 February 1912.

Stuckey Coles, with the devotion to his friends for which he was famed, wrote the obituary for the national press and celebrated the requiem mass. He told Mamerto's tale in brief but then touched upon what was always at the heart of the story of Mamerto Gueritz, the priest: Church principles, devotion to God and his people and the pursuit of holiness.

Postmortem

The family lived out their lives, some staying in Colyton, others going far afield. The church carried on under a new regime and the question at this point is, did Mamerto Gueritz achieve what he had set out to do, or did the results of his labour pass with his own passing?

The answer to this depends on how we view Gueritz' lasting intentions as they grew and matured from the convictions with which he arrived in Colyton into his agenda for the Church of England and for the parish. We have seen how that agenda changed and developed as different aspects of church life claimed priority. Initial moderation in externals, which appeared extreme at the beginning to Congregationalists, Unitarians and indeed some Anglicans, gave way to a clear-cut Ritualism formed in the "London School". This was accompanied by an adherence to Church principles which alienated dissenters and puzzled some Anglicans in the parish, yet which earned more than a grudging respect even from his opponents.

Just as Gueritz was shaped by his immersion in the Ritualism of London churches, so day-to-day life in the parish and the needs of his parishioners tempered his fiery zeal to bring all things Catholic to Colyton. What began as a consuming fire eventually became an illuminating flame. He always believed that worship should be offered according to correct usage and Catholic ceremonial, and while he was incumbent the services were so conducted. However, it should be remembered that his first and perhaps greatest battle was over a matter of principle and not liturgical practice. The storm which followed the Pavey funeral in 1864 was in reality all about whether or not the law of the land could or should compel a priest to act contrary to the teaching of the Church.

The early years of conflict over ritual eventually resolved into acceptance for some and a fervent loyalty for others. However, even as that was happening, there was an implicit acknowledgement by Gueritz and the clergy who supported him that if that was all the victory contained, if victory it should be called, then it would be hollow indeed. The coming of the Sisters of Mercy, the repeated parish missions and the weekday sermon series in Lent and Advent all tended towards one end. Of course, having had a sisterhood in the parish was a feather in the cap of any Anglo-Catholic priest, but even if that were somewhere in Gueritz' motives, their true purpose was both to serve the community and to infuse an example of prayerful dedication into the lives of the ordinary folk of Colyton:

> Time was on the side of the Colyton advance. Opposition ended . . . three missions have born their fruit. Vocations to the priesthood and holy lives in various walks of life were among the consolations of Mr. Gueritz's age.[13]

We have only to look at the publicity for those missions and to read some of Gueritz' pastoral letters to recognize that his overriding priority was to see the gospel rooted in the hearts of his people and then reflected in disciplined and holy lives.

If Gueritz' sole intention had been to bring Ritualism to Colyton, then his life's work would have been almost entirely a failure, at least in the short term. A most telling sentence appears in Coles' obituary:

> In the morning of his funeral the vestments which had lain unused in the sacristy since the time of his departure, were brought out by his second successor for use at his Requiem.

It seems a reasonable assumption, given this and other indications, that in sending Richard Turner to be the new incumbent of Colyton, Bishop Ryle intended to reduce the ritual and impose his own understanding of correct usage in worship. Turner was very familiar with church life in Colyton; as a member of the diocesan mission team, he had preached several sermon series for the parish and although his appointment was not initially broadcast, it seems that he was either effectively or actually the curate in charge as the parish waited for a new incumbent.[14] Superficially it may have seemed that Turner carried out the bishop's wish, but it proved impossible to turn the clock back entirely. In the preceding 70 years, the whole Church of England had undergone a profound change. Even those who opposed the Oxford Movement and its outworking held their position against it and therefore in relation to it. Even if reduced in externals the worship in Colyton was still recognizably the product of the Catholic Revival and thus in harmony with the vast majority of parishes in Exeter diocese at that time. Instead of a chasuble Richard Turner wore a surplice and stole to celebrate the Holy

Communion and reduced the number of sanctuary assistants, but the work of the choir, surpliced and seated in the chancel, continued without constraint. In other words, all that in 1860 was taken as evidence of the influence of the Oxford Movement on the liturgy was still in place.

Even if vestments were eschewed, the sacramental life of the parish was maintained. The Guild of St Andrew, formed to bring together the communicants of the parish in a body devoted to deepening the sacramental and spiritual life of its members, continued as before. On the feast of St Andrew 1902, the anniversary was celebrated as it always had been. Turner graciously allowed Reginald Mortimer to return and preside on that occasion and the report in the parish magazine indicates that the occasion was a particularly happy one even though Mamerto Gueritz, their founder, could not be with them. The guild continued through Richard Turner's incumbency and well into that of his successor.

During the time of Gueritz' illness just before he retired, the pattern of almost daily Eucharists had necessarily been reduced to once a week on Thursdays and early choral services on major feast days. This pattern continued throughout Turner's incumbency and that of his successor. There was some reduction in the number of services in Holy Week and around the Easter season, but the parish retained the Sunday morning pattern of early Holy Communion, later Mattins and another Holy Communion immediately following, but with only Mattins being the morning choral service: the early Eucharist was said.

In June 1907, Richard Turner was preferred to the living of Barnstaple and in September of the same year G. E. F. Molyneaux was instituted to Colyton. The pattern of services remained much as under Turner but with some significant differences. The practice of taking Holy Communion to the sick, scarcely in evidence in Turner's time, made a reappearance in the registers. In the year before his death, Mamerto Gueritz regularly received communion at home from the hands of his second successor. This was always entered as a "Private Celebration" rather than the designation "Private Communion", which Gueritz had used. It seems that the practice of reservation of the Blessed Sacrament had been discontinued under Turner and may not have been restored by Molyneaux. When it is remembered that the devotions of the members of the Confraternity of the Blessed Sacrament made explicit their belief in the doctrine of the real or true presence of Christ in the consecrated elements, it can easily be seen why a Protestant bishop wanted the practice of reservation stopped. However, Molyneaux did reinstate the full Holy Week and Easter services, with devotions being held daily until Low Sunday.

Under the Revd H. S. Wyatt, who arrived in Colyton in November 1920, there were yet more frequent celebrations of the Holy Communion, and the registers often record "Communion from the Sacrament reserved for the sick". That was a nice distinction to make, indeed a necessary one. The Sacrament was not officially reserved as a focus of devotion or worship; that was still a matter of contention, a cause of censure or even prosecution which some bishops would willingly exercise. The Communion of the sick, however, was increasingly recognized as a valid reason for reserving the Sacrament. If some people found their devotions in church aided by the knowledge of Sacramental presence, that was a private matter.

Wyatt was given the living of Teignmouth in 1935, and he was succeeded by W. G. Wilson. Since 1807, all the clergy of Colyton had been Oxford or Cambridge men, with the exception of Molyneaux, who graduated from Trinity College, Dublin. Wilson had trained for the priesthood at the College of the Resurrection, Mirfield. His training, therefore, had been steeped in monastic spirituality and a "Sarum" ritual with which Gueritz himself could have found no fault. This evidenced itself in Wilson's own prayer life and personal discipline, and the discipline he expected of his people. Saturday evenings were not to be spent in heedless recreation but in preparation for the Holy Communion on the Sunday. Although some of his parishioners found him harsh and unbending, strict over baptism and marriage discipline, there were still those who, many years later, bore witness to his great pastoral heart which brought him to their side in times of need and sorrow.

In the matter of liturgy, however, Wilson was content to exercise restraint. Vestments were not reintroduced, but a lace alb made its appearance at early celebrations and a plain one at any later Eucharists. The pattern was still to have an early Communion, followed by Mattins. The early service remained a low mass simply said and without music. On major feasts Wilson would also have a later celebration.

The main stamp of this incumbency, which lasted 28 years, was a renewal of the underlying disciplines of church life. Wilson enjoyed little in the way of popular acclaim or overt success, however that may be measured in a parish priest, but he left a legacy for his successor to build upon.

In 1964, Arthur Warne went to Colyton. A man of considerable intellectual prowess, he had just completed a doctoral thesis. Warne also had the common touch and quickly established himself as a man of the people. The worship changed considerably during his ministry. The musical aspect of the liturgy was renewed; the Eucharist was made the central act of worship on a Sunday; and the externals of Catholic liturgical practice began to make a reappearance.

The musical revival in the parish was aided by the presence of Professor Arthur Hutchings, who had held the music chair at Durham University. His influence on the music of the parish church was largely mediated through his friendship with Dr Warne, but there were times when his expertise with choirs was called into play. Wonderfully eccentric for most of his life, Hutchings made a fascinating if slightly unpredictable companion and supporter for Warne.

Placing the Eucharist at the centre of the life of the church, thus ousting Mattins from its accustomed place, was even more controversial than the reintroduction of vestments. Even Gueritz had been content with an early celebration, but in his day the early service was choral and suited the early rising population rather better than the parishioners of 1964 when folk were later abed. Warne was determined that the church in Colyton should reflect the nationwide movement to make the Eucharist central to the life of the congregation, and he had his way. What Gueritz had tried to achieve by teaching and by the forming of the Guild of St Andrew, Warne attempted by changing the nature of the services. He did so with the same level of consultation that Gueritz had exercised when he introduced Ritualism almost a century earlier and experienced the same, highly predictable reaction. However, the reintroduction of vestments, acolytes, processions and other elements missing for more than 60 years passed off with little enough complaint compared with the angry reaction to the downgrading of Mattins. At that time there were still septuagenarians who remembered with considerable affection the days of their childhood and the loving care afforded them by Mamerto and Anne Gueritz.

Mamerto Gueritz remained an ardent Anglo-Catholic, true to Church principles and discipline, but long experience had tempered his zeal with wisdom, well, most of the time. As he said concerning the actions of the Church

Association in their persecution of Bishop Edward King, defeating opponents and winning battles would never be enough. Winning hearts and minds was the key to establishing "the peace of Jerusalem".[15] He recognized that the ritual he had introduced and the traditions he had nurtured, while essential to him, were not an end in themselves but rather a means to an end. If his own modest revolution in Colyton was to be true to the great Movement within which it was set, then it had to be evidenced in changed and sanctified lives which bore witness to Catholic truth and the reality of saving grace. Changes in rite and ceremony might be accomplished in a relatively short space of time, but the working of grace in the life of a community is something that takes longer to show. At the end of 42 years in the parish, Gueritz had a generation of Colytonians active in the church who had known no other priest as their own. They knew no other way to worship, and most importantly they had been taught from the cradle upwards that although their faith should be expressed in beautiful worship, its crowning glory was their own lives, beautified by holiness. Again and again, this theme pervaded the parish magazine, the pastoral letters, and the pastoral labours among the people. The guilds and societies all offered ways for people of different types and temperaments to be sustained in their spirituality and discipleship:

> The Catholic doctrine of the Church tended to this one end. Christianity must be more than speculation about faith and more than mere philosophy but rather a life and a lived experience. The inevitable outcome of such a conviction was to make the pursuit of holiness the common ground and true hallmark of the Oxford Movement.[16]

By this and any other measure, Mamerto Gueritz was a true son of the Oxford Movement. Perhaps a fitting end to this attempt to tell the story of his life might come from the pen of a devoted friend who had known Gueritz from the days of his first curacy, had been there to support him in mission and had shared both family joys and sorrows; Stuckey Coles:

> This little record may seem uneventful, but others besides those who owe much to Mr. Gueritz may be interested in the romantic touch of the life begun at a convent in Jativa, the birthplace of the saintly Borgias, where

an officer's wife found shelter for her confinement during a march, and the
tranquil end in a little English town, where the faithful life had witnessed
for our Lord and His Church.[17]

The story did not end with the death of Mamerto Gueritz; he continued to affect
the world in the lives of those to whom he had taught the faith, in those whose
lives were touched by his ministry and, above all, in the lives of his children. To
them we must finally turn to complete his tale.

The Gueritz Family Tree

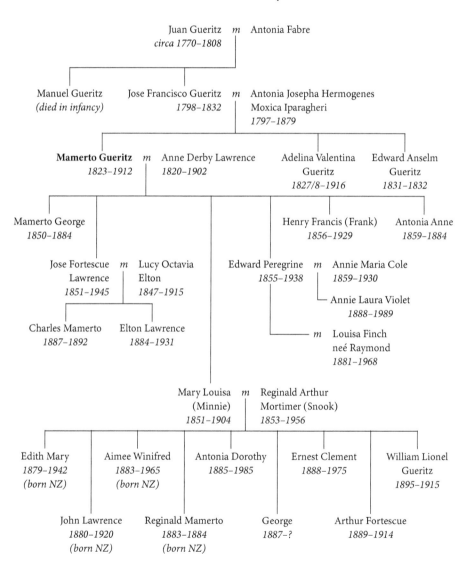

Juan Gueritz *m* Antonia Fabre
circa 1770–1808

Manuel Gueritz   Jose Francisco Gueritz *m* Antonia Josepha Hermogenes
(died in infancy)   *1798–1832*   Moxica Iparagheri
                                                1797–1879

Mamerto Gueritz *m* Anne Derby Lawrence   Adelina Valentina   Edward Anselm
1823–1912   *1820–1902*   Gueritz   Gueritz
                                                1827/8–1916   *1831–1832*

Mamerto George   Henry Francis (Frank)   Antonia Anne
1850–1884   *1856–1929*   *1859–1884*

Jose Fortescue *m* Lucy Octavia   Edward Peregrine *m* Annie Maria Cole
Lawrence   Elton   *1855–1938*   *1859–1930*
1851–1945   *1847–1915*
                                                          Annie Laura Violet
                                                          1888–1989

Charles Mamerto   Elton Lawrence
1887–1892   *1884–1931*   *m* Louisa Finch
                                                        neé Raymond
                                                        1881–1968

Mary Louisa *m* Reginald Arthur
(Minnie)   Mortimer (Snook)
1851–1904   *1853–1956*

Edith Mary   Aimee Winifred   Antonia Dorothy   Ernest Clement   William Lionel
1879–1942   *1883–1965*   *1885–1985*   *1888–1975*   Gueritz
(born NZ)   *(born NZ)*   *1895–1915*

John Lawrence   Reginald Mamerto   George   Arthur Fortescue
1880–1920   *1883–1884*   *1887–?*   *1889–1914*
(born NZ)   *(born NZ)*

Notes

1   *Colyton Parish Magazine*, April 1897.

2   *Colyton Parish Magazine*, August 1897.

3   The article in the *Devon and Exeter Gazette* ran to over 14 column inches.

4   *Devon and Exeter Gazette*, 22 March 1900.

5   A process often described by frustrated precentors as "herding cats".

6   *Devon and Exeter Gazette*, 22 March 1900.

7   R. J. E. Boggis, *The History of the Diocese of Exeter* (Exeter: Pollard, 1922), p. 573.

8   *The Royal Commission on Ecclesiastical Discipline 1904* (published 1906), refs 8079–80. The Good Shepherd, Seaton.

9   *Beverley and East Riding Recorder*, Saturday, 8 December 1900.

10   Boggis, *History of the Diocese of Exeter*, p. 540.

11   *Honiton Deanery Chapter Minutes*, 19 December 1901.

12   M. Gueritz, *The Office of Holy Communion set to Simple and Easy Music* (Exeter: Pollard, 1904).

13   V. S. S. Coles, Obituary of Mamerto Gueritz, *Church Times*, 16 February 1912.

14   The vestry minutes of the meeting held during the interregnum note Turner's absence from the chair of the vestry meeting. Only a curate in charge or an elected lay vice-chairman could take that role.

15   *Colyton Parish Magazine*, March 1889.

16   See p. 15 above.

17   V. S. S. Coles, Obituary of Mamerto Gueritz, *Church Times*, 16 February 1912.

The next generation

This penultimate chapter offers a limited account of how the children of Mamerto and Anne Gueritz found their place in the world. Some of what is written here has already appeared in earlier chapters but is necessarily restated so that the further stories of the Gueritz offspring, which if included earlier might have distorted the telling of Mamerto's tale, can be seen in context. Therefore if, in the reading of this chapter, there is occasionally a sense of *déjà vu*, that will be fully justified. Both within the immediate telling of the story of Mamerto Gueritz, and beyond it, the lives of his children, told in brief, remind us that a story, once we have joined it, can never be said to have ended "here" or "there". The road goes ever on.

Mamerto George Gueritz

1850–84

George, as the family called him, was born in Shepton Beauchamp during Gueritz' first curacy and at three weeks old was baptized on 6 April 1850. His early years were filled with movement from parish to parish, but much of it before he would have been able to recall. By the time George was seven years old, the family had moved five times. They were in Brixham for a year and then spent a year in Stoke Gabriel, where brother Jose Fortescue Lawrence was born. They stayed in Bigbury for almost five years, where his sister Mary Louisa and brother Edward Peregrine were added to the family. There was a brief interval in Yealmpton, which saw the arrival of Henry Francis, before the family moved again, this time to Penzance. It was in Penzance that some of the most formative of George's early experiences took place. An important one was his father's increasing links with the clergy of London and especially those of All Saints, Margaret Street. However, another, possibly profoundly influential, impression came from Mamerto Gueritz' lecturing activity, even if the effect was not immediately obvious. Mamerto was a great enthusiast on all things to do with Borneo and the career of Sir James Brooke, whom he had met briefly when Brooke was in Oxford for the presentation of an award. Later in his time in Penzance, he gave lectures on Borneo, dwelling especially on Sarawak, and the role of Rajah James Brooke. Members of the Brooke family lent him some valuable artefacts from their Borneo collection. This could hardly have failed to impress the ten-year-old George and his brother Edward.

As the Gueritz family prepared to move to Colyton from Penzance, so George also moved but even further east. The residential choir of All Saints, Margaret Street was re-formed and took up residence in the west wing of the vicarage early in 1860. Among the new boys was Mamerto George Gueritz. Life as a chorister at All Saints was very full. There was the daily round of choral services, the rehearsals and ordinary schooling all to be fitted into the day.

It seems that a musical life suited George, and the next we hear of him after Margaret Street is that his schooling continued in another choral setting at St Michael and All Angels College just outside Tenbury Wells in Worcestershire. The college had been founded in 1856 by Sir Frederick Arthur Gore Ouseley, whose intention was to provide the Church with a model for Anglican music and his students with an education which would fit them either for further education or a career in one of the services, either military or civil. Frederick Ouseley and Mamerto Gueritz had met during their undergraduate days in Oxford.

The door to a career in the Civil Service was open. In March 1868, George sailed on the *Lady Louisa* out of London with eight other passengers. He was on his way to Borneo to begin a career in the Sarawak Administration under Rajah Charles Brooke, who had succeeded his uncle Sir James Brooke. George arrived in Perth, Australia in June 1868 and having spent some time in Australia, arrived in Sarawak in early 1870. The Punan people found it almost impossible to pronounce "Gueritz", so George became "Tuan Goret" and remained so for the rest of his time there.

In 1874, there was an interesting juxtaposition of events. By this time, George was an acting resident in Sarawak. Edward Peregrine had also joined the Sarawak

Mamerto George Gueritz: Singapore 1879

Administration, and at the same time the curate of Sarawak, John Riley, spent October in Colyton.

We know that George was in Singapore in 1879 because the obverse of this photograph declares that this was where he had his portrait taken in his uniform. Then on 1 July 1882 the front page of the *Sarawak Gazette* carried the news:

> His Highness the Rajah has been pleased to grant Mr. George Gueritz leave
> of absence on full pay for twelve months, and an additional two months
> on half pay, dating from June 8th, 1882.

George went straight to Singapore on 8 June and, although he may well have paused at various places on the way, was back in Colyton by the spring of 1883. He took part in one of the parish entertainments and then had to return to duty.

Back in Sarawak, George picked up the traces and wrote his resident's report for October 1883.

In February 1884, it seems that discussions had begun about further responsibilities. The previous year Sultan Abdul Momin of Brunei had ceded Baram to Charles Brooke, and this new territory became the fourth division of Sarawak. The appointed resident, Charles A. C. de Crespigny, had returned to England in May in ill health and may not have been expected to return. In late June, George Gueritz was appointed to act in his stead.

George did not live to see Baram become fully integrated into the Brooke regime. He died on board the river launch *Bujang Baram*. The inscription on the reverse of a photograph of his grave says that he died on 23 December 1884, aged 34.[1]

The international telegraph service, by this time functioning even as far as Sarawak, may well have carried the news to England. Even so, the family in Colyton would not have the news immediately, but as the year turned into 1885, it would have been the saddest new year they had ever known.

Colyton 1883. This photograph was taken during George's last stay in Colyton.
It shows George in the doorway, Mamerto to his left and Anne Gueritz seated

Jose Fortescue Lawrence Gueritz

1851–1945

Just as Mamerto George was known as George in the family, so Jose Fortescue Lawrence was called Fortescue by his father and the rest of the household. This is how he is often referred to in the parish records and, after he was ordained, in the service registers written up by his father. Jose was the name of his paternal grandfather, and Lawrence was the family name of Anne Gueritz. Fortescue was born in October 1851, during his father's brief curacy at Stoke Gabriel, but the greater part of his early formative years was spent in Bigbury and then in Penzance. Fortescue was six by the time the family moved to Penzance. Little is known of his schooling either then or later. In Penzance, Mamerto Gueritz supplemented his income by offering residential tutoring to "a few sons of gentlemen" with a view to them gaining a place at a public school or, for the older candidates, university. These students would have been rather older than Fortescue, although he may well have gained a surprising degree of clandestine knowledge from sitting in on their lessons. His aunt Adelina, having remained in Shepton Beauchamp, was not with the family when Fortescue was born, but it seems that she joined them either in Penzance or beforehand. She was an experienced private tutor, having first taught Stuckey Coles and then the children of a Glastonbury doctor, so she may well have been Fortescue's main educator both in Penzance and later after they all moved to Colyton.

By the time the move to Colyton was settled, Fortescue was almost nine years old, and he and his siblings settled down to a new life in a new community. We do not know what, if any, other schooling was available to him at the time. There was the Feoffees' School, but the other establishments in the town and in nearby places were decidedly nonconformist or, in the case of the Lyme Regis school attended by H. P. Liddon, Calvinistic. It is difficult to think of Mamerto Gueritz being content with any of them for his son.

The next we hear of Fortescue, apart from tennis tournaments and cricket matches, is that he and his brother Edward Peregrine were working as commercial clerks and boarding with Mr Alfred Marsden, an accountant for an insurance office. This was in 1871 in Trafalgar Terrace in the St John's area of Hackney, scarcely two miles from St Matthias, Stoke Newington. Fortescue was 18 and Edward 16, and this was only three years after Mamerto's extended stay in Stoke Newington. It is therefore reasonable to see a link between the finding of employment for the two boys and the Gueritz family association with St Matthias. Five years later, when this portrait below was taken, Fortescue was in holy orders as a deacon. Even though we have little if any direct record of those years, several things must have been put in place for ordination to have been possible. Fortescue had not attended university and did not hold a degree. In previous generations, it has to be admitted, many men were ordained having taken degrees that scarcely fitted them for priestly ministry. This changed as the years passed and bishops increasingly required that their ordinands had read theology. The idea of vocational training for those who did not hold a theology degree, or indeed any degree, was in its infancy, and in the early 1870s vocational colleges for those seeking ordination were few. Cuddesdon College had been founded in 1854 and, as we have noted, H. P. Liddon was vice-principal there for a time. The *Scholae Cancellarii* in Lincoln had opened in 1874 and St Stephen's House, Oxford in 1876. However, there was an opportunity for vocational education of a different kind much closer to home. In 1854, the Exeter Diocesan Training School moved from the cathedral precincts to new premises in Heavitree, Exeter.[2] This establishment was founded to provide schoolmasters for the National Schools, and the Revd J. G. Dangar was the principal from 1869 until just after the turn of the century. Dangar was one of the clergy who assisted in Colyton; he was there for over a month in 1871.

Short of being able to examine a list of alumni from that period, the college having suffered great fire damage in the Second World War, all that can be said is that it is extremely likely that this is where Fortescue Gueritz qualified as a teacher, and with further study, this would have made it possible for him to be considered a *literatus*. The further study would necessarily include Greek and probably Latin, and the bishop's examining chaplain would determine when the appropriate standard had been reached.

Ordination by this route was not uncommon. For example, the Lord Bishop of Llandaff held an ordination in October 1832 when four priests were ordained, one of whom, Thomas John Griffiths, was of the *literati*. Three of the four who were made deacon on the same day were also *literati*.[3] The numbers of such ordinands grew as the theological colleges began to grow in number and were able to supply what was lacking in an ordinand's education for them to be equipped for ministry. By 1865, almost 25 per cent of ordinands were *literati*.

Fortescue Gueritz was curate of Colyton from 1876 to 1879, and from 1877 he also held the post of master of the Colyton Feoffee Grammar School.[4] This confirms the conclusion that he had undergone formal training as a teacher and to a considerable standard. The previously appointed master, the Revd H. J. Dodwell of Brighton, had been something of a disaster, neglecting his teaching duties, being seen intoxicated in public and treating his pupils with extreme violence. It cost the Feoffees a great deal in time and money to oust him from the appointment and remove him from the schoolhouse afterwards. The case was heard before Sir George Jessel, Master of the Rolls. Dodwell later discharged a pistol at Sir George in order to draw attention to the injustice of his situation and was consigned to Broadmoor. After the Dodwell debacle the Feoffees needed a known quantity as a successor, a safe and suitably qualified appointee. Such a candidate was found in Fortescue Gueritz.

In the normal course of events, being made deacon would be followed a year later by ordination to the priesthood, but Fortescue remained a deacon for almost all of his curacy at Colyton. Two factors would have influenced that, though there would have been others. As a *literatus*, Fortescue needed further study to satisfy the examining chaplain. The further training needed was undertaken during that time and perhaps, like many theological students, he found the Greek hard going! The second consideration is that for most of that period Fortescue was fully occupied with his mastership, for which priestly orders were not essential. There would have been precious little spare time for further study. He was ordained priest by Bishop Temple at Ottery St Mary on 8 June 1879.

In September, a mere three months later, there was an entry in the vestry journal:

> The Rev'd J.F.L. Gueritz officiated last time as curate, having been presented
> to the living of Templeton, near Tiverton.

Sir William Edmund Pole, ninth Baronet, was the patron of the living, and the Pole family, especially the Shute branch, were generous supporters of Colyton and,

Fortescue Gueritz at Templeton

latterly, of the parochial work of Mamerto Gueritz. Later in September, Fortescue moved to Templeton, which proved congenial and not impossibly distant from Colyton, about four hours by pony and trap, so he was able still to offer support to his father. In fact, he was back in Colyton for the harvest festival in October. He spent 1880 settling into Templeton, but towards the end of the year Mamerto Gueritz' health was failing once more so Fortescue, his parents, the archdeacon and the bishop devised a strategy for the next 12 months. At the end of February 1881, Mamerto and Anne Gueritz moved to Templeton, leaving Fortescue to act as curate in charge of Colyton. Templeton was a much quieter parish, with few occasional offices; Mamerto officiated at only one wedding during the year he was there. The secular and social life of the parish did not move at quite the pace of Colyton, and there were not the parochial organizations which took so much time and energy. The 1881 census shows Mamerto and Anne living in the Templeton rectory with two domestics, a gardener and a housekeeper. In Colyton, Jose Fortescue was living at the vicarage with his younger sister, Antonia, and the domestic staff, while Adelina, her mother and her husband were close by in Queen's Square. The year went well for all three of them. Mamerto's health improved, and Fortescue was increasingly appreciated as a priest by the people of Colyton who had known him as a schoolboy. His preaching earned particular praise, and the year was a good experience for him.

The 12 months passed, and during the first quarter of 1882 Mamerto assumed his vicariate once more. Fortescue was backwards and forwards to Templeton but was in Colyton for most of March. Evidently, support for his father's ministry was not his only motive and matters other than ministry had occupied his mind during the year. On 20 June, Jose Fortescue Lawrence Gueritz married Lucy Octavia Elton of Colyton House. Lucy Octavia was an accomplished and well-connected young woman.

Lucy's father, the Revd William Tierney Elton, rector of Whitestaunton, died in 1874. His wife, Lucy Caroline Elton, had borne him 13 children. Their firstborn, Julia Catherine Elton, was born in 1830 and died in 1871. Shortly after the death of her husband, Lucy Elton moved with those of her children who were still at home to Colyton House, the grounds of which bordered Colyton vicarage. Seven years later Mrs Elton was still living there with four of her children, Georgina, Agnes, Lucy Octavia and Edward, and a niece. Edward was paralysed and had a live-in nurse. Maude Young, who was recorded in the census as a "daughter", was actually niece to Georgina, Agnes, Lucy and their brother. She was 17 at the time and was the daughter of their eldest surviving sister, Frances. There were four servants, the youngest of whom, Rose Morris, had been born in Barrington, where Mamerto, Adelina and their mother had lived when he served his first curacy. There was sufficient income for the Elton family to live as befits gentry, and it shows something of their father's foresight that each of them had an income separate from the others.

Lucy was 27 when they moved to Colyton, leaving behind a large circle of friends and a decade of participation in the county life of Somerset. The Elton families had considerable lands and properties in the county. Lucy's uncle, Charles Isaac Elton, held the manor of Whitestaunton having inherited it from his uncle in 1869. William Tierney Elton, her father, was the son of Isaac Elton of Stapleton House near Bristol, who was the patron of the living of Whitestaunton. Lucy Caroline, William's wife, was an Elton by birth. She was the daughter of Charles A. Elton and the granddaughter of Sir Abraham Elton of Clevedon Court, Somerset. Obviously, the familial relationship between them was sufficiently distant for the marriage not to be prevented by the prohibited degrees of affinity; they were fourth cousins and great, great, great grandchildren of the first Baronet, Sir Abraham Elton. Incidentally William and Lucy Caroline were married in 1828 at The Hague by the ambassador's chaplain. There was probably a family affinity with the Low Countries because Lucy Octavia was born in Brussels.[5]

Lucy Octavia and her family were often present at Somerset county gatherings and events, but it seems her main enthusiasm as a young woman, indeed into her late twenties, was archery. Lucy was a member of the Sadbarrow archers and regularly shot in competitions all over south Somerset, including a meeting held in the grounds of the rectory where she lived and another in the nearby Whitestaunton Manor. This was no gentle game of "bows and arrows". The ladies taking part were expected to shoot two dozen arrows over 50 yards; that would take strength and stamina. In 1866, when she was 19, Lucy won a silver card case for the highest gross score of the season. Her sister Agnes gained the most hits and was awarded gold solitaire studs, while her cousin Louisa, having scored the most golds (bulls), won some gold earrings.[6]

It seems that the whole family were involved, or at least made family occasions of the meetings. When the Sadbarrow archers met in Chard in September 1873, not only were Lucy's own family out in force but other branches of the Elton families. She won a black and gold fan and a silver bracelet on that occasion. For ten years, there were regular reports of her skills and prizes won.[7]

The last record we have of Lucy taking part in a competition was in 1876, after her father had died, so the move to Colyton had not cut her off from Somerset life completely. Indeed, in 1874 her youngest sister, Henrietta, married the Revd Henry Antrobus Cartwright, who followed their father as rector of Whitestaunton. Henry and Henrietta were married in Colyton where Cartwright had appeared as a visiting preacher several times and where Henrietta was living at Colyton House.

For the years prior to 1874, although Lucy won several prizes for various achievements, she was always a close second to a Miss L. Clarke Bragge for the overall winner's trophy. It would be lovely to record that she won in 1876, but no, Miss Bragge did it again.[8]

Fortescue returned to Templeton with his new bride, but they were in Colyton often, especially in the December of their first year together when Lucy's invalid brother, Edward, died. Two years later, in 1884, their first son, Elton Lawrence, was born and a year later Fortescue was appointed rural dean of the Tiverton deanery when he had been in priest's orders for just seven years. In the diocese of Exeter, the appointment of a rural dean differed from most other places in the country. Elsewhere it was more usually a bishop's appointment, and while he may or may not consult the deanery clergy and his archidiaconal colleagues, the candidate was his choice. In Exeter diocese, the clergy would meet in local chapter and agree a nomination to the bishop who would then, unless he had reason to refuse, challenge or suggest alternatives, accept the nomination.

A year later, Bishop Bickersteth came to Templeton for a confirmation and stayed the night with Lucy and Fortescue. Within a month he had offered Fortescue the living of Swymbridge near Barnstaple. This was a prestigious move. A previous incumbent had been Parson Jack Russell, a friend of the Prince of Wales and breeder of the eponymous terriers. The dissident press lost no time in commenting, and in a rather incoherent article published on 1 April 1887 the *Western Times* repeated all its old inaccuracies about Mamerto Gueritz' relationships with the Calvinist clergy of Plymouth in his youth. The writer then proceeded to inform his readers that "the young divine is the fortunate son of the ritualistic vicar of Colyton" and then went on to point out that Fortescue had "got into the church as a Literate" as if it were somehow a suspect process instead of an increasing source of young clergy, many of whom ended up better fitted for parochial ministry than those who held a completely unrelated university degree.

Such reports seem not to have affected the life at Swymbridge vicarage, and later that year another son was born to Fortescue and Lucy, Charles Mamerto. In December, there was a meeting of the North Devon Sunday School Teachers Association where Fortescue was referred to as the "esteemed vicar of Swymbridge".[9]

Young Elton Gueritz continued his studies at what was then called the Devon County School, now West Buckland School. He was a good scholar and there are frequent notes of prizes won and achievements honoured, but just as life seemed set fair for the little family, tragedy struck. Aged only five, Charles Mamerto contracted diphtheria and died. The heartache can scarcely be imagined, and the emotional shock took its toll on the whole family. In April 1893, the bishop gave Fortescue leave of absence for a year and even provided a caretaker priest in the person of the Revd H. L. Pigot, who would be assisted by Fortescue's new curate, W. Ware.

At the end of the year, Lucy and Fortescue returned to the parish to carry on as well as they might. They did so for almost five years more, with Elton still excelling at his studies. However, plans were being laid for a change, but what was envisaged was a move of some complexity. Each element of the plan would have had to be in place before anything could be certain. A move of any distance would mean that the bishops of the dioceses concerned would have needed to give approval. Provision would need to be made for Elton's further schooling and that this had been addressed was made public in a report of 23 March 1899:

Elton Gueritz, (son of the Rev. J. F. L. Gueritz of Swymbridge) of the Devon County School, West Buckland, who in the recent Cambridge Junior Examination obtained first class honours, has been offered an exhibition eligible to sons of clergy, and of the value of £55 per annum, at the famous Glenalmond College near Perth.[10]

Perth was a long way from North Devon, over 500 miles away. From North Devon the journey was most often made by sea, up the Firth of Clyde and then overland from Glasgow. It seems that neither Fortescue nor Lucy were happy for their remaining child to be that distant from them, so a plan had been constructed during the previous two years. There had been signs for those who might read them. Before there was any public indication of a possible move it was noted that among those present at the Pitlochry Highland Games in September 1897 was the Revd J. F. L. Gueritz and his family from Swymbridge. At some stage, Fortescue had contracted an exchange of livings with the Revd H. Harrison, who was the incumbent of Holy Trinity, Dunoon, but whether Glenalmond School or the parish of Dunoon was the prior arrangement is not known. This exchange was not just a matter for the two clergy. It required the unequivocal support of the Bishop of Exeter and the Bishop of Argyll and the Isles. It appears that such support was forthcoming. At the end of March 1899, a final service was held at Swymbridge, with many leaving gifts and tokens of affection being given. The family then departed for Dunoon on the banks of the Clyde near Holy Loch in the diocese of Argyll and the Isles. The new incumbent, H. Harrison, took up his post in Swymbridge on 3 April 1899.

The parish of Holy Trinity, Dunoon was closer to Glenalmond than Devon, but it may not have felt like it. The northern land route was 100 miles through mountain passes; the southern route required a ferry across the Clyde, and then 100 miles through Glasgow and on almost to Perth. The parish of Dunoon was a thriving concern. In 1847, a design for a church had been commissioned and the first stone was laid under the altar on 31 March 1849 "in the name of The Holy, Ever Blessed and Undivided Trinity". The Right Revd Alexander Ewing, the new Bishop of Argyll and the Isles, carried out the consecration and Holy Trinity opened for worship according to the rites and ceremonies of the Scottish Episcopal Church on 11 September 1850. There was much about the building to attract Fortescue, including an ornate stone altar and font, vaulted chancel and "Minton" encaustic tiles in the sanctuary. Five years before Harrison left for Swymbridge plans were drawn up to extend the church to accommodate the large number of summer visitors. The nave was extended by nearly a third to the west, and a large narthex and the tower and bells were added over the next few years so that by the time the Gueritz family arrived any necessary rebuilding was complete. The church had been built to Ecclesiological Society standards at its inception, so the battles still being fought in Colyton must have seemed further away than the mere miles between.

Fortescue's tradition of hospitality to visiting clergy, learned from his father, continued in Scotland. Just as his father had provided a place for priests of uncertain provenance and future so, it seems, did Fortescue. Staying at the parsonage in Dunoon in 1901 was one John James Elphinston Robertson. Robertson had attempted to assist in various parishes in England, but each time the incumbent had become suspicious about the validity of his orders. Robertson told different stories in different circumstances, but the truth of the matter was that he had been ordained by Thomas Wimberly Mossman, who was one of the three clergy who claimed to have secretly been consecrated bishop and who formed the Order of Corporate Reunion. The other two were F. G. Lee and J. T. Seccombe. Mossman had been a contemporary of Mamerto Gueritz at St Edmund Hall some 56 years earlier. It is therefore possible that Robertson's orders were valid but highly irregular and certainly not Anglican.

Ministry in Dunoon continued for ten years until Fortescue moved to Montrose in 1909. The Episcopal Church in Scotland functioned rather differently from the Church of England. If the clergy in Scotland felt it was time for a change, for their own sake or that of the congregation, then rather than seek preferment they would consult their bishop and, with his agreement and facilitation, arrange matters. Fortescue exchanged livings with the Revd Charles Grubb of St Mary's, Montrose and was soon involved in the social as well as the ecclesiastical life of the town.

Elton was just finishing his university education. He had passed through Glenalmond College, taken a Classics MA at Glasgow University in 1908 and was awarded the Reid Stewart Fellowship in Economic Science in 1909. Having married Eleanor Dixon Valentine Findlay on 17 July 1910, he joined the Colonial Civil Service and began his ascent of the ranks of the service in Nigeria.

In 1914, at the beginning of the First World War, Fortescue was already acting as officiating chaplain to the Episcopalian troops among those stationed at Montrose. His last known engagement with the Army was in August 1915.

On 13 September 1915, Lucy Octavia died after a bout of influenza which was compounded by ulcerative tonsillitis; the combination of the two resulted in heart failure. On the day of her funeral, there was a requiem mass at 8 o'clock, followed

Fortescue Gueritz at Montrose

by the funeral in the afternoon taken by the Primus of the Scottish Episcopal Church. Among those who sent wreaths was Valentine, the wife of Elton Gueritz; their son Elton was auditor in the Gambia at the time of his mother's death.[11]

Fortescue carried on for another year but in September 1916 sent a pastoral letter to his congregation explaining that, because of his failing health, he must retire. He was 65. He returned to England and settled at Woburn Sands, near to his daughter-in-law and the younger generation of his family, assisting in the parish of Aspley Guise when he was able. In 1927, he moved to Charlton Kings and thence to Cheltenham in order to remain close to Valentine, who had earlier moved to Cheltenham, probably in April 1926. His son Elton returned early from service in West Africa, his health seriously affected. Elton died in 1931 aged 46.

Fortescue remained in Cheltenham, living in his own rented accommodation, relishing his independence and assisting in the local churches as long as he was able. In 1943 he moved to a nursing home in Ross-on-Wye, where he died two years later on his birthday, 18 October.[12]

Mary Louisa Mortimer née Gueritz

1853–1956

Mary Louisa, always called "Min" by the family, was born in 1853 during her father's time as curate of Bigbury. When in her nineties she was asked what her earliest memory was and replied that it was being given a ride in a donkey pannier on the beach at Bigbury. She was just three at the time. When she was four the family moved to Penzance, where her godmother, Miss Fortescue, lived and where they stayed until 1860 when the family moved to Colyton. There Mary's life unfolded both in the home and in the community. Her early education was in the school run by her father in the vicarage, where her brothers and several local boys were also taught. One of those boys was Reginald Snook, whose friendship would later grow into something rather more than being teased by the tom-boy Mary.

Before that, however, her father ministered as a *locum tenens* at St Matthias, Stoke Newington, and it seems that the whole remaining family (George was by this time in the far east) took up residence in London. There were frequent returns to Colyton and in March 1868, at a service conducted by Bishop Jenner of Dunedin, Edward Peregrine Gueritz aged 13 and Mary Louisa aged 14 were confirmed. They then returned to London, where she and her brothers, Edward and Fortescue, remained even after their mother and father had returned to Devon. Of her time at school in London, Mary recalled:

> When my people returned to Colyton they left me at boarding school in Stoke Newington, where I am afraid I was somewhat of a trial to the dear old maids who ran the school. They were very strict and proper and if we met even a brother whilst out on a walk we were not allowed even to look at him ... but I enjoyed life there and was sorry to leave school at the age of sixteen, to keep house for my mother ... and to help in parish affairs.

A particular memory from this time was understandably clear even in Mary's old age. One day Miss Houghton, one of the schoolmistresses, called Mary and told her she had a visitor. It was Reginald Snook, who had taken lessons with her at the school in Colyton vicarage. He was about to leave for New Zealand to join his cousins there and had obtained written permission from her father, Mamerto, to come and say goodbye. Uncharacteristically, Miss Houghton allowed them to go for a walk together, and Reginald gave Mary a gold pencil case as a token of his affection. Reginald sailed for New Zealand the following day, 22 February 1870. During the years he was there they were not even allowed to correspond!

After working for a bank and then as a gold buyer, Reginald began bible classes for miners and other church work. Eventually the Bishop of Dunedin suggested he return to England and prepare for ordination. Reginald had intended to go to Cambridge, but another path opened for him. He would marry Mary Louisa, return with his bride to New Zealand as a lay reader and be ordained there. The necessary letters dismissory were obtained from the Bishop of Exeter, and a new course was set for both Min and Reginald.

On 21 May 1878, Mary Louisa Gueritz and Reginald Arthur Mortimer were married. Reginald was the son of John and Elizabeth Snook. Snook senior, a local medical practitioner, died in 1871, and a new font was given in his memory.

However, just before the wedding Reginald and his brother Lionel took their mother's maiden name of Mortimer.[13]

Mary's memory of the day was still understandably vivid decades later:

> I wore white cashmere with a white silk train and a veil of Honiton lace given me by the women of the parish. My four bridesmaids wore pale blue cashmere . . . fifty people sat down to the wedding breakfast.

Mary's brother-in-law Lionel had been teasing her with the story that Reginald already had a wife in New Zealand and bet her a shilling that the wedding would not come off. At the wedding breakfast, in front of 50 witnesses, Mary claimed her shilling; she later pierced it to wear as a trophy and kept it lifelong.

After the ceremony, Reginald and Mary Louisa left for North Devon, a fortnight's honeymoon, then to a sea voyage to New Zealand and their new life. The night before they sailed brother Edward appeared to say he would be going on the same sailing. He had secured an appointment in the Bank of New Zealand.

They were six weeks at sea, which Mary thoroughly enjoyed but Reginald less so. He was not such a good sailor as she and had to study Greek every day so as to be ready for his further study in New Zealand. Three weeks into the voyage both Mary and Reginald celebrated their birthdays. He was 27 and she 24. The officers of the ship gave them a dinner with champagne to celebrate.

After working as a lay reader in the parish of St Luke in Christchurch, Reginald was ordained deacon, and late in 1879 their first child was born, Edith Mary Mortimer. Then in October 1880 Mary Louisa was delivered of a son, John Lawrence. During their time at St Luke's, an epidemic of diphtheria broke out in Christchurch. The rapidly rising infection and death rate meant that the doctors were soon overwhelmed, and Reginald was given a rudimentary medical training and the care of 50 cases in his parish. When the epidemic subsided, they were exhausted and spent recovery time with relatives "up country". A pattern of overwork and subsequent debilitation was already being formed.

The curacy at St Luke's, Christchurch continued until Reginald was ordained priest in 1882, whereupon he became the first incumbent of the newly created parish of St Matthew's, St Albans. The bishop allowed the parish to be formed when the working men of the congregation all pledged a week's wages every year to fund the stipend. He seems also to have been swayed by Reginald and Mary's record of selfless service to the people.

Life was not as it had been in England, but this seemed not to bother Mary at all. She liked the informality and welcome of "colonial ways", and although they could not at first employ a maid, she professed to enjoy doing all the work until they could.

The following year, on 17 April 1882, Aimee Winifred was born. A month later Mary was seriously ill with peritonitis. The two older children went to stay with an aunt until Mary was well again; then on 25 October 1883 Reginald Mamerto was born.

In theory, Reginald senior remained the incumbent of St Matthew's until 1885, but he, Mary and their family returned to England in June 1884.[14] One thing left behind in New Zealand as something of a legacy was a collection of Mamerto's musical settings for the Holy Communion. Mary and Reginald must have taken copies with them on their outward voyage, or had them sent by post. The settings were still in frequent use at St Matthew's more than 15 years later, and not only St Matthew's, but also at Holy Trinity, Lyttleton, All Saints, Prebbleton and the Church of the Good Shepherd, Christchurch. As late as 1929, the setting was used at St Andrew's, Tinwald for their jubilee service.

One of the reasons given for the family's return to England was health. It was inferred that it was Reginald senior who was the cause for concern, and given his propensity for overworking, that seems likely. However, later events also lead to the supposition that it may have been little Reginald Mamerto who was in precarious health. The international telegraph had been operating since 1876, so they could well have had the news of the death of Mary's sister, Antonia, which would only have intensified their desire to return.[15] Reginald was given a year's leave of absence by the Bishop of Christchurch, Henry Harper, and took ship in June. Whatever the cause for their leaving, Min, Reginald and the family did not return to New Zealand after their leave expired.

The family landed in England in late July, and in early August 1884 they arrived in Colyton. When the bellringers got to hear of their arrival the bells were rung to welcome them. They must have found little cause for rejoicing. Mary's sister, Antonia, had died on 26 May, and then little Reginald Mamerto, aged ten months, died and was buried at Colyton in a service taken by his uncle Fortescue on 27

August. Had they been told that their baby was unlikely to survive? Were they going home to be with family when the inevitable happened? There seem to have been several compelling motives to make the journey with such a small child, such that the arrangements for leaving might have been in place even before Antonia's death. Whatever their reasons, all of that, compounded by the death of George in Borneo, made 1884 a truly horrible year.

As Mary Louisa's story unfolds, it becomes the story of a wife and mother, in both of which roles she appears to have excelled, but she was even more than that. She was Mary Louisa, née Gueritz, Mortimer who had sailed off with her new husband to a new and unknown future in a far-off country to support him in his ministry. She knew that would be her lot before she married Reginald, and she appears to have embraced the challenge without hesitation, but in the autumn of 1884, they were home once more.

In Colyton, with surroundings familiar to them both, they decided to stay. The children, Edith, John and Aimee, had of course never known anything other than their home in New Zealand, but in 1884 Edith was five, John was four and Aimee just two, so perhaps they settled the more easily for that. Mamerto needed a curate, so Reginald entered a new phase of ministerial life. Mary was cast once more in her role as an expectant mother, and in 1885 Dorothy Antonia was born,[16] then George in 1887 and Ernest Clement in 1888.[17]

In April 1889, it was announced that the family were moving to Roborough in North Devon. There Mary would be only 15 miles from her brother Fortescue, in Swymbridge. In October, Arthur Fortescue Mortimer was born, and then there was a gap in arrivals. Mary had borne eight children thus far, but having lost baby Reginald, her fourth child, she was caring for seven of them and for her husband. With the help of local servants, a housemaid and a cook, all was managed happily. The family were to settle in Roborough for seven and a half years.

Soon Mary's own experience of grief and loss was echoed by that of her sister-in-law Lucy and her brother Fortescue when their son Charles died of diphtheria in 1892. Possibly it was Mary and Reginald's move to Exeter and the parish of St Mary Major in December 1896 that prompted Fortescue and Lucy to begin to think in terms of a substantial move; less radical than going to New Zealand but well away from the scene of their personal tragedy. As an aside, it was less than

a year after the Mortimers' move to Exeter that Lucy, Fortescue and the family
were seen at the 1897 Pitlochry Games.

The journey for Mary and Reginald was not as distant in geographical terms,
but moving from sequestered Roborough to busy Exeter must have been quite a
challenge, especially as their latest, and as it turned out their last child, William
Lionel Gueritz Mortimer, was born not long before they set up their new home.
The house in Colleton Crescent, Exeter was spacious and the residences among
which it was to be found were occupied by some distinguished inhabitants, not a
few of them clergy. The parish of St Mary Major was, however, another matter. Set
in what was then designated West Exeter it was, at the time, particularly deprived
and hugely demanding in its poverty and pastoral needs.

Not only was the parish highly demanding, so also were the calls for Reginald
to speak and preach for various bodies, churches and causes. This inevitably
meant that he was away from home rather more than had been the case in
Roborough. Thus, the day-to-day burden of the household fell increasingly on
Mary's shoulders.

Late in 1901, Mary's father formally resigned the living of Colyton, but he
had already been living with her in Exeter for much of the year, being cared for
in his illness. Anne Gueritz, who had stayed in Colyton at the vicarage while
Mamerto was still legally the incumbent, joined the family in Exeter when his
freehold ended. In August of the following year, Anne Gueritz died and was taken
to Colyton for her burial. Then, just under two years later, at the beginning of
July 1904, having contracted influenza and bronchitis during the preceding few
months, Reginald Mortimer died.

He was keeping a commitment to preach in Manchester and when that duty
was discharged, he went to Long Sutton to see his sister, Cora, and daughter
Edith, and there he passed away. On 6 July 1904, Reginald Mortimer, aged 54, was
laid to rest in Colyton. The years of overwork had taken their toll. Widowed at
50, Mary Louisa was left with seven sons and daughters at home. The youngest,
William Lionel, was nine years old. Clearly, they could not stay in the rectory
in Colleton Crescent, so Mamerto, Mary Louisa and her children returned to
Colyton and lived at Richmond House in King Street. It was a large house and
there was room for those of the children who remained at home. Soon enough
they began to fly the nest.

Later, Mary shared a house with Sara "Kate" White, a friend of many years, who also lived in King Street with her niece. Kate had been one of the prime movers, with brother Frank, in all kinds of entertainments and social activities as well as being a longstanding district visitor.

Adelina and Mamerto left King Street to take lodgings with the Matthews family who lived in Alexandra Terrace in North Street.

Seven years after the death of Reginald, with the children beginning to follow their own paths in life, Mary was still living with Kate White and her niece, Frances. Mary was still only 57.

Mary Louisa lived to a great age, outliving all her siblings and four of her children. Of those who died before her, beginning with the latest born, William Lionel was killed fighting in the Dardanelles, dying of his wounds on 10 August 1915. The sparse, sad entry in the army records of the return of his effects to his mother included remittances to the value of £41 16s. 5d.

The next youngest, Arthur Fortescue, became a solicitor's articled clerk, probably in the family business in Colyton. By the time he was 22, he had become seriously ill and spent some time in Nordrach House, a sanatorium in Somerset. This had been established by two doctors who had themselves contracted tuberculosis and had been successfully treated at Nordrach in Germany. The Somerset sanatorium must have been one of the best of its kind at the time. There were the two doctors, nurses, 20 servants and 37 patients, who came from all over the country. The treatment may have provided some respite, but Arthur died of pulmonary tuberculosis in 1914.

Little Reginald, the fourth child, had died in 1884, aged only ten months.

Mary and Reginald's second child, John Lawrence Mortimer, returned to New Zealand and was married there to Helen Burton in 1913. They had two sons, and he died at Christchurch in 1920; he too was a victim of tuberculosis.

Of those who survived their mother, Ernest followed his grandfather to St Edmund Hall and became a clergyman, living until 1975. It was he who wrote the letter to S. L. Ollard, vice-principal of St Edmund Hall, which so illuminated Mamerto's time as an undergraduate.

George became an engineer, working for a time in the Priestman colliery, near Winlaton, Durham, and boarding with the Revd Charles Snell and his family at Blaydon. Later he went to Canada and the United States.

Antonia Dorothy, who in later life was called simply Dorothy, also lived to a great age. Early in life she had become a schoolmistress in Exeter at the Episcopal School and was living with the other staff in Pennsylvania Road when in her mid-twenties. It is to her letter that we owe the family insight into the burning of clergy effigies in Colyton. She died in June 1985.

Aimee Winifred, like both of her sisters, never married. She lived for a while at Colyton vicarage in her teens and with her sister Edith when she returned to Colyton. We know that she and Edith were the prime movers in providing a memorial to their brother Frank in 1935. The next we know of Aimee is that she died at Sidmouth on 2 May 1965, leaving an estate of over £5,000. Her sister Dorothy was an executor.

At some point between 1887 and 1891, Edith Mary, the eldest child, went to live with her aunt and uncle, Cora Elizabeth (née Snook) and Samuel Mossop. They were in Long Sutton in Lincolnshire, where Samuel was a solicitor and another uncle, Lionel Henry Mortimer, had been an articled clerk. Edith would have been about ten years old when she went to live in Lincolnshire and was there when her father, weakened by overwork and illness, came to visit in July 1904 and died during his stay. Edith stayed with the Mossops for the rest of their lives. Cora Mossop died in January 1916, and Edith remained with her uncle until he too died in 1930. With the legacy she received from her uncle Samuel, Edith returned to Colyton and built "Barnes", a substantial detached house set on a hill between Colyton and Colyford. There she lived until she too died in 1942.

Edward Peregrine Gueritz

1855–1938

Of all the children of Mamerto and Anne, Edward gained the greatest public and international notice. Perhaps that pathway really did begin when he was five years old and heard his father enthusing about Borneo and the contribution of the Brooke family to that island's development. There were many years to pass, however, and many reversals of fortune between his early years in Penzance and Colyton, and those later achievements.

Edward Peregrine Gueritz in court dress as Governor of Labuan

Several sources state that Edward was educated at St Andrew's School, Stoke Newington. This establishment was not linked to any of the St Andrew's churches in the area but was rather a "Collegiate College", which, at that time, was a name for a school preparing its students for competitive examinations, entry to university or a commercial career.

St Andrew's Collegiate College was under the headship of R. V. Chilcott, who charged fees of between two and four guineas per term dependent upon the age of the pupil and offered a sound, systematic education to the sons of gentlemen.[18]

Next, we hear of Edward in 1871 when he and Fortescue were boarding in Hackney and working as commercial clerks. Three years later, when he was 19, Edward followed his brother George into the Sarawak Civil Service. He remained with the service until 1877, when he returned to England. He was in England for the wedding of his sister Mary Louisa in 1878, and then, having joined the Bank of New Zealand, he sailed for the Antipodes. Edward remained with the bank until 1881, when he returned to Borneo. He made that voyage on the *Cutty Sark*, reputedly the only person ever to sail as a passenger on that vessel. The captain had tried to dissuade him because the only accommodation was an apprentice's cabin, but Edward insisted, paid £25 for his passage and had to live on salt beef, ship's biscuits and milk-less tea for 46 days.[19] Either by fate or divine intervention he was saved from disaster. The ship he should have sailed on was wrecked with the loss of over 200 lives. Once arrived in Borneo, Edward worked first as agent for Captain John Ross, the writer. Ross called him "Gritz", just as the people of Colyton had called Mamerto. The following year Edward joined the newly formed North Borneo Company. The company was recruiting from among former officers of the Sarawak Service, so Edward was in familiar company. Until 1884, he served as assistant resident, and when the post was made redundant, he returned to England and was in Colyton at the time of the death of his sister Antonia.

From 1885 to 1890, Edward was collector and magistrate of the Malay States. It was during this appointment, in 1887, that he married Annie Maria Cole, and in April the following year, while in Singapore, they had a daughter, Annie Laura Violet. In 1891, Edward was appointed resident of Labuan in North Borneo, where he also served as a sessions judge and judicial commissioner. In 1903, he was made Governor of Labuan and of North Borneo, where he served until his retirement in 1912.

Although Edward officially retired in 1912, he was in England in 1911, living in Colyton before moving to his retirement home in Seaton. Living with him were his wife Annie Maria, their daughter Annie Pearson and her daughter Constance Betty, who had been born while she was in North Borneo. Annie had married Aylmer Pearson at Whimple on 23 August 1907. In 1911, Pearson was still serving in North Borneo.

In 1916, Edward and Annie Maria moved to Byfleet. They had only been there a matter of weeks when fire broke out in their new home. The collection of artefacts, almost 40 years in the gathering, was almost completely destroyed, but the Union flag which had floated over the governor's residence in Borneo survived.

Annie died in 1930, and in 1932 Edward married again. By this time, he was living in Seaton in Devon at Castle Cottage, and his new wife was Louisa née Finch, who had been twice widowed. Louisa was 50 and Edward 77. Later they moved to a house called "Labuan" in Cherry Drive, Seaton, which he had named after the place of his first residency in Borneo.

On 13 October 1937, Edward wrote to his brother Fortescue with a newspaper cutting and a note for Eleanor Valentine Gueritz, the widow of Elton Gueritz. Fortescue had assisted at the wedding of his granddaughter Lucy Valentine, and this gave Edward cause to remember the weddings of Adelina and Mary Louisa when he had been the one to note that the vicarage pomegranate tree had blossomed. It was a family legend that the tree would only bloom for a vicarage wedding and, according to Edward, it had not done so since Mary's wedding in 1878. In October, the wedding in Cheltenham of Lucy Gueritz was also marked in Colyton. *Pulman's Weekly News* of 12 October reported the "Pomegranate Coincidence":

> The tradition is broken as far as the Vicarage is concerned but it is a remarkable coincidence that this year's bloom synchronises with the marriage of another Miss. Gueritz—a great grand-daughter of the late Vicar—and she was married at Cheltenham on Saturday.

Edward died a year later at "Labuan". Louisa lived on until 1968.

Henry Francis "Frank" Gueritz

1856–1929

Frank, as everyone called him, was born in Yealmpton during the family's brief stay there in 1856. He was still a baby when they moved to Penzance and only four when Mamerto was preferred to the living of Colyton with Monckton.

To the casual observer it might seem that Henry Frank Gueritz did not make such a showing in the world as did his brothers George and Edward. He was not called to holy orders, as was Fortescue, neither did he leave children to mark the world, as did his sister Mary Louisa, and yet his contribution to the realization of his father's image of the Church was as profound as that of any of his siblings.

Frank's schooling and early life in Colyton was not much recorded. He became a competent tennis player and cricketer and was often named in reports of matches and tournaments. However, adventure was to come, and in 1879 he followed his sister to New Zealand, arriving on the *Hurunui* on 8 December at the port of Lyttleton. There Frank began to forge a life for himself, and by January 1880 he had taken the mastership of St Luke's Parochial Day School, under the incumbent E. A. Lingard, with whom Reginald Mortimer initially served as curate. In August 1881, Frank matriculated to the University of New Zealand, but whether that issued in a degree is not known.

Exactly when or why Frank returned to Colyton is not entirely clear, but during 1883 he began to feature once more in the social life of the parish, especially in those entertainments organized by church members. His skills as a cricketer and tennis player and his lively personality had rendered him popular with the young people of his generation. This enabled him to involve a number of them in the Easter entertainment that year. In a varied programme, the finale was a scene from *H.M.S. Pinafore* in which Frank took the part of the First Lord and gained many plaudits for both his acting and his singing.[20]

In a time when all entertainment was live and in person, such events took on great importance in the life of the community. The entertainment in June saw Frank not just taking part but directing the whole venture and doing so with considerable skill, both creative and managerial. Brother George, home for a short while, also took part and was roundly applauded for his singing.

George had been home on leave during 1883 and had to return to Sarawak. Several months later Frank sailed from Plymouth on 15 December, bound once more for Christchurch, New Zealand. Possibly his time in Colyton had been in the nature of home leave or furlough from his work as a schoolmaster.

The year 1884 was, as we have seen, a truly awful one for the Gueritz family. There was the death of Antonia Anne, followed by that of Reginald Mamerto, the infant son of Mary Louisa and Reginald Mortimer. Then, at the end of the year, George Gueritz died in Sarawak. Edward, who had been in New Zealand working for the bank, had returned to England before Antonia's death. Mary and Reginald too had gone home and would not return to Christchurch. Frank was still there, in New Zealand, involved in the life of the community and the church. He served on the Church Temperance Committee and was also noted as playing in tennis tournaments in the local area, but a year or two later at the most, he too returned to Colyton.

In 1887, when he was 30, Frank was sponsored to membership of the English Church Union by Edmund Drower and Henry Deane. Drower would serve many years as Mamerto Gueritz' churchwarden, and Deane was treasurer for most of the church-based associations in Colyton. Henry Frank Gueritz was one of over 300 people sponsored on that occasion. Membership of the ECU was a clear and unequivocal statement of commitment to the Catholic identity of the Church of England. Frank was proving to be his father's son in several different ways.

Mamerto Gueritz' skills as a musician had been handed down to Frank. He had not only learned to sing well himself but had inherited his father's talent for teaching and leading others. In 1889, the East Devon Choral Union could boast some illustrious names among its officers and alongside them were Mamerto Gueritz the precentor and Frank Gueritz the choirmaster. Frank had already made a substantial contribution to the work of the EDCU, and when the festival was held in Colyton in the same year, it was he who held the baton.

Frank was clearly active in the world of music, both secular and sacred, but was also breaking ground in the pastoral ministry of the church in Colyton. Hitherto the work of the parish or district visitors had been the preserve of the ladies. Striking a blow for male equality, he joined the ranks of the visitors, ministering to the poor of the parish in their homes.

So, from a brief beginning in 1883, and then after his final return in 1887, Frank Gueritz had begun to take his place in the story as it is told in Colyton and to establish himself as a character in his own right. Frank found his own way in society and in the Church, a way which differed from that of his siblings and which allowed him to exercise his musical and dramatic talents in the community and still to develop a pastoral and preaching ministry. We have already seen how Mamerto Gueritz was ahead of his time in valuing and developing lay ministries, an understanding which grew and blossomed during his time in Stoke Newington where he foresaw the much greater development of the ministry of the lay reader. On 3 October 1890, Frank Gueritz left Colyton to take up his duties as a lay reader at Shermanbury in Sussex, where he lodged with sisters Sarah and Patience Holder. While there he evidently integrated well into local life and there are notices of his presence as a guest at various events.

In 1891, Mamerto Gueritz was away touring Spain and France, and Frank returned from Shermanbury for at least one visit. He joined the choir outing of 18 June to Lyme Regis. There was great excitement as some of the junior choristers, living only three miles inland, had never seen the sea! A service was held in Lyme church at 4 o'clock and Frank led the musical parts of the day, both secular and sacred, and it was noted how much better the participants played and sang with Frank leading them.

The next month brought the annual Sunday school treat. The previous year Mamerto had been too ill to take much part, but this year he was very much his old self. The usual perambulation of the town took place. Mamerto was accompanied by Frank, who was home for a visit, and it was noted that one could tell where he was simply by following the sound of laughter: "The bringer of jollity".

November 1892 saw the return of Frank Gueritz to dwell in Colyton once more. He had served the equivalent of a first curacy as a licenced lay reader for two years in Shermanbury and was back in Colyton ready to exercise that ministry alongside his father. He instituted and led a bible class for men that was to meet on Monday evenings at 7.30. Then in January 1893 Frank started short weekday services for men, at which he was normally the one to give the address. He was also the prime mover in founding the working men's club which was to prove a great success, especially with those on the margins of church life. However, other aspects of the "exuberant talent" of Henry Frank Gueritz have already been remarked and could not long be kept unexpressed. That talent was to be exercised in ways that perhaps might not then have been deemed appropriate for a priest but acceptable in a lay reader.

January 1893 was to be a very busy month. On the second day of the new year, there was a "Juveniles Party" at which Frank, with Miss K. White and Mrs Edwards, "afforded a great deal of entertainment to a large company". Then three days later he organized a party at the vicarage for unmarried ladies and gentlemen. There were impromptu charades in which "Mr F. Gueritz, with his ever ready tact and merriment, was a leading spirit". And finally, for January at least, Frank and seven of his friends organized and hosted the Bachelors' Ball, with the stated aim of reducing the number of bachelors. Frank, however, stayed firmly among the ranks of the eligible but unwed.

During the year, Frank's activities with choir and choral associations continued and grew. Alongside his work with the East Devon Choral Union, of which he was the conductor, he was also working with the smaller associations within the union, particularly this year with the Ottery Choral Festival.

By this time, Frank was in his late thirties but showed no sign of waning exuberance. In fact, quite the opposite. At the entertainment just after Christmas 1893, Frank's dramatic flair was once more in demand. He and a friend from Exeter, G. H. Kingdon, with the assistance of Miss Evans, presented the farce *Cox and Box*, which from all accounts was a great success. With Miss Evans as "Mrs Bouncer", Kingdon as "Box" and Frank playing "Cox", "The audience was kept in roars of laughter by the eccentricities of the two lodgers, while Mrs Bouncer made a most excellent landlady."[21] They raised quite a sum for the restoration fund.

Then in February 1894 was the "Grand Christmas Pantomime", which Frank wrote and directed. It was staged in St Andrew's Hall, next to the church, and, according to local reports, it was such a draw that the audience overflowed into the churchyard.

Frank was clearly not averse to using theatre to make a point. The three acts of the pantomime were "The Dame School or Disorder", followed by "The School Board or Transition", and finally "The Board School or Order". When we recall the conflict engendered over the election of the school board and the transition from small local classrooms to publicly funded education, the point that was being made is obvious. The story loosely followed that of "The Old Woman Who Lived

in a Shoe" and was played in the main by the children of the choir and the Sunday
schools. At the last moment Frank had to step in and play the Old Woman, as well
as conduct the music. This earned him much praise, which was shared with his
faithful supporters, Kate White and Agnes Elton.

That year, just as the parish was preparing for Holy Week and Easter, Mamerto
Gueritz was taken ill. The family rallied round with Fortescue, Reginald Mortimer
and others helping with the services. As the lay reader, Frank was also involved,
and he led several of the devotional services.

The year 1895 began with the pantomime, which by then was a local tradition,
it being the second year it had happened. Once more there was great acclaim and
evidence of a growing number of people willing to be involved.

The year unfolded with Frank more and more involved with the ministry of
the parish. Before the end of the year, his increasing commitment to choral music
had grown to the point that he was involved at diocesan level. On 3 December,
the Exeter Diocesan Choral Association met in the chapter house at the cathedral.
The notes of the meeting record that "Mr. H.F. Gueritz moved that the holding of
a Gregorian Festival in the Cathedral in 1897 should be explored." The motion
was agreed.

In February 1896, the pantomime was, again, a great success. It was reported
not only in the parish magazine, which might be expected to be enthusiastic, but
also in *Pulman's Weekly*, which in the past had been highly critical of anything
to do with the name Gueritz. The report, exhaustive in its detail and lavish in its
compliments, commented on the "smoothness and precision" of the production
and then:

> When it is remembered that the performers were all amateurs, and for
> the most part school children, the significance of this fact becomes even
> more remarkable, and reflects the highest credit on the ability and energy
> of the organiser, Mr. F. Gueritz. The company, numbering in all some 65
> members, had been under Mr. Gueritz's training for the comparatively
> short period of two months, and it is safe to assert that, so far as the details
> of the stage business were concerned, could not have been surpassed on
> any professional stage.[22]

It hardly needs saying that Kate White and Agnes Elton made most of the costumes. This was, in its time, a striking juxtaposition of roles and one that no clergyman could have attempted without censure. On the one hand a theatrical impresario, while on the other an effective and valued layman who, for almost a decade, worked as a district visitor, secretary of the Church Lads' Brigade, Sunday school superintendent and secretary of the football club. In addition to all of which Frank was the accredited lay reader of the parish of Colyton.

That year was not to be without its accidents. In June, while at a rook shooting at The Grove in Colyton, Frank's gun burst and shattered his thumb. It had to be amputated. Many people sent their good wishes. He gradually recovered and did so well enough to step into role once again as the director of the pantomime, which was presented in February 1897 and was another of Frank's creations which he called *The Christmas Dream*.

As the next few years came and went, the pattern was repeated. Frank was very active in the various roles and ministries he had developed in Colyton. In 1899, he was especially concerned to raise funds for the working men's club, which pleased the ladies of Colyton. They commented that their Saturday evenings were so much more pleasant for knowing where their husbands were and that they would not be coming home "the worse for wear".

For several years, Frank had been living at the vicarage while his father had been absent through illness. His aunt Adelina was also living there in her widowhood, together with Aimee Mortimer. When Mamerto Gueritz formally resigned in 1901, they all, perforce, had to leave. Shortly afterwards Frank Gueritz was exercising his ministry as a lay reader in Calstock near Tavistock. In Calstock, he remained assiduous in his pastoral work. For example, in 1913 he wrote to the incumbent of Inwardleigh, the Revd J. Jones, about a former parishioner of his, then living in Calstock, who, if he were of the right age, would qualify for the old age pension.[23] However, the unfortunate parishioner, John Carpenter, had no evidence of his age and only thought he might be over 70, the qualifying age. Carpenter needed help to contact his old parish, so Frank did it for him. When the Revd J. Jones checked his baptism registers, it was found that Carpenter was only 67 and did not yet qualify for a pension. Nevertheless, the incident reveals just a little of the continuing pastoral ministry of Henry Frank Gueritz and of his willingness to go the extra mile.

Frank was still exercising his ministry as a lay reader when he died in 1929 aged 73.

Colyton was not allowed to forget either Frank's ministry or his personality. At the annual vestry meeting of 1935, Edith Mary Mortimer and her sister Aimee Winifred asked for permission to place a carved figure of the crucified Christ on the plain cross above the tower arch as a memorial to their uncle. The church council had already discussed the proposal but wanted to have a wider view from the annual meeting. Edith had returned to Colyton from Long Sutton in 1930 and was, at this stage, living in the house she built called Barnes. She and Aimee Winifred spoke at the annual meeting and reminded those present of all that their brother had done for the parish, pointing out that Henry Frank Gueritz was still held in affection by the older Colytonians. The older Colytonians remembered.

A faculty was applied for and was evidently successful. The figure was commissioned from an Oberammergau artist and hangs there to this day.[24]

Antonia Anne Gueritz

1859–84

Antonia was born in Penzance and was just 19 months old when the family celebrated their first Christmas in Colyton. Between her mother and aunt Adelina, she would have had a more than adequate preparation for life in such a setting. We know little, if anything, of her early years until, when she was 19, she was bridesmaid for her sister Mary Louisa when Minnie married Reginald Mortimer.

After that Antonia began to take an active part in the work of the church in Colyton. Between them the parish magazines, the service register and the vestry journal give a sparse but telling commentary. In her early teens, Antonia was among the first workers for the Dorcas Society, a commitment which continued throughout her life. Then she began assisting Agnes Elton in the infants' Sunday school, later becoming one of the superintendents. In her early twenties, Antonia would occasionally be a sponsor at the baptism of an infant who may well have later joined the Sunday school, where their "godmother" would be there to welcome them. She also got to know the children well through her work with them in the Children's Guild. In addition to all of this, Antonia worked as a district visitor alongside her mother, brother Frank and a considerable team, visiting the poor and sick in their homes and calling the Dorcas Society into action when such help was needed. However, by all accounts, Antonia's first and greatest love was the children of the parish. Her work in the Children's Guild and her role in the Sunday school put her into direct contact with the families of ordinary Colyton folk and, as they later amply demonstrated, the children of the parish adored her.

In 1881, Mamerto and Anne were living temporarily in Templeton, while Fortescue and Mary were at the vicarage in Colyton with Antonia. When brother George came home on leave in 1883, Frank put on one of his entertainments in which Antonia and George took part. As his time of furlough was ending, George took his leave and returned to Sarawak. She would never see him again.

During the spring of 1884 Antonia was ill. On 24 May, she died aged just 25. The family was devastated. So were the children of the parish. Friends gathered from near and far to support them and share in their grief. Stuckey Coles celebrated the requiem and took the funeral, and 50 of the children processed with the coffin from the church and up the hill to the cemetery, all carrying white blossoms to lay on it for the burial. Fittingly, Antonia Anne was laid to rest in the same plot as Antonia Josepha, her grandmother. Later, in July, the Sunday School Festival was held as usual, but this year it was a solemn occasion, quite unlike the usual party atmosphere. Edward Peregrine was home from Borneo and was able to see Antonia before she died. He was also there at the Sunday School Festival, assisting Mamerto as he gave each child a small gift as a token of Antonia's touch upon their lives.

Perhaps this is a fitting image with which to close these chapters of the Gueritz story; a child, standing at a graveside, holding a white flower and remembering Antonia Anne Gueritz.

In that same hillside cemetery where those children gathered now rests Antonia Josepha Moxica Gueritz, that indomitable Spanish lady. Close by are Mamerto and Anne Gueritz, and their daughter Antonia Anne. Near them lie the beloved son-in-law Reginald Mortimer and his infant son Reginald Mamerto. And awaiting the resurrection with them is Adelina Valentina Bartlett.

For Mamerto and Anne Gueritz, their children and their descendants

Oremus.

Requiem aeternam dona eis, Domine, et lux perpetua luceat eis.

Requiescant in pace.

Notes

1. *Sarawak Gazette*, 2 February 1885: "Domestic Occurrences. On the 18th ultimo, on board the S.S. Bujang Baram, in the Baram river, Mr George Gueritz, Resident in Charge of the Baram District, aged 35." For the purpose of this exercise and given the sometimes uncertain dating of the local press, the earlier date, attested by the record of the grave, has been preferred.

2. The first students at the Exeter Diocesan Training School were, inevitably at the time, all male, and according to the first prospectus they were expected "at the least to read English prose intelligently, to spell correctly from dictation, to write a good hand, and to work accurately with the first four rules of arithmetic, simple and compound and to have an elementary acquaintance with Scripture, History, the Church Catechism, English Grammar, English history and Geography. Any further knowledge he may possess will be so much in his favour."

3. *Celtic Quarterly Magazine* 18 (1832).

4. D. M. Bertie, *Scottish Episcopal Clergy 1680 to 2000* (Edinburgh: T & T Clark, 2000), p. 180.

5. South West Heritage Centre, Devon Archives, Ref. Colyton 3483A/PR14.

6. *Exeter and Plymouth Gazette*, 28 September 1866.

7. *Exeter and Plymouth Gazette*, 26 September 1873.

8. *Exeter and Plymouth Gazette*, 6 October 1876.

9. *North Devon Journal*, 6 December 1887.

10. *North Devon Journal*, 23 March 1899.

11. Eleanor Dixon Valentine Gueritz née Findlay.

12. Obituary, *Gloucestershire Echo*, 19 October 1945.

13. A more complete account of the change of name and the wedding can be found in Chapter 12. It should also be noted that Reginald Mortimer was related, through his mother, to Robert Cecil Mortimer, Bishop of Exeter from 1949 to 1973. Robert was the

grandson of John Mortimer, the youngest brother of Elizabeth Snook née Mortimer, who was Reginald's mother. Robert was two years old when Reginald died.

[14] Card index reference: Ref M 653 (Photocopy held).

[15] The first direct links with London were established in 1876, via Australia, Java and Suez. The first telegrams to London cost 15 shillings per word, around £120 in 2023. By 1884, prices had come down considerably, but the cost was still enormous.

[16] The writer of the letter confirming the burning of effigies. Some of the records name her as Antonia Dorothy, but she appears elsewhere as Dorothy Antonia. She certainly used the name Dorothy later in life, and this is how her descendants, notably Admiral "Teddy" Gueritz, spoke of her.

[17] The writer of the letter in Appendix 1.

[18] This is given in the *Sabah Society Journal* 15 (1998). It purports to be quoting from Edward Gueritz' diaries but acknowledges that they had to be reconstructed from notes after he burned the originals. It also appears in the *Malaysian Daily Express* obituary. An advertisement for St Andrew's Collegiate College appeared in the *Hackney and Kingsland Gazette* of 17 February 1872.

[19] Obituary, *Western Morning News and Daily Gazette*, 5 August 1938.

[20] *Colyton Parish Magazine*, May 1883.

[21] *Colyton Parish Magazine*, February 1894.

[22] *Pulman's Weekly*, as reported verbatim in the *Colyton Parish Magazine*, February 1896.

[23] South West Heritage Centre, Devon Archives, Ref. Colyton 3483A/PR14.

[24] The annual vestry meeting was reported in the *Devon and Exeter Gazette* on 15 March 1935.

The supporting cast

Having left Mamerto Gueritz and his family resting in resurrection hope we now turn to some of those whose interaction with his life and ministry merits their inclusion in a list of the "Supporting Cast". As we do so we should note that, in the world of theatre, characters who might appear in such a list will include allies and friends as well as enemies and opponents. Those who appear here do so on the basis of their place in the story of Mamerto Gueritz. As already noted, given that other writers have already done them justice, the best known of the Oxford men are not included here. These few who are given space interacted directly with Mamerto Gueritz, but some may not be known in the wider context of the Oxford Movement, even by the keen student of Anglo-Catholic history. With one exception, these notes are not truly biographies but rather vignettes. They are written around the encounters each of them had with Mamerto Gueritz, in the hope that this will help the reader to a more informed understanding of him either in his role as the vicar of Colyton or in the setting of the Oxford Movement, or just as Mamerto Gueritz.

William Henry Baptist Proby

1832–1915

Of all the supporting cast in this drama, William Henry Baptist Proby was involved the most deeply in the story of Mamerto Gueritz as it unfolded in the parish of Colyton, and therefore he is given first place. Where the playing of his part directly affected the ecclesiastical life of the parish and its incumbent, those incidents will only be briefly mentioned here because they have been more completely developed in the main body of the work. This is Proby's story.

According to the records of the Scottish Episcopal Church, in 1834 (sic) William Henry Baptist Proby was born in Barton-under-Needwood, Staffordshire.[1] He was the first child of Commander William Henry Baptist Proby RN and, in the style of the newspaper reports of the time, of "The Lady of Commander etc. etc." The lady's name was Louisa Mary née How, and she was the daughter of the Revd Samuel How of Southleigh in East Devon and of Stickland in Dorset. Commander Proby also had clerical antecedents, but his were even more exalted than those of his wife. His grandfather had been the Dean of Lichfield; he was great nephew to the first Lord Carysfort and the eldest son of the Revd John Baptist Proby of St Mary's, Lichfield. Around the time of the younger William's birth and for several generations, both before and after that event, the family had property and kin in Staffordshire. However, concerning their firstborn and given that there are several other errors in the Scottish records, a check of the birth and census records revealed that the younger W. H. B. Proby was born, not in 1834, for that is when his younger brother Charles was born, but in 1832.[2] The census records also reveal that William was born in Barton-under-Needwood in Staffordshire, which contradicts a local tradition that he was either born at or brought as an infant to Borcombe Farm, which lies south of Northleigh and east of Colyton in East Devon. Local tradition in Devon can sometimes be more powerful than feeble historical facts. Certainly, his mother Mary Louisa purchased the farm around that time, possibly during one of the many sea voyages her husband made. There was also considerable land and property which she had inherited in the parish of Northleigh nearby and that inheritance was the point at which the manorial rights of Northleigh passed to Louisa Proby. The *Imperial Gazetteer of England and Wales*, published between 1870 and 1872, noted that the manor had originally belonged to Lord Petre, had passed in 1794 to J. M. Howe (sic) Esq. and had subsequently passed to Mrs Proby.

Borcombe Farm figures much in this story. It was originally part of the estate of Sir William Petre, a staunch Catholic who contrived still to be welcome at court during the reigns of Henry VIII, Edward VI, Mary Tudor and Elizabeth I.[3] In the 1720 extension to the main house, a chapel was created which, during the nineteenth century, became part of the parish of Colyton. Within the chapel is a tabernacle intended for the reservation of the Blessed Sacrament, originally created for Roman Catholic use by the Petre family. This seems to date from the time of Sir Edward Petre, a Jesuit and confessor to King James II.

The house at Borcombe and the chapel appear again later in this tale, but, in defiance of local tradition, it is doubtful that the Proby family ever used Borcombe as their main domicile, although the house was substantial enough. For much of its history Borcombe was let to tenant farmers.

The Proby family home at this time was The Ryalls in nearby Seaton. Commander Proby will necessarily have been there as late as September 1833 because the *Bristol Mercury* of 7 June 1834, in its customary staccato style, reports: "At his seat, The Ryalls, Seaton, Devon, The Lady of Capt. W. H. B. Proby, a son."

This marked the arrival of Charles How Proby. It is interesting to note that from this point the rank afforded to Proby senior shifts between commander and captain. This is because, although officially he remained "Commander RN", during the periods when the Royal Navy could not use his services and thus declined to pay him, he also commanded various free trading vessels where he would have been afforded the title "Captain".

Even if he was at sea again in the intervening months, by the spring of 1835 Commander Proby was again in Devon and active in serving the community. He was concerned to provide shelter and work for the poor of the area and was engaged in correspondence with the Poor Law Commissioners to that end. He reported to them that a meeting had been held on 26 March 1835 when a committee had been formed with the intention of exploring the provision of a workhouse for the paupers of Seaton and Beer. He asked what immediate intentions the Commission had in this respect and whether or not they would sanction building a workhouse within the parish. A reply was received within the month, confirming that the Commission would like an efficient workhouse for the parish of Seaton and Beer and requesting a report from their Assistant Poor Law Commissioner appointed for the task. They further commented that they would not allow any private or partial advantage of local businessmen to be exercised to the detriment of those for whom the work was to be carried out, namely the poor of the parish. This was not an accusation against Proby or any of the other proposers, merely an indication that the Commissioners were aware of the possibility.

The outcome of the correspondence is entirely another story, but this brief example indicates something of the family milieu into which the infant William Henry and his brother Charles were born.[4] Then in the autumn of 1836, "Oct 25 At the Ryalls, Seaton, Devon, the Lady of Capt W.H.B. Proby, a daughter."[5] This was Sarah Louisa, whose arrival was followed by that of her sister Mary the next year. The little family was complete, for all too brief a time. The *Gentleman's Magazine* of April 1840 contained the obituary of "Capt W. H. B. Proby R.N. who died aged 45 on November 26th 1839 at The Ryalls near Seaton."

It was a stirring account of a life full of adventure and voyages, of talent, and of merit recognized but not always fully rewarded. William the younger was eight years old when he became the "man of the house", his brother Charles only six, their sister Sarah just four and Mary still an infant. Without underestimating in any degree the grief that was theirs, the little family was not without means and the boys could be given opportunities that befitted their station in life and the girls enabled to live as gentlewomen.

Louisa Mary, her children and six servants were still at Ryalls the following year. At various times she visited family in Staffordshire, taking her daughters with her. Time passed and just over a decade after the death of her husband Louisa Proby was engaged in a legal exchange of some of her Northleigh lands and property with Sir Edmund Prideaux of Farway. The Inclosure Commissioners for England and Wales deemed the exchange to be mutually beneficial. Having noted Mrs Proby's skills at buying and selling land to advantage, this can hardly be doubted.

In 1851, Louisa Mary and Sarah Louisa visited relatives at Milwich in Staffordshire, leaving Mary, aged 12, at The Ryalls in the care of her governess. William, aged 19, was boarding as a scholar in Brighton either prior to going up to Trinity College, Cambridge, where earlier generations of Proby clergy had gained their degrees, or as a congenial place to be between terms. In using the term "congenial", it should be remembered that the great wave of Anglo-Catholic church building had not yet fully arrived in Brighton. St Paul's had opened in 1848 and was gaining ground. The ancient church of St Nicholas would be rebuilt in 1853, but plans had been laid and the work of the architect, R. C. Carpenter, was thoroughly rooted in Cambridge and the Camden Society or, as it was later known, the Ecclesiological Society.

In June 1854, William's younger brother Charles purchased (or had purchased for him) a commission as an ensign in the First West India Company, a rank replaced in 1871 by that of second lieutenant.[6] In August of the same year, he was promoted, without purchase, to be ensign in the 1st Regiment of Foot, otherwise known as "The Royals". That promotion took him to the Crimea, where further promotion in the field to full lieutenant quickly followed.

William, by this time, was immersed in his studies at Cambridge. He was by all accounts an assiduous and talented scholar. However, his happiness at Cambridge was to be sadly marred. In August 1855, Charles Proby fell ill at Sebastopol with the "Crimean fever", now known as brucellosis. He was sufficiently ill to be sent home to England and then, as his condition deteriorated, was obliged to interrupt his passage in Malta. In the hospital in Malta, on 10 September 1855, Charles Proby died. He was just 21 years old.[7]

William resumed his studies, having already been awarded a Bachelor's degree, first class, and winning first place in the Tyrwhitt's Hebrew Scholarship in that same year. At this time, the Bachelor of Arts degree was mainly classical in content. In 1856, William took the Theology Tripos and in addition won the Carus Greek Prize. It may have seemed that a life in academia beckoned, but that was not, apparently, where his heart was taking him. As was the custom for those destined for holy orders, as soon as his studies were complete, he was made deacon by the Bishop of Winchester and began to serve his title at East Hatley and Tadlow in Cambridgeshire. Ordained priest in 1857 by the Bishop of Ely, William remained in his first curacy, living as a lodger at Parker's Farm, East Hatley until 1861.

By this time, his mother and sisters had moved to 4, Chesterfield Place in Melcombe Regis in Dorsetshire, where they managed with just three servants. Sara Louisa managed the household in Chesterfield Place when her mother was absent dealing with affairs in East Devon. When visiting Seaton and Northleigh, Louisa Mary no longer lived at The Ryalls but lodged elsewhere with her younger daughter Mary. The old home was either sold or let.[8]

Having served for five years, William Proby resigned his curacy in Cambridgeshire and moved to Scotland to serve in the diocese of Brechin in the Scottish Episcopal Church. He was first appointed curate of St Ternan, Muchalls, then curate in charge and then incumbent.

This move may seem at first surprising, but William was not alone in making such a departure, as we have seen in the case of Jose Fortescue Gueritz. Sustainable inferences may be made, especially in the light both of William's later development and what the Episcopal Church of Scotland offered Anglican refugees from the south:

> Not a few of the younger English clergy of that time were depressed and
> unsettled by the Erastianism and worldliness of the Church of England and
> were greatly attracted to the Church in Scotland by reason of its greater
> freedom.[9]

Another, possibly even more powerful, incentive lay in the person of Bishop Forbes of Brechin, once described as "A Scottish Pusey". When Forbes went up to Brasenose College in 1840, Newman was all but lost to the Church of England; he was already thinking of resigning St Mary's and retiring to Littlemore. It was with Edward Bouverie Pusey that the young Forbes formed a deep and lasting friendship, a bond that was to shape and grow his own discipleship and ministry:

> But it was the saint in Pusey more than the scholar that brought him
> (Forbes) constantly to Tom Quad and Christ Church . . . here was religion
> in a life, not in a book.[10]

Forbes' curacy at St Peter's, Oxford was followed by an attempt, at Pusey's invitation, to sort out the difficulties at St Saviour's, Leeds. This was a task beyond the strength, if not the abilities, of Alexander Forbes so, again at Pusey's prompting, he took up an earlier, less demanding, invitation to take charge of the Scottish Episcopal Church at Stonehaven. Forbes had only just arrived there when W. E. Gladstone, who was in Scotland visiting his father, suggested him for the vacancy in see of the diocese of Brechin. With support from the majority of the clergy, especially after Gladstone's persuasive urging, Forbes was consecrated bishop on the feast of St Simon and St Jude 1847. There were few church buildings and very little money, but clergy who were committed to the sacraments, to their people and to Church principles would find unwavering support from their father in God. It was his commitment to the sacrament of the altar, expounded in a charge to his clergy, that caused Forbes to be charged with heresy. When he was tried in 1859, his opponents were not prepared for the considerable reaction against them that their charges had provoked. The trial resulted not even in a demand that Forbes retract his teaching but in an admonition. To an onlooker it might have seemed something of a damp squib. For Forbes, it left emotional scars that were with him lifelong. It was to this battle-proven bishop, to the diocese of Brechin and to the people of Muchalls that in 1861 William Henry Baptist Proby pledged duty and service. It was here also that his combative instincts, which later proved to be central to his nature, began to emerge. That, however, developed alongside his maturation as pastor, preacher and priest.

Parochial ministry in the Episcopal Church in Scotland differed considerably from that in the Church of England. Having noted some of the advantages for catholic-minded clergy, there were still comparative disadvantages. This was not the Established Church of the country; it did not have the same status in law as its English relation; clergy did not enjoy the same rights and social privileges as their English counterparts. It was a minority ministry, which brought its own challenges, and although as such it was never easy it did offer a sense of authenticity to the so-called "Puseyite" clergy. They were responding to their calling as priests rather than filling the societal role occupied by clergy.

Muchalls was no easy cure. There was no church building, simply a small chapel. Proby was starting, quite literally, from the ground up. However, his labours and the support he had from his bishop began to bear fruit and a church building was planned. Meanwhile, the plight of his diocesan bishop began to weigh upon Proby. Forbes was ill housed and in addition to his episcopal duties had the care of a parish. Characteristically, having devised an answer to the problem, without waiting for approval from his bishop, Proby acted. At the August synod of 1862, Proby proposed a motion to provide adequate income and housing for Bishop Forbes by the opening of a fund with the intention that once the housing had been provided and once the interest of the fund reached £400 the fund would be closed. He also proposed: "It shall be incompetent for the bishop to hold any incumbency either within or outside the diocese."

It was well meant but precipitate, a tendency which was to be repeated in future years. Proby would have done well to consult the bishop prior to proposing the motion because Forbes refused to allow the plan to be acted upon.

In 1864, there was a correspondence between Proby and a certain Revd Dr Begg.

Begg had asserted, in a letter to the *Montrose and Brechin Review*, that an analysis of the religious affiliations of imprisoned criminals showed that those claiming to be Episcopalian made up a disproportionately high number of the prison population when that denomination's overall membership was considered. He claimed that the Free Church of Scotland, the United Presbyterian Church (to which he belonged) and the Congregationalists provided 154 criminals, which compared favourably with the 220 supplied by the Episcopalians. It was patently an absurd claim, which exposed Dr Begg to ridicule and would have been much better ignored. However, the combative element in Proby would not allow him to let it lie. He engaged in the correspondence with a will and his first salvo clearly revealed his underlying convictions.

He first showed that Dr Begg was working with out-of-date information, thus challenging the integrity of his assertions, and then replied:

> Our Presbyterian brethren will naturally attribute so large a proportion of criminals to what they consider erroneous in our principles . . . I cannot help entertaining the belief that the greater number of our (Episcopalian) criminals is principally furnished by those two dioceses where what we call "Church Principles" (i.e. what is commonly called Puseyism and Tractarianism) are lowest viz Edinburgh and Glasgow. Such a view may at all events be considered probable.[11]

Proby's stance was as partisan and partial as that of Dr Begg. All other considerations were set aside; density of population, poverty, the inevitable tendency of large cities, especially those with ports, to have a higher incidence of crime. All instead was attributed to the woeful lack of "Church Principles".

Such skirmishes notwithstanding, the work in Muchalls grew until, on Thursday, 20 April 1865, the foundation stone of the chancel of St Ternan's Church was laid. The clergy were vested in surplices and stoles, and Proby was the celebrant. As the inscription records, the stone was laid by:

The Very Rev Robert Kilgour Thom, Dean of this diocese of Brechin and
Incumbent of St. John the Baptist Church, Drumlithie on Thursday in
Easter week, April 20th in this year of grace 1865, in the episcopate of the
Rt. Rev Alexander Penrose Forbes D.C.L. and in the incumbency of the
Rev. W. H. B. Proby M.A.

Later in the same year, on 2 August, a diocesan synod was held at which Proby
was the preacher. The synod was worthy of note simply because, as the dean
reported, there was no agenda because there was no special business to transact!

From this, it might have seemed that Proby was an ascendant star in the
Scottish firmament, but on Thursday, 18 January 1866 it was noted in the local
press:

The Rev W. H. B. Proby having resigned this living and returned to England,
the Vestry, with the Bishop's sanction, have unanimously presented the Rev
W Hall, Curate of Newtonhill to the incumbency.[12]

It may have been that the Episcopal Church of Scotland was beginning to have less
of an appeal to one of Proby's convictions than it had formerly. As he himself had
noted, there were Scottish dioceses where the bishops were vehemently opposed
to the teaching of the Tractarians. Matters came to a head when Frederick George
Lee was condemned by the Bishop of Aberdeen. Bishop Forbes had warmly
welcomed Lee to Scotland, urging him to proceed with caution and tact. However,
Lee was never easy to direct and caution and tact were not natural attributes
for him. He had first been incumbent of St John's, Aberdeen and then, when he
resigned because of opposition to his teaching and liturgy, the priest of St Mary's
Mission Chapel. The Bishop of Aberdeen's condemnation of Lee was conducted,
not in the courts where it could have been challenged, but in a circular letter to
the clergy. In spite of Lee's habitual recalcitrance, he might have hoped for better
from his bishop, perhaps for more pastoral integrity. It was not forthcoming, and
Lee left for England not long before Proby.

In the event, it was family responsibilities that called Proby home to England.
His mother had been ill and died on 12 January 1866 in the house at Melcombe
Regis, and William, as the new head of the family, had responsibilities to discharge.

Proby was now of the "landed gentry" in that there were properties and farmland in East Devon, Staffordshire and Dorsetshire. Moreover, he was now Lord of the Manor of Northleigh and of the considerable acreage there which his mother had acquired and to which he later added.

While organizing his affairs in East Devon during 1867, Proby was listed as "Officiating Priest" in the service registers at Colyton. His assistance in the absence of the vicar, Mamerto Gueritz, was not an unalloyed success![13]

The title "Officiating Priest" tells more than at first appears. William Proby's precipitate return to England was made necessary by family circumstances. Either because of the resulting pressure of time or because he had been unsuccessful in his attempts, Proby lacked a "living". To be offered a "living", that is a parish and its income and parsonage house and incidentally the place it afforded in society, signified the support of a patron and, at the very least, the toleration of the diocesan bishop. Given Proby's brief experience as a curate at East Hatley and Tadlow and possibly also given the distinctly "Puseyite" character already evident in his ministry, it was unlikely that he would find a parish immediately. He would have to be content to serve another curacy and obtained one in 1867 in a setting entirely congenial to his Catholic convictions, that of senior curate of St Augustine's, Haggerston, in London.

The incumbent, the Revd George Hervey, had been presented to the living three and a half years earlier. St Augustine's was to be one of three new parishes in Shoreditch, but it was not until Friday, 12 April 1867 that Dr Anderson, formerly Bishop of Rupert's Land,[14] consecrated the magnificent new church. More than 30 clergy assisted at the ceremony and in the evening the preacher was the Revd Charles Lowder. At this point, Fr Lowder, as he became known to his people, was the perpetual curate of St Peter's, London Docks, which had been consecrated the previous year. Fr Lowder was the founder of the Society of the Holy Cross (SSC), an order for Anglican priests after the model of St Vincent de Paul and the Lazarists.

Haggerston was one of the great centres of the Ritual Revival. There Proby gained first-hand experience of the work of a sisterhood in the parish. He was caught up in the great surge of church building which resulted in there being a curacy for him to serve.

Here he met Robert Brett, a layman and a medical doctor, for whom the Catholic Revival had provided the heart and centre of his religious life and who was largely responsible for the great plan for Haggerston which resulted in the building of St Augustine's, followed by St Chad's in 1869 and St Columba's in the same year. By the turn of the decade, this area was described as "the most extensive and closely concentrated Anglo-Catholic outpost in the whole of London".[15]

This was the ecclesiastical milieu into which William Henry Baptist Proby entered on his return to England. He held his licence at Haggerston for two years, until 1869, although he was often absent from the parish. In 1870, he is again noted as an "Officiating Priest" in Colyton. Then there followed another ministry at Hitchin in Hertfordshire from 1870 to 1871, but that seems never to have been a formal appointment and *Crockford's Clergy List* of 1901 is clear that his final curacy was at Haggerston. Additionally, in the 1871 census Proby is registered as living at 47 Hitchin Hill in the company of a servant and a housekeeper, where he is described not as a clerk in holy orders, as might have been expected, but rather as a "Landowner".

This was the period in which Proby began a journey from mainstream Anglicanism into the Catholic Apostolic Church. It was partly provoked by the pervasive Protestant element in the Church of England which denied, as it seemed to him, the catholicity of the Church. This was anathema to Proby. There will necessarily have been other factors, but more anon.

During 1872, Proby had three short works for children published.[16] We might imagine that books for children would be uncontentious, but not when W. H. B. Proby was the author! That which caused the greatest reaction was *The Church Catechism Made Easy*.[17] There were numerous negative comments in the press, but a critic, writing in the *Carmarthen Weekly Reporter*, inadvertently reveals both the negative and the positive in showing just how widespread the pamphlet's use had become in only a year.[18] The title of the article was "Ritualism Developing Itself in Carmarthen". It referred to a small pamphlet which had been extensively circulated among Carmarthen's confirmation candidates. The complainant wrote:

> The author states in the preface that it was, "Prepared for such persons who as, either from age or smallness of ability are unable to master the long and sometimes intricately constructed answers in the Catechism".

Among the many elements complained of was Proby's assertion that the Prayer Book Catechism was inadequate because it failed to assert that not only had the Lord commanded bread and wine to be received but that he had commanded them to be consecrated and offered. Another cause of offence was that in the question-and-answer section of the pamphlet it was asserted that "Romish" doctrine was proclaimed:

> "What is done with Christ's body and blood in the Lord's Supper?"
> "They are taken and received by the faithful."
> "Are they taken and received after the manner of a figure only?"
> "No, they are taken and received verily and indeed."

Another affront to the complainant was the affirmation of the place of the Blessed Virgin Mary in the plan of salvation, but following that, something that would have been of considerable annoyance to Proby and others of his persuasion, was the challenge "Is this the teaching of our Protestant Church of England in the nineteenth century?"

Quite simply, for those who considered themselves part of what has been called the Oxford Movement—the Tractarians, the Puseyites, the Ritualists—the reply would have been the same: "The Church of England is not Protestant. It is both Catholic and Reformed."

Sometime in 1872, Proby was again in Colyton and assisting with the services. He was most active in the second part of the year, taking a large proportion of the services in the final quarter of the year. In 1873, he was still in East Devon and Northleigh, where he chaired the Farway, Northleigh, Offwell and Widworthy Agricultural Association annual meeting. The following year he was present at the association's annual ploughing match, of which he was a patron. Whatever else was occupying his energies, Proby maintained a close interest in the lives and wellbeing of the farmers and tenants on his lands and in the surrounding parishes. However, as far as the church in Colyton was concerned, Proby was taking services until April 1873 and then disappears from liturgical view. This reflects not only his growing attachment to the Catholic Apostolic movement and his increasing opposition to the Protestantism rife in the Church of England, but also the degree of estrangement his actions had created between himself and Mamerto Gueritz.

During the next few years, when in London, Proby resided at River House in Duncan Street, Islington. An affinity with the Irvingite Church had been in gestation for some time, possibly since or even before the year in Hitchin. It was a development which was to change Proby's spiritual and ecclesiastical life both in London and in Devon, and it was most opportune that there was also on Duncan Street a Catholic Apostolic church. In 1889, to look forward a little for a moment, the Ordnance Survey showed a Catholic Apostolic chapel in a building adjoining Colyton House in King Street, Colyton. It had clearly been there for some time because, as reported in the newspapers,

> At half past four in the morning of Wednesday 10th February 1875 the "Irvingite" Chapel, the property of the Rev. W.H.B. Proby, King Street, was discovered to be on fire.[19]

The source of the fire was in a stove on the upstairs floor. The chapel was repaired and returned to Irvingite use. It was obviously in use earlier than the time of the fire in 1875 and probably by April 1873 when Proby's public ministry as an Anglican priest came to an end. In opening a private place of worship in the parish of Colyton Proby placed a divide between himself and Gueritz. That separation was occasionally acrimonious, but it did not prevent the two of them engaging fully in the life of the community. To the end of his life Proby was careful to defend the role of the "lawful parish priest", even though he had eschewed that authority himself.

Before we examine Proby's growing relationship with the Catholic Apostolic Church, there is yet another skirmish to be noted. Although often in Colyton and Northleigh, Proby maintained his *pied-à-terre* in Duncan Street, and in 1878 he rose once more to a Protestant challenge. The *London Evening Standard* of 9 October carried a letter from Proby defending the Revd Alexander Mackonochie against the charge that he "perverted" to Rome some sisters of St Mary's Priory, Hackney. At that time, those Anglicans who joined the Roman Catholic Church were labelled "perverts" rather than converts. Mackonochie was still perpetual curate of St Alban's, Holborn but also warden of the priory. The heart of Proby's letter, given here, reveals something of him as he was in his mid-forties:

> Having been at the time curate of the parish in which the sisterhood was working—St. Augustine's Haggerston—I may also state that I have often heard the late incumbent, Mr. George Hervey, deplore the ways in which the sisters and their chaplain interfered with him in his work, instead of confining themselves within their proper limits; and his satisfaction at the way in which the sisterhood after the secession, worked in the parish under their present respected Mother and Warden. [The warden was Mackonochie.] Your readers will now have one item of information towards judging the reasonableness of Mr. Weldon's attack on sisterhoods generally; an attack which I conceive to be mean and cowardly, though quite characteristic of Protestantism.
>
> River House, Duncan Street, Islington. October 8.

The previous warden, himself an ardent Romanist, the mother superior and several sisters of the priory had all seceded to Rome and attempted to take many parishioners with them. Evidently Proby considered both their "Romanizing" behaviour and their departure as something of a betrayal, but his main intent in the letter was twofold: to counter Protestantism in the Church and to defend a brother priest against injustice. Alexander Mackonochie had already seen much of that and was to see more in the years to come.

After 1869, Proby never again held an appointment in the Church of England. His interest in and subsequent allegiance to the Catholic Apostolic Church was evidently germinating before then, but given the evidence so far of his capacity for precipitate action, the shift, when it came, may well have been quite rapid given that within no more than four years he had created an Irvingite chapel in his erstwhile colleague's parish of Colyton. Some of the motives for this realignment of loyalties are evident. On the one hand, there was Proby's antagonism to the forces of Protestantism, which he saw primarily as a contamination of the life of the Church of England, and ultimately as a serious hindrance to the defence of its catholicity. On the other hand, Proby was not simply a Romanizer. He did not adopt, as many of his colleagues had, the use of the title "Father". His use of ritual was based on a desire for authenticity which did not allow simply for a blind acceptance of Roman practices. But more than this, he had lost faith in the integrity of the Established Church and its basis in the Prayer Book. Proby was still partially resident in Duncan Street for some years after 1878, but this was a period in which he travelled in the Middle East, and as far afield as the north-western frontier of India.[20] On his return, probably in 1880, he settled down to another task.

In 1881, Proby was beginning work on his next book, *The Annals of the Low-Church Party in England, Down to the Death of Archbishop Tait*.[21] Part of the work involved research into the "surplice riots" in Exeter, and this resulted in a request for information to Dr Thomas Shapter, formerly of Exeter and a witness to the events in view. Shapter, whose main work was medicine, grudgingly complied:

> My dear Sir, Accompanying this is the account I promised of the surplice question etc. in Exeter, 1844 and 1845 . . . You will understand that I have nothing more to do with it than assisting you with your enquiries by giving you what is otherwise open to you or to anyone to arrive at. As I said before, my feeling is that it is such a sorry affair the less said about it the better.[22]

Thomas Shapter's implied disapproval of the project notwithstanding, the work continued but not to the exclusion of all else. An inserted page in the family Bible has a note, in his own distinctive hand, of Proby's marriage on 6 September 1883 in the Catholic Apostolic Church, Duncan Street, Islington to Blanche, eldest surviving daughter of George Alderman Arnald, commercial manager, and the late Julia his wife (née Parker). Proby was 51 years old and Blanche 36.

The address given for the marriage registers was Acacia Cottage, Albury. Albury was where the leaders of the Catholic Apostolic Church had "separated" themselves as they planned the great work. If Proby was driven to seek another spiritual home by his disgust with the Church of England, he may also have been guided by more tender feelings. The Arnald family were staunch Irvingites.[23]

The highly provocative *Annals* was published in 1888. Proby declared in the preface that the Prayer Book had been "marred by the Zwinglianism of another set of men" and that "the distinctive tenets of Calvinism and Zwinglianism must needs be deemed erroneous".[24] In thus damning the Book of Common Prayer,

WILLIAM HENRY BAPTIST PROBY, Clerk in Holy Orders, M.A. of Trinity College, Cambridge, eldest son of the late William Henry Baptist Proby, Commander in the Royal Navy, and Louisa Mary his Wife (née How), was married, September 6th 1883, in the Catholic Apostolic Church, Duncan Street, Islington, to BLANCHE, eldest surviving daughter of GEORGE ALDERMAN ARNALD, Commercial Manager, and the late Julia his Wife (née PARKER).

The inserted page in the Proby family Bible. Note the lower quarterings have been cut out and reversed rather than completely reworking the armorial shield.

he effectively and publicly set himself against the Church of England. Of his Protestant opponents Proby wrote: "Evangelical . . . I could never use it in reference to them without implying that I myself am not evangelical."

He described the formation of the Church Association in 1865 as the end of the "Polemic Period" and the beginning of the "Immoral Period" of the Evangelical party.[25] Perhaps one of the most telling passages is this:

> But we mean that if a man denies Baptismal Regeneration, the validity of
> priestly absolution, or the authority of the Church in controversies of faith,
> he ought not be admitted to holy orders; that when a man has preached
> against the doctrine of the Real Presence . . . he should not be admitted to
> any office of rule.[26]

The reaction to the book was predictable and long-lasting. Over a decade later, the Evangelical polemicist Walter Walsh described Proby as "one of the most bitter writers against the Evangelical party".[27]

If the Gorham controversy of 30 years earlier, a time when men like Archdeacon Manning had judged the Church of England to be Erastian and departed, had not convinced Proby of the irredeemably flawed state of the Church of England, the constant drip-feeding since his return from Scotland of what he considered to be Protestant heresy had its effect.

Unlike Pusey before him, Proby could no longer believe in the Church of England. Unlike Newman before him, he could find no justification for seceding to Rome. The Catholic Apostolic Church offered not only refuge but also opportunities. The Irvingite Prayer Book of 1842 blended Roman Catholic and Greek rites with elements of the Anglican tradition. The movement was based in a Trinitarian understanding of God, and it affirmed all the baptized of any and every tradition as members of the one body. All the other denominations had to do was settle or ignore their differences. One of the central tenets was the imminent "Second Coming" of Jesus Christ, which led to an evangelistic urgency in preaching which marked Proby's public ministry for the rest of his life. By the time he became Irvingite, there was a highly developed ritual with all the Catholic "privileges" which were almost identical to those Proby would have used at Haggerston. Perhaps even more importantly he no longer needed to struggle with the validity of those priests he saw as heretical and bishops he regarded as Erastian.

Well before the publication of *Annals*, indeed before 1875 when his chapel in Colyton caught fire, Proby had evidently become missional about this new allegiance. The existence of the chapel is evidence for this. Activity in London was to continue but gradually life in Devon began to claim a greater part of his energies.

It is noteworthy that neither Proby's espousal of the Catholic Apostolic Church nor his establishment of a chapel in King Street distanced him from the daily life of the parish, or his wife from the activities of the parish church. Proby and Gueritz would inevitably have points of conflict and various skirmishes, but Blanche Proby and Anne Gueritz established common cause on several fronts and the Probys continued their financial support for much of the pastoral work.

Although Proby had purchased Colyton House on 1 June 1869, and later established his chapel in a cottage in the grounds fronting on King Street, he had never lived there. The house was occupied for a long time by the widow, daughters and invalid son of the Revd William T. Elton, lately rector of Whitestaunton. It was a considerable household with five family members and five servants. In 1885, Lucy Caroline Elton, the widow, also died. Over time, the remaining daughters created separate households. Two of them, Georgina and Agnes, made a home with their servants in Road Green, Colyton, just a five-minute walk from their old home. Another, Lucy Olivia, married Fortescue Gueritz when he was rector of Templeton. Thus, Proby was able to move into Colyton House in 1887.[28] It was one of the most prestigious residences in the town and bordered the grounds of the vicarage on one side and King Street and Vicarage Street on two others. The property was separated from the neighbouring vicarage by a high stone wall which also ran along the roadway. For reasons of his own, Proby doubled the height of the wall on Vicarage Street.[29]

It may be that his own experience of fire in the chapel on King Street had led to a personal interest in the work, but in 1889 Proby was elected chairman of the Colyton Vigilance Committee, a body set up to guard against fires in the town. His report to the meeting speaks for itself:

It is a matter of regret that more of the parishioners were not present to meet the Committee. When incendiary fires were so frequent as to cause a general feeling of insecurity in the town the inhabitants were enthusiastic in their efforts to promote the formation of the Vigilance Committee . . . the danger has passed . . . and the inhabitants, now that they once more feel secure, show themselves indifferent about recognising the effects of the Committee.

In 1890, Proby added to his already considerable landholding by buying another overland tenement in the parish of Northleigh, an area of just over 35 acres.

In 1891, at the time of the census, W. H. B. Proby was visiting the vicarage in Desborough and was described as "Clerk in Holy Orders living on own means". No accompanying visitors were shown. Blanche Proby was at home in Colyton House with her sister Ellen Arnald. The incumbent of Desborough, Edgar Campbell Channer, was also a Cambridge man and had served his first curacy at Halwill in Devon. That may partly have been the connection with Proby, but more likely it was the time Channer spent in curacies in London. Channer was at St Luke's, Hammersmith from 1874 to 1878 and several parishes nearby to Desborough were identified with the Oxford Movement.

The year 1892 was marked by an objection Proby made to a public meeting called by the incumbent, Mamerto Gueritz, in order to discuss the reordering of the church. This objection was based on Proby's belief that it should not be the business of the general populace, many of whom were dissenters or Unitarian in allegiance. There is a delightful irony in this. Although he had moved away from the Church of England, Proby was still concerned to defend it against people he saw as heretics!

Alongside local church politics, he was still active and involved in local agricultural life. In September of that year, he publicly lamented the lack of encouragement to apple growers in the area, and at the Honiton Agricultural Show there was a special prize for orchards, awarded to G. F. Snell of Sidbury and donated by the Revd W. H. B. Proby.[30]

The next year was memorable because of Proby's opening of the Chapel of St John the Baptist in Pottlelake, a hamlet a few miles north of Colyton. This was clearly advertised as a chapel of the Catholic Apostolic Church and therefore was opened without need for any legal sanction from the local clergy or the Bishop of Exeter. However, it was still the cause of considerable contention and the assertion by Mamerto Gueritz that the chapel was neither Anglican nor Irvingite in nature but rather "Probyite". That argument forms another part of this history.

The year 1895 was eventful. It began with unremarkable domestic incidents. For example, in March Blanche Proby advertised for a "General Servant, understanding plain cooking".[31] Later, however, in October, there was another row brewing. The Colyton Volunteer Band had played for the harvest celebration, which had included a procession through Proby's own grounds at Colyton House. After the procession and church service, the band went on to various other events, including, to Proby's disgust, the service at the Unitarian Meeting House. Several local papers carried a report of the letter that Proby sent to the secretary of the band. The papers were at pains to point out that Proby was "[a] clergyman of the Church of England, in no way connected however with the parish church of Colyton".[32] Evidently Proby's stance on local heretics was well known because another paper, with the story still running a week later, prefaced the letter with:

> The Rev. W.H.B. Proby promised at his ordination to "banish and drive
> away all erroneous and strange doctrines" and as he could not get Sergeant
> West banished into exile he sent them the following letter.[33]

The letter informed Sergeant West, the bandmaster, that as the band had seen fit to perform at the Unitarian service, Proby was withdrawing his financial support from them:

> It can hardly appear reasonable that an institution supported in the main by
> Church people should be used for the purpose of glorifying the functions
> of dissenters or other heretics.

Colyton was then, as it is now, a small community, and by this stage Proby's occasional outbursts against heretics were simply part of community life. They had, after all, marked his presence for almost 30 years and resulted in him being burned in effigy on one occasion.[34] Most people had come to take such criticisms lightly, especially when they considered Proby's support for the community. It was not entirely unheard of for those with whom he had been at "daggers drawn" over theological issues to stand shoulder to shoulder with him over community and welfare matters.

Then from social conflagration to a fire of another kind. On 23 November, Borcombe Farmhouse and some of the surrounding barns were on fire. This was the farm purchased by Proby's mother around the year of his birth. The flames took hold rapidly, the roof of the house fell in within the hour and most of the furniture and a great deal of the produce was lost. The tenant at the time was Richard Pearcey and, although the loss was great, he had had the foresight to insure his furniture and the stored produce. The building, which was Proby's as landlord, was also insured so, after an interval, life at the farm resumed, as did the use of the chapel of SS Simon and Jude which was attached to the house.

The Monday after the fire Proby was at the Colcombe Castle Hotel in Colyton for the annual dinner of G Company of the Third Volunteer Battalion of the Devon Regiment.[35] He evidently had a respected place in the company and was well known to the men and the officers in that he was the proposer of the toast to the chairman, Sir Edmund de la Pole. The toast was received significantly with "musical honours". Several of those musicians were members of the town band whose interfaith activities Proby had roundly condemned only a month earlier! He was thanked by Sir Edmund for his address and especially for his acknowledgement of the way in which the baronet had discharged his duties as a landlord. However, Proby's connection with the regiment was not limited to attendance at dinners. Colyton men who served in India during the Second Afghan War, which lasted from 1878 to 1880, brought back memories of his visits when Proby, on his travels, would seek out the men from Colyton and bring them news and home comforts.[36]

The following year, 1896, saw Proby approaching the age of 65 and yet still active and involved in many things. In addition to his life in the community, he was to be found lecturing for the Palestine Exploration Fund, and the second quarterly report of the fund for 1896 carried a note of various reports and addresses given. There was one on the excavations in Jerusalem. Another described the house of Veronica, the woman reputed to have wiped the face of Jesus on the Via Dolorosa. Among them was Proby's paper on "The Construction of the Tabernacle".[37]

The year 1899 was marked by demonstrations and even riots in Anglo-Catholic churches all around the country. It was also the year in which John Kensit, leader of the anti-ritual forces and founder of the Protestant Truth Society, created something of a political storm by announcing that he was going to stand for Parliament against the leader of the House. In Torquay, church folk were so exasperated by the "agitations" that it was proposed to ban all collections for both the Church Association and the English Church Union. As a measure of the level of activity, in Liverpool there were anti-ritual demonstrations in no fewer than seven churches on Sunday, 26 March.

On 24 March, Proby gave a lecture on "Some features in the present agitation" in St Andrew's Hall, Colyton. In Colyton, by this stage, such battles had largely passed into history and the meeting was poorly attended. The lecture is mainly significant for our understanding of Proby's relationship with the Church of England and the Book of Common Prayer in his later years. By this stage, many of even the most vehement Unitarians in Colyton had accepted that there were elements of the life of the Church with which they would never be in accord and, more significantly, did not need to be. They had reached a point of acceptance of the incumbent, Mamerto Gueritz, and recognized that his position was held not so much against them but rather in support of his Church principles. There were still, however, one or two old Unitarian warhorses in the field, and the presence of W. H. B. Proby was sufficient to draw them out.

Gueritz did not attend the meeting. In 1899, he and his wife had endured repeated ill health. However, he had firmly instructed the chairman of the meeting, who was also the master of the grammar school, that while the lecture could be given and questions answered, there was to be no debate. The chairman kept that injunction as well as he could.

Proby began by branding the Protestant (Kensitite) objectors to ritual as bullies in that they depended on irreligious force rather than argument to win their aims. He went on to claim that the general public was incompetent in such matters which should be left to learned divines and that the "Low Church" party had hardly anyone who could be so described. Then he claimed that they were ignorant of the true nature of the Church of England, which was simply not Protestant. It had always used confession, and the Prayer Book itself taught the doctrine of the Real Presence, baptismal regeneration and the effectiveness of priestly absolution. Proby favourably compared the Anglo-Catholic clergy, who unreservedly held to the doctrines expressed in the Prayer Book with integrity and honesty, with the Protestant clergy, who made their ordination declarations with mental reserve. Then he claimed: "Dissenters being in separation from the Church have no moral claim to interfere in her domestic concerns." This was aimed not at the Evangelical Anglican clergy who were, in Proby's eyes, the betrayers from within the Church, but at the very people sitting in front of him. The reaction was predictable, especially from a Mr Mountstephen who was a longstanding opponent of Proby. Incidentally, the two of them together had enjoyed the dinner at Colcombe Castle for the Volunteer Battalion of the Devon Regiment.

What this shows is that Proby had not rejected the Book of Common Prayer as completely as his earlier comments in *Annals* might have indicated. His separation from the Church of England never had been complete. Indeed, a large proportion of the beneficed clergy who allied themselves to the Irvingites held both identities in greater or lesser contentment. All of which helps us to understand the final scenes in this history.

The next few years were remarkably quiet. Proby's oft-altered relationship with Colyton's incumbent of 42 years, Mamerto Gueritz, changed yet again when Gueritz retired because of ill health in 1901. The next incident worthy of note takes us to 1909 and back almost to where the journey began, the farm and chapel at Borcombe. The "Borcombe Homily" is reproduced in its original form in Appendix 3. It is written in the same "calligraphic" style that Proby used to inscribe the family Bible with his wedding details and contains within it several indicators of Proby's mind, not just on matters ecclesiastical at that point in time, but also his personal journey. The homily is addressed to "My fellow parishioners residing in the neighbourhood of the chapel of St. Simon and St. Jude Borcombe" and begins by noting that the rector of Southleigh would take services from time to time in the chapel and that this was being done with the " . . . sanction of our Vicar who is still your lawful parish priest". He is referring to the Revd George Molineux, who had arrived in Colyton in 1907 and in whose parish the chapel was situated. However, note the use of "Our Vicar" and "Your lawful parish priest". Proby maintains his own ambivalent relationship with the Church of England but by this stage is keen to point out where the parishioners' loyalty should lie.

The next thing to be revealed is the lasting effect on Proby's preaching of the Irvingite expectation of an imminent "Rapture" or the second coming of Christ. Proby points out the words over the altar, "Behold I come as a thief", and declares his own belief that "The Lord may fulfil them any day now". This is an echo of his urging to the people of Pottlelake when the chapel there was opened but also in this homily, having adjured the people to live as befits Christians:

> And when he comes again (which I beg you always to remember, may be before you and I have time to die) He will wish to find us so living.

All this was in the context of an affirmation that this message was being addressed to:

> His Church—to that company of baptized people of which you all (I suppose) as well as myself are members; and of which the Church of England is the chief branch in this country.

The Church is here equated with the company of all the baptized, of every denomination, which was one of the basic tenets of the Catholic Apostolic Church. The Church of England is the "chief branch" of that Church in this land but not the only one. Then follows a moving plea for Eucharistic centrality in the life of the people and for those lives to be centred in Christ:

> And we must not be content until there is celebrated, at the Altar in the Chapel that chief deed which is our Christian Sacrifice—I mean, of course, the Holy Eucharist. Our communion therein, too, is, according to New Testament teaching, the means by which our oneness with Christ, begun in our baptism, is to be kept up. It is important for us to remember that we are saved, not by hearing about Christ, or thinking about Christ, or even praying to Christ; but by being one with Him, and keeping our oneness up.

Proby then again refers the people to the incumbent of Southleigh, who will be caring for them within the Anglican fold, as the authority to which they must now turn and closes with an injunction to his hearers to take financial responsibility for the future work of the chapel:

> Most good things in this world have to be paid for . . . in fact a religion which costs nothing is worth nothing.

From this, we can see where the journey we have traced since 1832 finally took W. H. B. Proby. He remained true to Church principles. The Trinitarian faith which was anathema to his Unitarian opponents was declared yet again in the homily:

> May I remind you that He who sent the above message is no other than God the Son, the Second Person of the ever blessed Trinity, One in Godhead with the Father and the Holy Ghost.

Proby's experience in the Catholic Apostolic Church gave him an expectant belief in an imminent second coming of Christ and confirmed his faith in baptismal regeneration as the only necessary hallmark of those who belong to Christ's body, the Church.

The homily was signed in his normal cursive hand and dated Colyton House, Colyton, 17 September 1909. Shortly afterwards the legal transfer was made, and the chapel at Borcombe passed from the care of the incumbent of Colyton to that of the priest of Southleigh.

When William Henry Baptist Proby died on 8 May 1915, he left a not inconsiderable fortune and a number of minor gifts and legacies. To Church House Westminster, a manuscript of his revision of the Anglican Psalter. Colyton Grammar School received a number of books. The Trustees of St Andrew's Hall (note: not the churchwardens or the incumbent) received "a box of silver vessels for private communion and all such articles, vestments, books and furniture as may be found in the chapel at Pottlelake".

His manuscript of "Papers on the Holy Eucharist" went to the Bishop of Willesden, and as witness to his wider travels in the Church both the Bishop of Korea and the Anglican Bishop of Cairo were remembered.

Blanche Proby survived her husband and lived locally at Hillside, Colyton until her death in June 1933.

If Proby ever did function as a priest in the Catholic Apostolic Church, he latterly abstained from the exercise of a Eucharistic ministry in public services in the chapels he established. His statement at the opening of St John's Chapel in Pottlelake confirms this.[38] He seems to have ended his life still a communicant of the Church of England but personally occupying a kind of ecclesial no man's land in which he was not fully Anglican and not exclusively Irvingite but very definitely W. H. B. Proby.[39]

Harry De Spencer Kingdon

1815–1902

Harry De Spencer Kingdon became, in later life, one of Colyton's more notable eccentrics. He and Mamerto Gueritz were opposed over many issues. There was the doctrinal conflict between Anglicans and Unitarians, although Kingdon was only nominally a Unitarian for the last 30 years of his life. Then there was the argument over burial rights and rites in the case of John Pavey which achieved national, even international, notoriety. The formation of the first school board in 1874 descended into open warfare over the inflated price of land for the school. The same happened earlier over the cost of land for the gasworks in Colyton. However, the issue which kept the antagonism between Kingdon and Gueritz simmering for decades was the matter of *Pues*. In summary, Kingdon "owned" a pew in St Andrew's Church, which had been purchased and built by his father. Mamerto Gueritz believed that there should be no such thing as a private pew and that all seating in church should be free to all comers. That argument went on, with periods of respite to allow other battles to be fought, for almost 40 years.

Harry Kingdon was the son of James Kingdon and Jane, or Jenny, Spurway. Kingdon's father practised law and was later described by his son as an "eminent solicitor and pew builder".[40] James Kingdon had settled in Colyton in 1807 and it was he who, under the faculty of 1817, had purchased the rights and built the pew that was the later cause of such contention.

Harry De Spencer Kingdon c 1860

At the time of Harry's birth, the Kingdon family were members of the congregation of "Protestant Dissenters" which met in George's Meeting House. He was baptized there on 13 May 1816 by Dr Joseph Cornish, who became an intimate friend of the Anglican incumbent, Frederick Barnes.[41]

The reasons for James Kingdon moving to London have not been explicitly recorded, but the almost total lack of contact over the following years indicates a level of estrangement. Harry and his mother stayed in Colyton in their house in Regent Street. When his elder brother Frederick William died in 1839, he left a son, Frederick William Washington Kingdon, who came to live with the family. He was always known as Washington and in later life was active in the town alongside his uncle at vestry meetings, in the work of the Feoffees and in trying to wrest power from the supporters of Mamerto Gueritz. Washington and Mamerto seemed to enjoy a more amicable relationship once the school board battle was over.

In 1851, Harry and his mother were living in Cuckoo Street, Colyton with a servant, but the year was to bring changes. In November of that year, Harry De Spencer Kingdon and Sarah Jane Gibbs Withycombe were married in Colyton.[42] The family soon moved to Willhayne, where on 12 February 1853 their first daughter was born: Sarah Jane Rebecca Spurway Kingdon. Her arrival was followed three years later by Elizabeth Patience Ursula Spurway Kingdon.

Living at Willhayne with its grounds and buildings and holding land and property in various places in the parish, Harry's mother, Jenny Kingdon, was a woman of some substance. After she died in 1858, her heir, Harry Kingdon, was able to describe himself as a "Landowner and Fundholder".[43]

Kingdon was 43 in 1858, and it is around this time that his more notable eccentricities began to emerge. He refused to have his mother buried. Instead, she was embalmed and placed in a hermetically sealed coffin in his curio room, which had previously been the summer room. The leaden coffin had a glass plate set into it over the face of the corpse, and Kingdon would visit from time to time. For years, he had been an avid collector of books, china and furniture, so that his collection filled not only the curio room but several other parts of the house as well. Any visitor who showed even a passing interest was enthusiastically shown the collection. What later visitors felt when they found an occupied coffin among the artefacts might not have been expressed at the time but was certainly shared later! One has to wonder what the little daughters, Sarah Jane aged five and Elizabeth aged two, made of it all. Kingdon's father, James, died ten years later in 1868 in Wandsworth, London, but little or nothing is heard of him in the intervening years.

One of Kingdon's passions was the breeding of mastiffs. At one stage, he had more than 40 in his kennels at Willhayne and was absolutely adamant that he would not allow their bloodline to be lessened by interbreeding with modern strains. The line of one of his bitches, Dagmar, could be traced back to 1415. A report of his life as a breeder shows that while in one context he might well have earned the label "eccentric" and even "obnoxious",[44] in a different setting he would be quite differently regarded:

> Frequenters of dog shows of thirty years ago (late 1860s and early 70s) will not have forgotten the pleasant personality of Mr. H. S. Kingdon, of Wellhayne (sic) Colyton, Devon ... As an exhibitor at the shows his attention was entirely confined to mastiffs, his strain tracing back to the old Lyme Hall breed ... he was retained as a reporter on the Sporting Gazette, which at that time had a considerable reputation ... (his accounts were) ... readable, scholarly and practical ... and invariably anticipated with considerable pleasure.[45]

This provides quite a contrast to the combative Kingdon we have seen in his encounters with Mamerto Gueritz.

There was more to Harry Kingdon than either his earlier passions or later eccentricities might lead us to believe. During his earlier life, he had gained a respected place in the community of Colyton and for many years he was the senior Feoffee, by all accounts serving that body well and faithfully. He had a considerable following among the ratepayers of the town; those who owned property. That following persisted for many years, which was how Kingdon was able, in the vestry meetings, to vote down all Gueritz' proposals for the reordering of the seating in church. It was in those meetings that the power plays were made and where the first signs that Kingdon's influence was waning appeared.

At that time, churchwardens were powerful people in a small community and their election a matter of some import. When Kingdon could not ensure the appointment of one of his faction, not even his own nephew, his campaign against Gueritz became more furious but less and less effective.

The 1875 battle for control of the school board in Colyton has been examined in some detail, and the delight of Kingdon and his allies when the Gueritz party was defeated is a matter of record. But 1875 was not totally taken up with school matters and local politics because in that year Harry's elder daughter, Sarah Jane Kingdon, was married to James Noakes, who was 20 years her senior.

James Noakes was a widower, originally from the Isle of Man but more recently living in Seaton, Devon. He had three children from his first marriage, who when he married Sarah Jane Kingdon were 13, eight and seven years old. The couple moved to Islington, where their first son, James, was born the following year. His brother Arthur arrived in 1877, when they were living in North Finchley. Over the years, the family seem to have moved repeatedly between Stanley Villas, Finchley, and Miranda Road in Islington. Their only daughter, Constance Sarah, was born in 1879, but in that same year James Noakes died. Sarah was left to bring up her own three children, and although her stepdaughters had lived for a while in Nottingham, they also later came to live with her. Harry Kingdon took a special interest in his first grandson, intending to leave the bulk of his property to young James.

Family affections notwithstanding, the conflicts in Colyton continued. In 1880, the school board election came round again and with it accusations of mismanagement and profiteering. The accusations were evidenced and believed, and Kingdon and his party were ousted.

The tale of the battle over the reordering of the church and the removal of the pews is fully told in the main body of this work and does not need repeating here, but one insight into the difference between Kingdon and Gueritz does bear further comment. One of Kingdon's objections to the removal of his pew, quite aside from the question of legal ownership and inherited rights, was that Gueritz was wrong in disturbing the divinely ordered social structure which was demonstrated by where people sat in church. In fairness to Kingdon, tradition was on his side. There is a, now discarded, verse in a much-loved hymn which runs:

The rich man in his castle,
The poor man at his gate,

God made them high and lowly,
And ordered their estate.[46]

This was emphatically not the position of those who might be called the champions of the later Oxford Movement or second-wave Tractarians. Gueritz' egalitarian attitude echoed that of his brothers in the slums of London. His approach to who could sit where in church seemed to Kingdon to strike at the very heart of English society and the Victorian pyramidal concept of hierarchy. That Gueritz' position was entirely scriptural and clearly in accordance with the teaching of St Paul was not for Kingdon a valid argument.

Gradually Kingdon withdrew from the community life of Colyton. He was, however, still engaged enough in matters to attend when Gueritz called a public meeting to discuss the reordering of the church in 1892. There is a certain pathos that attaches to the image of this septuagenarian, still defending his position and what he saw as his rights even when the tide of local opinion had turned and left him without support. There was laughter recorded at the meeting when he repeated his old arguments, but still he did not give in. His battle of words with the bishop and the diocesan registrar, Arthur Burch, was only just beginning.

In February 1893, just over a year after the public meeting in church, Sarah Jane Kingdon, Harry's wife of 42 years, died. Kingdon had determined that he, his mother and his wife would all be buried together in the mausoleum he had built in the cemetery, which could be seen from Willhayne. So he had her body embalmed like that of his mother and placed in a sealed lead coffin, but this time without a window. It was kept in the greenhouse.

Kingdon's isolation and eccentricities grew with the passing of time. His days were spent alone at Willhayne with only his housekeeper, Mary Brooks, and a manservant for company. Then, in 1900, there was another blow to his increasingly fragile grasp on present reality. James, the grandson whom Harry Kingdon had chosen as his heir, died on board the SS *Dunolly Castle*, aged 24. His remaining grandson, Arthur Noakes, became his new heir and beneficiary.

On 2 January 1903, Harry De Spencer Kingdon died. The *Western Morning News* reported "an unmourned, if peaceful death in the Great Hall of Willhayne House", commenting on his intellectual gifts and eccentricities. However, the reporter managed to get several details wrong, which is hardly surprising, given the strangeness of what was being reported. It was said that it was Kingdon's sister and wife whose coffins had been kept at Willhayne when, as we have seen, it was his wife and mother who had waited out the years for their burial.

And Harry De Spencer Kingdon was not "unmourned", not quite. His passing might not have exactly inspired grief in the community but the death of such a remarkable character could not go unremarked. The funeral service was attended by many local people, in spite of the pouring rain and the attempts that had been made to keep it a private matter. News of the strange event had spread, and Colyton people would not miss a once-in-a-lifetime experience such as this. From the hillside cemetery, they were able to see the progress of the funeral procession as it approached from Willhayne. The cortege consisted of the mourners and bearers but only one coffin, that of Harry Kingdon. Those of his wife and mother had been placed two days earlier in the sarcophagi prepared for them in the mausoleum.

Kingdon's daughter, Sarah Jane, was in the cortege with her son Arthur, who was heir, apart from a few legacies, to the whole estate. George Eyre Evans, the author and son of a former Unitarian minister, was present, as was Ravenor E. Rose, for 12 years the Congregational minister of Colyton. For years, Harry Kingdon had refused all religious ministry of any kind, and it had been decades since he had attended George's Meeting House.[47] The Prayer Book burial service would have sat uncomfortably with everyone; with the Unitarians because of its Trinitarian theology, with the Anglicans who could not see how it could be said with integrity over the deceased, and with anyone who had even an inkling of Kingdon's mind on religious matters. The priest who had followed Mamerto Gueritz as incumbent, Richard Turner, took the service in a manner which was both pastorally sensitive and also took advantage of the Burial Laws Amendment Act of 1880 which removed any penalty for Anglican clergy who used a burial service other than that in the Book of Common Prayer.

The Prayer Book service was adapted for the occasion. In fact, it was altered out of all recognition. The *Western Morning News* reported:

> In consequence of the religious views the deceased held, the funeral service
> was shortened. The 130th Psalm was read and then followed that portion
> of the service commencing, "Man that is born of a woman." The committal

Harry De Spencer Kingdon at Willhayne c 1900

portion was omitted. The Lord's Prayer was said and the service concluded with the last part of the Litany. The body was not taken into the church. It was a strange service and will be long remembered by those who were present.

The three coffins and their contents were finally placed where they could await the resurrection together and the doors of the mausoleum were sealed. There is, however, one final thread to the Kingdon story which may seem just as unexpected as the behaviour of Harry Kingdon himself.

Kingdon's second daughter, Elizabeth, lived with her sister Sarah for several years and was with her at the time of the death of her husband, James Noakes. Elizabeth stayed with Sarah for the most part, when she was not at Willhayne. Later she moved to Alton and thence to Arundel. Elizabeth was in Colyton during 1891, but after her mother died in 1893 she seems to have felt free to follow her own vocation in life. She took a path that would sunder her from her father and family entirely, first by becoming a Roman Catholic and then by joining an order of nursing sisters in Alton. The sisters had set up their work in 1899 in Normandy Street, Alton in buildings attached to St Saviour's Church. Elizabeth was part of that community until it was dispersed. When the work in Alton was closed by the Roman Catholic hierarchy of the diocese of Portsmouth, some of the sisters moved to St Wilfred's Priory in Arundel. There they ran a school and Elizabeth, as one of the sisters, worked as cook for the convent. When she died in 1933, aged 77, Elizabeth was living once more in Islington in the house she had shared with her sister.

Vincent Stuckey Stratton Coles

1845–1929

Stuckey Coles' part in this story begins with him as a small boy being tutored by Adelina Gueritz in the parsonage at Shepton Beauchamp, while Mamerto Gueritz was learning how to be a parish priest in Shepton and Barrington. It continues with frequent appearances in Colyton both sharing in the joys and sorrows of the Gueritz family and in lending support to the work of mission. The strength

Elizabeth "Bessie" Kingdon, c 1894

of the relationship and the mutual affection between Stuckey and the Gueritz family is perhaps best illustrated in the obituary he wrote for the *Church Times* and the national newspapers, but that warmth was not diminished by Mamerto's death. Coles' initial attachment to Mamerto and Anne and Adelina was not only maintained but extended to the next generation and the generation after that. Gueritz' grandson, Ernest, when writing to S. L. Ollard, his vice-principal at St Edmund Hall, refers to Stuckey Coles as "our mutual friend".[48]

In 1855, Stuckey went to a preparatory school in Exmouth, where he was rather unhappy. He later attributed this partly to the fact that he was frequently unwell, which cut him off from the usual sports enjoyed by young boys. Another element in his alienation from the school was his stoutness, which made him an occasional object of derision. These two disadvantages were to be with him lifelong, although, as the years passed, he learned to concern himself less with what others might think about his girth. Sometime before Stuckey went to school Adelina Gueritz left her employment with the Coles family for an appointment as a governess in Glastonbury, but after a year or so she returned to the Shepton and Barrington community. Adelina resumed her work in the Coles household after Glastonbury and was able to teach the young Stuckey up to a point, but he would need more than the teaching of a governess, be she never so skilled, for the next stage of his education. Every day he would ride over to a nearby village where the vicar taught him Latin. This was when he was just ten years old.

Aged 13, Stuckey Coles was confirmed in Martock Church and in the same year went to Eton College. Even before this, Stuckey had become noted for his "genius for friendship" and his ability to relate to people of all classes and stations in life. This characterized him lifelong and indeed became a major element in his later ministry, but such a capacity for affection brings with it its own dangers. Those closest to him recalled his growth in self-awareness and his alertness to the potential for sin while still a schoolboy at Eton:

> He soon realised that this love for his friends might co-exist with much
> that is faulty and ill-regulated, and even with much that is corrupt, and that
> (while) it has untold capacities for good, also carries within it possibilities
> for evil. While still a schoolboy Stuckey set himself the task of sanctifying
> his friendships, and thought out a philosophy of conduct in these matters.[49]

Of course, recognizing that there is a battle to be fought is not the same as winning the fight, but when others note the struggle and take courage from it themselves, that is, of itself, something of a victory. So it was both at Eton and in the years that followed. Those who struggled with what might be called "inordinate affection" may have sought to hide it from friends and acquaintances but would somehow find themselves sharing their difficulty with Stuckey Coles.

At Eton, Coles was already beginning to reveal what were to become the two main themes of his life, relationships and religion; indeed, they were to become inextricably intertwined. Robert Bridges, poet laureate from 1913 to 1930, later wrote of himself and D. M. Dolben, another friend of his schooldays:

> We were both Puseyites and members of a small group of "High Church" boys. Coles was pre-eminent for his precocious theological bent and devotion to the cause, was indeed the recognised authority and our leader in so far as universal esteem and confidence could give anyone such a position among us.[50]

It was during his time at Eton that Coles' idea of vocation to the priesthood grew into a conviction. He had imbibed the ethos and teaching of the Oxford Movement as he had experienced it in Shepton Beauchamp during his childhood, and there was a particular memory which, for him, seems to have marked the public affirmation of his place in the Catholic Revival, as he habitually called it. He was addressing an Exeter gathering of the Church Union when he said:

> I was either eighteen or nineteen when, on the nomination of Mr. Gueritz, then recently become Vicar of Colyton, I joined the English Church Union. I am now sixty-eight. I had felt myself to be a young and humble member of the fellowship of catholic revival some few years before I became a member of our Society.[51]

An underlying assumption of the opening statement in this paper is that members of the English Church Union would know exactly who Mamerto Gueritz was; not only because it was less than a year earlier that Coles' obituary of him had appeared in the *Church Times* and not only because they might recall the Pavey burial controversy of 1864 and 1865, but because Gueritz was known, in his own right, as a champion of the Movement.

Coles went up to Balliol in 1864 with his course already charted. To the surprise of his tutors, he achieved only a third-class degree but as Charles Gore later wrote of him:

> He was never a student and always preferred persons to books, though he had a great faculty for tearing the heart out of a book.[52]

Balliol was followed by a year at Cuddesdon Theological College, where Edward King was principal. King later founded St Stephen's House, Oxford and went on to become Bishop of Lincoln. From Cuddesdon Stuckey was ordained in 1869 and went to serve his title at Wantage under the tutelage of W. S. Butler. This was a profoundly formative experience, and the influence of Butler could long be detected in Coles' own exercise of priestly ministry.

In December 1872, Stuckey's father, James Coles, rector of Shepton Beauchamp and Barrington, died suddenly, and Stuckey was presented to the living. Concerns about the validity of inheriting a cure of souls, which he had expressed previously to D. M. Dolben, seem to have been laid to rest. Stuckey's labours in Shepton and Barrington and his development of worship and catholic teaching seem to have been a natural extension of the work his father had begun. The work also mirrored that of Mamerto Gueritz some 23 miles away in Colyton which had been developed over the previous decade. This should not be surprising on several counts. An important thing to note is the increased cohesion and commonality of the later Oxford Movement as it spread in rural areas. Of course, local traditions remained, and there were still wonderfully idiosyncratic clergy to be found, but earlier, sometimes wild, liturgical divergences were being balanced by a growing desire for legitimacy and authenticity.[53] On a more personal note, given the continuing and mutual affection between Stuckey Coles and the Gueritz family, it is demonstrable that the aspirations and practices of each were mutually formative.

It was during these years at Shepton that Stuckey's reputation as a preacher and a leader of missions grew until it reached far beyond the confines of a remote Somerset parish. Perhaps Coles' sister's perception of his ministry at Shepton illuminates the process a little. She once said to the rector of Bagborough that she considered the 12 years of her brother's rectorship of Shepton to be like a continuous mission. At home or abroad, Stuckey was simply himself, but that selfhood was realized in his bringing together the love of God and the love of people and making them one:

> For many years there was hardly anyone in the Church of England more sought after as a missioner. At best he was truly eloquent and his obvious sympathy and sincerity made him almost irresistible, particularly to simple folk. To see Stuckey walking up and down the aisle, talking to the country folk in a dialect that they loved and understood, was something never to be forgotten.[54]

The country folk referred to here were Somerset people, but it was equally true of the Devonians of Colyton, who took Stuckey very much to heart. While he always had episcopal sanction for ministry in the diocese of Bath and Wells, either as an incumbent or as the holder of a preacher's licence, Coles does not seem to have concerned himself overmuch with such niceties when he crossed the boundary to preach and lead missions in the diocese of Exeter.[55]

Stuckey's appearances in Colyton were not limited to invitations to share in the mission and ministry. When he was in residence in the flat that he and his sister rented in Seaton he was a frequent caller at Colyton vicarage, it being a mere three miles inland. However, there were at least five occasions when his skills as a leader of missions and a preacher were requested and joyfully shared.

In November 1875, as a preparation for Advent, Coles led a mission assisted by A. H. Drummond. Then, in Lent 1876, he was assisted by H. J. Dodwell, and in Advent he returned with a larger team. J. Izod, the curate of Honiton, was assisting alongside H. A. Cartwright, the incumbent of Whitestaunton. As we have seen, Cartwright had visited Colyton a number of times, first as an assistant secretary of the Additional Curates Society, later as a visiting preacher, and then, in 1874, to marry Henrietta Elton, the youngest sister of Lucy Octavia Gueritz.

Lent 1877 saw Izod and Cartwright return with a different team and without Stuckey Coles, but in Advent they were together again in mission. Then the following year missions gave way to a sermon series in the penitential seasons, with Stuckey leading during Lent. He was still in Colyton, or had returned, in May when he officiated at the wedding of Mary Louisa Gueritz and Reginal Mortimer, and was then described as "so well known and loved in this parish". Five years later Stuckey was still responding to requests to come to Colyton and was alongside Mamerto Gueritz in preaching a "Call to Repentance" in Advent 1883.

Stuckey himself did not share in the glowing assessment of his abilities as a preacher and a leader of missions. Friends acknowledged that he was always a more effective preacher when he preached extempore, and Stuckey lamented that some of his missions were more like parish retreats than a call to conversion. This notwithstanding there were remarkable stories of conversions to be told. Often these were revealed well after his missions were over, and when his preaching had taken root. Just as frequently change came about for people as a result of a personal encounter with Stuckey and with his ability to reach into the heart of the person before him, be that person peer or ploughman.

The year 1884 was tumultuous both for Coles and for the Gueritz family. In May, Antonia Gueritz died after a short illness. She had been universally loved in the town, and the grief of the community was palpable. Stuckey Coles was there to preside at her requiem and to comfort the family. In July, the children of the Sunday schools were all given gifts in Antonia's memory, and at the same event it was announced that Stuckey Coles would be leaving Shepton Beauchamp to take up a new post in Oxford.

Coles was to be one of three librarian priests or custodians of the Pusey Memorial Library. Charles Gore, a Fellow of Trinity and lately vice-principal of Cuddesdon, was to be the principal; Frank Brightman, who had been chaplain of University College, was to be the librarian proper; and Vincent Stuckey Coles was to be chaplain.

Pusey House was opened with due ceremony on 9 October 1884 by the Bishop of Oxford, John Mackarness, who, while he was incumbent of Honiton and prebendary of Exeter Cathedral, had been a friend and supporter of Mamerto Gueritz. On the same day, there was a note in the Colyton vestry journal which simply read "Pusey Memorial". There were no services in Colyton that day so perhaps Mamerto Gueritz was among the "fifty or sixty" of the friends who were gathered for the occasion. There is no extant list of attendees, but several champions of the Oxford Movement were in attendance, among them Henry

Parry Liddon, who was one of Stuckey's closest friends, and Edward King, who was consecrated Bishop of Lincoln the following year. It was King who is rumoured to have said that he imagined F. E. Brightman would dust the books, Charles Gore would read them, and Stuckey Coles would talk about them. Another version of the story has it that Gore would read the books, Brightman would write about them, and Coles would indeed talk about them. As Gore later wrote of him, Stuckey had a great talent for "tearing the heart out of a book".

It was in his time at Pusey House, first as chaplain and later from 1897 to 1909 as principal, that Coles was able to use his innate and consciously fostered gift for empathy to its full. One of the founding purposes of the house was to provide spiritual counsel and comfort to members of the university. Edward King said to Stuckey at the outset, "you have learned to be a friend of country lads, and now you will have to be the friend of undergraduates". Stuckey's fine disregard for class and station in life stood him in good stead in such a work. He always empathized more with those who felt themselves to be out of their depth in the world of Oxford undergraduates and, indeed, could be firm, even daunting, with those who appeared to consider themselves part of an elite. It was said of him:

> the Bullingdon tie and Leander coat were hindrances to intimacy with him.
> He was always inclined to look askance at Isis idols, and to exalt the humble
> and meek, yet no one bore the stamp of Eton and Balliol more than he.[56]

However, there are many incidents recorded where Coles' capacity to discern the "inner man" allowed him to see past the urbane veneer to the devout heart within; moments when he knew it was necessary to challenge the superficial for the sake of nurturing the nascent spiritual life. This gift was at the service of generations of students and scholars for 25 years, until Stuckey finally relinquished his role as warden of Pusey House. By then many hundreds of Oxford men had received his guidance and care. For many the marks were indelible.

M. R. Newbolt was one such undergraduate who relied on Coles for spiritual guidance until well into his priestly ministry, indeed until Coles was no longer able to offer such a ministry. Newbolt later became principal of the Missionary College at Dorchester where, in 1911, Ernest Clement Mortimer, a grandson of Mamerto Gueritz,[57] was one of his students. The influence of Stuckey Coles on

*V. S. S. Coles showing his distinctive white eyebrow
(reproduced by courtesy of the Librarian of Pusey House)*

Newbolt and on Ernest Mortimer may have operated in different spheres, but both felt him to be a link connecting the two.

After 11 years at St Michael and All Angels, Brighton, Newbolt was made a canon of Chester Cathedral. It was from there that he wrote, following the death of Stuckey Coles:

> For myself, I owe everything to Stuckey as a confessor and spiritual guide from my confirmation at school to well on in my priesthood. If what he did for me were taken out of it, my whole life would have been a very different and a far poorer thing.

And of a friend whom he had taken to see Coles 30 years earlier:

> I do not believe that X ever forgot that interview. He carried away with him from Oxford an impression far different from anything he had anticipated. He knew he had been in touch with a real spiritual force, a priest who would flash upon him in a short interview a stronger and more humbling conception of the priestly vocation than he had ever been able to reach before.[58]

There were other equally far-reaching aspects of Coles' ministry while he was in Oxford. Not least was his work with the Society of the Resurrection, a company of celibate priests living by rule in the world. This was originally formed by Gore at Radley, and later became the Community of the Resurrection based at Mirfield. While he was at Pusey House, Coles was elected superior and held that role for some years. His work of preaching and teaching, of leading missions and retreats, carried on, and he was often to be heard at St Barnabas, Jericho or in the chapel at Pusey House, where his addresses became something of an institution.

In 1909, as his health seemed to be deteriorating, Coles decided to relinquish his role as principal of Pusey House. In 1906 and 1907, he had endured a period of episcopal disapproval because of his criticisms of the recommendations of the Royal Commission on Ecclesiastical Discipline and also because of his Eucharistic theology, especially as it was made manifest in his hymns. It is entirely possibly that this disapproval was also a contributing factor in his decision to lay the burden down. Coles was not unsupported in that controversy, however, and over 500 of his friends signed an address of sympathy and gratitude for all that he had done in many ways but particularly as the "never failing guide of generations of men who have sought your advice and profited by your example".

For a brief period after leaving Oxford, Stuckey Coles made his home in the apartment he had leased for some years in Seaton. In previous years, he had been able to use the flat as a base for local missions and from where he could be in close contact with the Gueritz family but still have his independence and freedom. Over the years, many undergraduates, ordinands and clergy had sought Coles out in Seaton, receiving both hospitality and spiritual wisdom in equal measure. Others had taken up his offer to use the place for rest and recuperation. However, by 1909, the Gueritz family had largely dispersed from Colyton. Fortescue was in Scotland, and Frank had moved to Calstock; Reginald Mortimer, Antonia Gueritz, Anne Gueritz and George had all died. Nevertheless, there were still ties to the past. Mamerto was living with Mary Louisa and several of her children in King Street and Adelina, Stuckey's first and much-loved teacher, was also in the town.

For many years, Stuckey had been a staunch supporter of the religious life and had close links with several religious communities. In 1910, he became warden of the Community of the Epiphany in Truro, a role for which he was eminently suited and an ethos within which he was completely at home. The community had been founded by George Wilkinson in 1883, when he was Bishop of Truro. He relied greatly on Stuckey Coles for spiritual guidance and advice, and this continued when Wilkinson was called to be the first Bishop of St Andrews, Dunkeld and Dunblane and then, in 1904, Primus of the Scottish Church. On one occasion, when Wilkinson was ill and much in need of support, Stuckey caught the night train to Perth to see him and then had to be persuaded to rest overnight instead of returning immediately as he had intended.

Charles Gore, with whom Stuckey had worked closely for some years at Pusey House, returned to Oxford as bishop in late 1911. In 1912, he appointed Coles as diocesan chaplain and honorary canon of Christ Church. A major part of his work as diocesan chaplain was to hold short missions in country parishes, with the dual intent of invigorating the spiritual life of the populace and encouraging the isolated priest of a remote parish. It was a task in which he delighted and at which he excelled.

When Gore resigned the see of Oxford in 1919, Stuckey Coles returned to the West Country. For decades, he had been a byword for immoderate generosity, both with his time and with his money. Possessed of a considerable income, he used much of it in support of friends and others in need, being content to live frugally himself. When he retired, he found he could no longer sustain his levels of giving and retain his apartment at Seaton, so he gave up the apartment. Stuckey returned to Shepton to live with his sister, where he held a licence as assistant curate. He died in 1929, lamented by people of every walk and station in life.

One of the characteristics which endeared Stuckey Coles to all who knew him, not least to three generations of the Gueritz family and the people of Colyton, was summarized by Charles Gore:

> In his (Stuckey Coles) mind the grave and the gay lay close together. This gave a singular charm to his conversation. One moment he would be telling an amusing story with the greatest gusto or shaking with laughter over some funny incident, and the next would find him sinking into the depths of solemnity or rising to the heights of aspiration without either feeling or giving any sense of incongruity.

Stuckey Coles played a considerable part in the story of Mamerto Gueritz. Vincent Stuckey Stratton Coles, a man who loved much and was much loved.

St Matthias, Stoke Newington

The significance of this brief period, from 1868 to 1869, in Mamerto Gueritz' formation as a priest has already been established. Again, in the words of Stuckey Coles' obituary for Gueritz:

> he once served at Mr. Le Geyt's place in Stoke Newington and won the valuable acquaintance of Robert Brett.

To those names must be added that of W. H. Monk, the organist and choirmaster of St Matthias, Stoke Newington.

Charles James Le Geyt
1828–77

C. J. Le Geyt is important for this study for rather more than the attraction of a tragic figure, dying too young and burnt out in the cause for which he lived. His influence and that of the ethos which he helped to create at St Matthias, Stoke Newington were particularly formative in the ministry of Mamerto Gueritz. That effect has been explored, in some measure, in the main body of the work; now for the man behind the effect.

The name Le Geyt has been recorded in the Channel Islands since the thirteenth century. It first appeared in the history of Jersey in the *Short Inquisition* of 1274 and again in the late medieval records of Guernsey, and according to G. F. B. de Gruchy, was "one of the old Jersey names still surviving. It means 'watchman'."

There are many branches of the Le Geyt family, and one would have to go back five or six generations to establish any substantial links between, for example, the Charles James Le Geyt of Stoke Newington and Charles Arthur Le Geyt, curate of Beer and then of Truro Cathedral.

Charles James Le Geyt's grandfather, Robert, was born in St Helier, Jersey in 1730. Robert left Jersey and was married in Canterbury Cathedral. One of his sons, Philip, was born and baptized in Canterbury in 1776 and also later married in the cathedral. Before his marriage Philip was a Fellow of Magdalen College, Oxford. His marriage to Jane Cairnes produced 12 children, of whom Charles James Le Geyt was the youngest, born in 1828. It is often lamented that Charles died young, but this was, sadly, a family trait. Three of his siblings died in infancy, six in their twenties and thirties, with just one brother surviving until almost 60 and a sister who reached 70. Charles James Le Geyt died when he was 48.

From 1803 until 1816, Philip Le Geyt was incumbent of Chislet in Kent. During that time, he visited Macao in China at least twice, spending almost three years there in total, and there three of the children were born. In 1817, he became rector of Marden in Kent, an appointment he held until his death in 1847. For part of that time, he was also chaplain to the Duke of Kent.

It is reported that in his late teens Charles James travelled to India.[59] Certainly the family had considerable connections in the Far East and China as we have seen, but India also figured largely in their story. An older brother, Robert Cairnes

Le Geyt, was serving with the 1st Regiment of Lancers in Afghanistan when he was killed in action in 1842. Another brother, James Cairnes Le Geyt, was serving in India but died two years earlier in 1840. However, their eldest brother, Philip William, served in the Indian Civil Service and in 1834 had married Caroline Anderson in Bycullah, Bombay. He survived until 1860, which made him the second longest lived of all the siblings. It was noted, in one of the many obituaries, that Charles "after a brief career in India entered Exeter College, Oxford".[60] It is not recorded how long that brief career lasted or what part his elder brother had played in the adventure, but Charles returned from India in time to matriculate in 1850.

Charles graduated in May 1853, but before then, on Saturday, 18 September 1852, he and Janet Phillis Monro, a daughter of the late Alexander Monro, were married. Janet's father had died some years before and, although her mother and some of her sisters were in Twyford, Janet had been living with her uncle, Robert Monro, the rector of Aston Sandford. The wedding took place at Hursley, where John Keble had been incumbent since 1836, and the Revd Edward Monro officiated at the wedding. Marrying before graduation would have required the permission of Exeter College and the university authorities and would automatically have debarred Charles from a fellowship. This seems not to have hindered his academic career in the immediate.

Graduation in May 1853 was followed by ordination to the diaconate in September and a first curacy at St Peter's, Oxford. In October of the same year, Charles was appointed chaplain of Magdalen College and given sole charge of the parish of Clifton Hampden. In January of the following year, a daughter, Janet Madaleine, was born. When they left just over three years later, the generosity, especially of the poorer members of the parish, revealed just how well the family had won their hearts. Two of the servants who were native to Clifton Hampden left home and moved with them to Hursley and then later to Stoke Newington.

In 1857, Charles went to Hursley to serve as curate to John Keble, but he had been there little more than a year when, at the prompting of Sir William Heathcote, the Prime Minister, Lord Derby, offered him the perpetual curacy of St Matthias, Stoke Newington. John Keble and William Heathcote were close friends. J. T. Coleridge's *Memoir* of Keble was dedicated to Heathcote as "a favourite pupil of John Keble; who became his fast friend and only patron".[61]

It seems that Heathcote was willing to extend that patronage to Keble's protégés and in this instance to Charles James Le Geyt.

The first incumbent of St Matthias, T. A. Pope, had seceded to the Church of Rome while on holiday in Belgium. The second, S. W. Mangin, had been caught between the "Scylla and Charybdis" of the wishes of his congregation and the demands of the newly appointed Bishop Tait. The bishop had required Mangin to remove the ornaments of the altar and reduce the ceremonial, which anyway was moderate by later standards. The congregation were outraged and sent a deputation to Bishop Tait not only to protest but to challenge the legality of his Lordship's instructions. Bishop Tait did not always deal with such matters in the same way as had his predecessor Bishop Blomfield. In his article in the *Dictionary of National Biography*, written in 1886, W. R. Wroth writes of Blomfield:

> His genial and kindly nature made him a lovable mediator in the controversies arising out of the Tractarian Movement.

The deputation from St Matthias, led by Robert Brett, might have hoped for a similar willingness to engage on the part of Tait; however, the bishop would not be moved and unable, in all conscience, to satisfy either the bishop or the people of St Matthias, Mangin determined to leave, but not until he and his congregation were sure of a successor who would champion their cause.

So began Le Geyt's ministry at St Matthias and with it, initially at least, the judicious restoration of ritual and the ornaments of the sanctuary. Although the altar lights were not restored immediately, it was not long before they reappeared, and the worship at St Matthias, over the following seven years, developed to a point that S. W. Mangin had only dreamed of. At the dedication festival in 1859, the altar candles were lit. In the same year, Lent and the rites of Holy Week were fully observed with visiting preachers such as Archdeacon Denison, Benson of Cowley, and John Mason Neale.

Over the next two or three years, the family settled into Ebor Lodge, the house which had been secured as a parsonage, and visitors were frequent.[62] By 1865 vestments and incense were being used at Easter and the use of copes, gospel lights and the sanctus bell were introduced before Whitsunday. Of course, there was a reaction. The Marquess of Westmeath, George Nugent, visited St Matthias on Whitsunday 1865 and carried a report back to the House of Lords concerning the ritual at Stoke Newington. For a man with his history to assume the role of a critic of those who saw themselves as defending Church principles was galling in the extreme. He had fathered an illegitimate daughter many years previously, which might have been seen as youthful error had he not since been divorced twice and married three times.

In 1867, Le Geyt was called to appear before the Ritual Commission. The examination itself was daunting enough but it was only the early rumbling of a gathering storm. Recent history was repeating itself. In 1850, anti-ritualist mobs had attacked St Barnabas, Pimlico. A decade later there were riots at St George in the East. The rioters called themselves defenders of Protestantism. Their methods and violence, the way in which the leaders fed the fury of the mob and the disregard they showed for life and property, gave that claim the lie. Seven years later in Stoke Newington it was all happening again. For several Sundays in the autumn of 1867, mobs gathered around St Matthias. On 29 September, Robert Brett's house was attacked by the mob, threatening his wife and daughters. On another occasion, there were over a thousand rioters. On 19 October, an even larger mob formed with the intention of burning down the vicarage and wrecking the church. The police held them at bay but what really changed the mood was the sight of the huge congregation of men and women gathered silently outside the church, refusing to be moved:

> To rulers in Church and State it was an evidence of ecclesiastical strength, and unity of purpose, which no assembly of bullies or cowards could shake.[63]

So it was that when Mamerto Gueritz came to assist at Stoke Newington early in 1868, the events of the previous autumn were still fresh in the minds of people and priest. Gueritz was there for the dedication festival that year, which was the first occasion that six additional candlestands were placed on a gradine behind the altar. The following year two new nearby churches were consecrated, St Chad's and St Columba's, and shortly afterwards Le Geyt was the preacher at St Columba's harvest festival. A member of the congregation reflected the understanding of many of his hearers that while Le Geyt was a most gifted preacher, the path he had taken had destroyed any hope of preferment: "What a flat he was to turn ritualist! He might have been a bishop but there's no hope for him now!"

C. J. Le Geyt contributed a great deal to the cause of ritual revival, not only by his own practices and example at St Matthias but also in his work of instructing others. He was called upon to preach and address meetings all around the country. His lecture to the Oxford branch of the English Church Union, entitled *Catholic Ritual in the Church of England*, was published in 1866. Then the following year he wrote *On the Symbolism of Ritual; in the Church and in the World*. His writing on ritual, however, was but one facet of his contribution to the shaping of the later Oxford Movement. His emphasis on mission, nurture, spirituality and the development of lay ministries lay firmly alongside his commitment to ritual, providing something of a check to the inherent tendency that the promotion of ceremony had to become an end in itself. Ritual was to be the means to introduce the poor and the privileged alike to the mystery and wonder that should be found in worship and thus to a deeper understanding of themselves in relation to that mystery. It was a fine line to tread and the behaviour of some of those who were passionate advocates of the Ritual Revival sometimes seemed to cross it, but the line was always there.

Le Geyt was also a committed ecumenist of a particular kind. He was active in the Association for the Promotion of the Union of Christendom, and before the association was condemned as heretical by the Inquisition in 1864, he was among 200 Anglican clerical members of the APUC who had engaged in conversations with the Holy See, corporate reunion being the desired end. With him in those attempts were men such as Sabine Baring-Gould, Robert Liddell, R. F. Littledale, W. J. E. Bennett, Stanton of Holborn, Alexander Mackonochie and R. F. Lowder. Of course, in the vanguard was Frederick George Lee. For them all, the "Union of Christendom" meant reunion with Rome in some form. Those Protestant branches of the Church which had eschewed the ancient orders of ministry and the sacraments had first to address those errors before any further steps towards them could be taken.

Le Geyt's work was hard and the conflicts frequent, both in Stoke Newington and in the many places in the country where he was asked to speak. This took its toll. There was the prosecution of John Purchas in 1871 when the Privy Council ruled that facing eastwards to celebrate the Holy Communion, mixing wine and water in the chalice, using wafer bread and wearing vestments were all illegal in the Church of England. Le Geyt and more than 40 of the London clergy made public their intention to disobey the order of the court. It was around this time that Janet Phillis Le Geyt and their daughter moved to live in Ryde, on the Isle of Wight, where the family had connections. Then in 1874 came a double blow. Early in January, Robert Brett, his trusted friend and tireless supporter, died. In May of the same year, for reasons possibly not unrelated, Le Geyt was obliged to file for bankruptcy. He had assets of £200 and debts of almost £4,500. Eventually, during 1877, the living of St Matthias was sequestrated for the benefit of Le Geyt's creditors, and a curate was placed in sole charge. Janet Le Geyt was in possession of more than enough money to have assisted, but either she was unwilling or Charles would not accept her help.

The stress of all this and the effects of years of overwork resulted in repeated illnesses which, in turn, meant that he had to be away from the parish for long periods, sometimes in the Isle of Wight and sometimes in France. Le Geyt attempted to return to Stoke Newington in the summer of 1877 but had to leave again in the autumn and went to Calais. While there he was confined to bed, but even so his death on 27 December was unexpected. His body was brought back to St Matthias, where a solemn requiem was celebrated before burial at Highgate Cemetery.

Obituaries and tributes appeared in many publications, but perhaps the most insightful was written almost 20 years later by the Roman Catholic priest of Lubbeck, near Louvain, Austin Richardson. He had known Charles James Le Geyt for around eight years before his death, and his article "Un Prêtre Anglican" appeared in the *Revue Anglo Romaine* in 1895.[64]

In his praise for his friend, Fr Richardson was careful to avoid any appearance of seeming to affirm Anglican orders and emphasized that his use of the word *Prêtre* in relation to Charles Le Geyt should not be construed as doing so. This was the year before the Papal Bull *Apostolicae curae* declared Anglican orders "absolutely null and utterly void", and Richardson, in common with a considerable body of French Roman Catholics, still entertained hopes for deepening Anglican and Roman relationships. He claimed that if only people would take the trouble to understand each other "on both sides there will be surprise to see how narrow is the land that remains to cross".

Richardson points out that he has chosen to write not of the great ones of the Oxford Movement such as Pusey, Keble or Liddon, but of "a man no longer of this world though his memory will stay forever dear and alive to his friends". He mentions Le Geyt's marriage and the birth of his daughter, all of which, as he carefully points out, took place before ordination. Then he makes an assertion which, if true, explains some later aspects of the Le Geyt household arrangements:

> If I recall this fact (the marriage) it is because my friend was sympathetic to the celibate ecclesiastic and I have every reason to believe that, from the point of his ordination, he practised what he preached.[65]

Le Geyt's daughter, Janet Madaleine, was born in January 1854. Charles had been ordained the previous May.

The worship and ritual at St Matthias are briefly described in Fr Richardson's article and it is interesting to note what he felt it appropriate to include:

> In St Matthias Church, as in all other ritualist churches, the men are on one side and the women on the other following the ancient usage. But all classes of society are mixed, gentlemen sit next to the workers, the ladies next to the most humble maids. Each sits where he likes (First come first served).
>
> At St Matthias the offices are said as closely as possible to the style of the Roman Church. The ministers wear Catholic vestments in Gothic form. The celebration of Communion had every appearance of the Mass. The altar was decorated with candles and with flowers; incense burned as at home.[66]

Le Geyt's views on the Reformation, which he called the "Deformation", are set out in brief. He regarded the separation from Rome as schism and therefore a grave sin, but believed that it had in no way extinguished the spiritual life of the Anglican Church. He believed the primacy of the successors of St Peter to be divinely instituted and held, as a hope for the Church of England, the examples of churches separated from communion for a time which nevertheless remained recognized as part of the Church Catholic. Richardson refrains from affirming or denying this view: "Now is not the moment to refute this teaching. I am writing a simple biography."

However, in commenting on Le Geyt's hope for corporate reunion, Richardson acknowledged that although English Roman Catholics may have regarded the idea as absurd, the example of the reunion of the oriental churches with Rome after centuries of separation was something that gave hope to a considerable number of Anglican clergy. Fr Richardson, although bearing an English name, was a priest of the Roman Church in France. The English Roman Catholics, perhaps as a legacy of the long years of persecution and exclusion, were far less sympathetic to the Church of England than their continental brethren. There were exceptions, of course, but many of them, as Gueritz discovered, regarded Anglican clergy as no more "Catholic" in its proper sense than, for example, a Congregational Church minister.

Charles James Le Geyt did not live to see his Anglican priesthood utterly denied by the Bishop of Rome and the decay of hope for corporate reunion, but his memory survived in the heart and mind of at least one Roman Catholic sympathizer. He also lived on in the memories of the people he had served and the lives of priestly service that he had shaped and influenced. Mamerto Gueritz was one of many who could claim a share in that inheritance.

Janet Phillis Le Geyt and her daughter moved, for a short while, to Stamford Baron in Northamptonshire and eventually to Winchester, where they lived in a substantial house at 12 St Swithun Street, with two servants. Charlotte, Janet's sister, joined them for a short while but died in 1905. When Janet Phillis died in 1908, she was buried in Camden and her daughter went to live at Bromley in Kent. Evidently money had not been lacking for either mother or daughter in spite of C. J. Le Geyt's bankruptcy. When Janet Madaleine also died in 1942, she left an estate worth over £17,000. Her passing was noted by the Guild of All Souls, of which she had been a member all her adult life.

Robert Brett

1808–74

When Robert Brett died on 3 February 1874, there was an immediate outpouring both of sorrow at his passing and thanksgiving for his life. That response came from people in every walk of life and station in society, from baronet to barrow boy. It came from the countless lay people whose spiritual lives had been substantially enriched by Brett's devotional writings, and from the large number of Anglo-Catholic clergy who recognized the service he had given to their cause and the debt that was owed.

Robert Brett was born near Luton in Bedfordshire on 11 September 1808, the son of a John and Martha Brett. Brett senior was a farmer and churchwarden of their parish. Robert's early education culminated in his apprenticeship to a relative, Dr Waller, who was a surgeon in Luton. In his late teens he began further medical studies at St George's Hospital in London and was made a member of the Royal College of Surgeons in 1830. In the same year, when he was just 22 years old, he became a Licentiate of the Society of Apothecaries of London.[67] Having qualified, Brett began to develop an aspiration towards ordination and missionary work, something in which all his talents could combine. However, in August 1831, hardly a year after qualifying, he married Elizabeth Braddock, a lady some 12 years his senior and with whom he had an attachment for the previous seven years. Brett settled once more to medicine as his first calling, and the following year they had a son, Henry Robert Brett. Henry was born in Luton, where Robert Brett had a medical practice, but the fact that Robert and Elizabeth were married in St Mark's, Kennington indicates that he was also still working at St George's Hospital, which was then situated at Hyde Park, only some two and a half miles away. Not long after Henry's birth Elizabeth Brett died, leaving Robert with an infant son to care for.

Around 1832 Brett removed from Luton to London, and then in 1835 he left hospital work and went as an assistant surgeon and then partner to a friend, Samuel Reynolds, who had a practice in Stoke Newington High Street. He had already established close and affectionate ties with Reynolds' family, his wife and children and his sister, Maria, who was living with them. After a few years, the professional partnership with Reynolds also became a familial one. On 9 October 1838, Robert Brett and Maria Hill Reynolds were married at the parish church in Diss, Norfolk. The marriage register shows that Maria's father, John Reynolds, was a Wesleyan minister. He was one of the witnesses, and Charlotte Fison née Reynolds, Maria's sister, was the other.[68]

Robert Brett was greatly influenced by John Keble's Assize Sermon and the *Tracts for the Times* which followed it, and his life as a churchman took on a new dimension.[69] He entered the lists in the Tractarian cause with a commitment and enthusiasm that earned him the friendship of its leaders and, as their interchange of correspondence during the early 1840s shows, first among them was Edward Bouverie Pusey. Brett's involvement in the Tractarian movement was dated "from its commencement" by one of his biographers. As we have seen, the label Tractarian was initially attached mainly to the authors of the *Tracts* themselves until after *Tract 90* was published in 1841. Then it was used more widely to refer to those who joined the ever-growing body of supporters and then later to those who remained after the departure of John Henry Newman. Brett was in correspondence with Pusey well before that departure took place.

Brett had written openly about his sense of "conversion" in a letter to Maria Reynolds some two years before they married. In a second letter, he spoke of the serious illness of his son Henry and of his belief that God had used that trial to make him more keenly aware of the divine life and presence. All this was about Robert Brett's relationship with God. He was clear that his espousal of the Tractarian movement was an outworking of that prior relationship. Small wonder, then, that Maria Reynolds was captivated by a man who could unashamedly share such a depth of feeling.

In Stoke Newington, the family began to grow as children arrived in rapid succession. Maria Charlotte was born in 1840, Eliza in 1841, John in 1842, and Mary in 1843. Then came a slight pause before Frances arrived in 1845, Catherine in 1846, and finally Helen in 1848. During this time, Robert's son by his first marriage was also living with them, and by the time he was 18 was a medical student assisting his father.

In 1846, Maria's sister Charlotte Fison, who had been a witness at their wedding, died. One of Charlotte's children, Eliza, also came to live with the Bretts. That made a household of 11 with, aside from Maria and Robert, ages ranging from just born to 25, the latter being their niece Eliza. At least they had two servants to look after them.

The medical practice grew, as did Robert Brett's reputation as a surgeon, and work occupied much time and energy. The partnership with Samuel Reynolds lasted until just before 1850, after which time it seems that Brett established his own practice and Reynolds continued in his. Reynolds was certainly still in general practice in 1860 and possibly later.[70]

Brett's espousal of Tractarian ideals fired his zeal not only for Church principles and the restoration of the ritual but also for the provision of church buildings that would serve the liturgy of the Church of England in its recovered catholicity. This gave rise to the great church building projects in which he engaged for the rest of his life.

However, before that later work began, almost by accident Robert Brett was the instigator of another great project. This was to bring him new contacts and strengthen existing ones in a way which would aid all his future endeavours. In 1843, Brett was on a holiday tour which took him to Canterbury. Quite by chance he went to see the ruins of the Augustinian monastery there and discovered that the land, the ruins, and such buildings as remained were available for purchase. The buildings were, at the time, being used as a brewery, a pot house and billiard rooms.

Brett wrote about his visit and his desire to see the monastery reclaimed for a better purpose in an article in *The English Churchman* in September 1843, having already shared his hopes with a close friend, Edward Coleridge of Eton School. The article was passed to Alexander Beresford Hope, who purchased the buildings, ruins and grounds, and then set in motion the creation of the Missionary College, which was to provide, according to its charter, "an education to qualify young men for the service of the Church in the distant dependencies of the British Empire". Coleridge was the first secretary of the provisional committee set up to take the project forward. Both of those names, Beresford Hope and Edward Coleridge, appear repeatedly in connection with Robert Brett.

The first great church building project with which Brett was associated was St Matthias, Stoke Newington. When Lord Nelson laid the foundation stone in 1851, it was noted that "for as many as twelve years, Mr. Brett, who may also be considered the founder of the church, has steadily pursued this one object of building a new church".[71]

Brett had been committed to the building of the new church since at least 1839, and his support of the movement which engendered the project will have predated that. Thus, Robert Brett was indeed among the earliest of the Tractarians, even before they were widely known as such.

In the many memorials and obituaries of Robert Brett, there was an oft-repeated refrain that he was "unendowed with the gifts of fortune"[72] and had "neither rank nor temporal wealth".[73] Although Brett had adequate means to maintain his considerable family and his place as a surgeon, his persistent generosity meant that his spending power was limited. Knowing this, and recognizing his health was being affected by the long journeys he made on foot in all weathers to tend his patients, friends conspired to buy him a carriage; among them were T. A. Pope, his incumbent at the time, and T. S. Evans of Shoreditch. Brett was moved to tears by their kindness.

What this also shows is that Robert Brett did not have the kind of money it would take to realize his dream of building churches sufficient for the need of the people and appropriate to the liturgy he espoused. What he did have was a wonderful talent for persuasion and for making his own zeal and conviction contagious. He may not himself have possessed rank or great wealth but was able to commune both with those who did and also with those who emphatically did not. His contacts and willing donors ranged from baronet to barrow boy.

The same report which noted his role in the building of St Matthias also informed the reader that over £1,000 had been raised in the previous 18 months by the weekly offerings of the congregation alone. It reported Brett's speech, made in reply to the praise of Lord Nelson, in which he revealed the names of some of the other supporters who were pledged to the cause. There was Alexander Beresford Hope, Mr Twells the banker and Mr Hubbard the deputy governor of the bank, along with the Revd E. Coleridge of Eton and Mr Markland of Bath "as well as those anonymous ladies who are said to have contributed largely to the building fund".

Perhaps only the names of Beresford Hope and Coleridge will be widely recognized now. All those names were immensely significant at the time, but equally important, not only in this instance but in the unfolding of the whole Church Revival, was the work of those "anonymous ladies". We have the names of the greater and lesser men of the movement, but without women like Eliza Coles, Charlotte Keble, Anne Derby Gueritz and countless wives, daughters and sisters who were just as fervent and sacrificially committed as their menfolk, the Oxford Movement may never have taken hold in the way it did.

The construction of St Matthias continued and the substantially completed building was consecrated in June 1853. The total cost was just over £7,000, and it should be remembered that less than a third of that had been raised at the time of the laying of the first stone in 1851. During this time, Robert Brett worked closely with William Butterfield, the architect, cementing a friendship which was to be most valuable in later years, not only for access to Butterfield himself but also one of his pupils, Henry Woodyer. Brett, however, was taken ill in 1852 and was obliged to convalesce for part of the year in Brighton in obedience to the instructions of his own physician. He returned in time for the consecration but was still not fully restored.

Although committed to Tractarian ideals and the Ritual Revival, Brett was not a narrow party man. He was loyal to the light he had been given but also open to the worth to be found in people holding very different views from himself. This meant that while he was firmly committed to organizations such as the English Church Union, he was also concerned to serve the wider interests of the Church. The 1862 Church Congress was held in Oxford and the photograph of the event shows a large number of eminent divines, bishops and archdeacons, together with the leading laymen of the day, among whom was Robert Brett. Another example was Brett's membership of the Church Institution for Defensive and General Purposes. This was created to bring together churchmen of every shade of religious and political opinion. Theological differences were to be set aside and a rule was made that "no question touching doctrine shall be entered into at any meeting". The sole purpose was to defend the Established Church against a growing voice in Parliament, that of the Liberation Society, which was strident in its opposition to the influence that the Church of England still had in the country and in government. At a meeting of the institution in December 1864, there were present Lord Robert Cecil, Earl of Dartmouth, 12 Members of Parliament, a Queen's Counsel, two baronets and a viscount. There were many others and among them were Alexander Beresford Hope, MP and Robert Brett.

Engagement with wider questions did not lessen Brett's focus on the needs of an ever-growing populace for adequate places of worship in his own locality. Neither did it take away from his commitment to the life and worship of St Matthias. All this, in the early years at least, was happening while he was still working at his medical practice and caring for his family. In later years, he was able to focus less on his medical work and more on his work for the Church. The fact that his family and the building of the kingdom of God in his part of London had jointly become Brett's *raison d'etre* was demonstrated in many ways, but is perhaps best summarized in a comment made by his wife, Maria:

> He is as meek as a lamb in most things; but for his children or his church he is a lion.[74]

Another indication was perhaps shown by Brett's use of his carriage to promote the cause. It was entirely usual for a family motto to be blazoned on the side of a private vehicle whether a person was armigerous or not. At around the same time that Brett received the gift of his carriage, horse-drawn omnibuses were having modesty boards installed on their upper decks in order to "prevent over-exciting passing pedestrians", thus providing blank spaces for mobile advertising. Whether Brett ever consciously combined the two ideas or not we may never know, but on both doors of his carriage was inscribed the motto, *Pro Ecclesia Dei*.

Before we look further at Robert Brett's part in the building of new churches, there was another way in which he was building the kingdom of heaven, not in bricks and mortar but in the hearts and minds of people. He wrote devotional books, some of which were based on his experiences with the sick and the dying as a surgeon, and others from his experience as a father of small children. Among the earliest were *Devotions for the Sick Room and for Times of Trouble*, published in 1843, and *Simple Prayers for Little Children* in 1848. He also drew on his own spiritual journey in *The Churchman's Guide to Faith and Piety* and *A Pocket Companion for Lent for Busy Men*.[75]

The income from the sale of these books was devoted to the building funds of the projects in which he was involved, something which continued after his death. Within a month of his death, Masters, one of his publishers, had re-issued his *Churchman's Guide to Faith and Piety*, which had already run to four editions.

Brett was involved in the building of St Michael's, Shoreditch, which was consecrated in 1865. While this project was in hand, a daughter of the incumbent, T. Simpson Evans, died. At almost the same time, Maria Charlotte, the eldest daughter of Robert and Maria Brett, also died on 6 April 1864. Her passing was marked by a solemn requiem at St Matthias, which was the first time incense was used there.

Brett first expressed his own deep grief by publishing *The Power of the Catholic Faith: A Memorial. (In loving remembrance of Maria Charlotte B.)* Then, he and Evans, in their shared sorrow, gave the reredos at St Michael's as a memorial to their daughters. Brett was deeply affected, but this was not to be the last blow dealt him in that year. His wife, Maria, also devastated by the death of their eldest daughter, contracted bronchitis towards the end of the year. It was an acute attack which did not respond to treatment, and she died on 20 December and was buried on Christmas Eve 1864.

Grief-stricken, Brett threw himself once more into the work of the Haggerston Church Scheme. This was begun by T. S. Evans and, in 1860, John Ross, the newly appointed vicar of Haggerston, had appealed for help to provide adequate worship space for the population of over 30,000. The first objective was the re-shaping of the parish church of St Mary, but that was just the beginning of a plan to provide more churches. Richard Foster, "one of the most devoted and munificent sons whom the Church in London has ever had",[76] responded with large and unprecedented financial help. Brett joined him, offering the wisdom gained by his experience, his capacity for persuasion and his contacts throughout the Church. Although he could not match Foster's finances, the income from Brett's books and the extra donations which came from his readers added considerably to the fund. James Brooks was the architect chosen for the work on St Mary's. He, Evans and Brett had worked together on St Michael's, Shoreditch.

Three more district churches were envisaged for Haggerston, and in a letter sent to possible donors in November 1866, Brett wrote:

> Mission Chapels have been opened and a sufficient sum has been set apart for each of the three churches, so that the small sum of £4000 will ensure their completion and leave some for finishing the Parish Church. One of the three churches (St. Augustine) is now nearly built and it is of the *utmost consequence* that the other two should be commenced *this autumn.*[77]

So it was that St Augustine's, Haggerston was consecrated in 1867, then St Chad's and St Columba's in 1869. This was the outcome of the work of many people, but among the leaders was Robert Brett, whose powerful letters of appeal and whose talent in dealing with sometimes obstructive officials and hierarchies contributed largely to the success of the scheme.

All was not peace in Stoke Newington in the autumn of 1867, and as St Augustine's, Haggerston neared completion, the anti-ritualist preachers inflamed large gatherings of protestors around St Matthias. The clergy and churchwardens of the parish were the primary targets. Brett, however, was a veteran of such conflicts and had gone weekly to St George in the East to support Bryan King in the rioting that took place there seven years earlier. Together with his colleague churchwarden, Robert Porter, they put plans in place to counter any disturbance inside the church.

On 22 September, a large group of men entered the church at the time of the service, and on being told they could not sit in the seats reserved for women, they became obstreperous. One of their leaders, a Mr Langston, repeatedly challenged the churchwardens to "lay hands" upon him and made no secret of his intention of finding an excuse to have them charged with assault. The *Evening Standard*, a publication sympathetic to the rioters, claimed that they were "violently ejected . . . as saintly men not even attempting to defend themselves". None of the intruders were worshippers, most were not members of the Church of England, and they were demonstrably there with the intention of disrupting divine worship. This indicates that the reporting of the *Evening Standard* was less than honest and somewhat partisan. The following Sunday there was an even larger mob, this time kept away from the church by a substantial police presence. The congregation of St Matthias had turned out in force, men, women and children refusing to be cowed by the mob. Infuriated that they could not get into the church, the rioters crossed the green to Robert Brett's house and having thrown stones at Brett himself on his way home, then began to heave pieces of granite, left by the roadbuilders, through his windows. Fortunately, the windows had already been barricaded otherwise Brett's daughters might well have been injured. Again, the *Evening Standard* reported the incident, carefully omitting the scenes of near carnage and maintaining that, although there were plentiful supplies of granite stones by the road, these were not thrown at the house. A pattern of selective reporting emerges.

October saw a continuation of the riots, with stones being thrown at the visiting preacher on Sunday, 6 October, but there was something of a lull the following weekend which might have resulted from a setback experienced by Langston, one of the main instigators of the riots. The *Weekly Dispatch* of Sunday, 13 October carried a report of a prosecution brought by Langston against Robert Brett and Robert Porter on charges of assault. The principal witnesses for the prosecution unintentionally provided the best defence, their testimony revealing much of the dubious motive for their and their leader's presence in St Matthias. The case was dismissed and the complainant, Langston, ordered to pay the costs. The lull was short-lived and the following Saturday a large crowd gathered with the intention of wrecking the church and burning down the vicarage. Again, the police held them in check. Finally, on Sunday, 27 October:

> At the close of the services the mob, as usual, made its way to Stoke Newington Green, and surrounded the house of Mr. Brett, the churchwarden. Where they howled and hooted, but carefully avoided throwing stones ... The police, of whom there was a strong force, kept the people moving about, and, as the night was cold, the majority of the roughs went away without even waiting for Mr Brett's return home.[78]

And so the riots petered out. A mob will willingly respond to the invective and malice of a leader until it, the mob, becomes bored and, in this case, cold. Obviously four weeks of it was enough for them.

Just after the death of Brett's daughter, Maria Charlotte, John Keble wrote to Brett in a sympathetic and warmly affectionate letter. One of Keble's concerns was for Brett's youngest son:

> I trust that our friend Jonny continues to be a comfort to you in every way—in health and in work—as always in conduct.[79]

Keble's concern was justified because John Brett was never a robust child, and while an undergraduate at St Mary Hall, Oxford, his health began to fail.[80] Just four years after the death of his mother and sister, John was taken seriously ill. During his illness, his godfather, John Jackson, who was Bishop of Lincoln and would later become Bishop of London, made the journey to Stoke Newington to see him. After lingering for three months, John died on Palm Sunday 1868, a day before the anniversary of the death of his sister.

The last of Brett's projects was the building of St Faith's, which was to be a district church within the parish of St Matthias. The provision of another church to match the growing population was not, however, the only motive for the work. While Charles Le Geyt was the incumbent, the worship and Catholic teaching at St Matthias were secure. However, the right of presentation was due to revert to the bishop at the next interregnum, and although Brett's close friend and his son's godfather, John Jackson, would soon become Bishop of London, when the plans for St Faith's were laid, Bishop Tait was still in office. The memories of the more or less forced departure of S. W. Mangin and the bishop's opposition even to candles on the altar were still near the surface even after ten years had passed. St Faith's was founded in the awareness that the Bishop of London could still move to suppress the ritual in the parish by appointing a priest to St Matthias who would follow Tait's instructions in the matter. In order to guard against this, the deeds of St Faith's required that the right of presentation should be vested in trustees who were bound to maintain the tradition, the teaching and the ritual.

First, a mission chapel of St Faith was opened in 1868, and then, when the land on which it stood was needed for the building of the new church, Richard Foster came once more to their aid. With the help of some friends, he paid for the erection of a temporary "Iron Church" close by, which opened in 1872. Later that year, in the middle of a snowstorm, John Hubbard, later to become Lord Addington, laid the first stone and building progressed rapidly. On 17 May 1873, the relatively new Bishop of London, John Jackson, consecrated the chancel and the completed part of the nave.

For Robert Brett, it was a time of hugely conflicting emotions. The new church was open, the consecration service had been all that could be desired, many supporters attended and a large number of priests processed, but there were absences that could not be remedied and a sorrow that could not be assuaged. After the death of her mother and sister, Brett's daughter Catherine had been his main domestic support and emotional sustainer during the work on St Faith's, until she too was taken ill. In the hope of recovery, she had gone to Torquay, but there, in March 1873, she died. Her body was brought back to Stoke Newington and, as there had been for her brother, sister and mother, there was a solemn requiem at St Matthias after which she too was buried in Tottenham cemetery.[81]

Brett never really recovered from this last blow, and although he carried on with his work and fulfilled all his commitments, he was visibly in decline and finally became too ill to leave his house. In the late afternoon of 3 February 1874, C. J. Le Geyt visited, administered the sacrament, and at 15 minutes to five, Robert Brett passed from this life aged 65.

As in life, so in death. The great and the good of Church and society flocked to the requiem on 7 February, and so did many of the poor for whom he had given freely of his skills and indeed of himself—from baronet to barrow boy. So many wanted to be there that admission had to be by ticket only.

Several of the obituaries noted that Brett had been churchwarden at St Matthias for many years:

> where the practices now associated with the Ritualist School have been gradually adopted. Mr. Brett, however, it was stated, was by no means a supporter of later developments in this direction.

What lies behind that is important for our understanding of Robert Brett's relationship with the Church. He was quintessentially Anglican. For him, the Church of England was and always had been Catholic, and the liturgy should reflect both its catholicity and its Englishness. Therefore, later developments which introduced Roman-style vestments of the "fiddle back" shape, or which used the Roman rite in translation, or which seemed to require an almost idolatrous attitude to the Blessed Virgin Mary, were to be resisted. It is therefore perhaps an irony that one of Brett's sobriquets was "The Lay Pope of Stoke Newington". This was a title affectionately given him by W. J. E. Bennett of Frome, who was often at St Matthias, and it was coined to reflect Brett's capacity to lead and guide, both in spiritual and temporal spheres.[82]

As already noted, Brett was able, freely and easily, to work with those who held opinions very different from his own. There is so much more that could be said on that score but Brett's own words at the Church Congress in Leeds in September 1872 are probably the best reflection of his convictions:

It is certain we cannot adjust all our differences, but let us treat each other
in a spirit of toleration and forbearance, and try to bring one another by
conciliatory means to be, if possible, of one mind, and God will give His
blessing to our efforts and overrule all to His own purposes of love and
mercy. There is room for High Church and Low Church; there is room
for Ritualists and for others; and no power on earth, no Privy Council, no
Parliament, no Tribunal, shall ever drive me out of the bosom of the old
Catholic Church of England.[83]

This was the man whose "valuable acquaintance" was won by Mamerto Gueritz
when he came to assist Le Geyt in Stoke Newington. The extent of Brett's influence
on Gueritz cannot be easily judged, but working in close proximity to such a
man for 18 months could hardly have been without effect and at the very least
the liturgy at Colyton remained essentially English rather than Roman and the
vestments were Sarum-Gothic throughout Mamerto's ministry there.

W. H. Monk
1823–89

Immediately following the death of William Henry Monk in 1889, there was a
great flurry of newspaper activity. Of course, there were the obituaries, memorials
and tributes, but also, and in great number, there were advertisements from music
teachers, all claiming to have been trained by W. H. Monk. It was obviously felt,
probably with justification, that a share in the reputation of the great man, even
at such a remove, would attract pupils, or the parents of pupils.

The name of Monk was not exactly rare in the Victorian musical world, and
this gave rise to occasional errors of identification. In 1857, it was reported that a
Mr Monk, organist and choirmaster, had accidentally drowned while bathing. The
report also noted that he was the brother of Dr Monk, the precentor of St Peter's
College, Radley.[84] The latter was Dr E. G. Monk, who was at Radley before he went
to York. In the year that W. H. Monk died and in the notices which followed his
death, there was even more confusion. A Dr Mark J. Monk was appointed organist
and choirmaster at Truro Cathedral in 1889. He had been a chorister under Dr E.
G. Monk, organist and master of choristers at York Minster, and later went on to

become organist of Banbury parish church. As if this multiplicity of "Monks" were not enough to create confusion of itself, in some newspapers the names of E. G. and W. H. Monk were interchanged in the death notices and a clarification had to be published. Edwin George Monk felt that his obituary was rather premature:[85]

> At the time of the lamented death of Dr. W.H. Monk, one or two notices confused his name with that of Dr E. G. Monk, and on the most regretted death of Sir F. A. Gore Ouseley the mistake was again made. Dr. E. G. Monk, organist of York Cathedral was co-compiler with Sir Frederick of the Anglican Psalter. Dr. W. H. Monk, Professor of music at Kings College, was co-compiler with the late Sir H. W. Baker of 'The Psalter and Canticles to chants A & M.' The mistake which we wish to rectify is very pardonable. Two Psalters, two musical doctors, two Baronets and Priests as their co-compilers. It was very easy for their several associations with their work to be confused in the mind of the uninitiated.[86]

William Henry Monk was born in Brompton on 16 March 1823. By the age of 18, he was organist at Eaton Square Chapel, Pimlico. Two years later, in 1843, he was appointed to St George's, Albemarle Street and two years after that to St Paul's, Portman Square. Monk's early talents as a musician were most apparent in his skill at the organ, but as time passed his worth as a composer began increasingly to be recognized. While he was still at Portman Square, W. H. Monk married a lady with the delightful name of Hope Isidora Pillow. Intriguing names seemed to run in her family, her mother having been Hopestill Harland before her own marriage. William and Hope Monk set up home in Upper Stamford Street, Lambeth.

The following year, in 1847, Monk was appointed choirmaster of King's College London, and there he met Professor William Dyce. Dyce was primarily an artist; his chair at King's College London was that of Professor of Fine Art. Dyce's appointment at King's followed a distinguished career in Scotland and, latterly, in London. However, his main influence on W. H. Monk was in liturgical music. In the same year that Monk was appointed to King's College, Dyce helped found the Motett Society, whose initial purpose was to create "a Collection of Ancient Church Music, adapted to English words, with a compressed score, for the purpose of accompaniment". The work of this society and his friendship with

Dyce had a profound influence on the development of Monk's understanding of the relationship between the liturgy, the music of the liturgy, and the role of the choir and the congregation in relation to both. This was to be given full scope for development in his next appointment outside the college.

In 1849, there were two further developments. Hope Monk gave birth to their first child, Florence Emily Monk, and, in addition to his role as choirmaster, Monk was appointed organist of King's College. Three years later, in 1852, there was another birth and another appointment. Constance Anna Colman Monk was born, and Monk was appointed organist and choirmaster at St Matthias, Stoke Newington. Soon the family moved to Park Road West in Stoke Newington, where they lived until the 1860s, when they moved to 53 Clissold Road, and thence to a commodious house called "Glebe Field".[87]

Monk's appointment as organist and choirmaster of St Matthias was during the incumbency of T. A. Pope, who had already made a considerable impression on the community of Stoke Newington. At that time, worship was still being conducted in the school and the church would not be consecrated until the following year, 1853. Monk's roles at King's College afforded him considerable standing in the musical world, and further appointments simply increased that influence, but his work at Stoke Newington was to provide an example of a musical policy and tradition that would help to shape the worship of the Catholic Revival in the Church of England.

There were two emerging schools of psalmody, described summarily in the same article that clarified the confusion between W. H. and E. G. Monk. In comparing the two psalters, that of W. H. Monk was described as "essentially Gregorian, though it embraces a large and well chosen variety of Anglican chants", while that compiled by E. G. Monk with Sir Frederick Gore Ouseley was "Anglican pure and simple". In an interesting link, Gore Ouseley founded the school at Tenbury to which Mamerto Gueritz sent at least one of his sons.

From the outset, Monk insisted on a choir of volunteers believing, as we have noted, that a polished "performance" style was of less importance than the willing involvement of those who were actively engaged in worship. Soon he had instituted daily choral worship at St Matthias, something which many churches with a professional choir could not maintain. On the same principle, he also worked to create a singing congregation, something which a number of churches lost as the music became more and more esoteric. This blend of plainsong and hymnody, which became such a feature of the daily offices and the Eucharistic liturgy at St Matthias, Stoke Newington, was the style which Mamerto Gueritz had taken with him to Colyton, albeit in embryo. Gueritz had evidently embraced this liturgical style when it was still in its infancy, as his work with the choral associations in Cornwall confirms. That was some years before he spent 18 months working alongside W. H. Monk and Robert Brett but nevertheless his time in Stoke Newington provided a solid affirmation of the choral work that he had already begun and an opportunity to enhance it. This influenced not only the worship in Colyton, where he trained both choir and congregation in singing, but also the development of the numerous local choral associations in East Devon in which Gueritz was a leading influence. That work eventually issued in the East Devon Choral Union.

The work at Stoke Newington was just one facet of Monk's influence on the world of church music. His place in the wider musical world is demonstrated by the appointments he held and his other activities, his lectures on opera being one example. By the time he went to St Matthias, he was already Professor of Music at the School for the Indigent Blind. Over two decades later he was made Professor of Vocal Music at King's College in 1874, then Professor at the National Training School for Music in 1876, and in 1878 Professor of Bedford College, London. Finally, in 1882, when he was almost 60, Monk was awarded an honorary Doctorate in Music by Durham University.

During Monk's first decade at St Matthias, Stoke Newington, three more children were born, Ernest Kempster Monk, Leonard Pillow Monk, and finally, in 1863, Florence Hopestill Monk, named for her maternal grandmother. Sadly, Ernest died when he was only 25, but his younger siblings lived to ripe old age, Florence dying in her ninetieth year. This was a demanding decade for W. H. Monk; a multiplicity of appointments, a growing family and yet another task looming.

Perhaps his greatest legacy, or rather that for which he is most remembered, is Monk's work on English hymnody. He is, of course, remembered for the many tunes he composed for new and existing hymns, and his "Eventide" is now arguably among the most famous of hymn tunes worldwide. Legend has it that Monk composed the tune in ten minutes, at a committee meeting, during which he realized that H. F. Lyte's hymn "Abide With Me" did not appear to have a tune.[88] Then there was the music he borrowed, adapted and arranged; for example, the tune "Victory" was taken from Palestrina and reshaped for "The Strife is O'er, the Battle Done". And again, there were newly translated ancient Greek and Latin texts, the work of scholars such as John Mason Neale and Edward Caswall, which needed either new tunes or accompanied congregational settings for the plainsong. The Advent hymn "Hark a Herald Voice is Calling" was translated by Caswall and then set to the tune "Merton" by Monk.

At the end of the 1850s, the Church of England had nothing to compare with the major, authorized, nonconformist hymnals. Once again, the Established Church was the victim of its own system wherein parochial clergy had considerable autonomy, a situation sometimes unkindly described as having a pope in every parish. One result of this, for example, was that in 1859 the five parish churches in central Nottingham were using five different hymn books, some of which were local compilations.[89] The very commonality of doctrine, discipline and worship which the Tractarian Movement had begun to establish within its permeable bounds was, in some places, subjected to idiosyncratic hymnody which spoke more clearly of the compiler than of the worship of the Church. Moderately successful attempts to supply the lack had been made by people who perceived the danger, and it was with the men behind two of those attempts that something new was begun. In 1852, Francis Murray, rector of Chislehurst, had edited a *Hymnal for Use in the Church of England*. William Denton, at the time incumbent of St Bartholomew, Moorfields, published his *Church Hymnal* in 1853. By the time Murray and Denton began to collaborate in 1858, Murray's book had already gone to three editions and sold 20,000 copies.

A chance meeting of the two of them on a train and subsequent correspondence resulted in the conclusion that the interests of the Church would be best served if the many clergy who were currently engaged in compiling their own hymn books could be persuaded to "unite in an endeavour to produce one good one".[90]

That endeavour resulted in the publication of the first words-only edition of *Hymns Ancient & Modern* in 1860, with 273 hymns, rapidly followed by the words and music edition in 1861. W. H. Monk was the musical editor for the 1861 edition and is credited with having conceived the title which, indeed, reflected the contents.

Initially Denton and Murray called together a committee of over 20, most of whom were parochial clergy, with Sir Henry Baker, the vicar of Monkland in Herefordshire, as secretary. By the time of the publication of the first edition, the committee had been superseded by 11 "proprietors" with Sir Henry in the chair. An appeal in *The Guardian* newspaper produced an overwhelmingly positive response from parochial clergy who had been engaged in gathering material for their own collections.[91] It also generated much advice as to what should be included in the new hymnal.

From the outset, the stated intention was to provide hymns suitable for singing not only in church but at mission services and lectures, at meetings of guilds and brotherhoods, and for all seasons of the Church's year and its festivals. It was conceived as a musical enrichment or extension of the Book of Common Prayer. However, as every parish priest has discovered, it is impossible to please everyone with the selection of hymns. The compilers of *Hymns Ancient & Modern, for Use in the Services of the Church* encountered exactly the same difficulty. Tractarians of the old school distrusted hymns which focussed on subjective and emotional religious feeling. The more extreme Protestant clergy wanted anything that seemed even slightly "Romish" deleted, and the Church Association published a tract by the Revd James Ormiston on the "Jesuitical stratagem" of the book. Some critics felt that many of the hymns were not poetical enough, others that they were too literary. However, by far the greatest response was one of affirmation and gratitude from clergy of all shades of churchmanship (save the extremes) for the provision of a resource which enhanced the worship of the Prayer Book and actually drew congregations back to the services of the Church. One Dorset priest reported that, once the music had taken hold, his congregation grew from a mere dozen to over 150, while regular communicants increased from three to 25 and dissent in his parish all but vanished. All that from a hymn book!

Some contemporary reports seemed to imply that the editorial work on the first edition was carried out by a team headed up by Sir Henry Baker. Sir Henry was indeed greatly involved and has been justly described as the "editor-in-chief", but it has to be acknowledged that the actual editorial work on the music of the second edition was carried out exclusively by William Henry Monk, and only when an enlarged edition was being produced did he have any help.

Hymns Ancient & Modern (*A & M*) was not Monk's only contribution to the hymnody available to the Church, far from it. He remained committed to A & M for the rest of his life, but, broad though its bounds were, there were other musical and liturgical needs to be met and he encouraged and participated in other ventures. He acted as editor for the Church of Scotland's psalter and its hymnal and book of anthems. He also edited the music for Bishop Wordsworth's *Hymns for the Holy Year* and *The Book of Common Prayer with Plain Song and Appropriate Music.*

Sadly, but fittingly, Monk had just completed the revisions and additions for the *A & M* edition of 1889 and sent it to the publishers when he died. The additional material for that edition included hymns by Wesley and other eighteenth-century writers which had not been included earlier.

The first music edition of the hymnal had sold 4.5 million copies within eight years. On the day of the publication of the 1889 edition, one million copies were sent out from the publishers.

Many of these achievements were incorporated into the plethora of memorials to William Henry Monk that appeared in the press following his death. However, for the purposes of this story, the telling of the tale of Mamerto Gueritz, perhaps a fitting remembrance is the photograph of Monk that hung for decades in the Bear Inn in Colyton; a renowned musician and hymn writer in rather disreputable holiday attire after fishing along the Coly River. Monk would have been welcome to holiday at the Gueritz household but equally that of Stuckey Coles three miles away in Seaton. Another example might be his kindness over the use of a hymn at the wedding of Mary Louisa Gueritz and Reginald Mortimer. Perhaps most of all, the welcome Monk gave to a musically talented country catholic, bruised and battered in his defence of Church principles and in need of the spiritual and musical refreshment St Matthias could afford.

All of this Mamerto Gueritz found in Stoke Newington in the company of Charles James Le Geyt, Robert Brett and William Henry Monk.

Sabine Baring-Gould

1834–1924

The number of different ways in which it is now possible to encounter Sabine Baring-Gould is really quite impressive, though it should not be surprising given the history of the man and his unique personality. First, and most profoundly, he is to be met in his own writings. He is also to be known in the ways in which his research and writing affected the work of others, for example in the field of archaeology, where he transformed the understanding of the pre-history of Dartmoor, and in the discovery of folk songs and tunes which, even today, permeate our culture. In addition, Sabine Baring-Gould is to be understood in what others have written about him,[92] and then, perhaps less accurately but no less entertaining for that, in the ways in which he has shaped, and even appeared in, fiction.

It is claimed that his friend George Bernard Shaw was so taken with the story of Baring-Gould's wooing and subsequent marriage with Grace Taylor, a young mill worker, that it inspired him to write *Pygmalion*. The play took to the musical stage and cinema as *My Fair Lady*, which is arguably even more famous. In Yorkshire, Baring-Gould encountered a local legend of werewolves which stimulated a great fascination and prolific research. The result in 1865 was *The Book of Were-Wolves: An Account of a Terrible Superstition*. It has long been acknowledged that anyone wishing to write a story or a screenplay or direct a film about the curse of lycanthropy, and there are now hundreds, ought first to consult Sabine Baring-Gould's seminal work. As an example of the shaping of fiction, Baring-Gould's grandson, William, wrote an imagined biography of Sherlock Holmes in 1962.[93] Lacking any detail of the fictional detective's early life, he simply transposed part of his grandfather's life story into that of Holmes.

As for appearances in fiction, it could be said that the most entertaining is in the work of Laurie R. King in her books about the retired Sherlock Holmes and his much younger wife, Mary Russell. In *The Moor*, Baring-Gould appears as a splendidly drawn character in the person of Holmes' godfather. King's research and the resulting writing are such that her characterization makes possible the reader's suspension of disbelief.[94] The disparity between the ages of Holmes and

Russell was, in some measure, echoed by that between Baring-Gould and Grace Taylor. It was not an infrequent feature of Victorian marriage.

Diana Amelia Sabine was Baring-Gould's grandmother, and it is for her and her family that he was named Sabine. Through his paternal great grandmother, the line of Gould could be traced back through several changes to John Gold, a crusader at the siege of Damietta in 1217. Sabine was born in Exeter in the winter of 1834, but much of his early life was spent travelling the Continent with his family. This meant that he had little formal schooling, which may have been a blessing given that his enquiring mind and voracious appetite for reading were only moderately constrained by a succession of private tutors. By his late teens, he was fluent in five languages, but on his travels he had acquired a bronchial condition which was to remain with him lifelong. His father, a somewhat domineering parent, decided that this was a reason for yet more travels in the warmer countries of Europe.

In 1852, Sabine matriculated at Clare College, Cambridge, graduating with a Bachelor's degree in 1857. It was there that he first felt a call to the sacred ministry, but his father was appalled at the idea. In spite of his father's disapproval, after his graduation he spent a short time as a master in the choir school at St Barnabas, Pimlico, and while there became closely acquainted with men such as Bryan King, Alexander Mackonochie and Charles Fugue Lowder. Baring-Gould had already discussed his sense of vocation with Nathaniel Woodard while at university and shared his frustration with him when Baring-Gould senior would not allow him to proceed. However, it was Charles Lowder who secured him a place at the Woodard School at Shoreham when financial constraints forced him to leave London. That was not an entirely happy appointment, and soon he transferred to Hurstpierpoint School, another Woodard foundation, where he remained as assistant master until 1864. There his studied eccentricities became more and more apparent.

The call to priesthood reasserted itself and, parental disapproval notwithstanding, Sabine Baring-Gould was ordained in Ripon Cathedral at Whitsuntide 1864. He served first at St Peter's, Horbury, where he met Grace Taylor, the young mill worker who would later become his wife. Then he moved to be assistant curate at "Dalton i't muck" as the locals called it. While there, he married Grace, who had been suitably prepared for her new station in life. All this time, his literary output was prodigious, as it ever was. When Gladstone read

Baring-Gould's *Origin and Development of Religious Belief*, he was moved to offer him the living of East Mersea on the windswept Essex coast. This was in 1871, when Sabine was 37. In 1872, his father died, and he inherited the estate, manor and patronage of Lew Trenchard, where his uncle Charles was the incumbent. When his uncle died in 1881, Baring-Gould waited for a respectable interval and then, as patron, presented himself to the living.

As the pattern of his ministry and work at Lew Trenchard took shape then, so it remained. Baring-Gould would visit his parishioners from early morning, and then, as the morning waned, he would be found standing at his desk and writing; that is when he was not being called out to a parishioner in need, or wayfaring around Devon and Cornwall obliging bewildered yeomen to sing for him and, in the process, creating one of the most important collections of English folk songs and tunes ever compiled.

Book after book flowed from his pen, and it was during this period at Lew Trenchard that he completed his 16 volumes of *Lives of the Saints*. It is a remarkable work on many counts, not least for Baring-Gould's capacity seamlessly to blend historical truth with devotional speculation.

Scholarship and ministry were not his only concerns. By the time Grace and Sabine arrived in Lew Trenchard, they had already produced eight children. One, Beatrice Gracieuse, had died when she was only two, and it has been suggested that the hymn "On the Resurrection Morning" was penned as an expression of the pain that loss inflicted and the faith in which it was endured. Of the other children, Mary and Margaret were born in Yorkshire, and Edward, Veronica, Julian, William and Barbara arrived while the family was in Mersea. Diana Amelia, named for Baring-Gould's grandmother, was born the year they moved to Devon. Then came Felicitas, Henry, Joan Cicely, John and finally Grace in 1891. Seeing them, or rather their names, all ranged together gives some credence to the oft-told anecdote of Sabine Baring-Gould at a children's party asking one small child "And whose little girl are you?", which produced much weeping and the response "Daddy, I'm one of yours!".

This vignette of Sabine Baring-Gould offers the scantiest glimpse of his parochial ministry, his work as an author, as a preserver of endangered songs, and his life *en famille*, and does not even begin to express the height and depth of the man. However, there is one aspect of him which is not yet mentioned, and yet is necessary to this study. Sabine Baring-Gould has been claimed by some as a hero of the Oxford Movement and an exemplar of the "Country Catholic". That is only part of the truth, and this slight summary is offered in the hope that it will allow some insight into what Mamerto Gueritz experienced when he found himself working alongside Baring-Gould and John Gilberd Pearse as vice-presidents of the Devon branches of the English Church Union.

For many years, the English Church Union was arguably the keel which held the vessel of the Catholic Revival upright, so we can see how Baring-Gould's presence and active membership should have been interpreted as it was. That was part of the truth, but a greater truth was that Sabine Baring-Gould was ever his own man, and once he had found a liturgical mode of expressing his catholicity, changing fashions in liturgy and ritual were of little interest. It was said of him:

> He remained a second generation Puseyite to the end of his days, so that those who penetrated his Devon wooded fastness in later times had the interesting, if faintly alarming experience of meeting a genuine Rip Van Winckle of the Tractarian Movement.[95]
>
> He was deeply Catholic in mind and spirit, but he was also a countryman; and in his understanding heart the needs of his people and a sense of their limitations came first.[96]

By the time Baring-Gould and Gueritz worked together, particularly in their roles as vice-presidents of the English Church Union, Mamerto Gueritz had come to something of the same mind, even though he was more of a ritualist than Baring-Gould would ever be.

It was this ability to empathize with his people which was a distinguishing feature of Baring-Gould's pastoral ministry in Horbury, Dalton and Lew Trenchard. This did not, however, extend to the people of East Mersea, where, with few exceptions, he felt that he had neither understood them nor they him. In Devon and in Lew Trenchard, matters were different. He could be remote, austere and occasionally ill-tempered, but that did not mean he failed to understand his people. Earlier, in Dalton, where he served from 1867 to 1871, his curacy followed that of Algernon Emeric Clementi Smith, who was an "Advanced Ritualist".

Clementi Smith's uncompromising attitude had proved too much for the local people and Baring-Gould's first task was to win them back:

> I reduced the ritual as much as I could without breaking with the procedure of my predecessor too violently, and, for teaching, I began with the inculcation of first principles.[97]

Time and again, emerging like a leitmotif in this work has been the assertion that in order to be true, not only to the Oxford Movement but to the faith thereby proclaimed, the ritual should never be an end in itself. Possibly Clementi Smith saw that less clearly than Baring-Gould.

The empathy Baring-Gould established in Yorkshire and later in Devon was not always extended to other clergy, and it was a rare bishop indeed who won his approval. He disliked Temple's voice intensely and was very cutting about Bishop Ryle, calling him "injudicious and dictatorial". When writing of the way in which his half-brother had been served, Baring-Gould summed up most of the bishops and not a few of the clergy thus:

> Being a man of exceptional gifts, no efforts were made by successive bishops of Exeter to retain him in the diocese where all the favour is—or at the time was—accorded to the flat fish, one sided, one eyed, who flop about but do not swim and breast the wave.[98]

Strangely enough, Baring-Gould seems to have disliked Bishop Bickersteth the least, even though their churchmanship differed markedly. He admired the bishop's common touch, which he had seen at work during some of the large luncheons Bickersteth would give from time to time at the palace to diocesan bellringers, Sunday school teachers and gatherings of churchwardens. The ease with which the bishop welcomed his rustic guests and found common ground with them counted for much with Baring-Gould. However, when Bickersteth wanted to change some of the wording of the hymn "Onward Christian Soldiers" the bishop's suggestion was met with one word, "Twaddle!". Ever his own man!

Grace Baring-Gould, who had been a constant source of wisdom and strength for her husband, died in 1916. In 1924, just short of his ninetieth birthday, Sabine

Baring-Gould also died and was laid to rest next to his wife. In the words of his hymn "On the Resurrection Morning":

> No more sorrow, no more weeping,
> no more pain.

A priest in parenthesis: Charles Arthur Le Geyt

1851–1935

When, in 1882, it was announced that Charles Le Geyt was to be the curate at Seaton and Beer in East Devon the news provoked something of a local reaction, especially in Colyton vicarage. It had been only five years since the death of Charles James Le Geyt of Stoke Newington and Mamerto Gueritz' time at St Matthias in 1868 and 1869 had only been one of a number of visits he made to gain, as Stuckey Coles put it, "refreshment". However, it is certain that the existence of this new Le Geyt was not unknown to Mamerto. We know that he assiduously kept up his university links and therefore could hardly have missed the graduation of Charles Arthur Le Geyt in 1876 from his own *alma mater*, St Edmund Hall.

C. A. Le Geyt is included among the "Supporting Cast" partly because of the coincidence of his name, which is possibly a touch of whimsy, but also because he provides an example of the way in which local clergy of like mind were prepared to support each other, learn from each other and come together in common cause. Any one of the local clergy repeatedly named in the Colyton service registers would have qualified, indeed some were there more often than he, but they were not named Le Geyt.

Until the death of his father, Charles William, in 1879, C. A. Le Geyt of Beer avoided the use of the first of his baptismal names and frequently signed himself Arthur Le Geyt. Like Le Geyt of Stoke Newington, he was from an ancient Jersey family but from a branch even closer to the root than his more famous namesake. Charles Arthur had been born in St Helier on Jersey in 1852. His father, Charles William, was a lieutenant colonel in the Royal Jersey Militia and was a direct descendant of Charles William Le Geyt, Jersey's first postmaster, who fought at the battle of Minden in 1759.

By the time Charles was in his teens, the family was established on the mainland at Corston in Somerset, and it was from there that he went up to St Edmund Hall and, graduating in 1876, was ordained deacon. Charles served his title in the Welsh parish of Cadoxton-Juxta-Neath and was also private chaplain to the Lee family of the nearby Rheola house and estate.[99] He was ordained priest in 1878 and a little later went to serve a second curacy on the Isle of Wight at All Saints, Ryde. We know that Janet, the wife of C. J. Le Geyt of Stoke Newington, and their daughter had gone to live in Ryde in 1871. Possibly they were still there in 1878 when another Le Geyt arrived, but that is mere speculation. From Ryde in 1882 Charles Le Geyt went to Seaton and Beer as the curate with responsibility for St Michael's, Beer, which is where he enters this story.

In Beer, a new church had been built on the site of the old Norman building, which possibly dated from 1122. The Norman work had been partly replaced by a sixteenth-century chapel which was inadequate in size and in considerable decay by the mid-1870s. The lord of the manor, Mark Rolle, gave a new church designed by the architect Hayward of Exeter in a style which entirely accorded with the pattern developed by the Ecclesiological Society and which fitted the liturgy of the "Oxford Revival". Built into the side of a hill, the altar and sanctuary were reached by an impressive flight of steps, with the high altar, complete with six candles, dominating the view from the nave. Bishop Temple consecrated the new church in August 1878, and both Mamerto and Fortescue Gueritz were reported to be among the robed clergy.[100] By the time Le Geyt arrived four years later in 1882, the tradition was well established, but some tasks remained outstanding. The stained-glass windows had yet to be installed and the transept set aside for an organ was still empty.

With much local support, Le Geyt ensured that a new organ was built and paid for, and its arrival was celebrated with a series of recitals in August 1885. The organ, however, was only a part of the plan. Le Geyt was an accomplished musician and had fully embraced the choral tradition which had already been established, under the leadership of Mamerto Gueritz, throughout East Devon. He recruited and trained a choir which was soon taking part in the East Devon Choral Union festivals. Such a body of singers needed somewhere to develop and rehearse, so Le Geyt raised funds of over £200 and oversaw the building of a music room for that purpose.

Another element of Le Geyt's ministry was to recognize and affirm the energies of the women in his congregation, in much the same way as Gueritz had done in Colyton in the work of the parish visitors and the Dorcas Society. A women's guild was formed in Beer which engaged in much good work. The guild, at the prompting of their priest, gave a stained-glass window, called "The Women's Window", which gave visual recognition to their part in the mission of the Church. In addition to this, the Rolle family provided the east window, a representation of St Michael, by Wood and Hughes of London. This was in June 1889.

Charles Arthur Le Geyt stayed in Beer for 12 years until 1894, when he went to Truro as honorary priest vicar at the cathedral. During his time in Beer, and indeed after he had left East Devon, he was a frequent visitor to Colyton, occasionally also preaching and taking services. In Truro, he was immediately involved in its musical life and the work of the local choral associations. The organist and choirmaster was Dr M. J. Monk, who had been appointed in 1889, an appointment which was hailed as "full of good omens" especially because of the lustre afforded the name by Dr E. G. Monk of York and the sadly deceased W. H. Monk. With such phrasing the *West Briton and Cornwall Advertiser* carefully avoided the confusion which followed the death of W. H. Monk and so disconcerted E. G. Monk. The year 1894 saw the seventh anniversary of the consecration of Truro Cathedral, which was celebrated with solemn, choral services. In the evening, Charles Le Geyt, according to the *Royal Cornwall Gazette*, "entoned (sic) the service most impressively". In July of the same year, the Powder Deanery Choral Association held its annual festival. It is a mark of the growth of such choral associations that in remote Cornwall one deanery could call together just under 300 choristers, 116 of whom were surpliced. C. A. Le Geyt chanted the second part of the service.

After Truro, there was a period as incumbent of Galmpton, South Huish. For a time, Charles Le Geyt returned to Jersey, and he was on the list of preachers at St Brelade's in 1904 and 1905. In 1906, while in Tenby, he married Harriett Thompson Prior, of Carisbrooke, Isle of Wight, and after the marriage he took the living of Marazion. St Michael's Mount was part of the parish and, in a separate appointment, he was also made chaplain to the Mount and in that role officiated at the funeral of Lady St Leven in 1911.

In 1912, Charles Le Geyt retired, aged 61, and he and Harriett moved to The Gables, Weston-super-Mare. During retirement, he was active in support of the local parish and clergy, but increasingly Harriett, who was 19 years younger than he, was becoming an invalid. They were still living at The Gables when Charles died in 1935 aged 84. Several West Country newspapers carried the headline "Death of an Octogenarian Clergyman".[101] Charles Arthur Le Geyt was not forgotten by the people he had served in Cornwall and neither had his memory passed from the folk of Beer. They remembered him at Mattins the following Sunday and sang John Ellerton's hymn "Now the Labourer's Task is O'er" as they did so.

Notes

1 D. M. Bertie, *Scottish Episcopal Clergy 1680 to 2000* (Edinburgh: T & T Clark, 2000), p. 406. There are sufficient errors in this work for it to be received with caution.

2 Several other sources, including the 1871 census, have W. H. B. Proby's birth date as 1832. Part of the entry referred to in note 1 reads: "He purchased the estate of Colyton in Northleigh, Devon about 1869 near which he built an Irvingite Mission Church in 1893." This is almost entirely erroneous. There is no "Estate of Colyton" in Northleigh parish. Proby certainly purchased land there in 1890. In 1850, his mother had engaged in a legal exchange of lands and dwellings with Sir Edmund Sanderson Prideaux, all in the parish of Northleigh, which Proby would have inherited as the surviving male heir. The manorial rights had passed to Proby's mother, thus making him lord of the manor after her death. This entry in the Scottish record may have been a confusion with his purchase of Colyton House, a prestigious dwelling in Colyton itself, although Proby himself was not living there in 1869. The 1893 Irvingite Chapel was St John's, Pottlelake which, from Colyton, lies some miles in the opposite direction to Northleigh. The chapel ultimately returned to Church of England use before being sold as a dwelling.

3 The research on the Borcombe chapel was carried out by the late Revd Christopher Leech, author, scholar and, in retirement, honorary curate with the care of Southleigh parish.

4 Kew Records, National Archive, Folios 18–19 and 1–3.

5 *Bath Chronicle and Weekly Gazette*, Thursday, 10 November 1836.

[6]   *The Sun* (London), Wednesday, 28 June 1854.

[7]   *Evening Mail*, Monday, 14 August 1854.

[8]   The census of 1861.

[9]   W. Perry DD, *The Oxford Movement in Scotland* (Cambridge: Cambridge University Press, 1933), p. xiv from the foreword written by the then Primus.

[10] Perry, *The Oxford Movement in Scotland*, pp. 64–81.

[11] *Montrose, Arbroath and Brechin Review, and Forfar and Kincardineshire Advertiser*, Friday, 25 November 1864.

[12] *Stonehaven Journal*, Thursday, 18 January 1866.

[13] See Chapter 7 and the references to the Woram funeral.

[14] Rupert's Land, or Prince Rupert's Land, was formerly owned by the Hudson Bay Company and formally transferred to the Dominion of Canada by the Rupert's Land Act of 1868. It was a vast territory of northern wilderness and makes up a third of Canada's land mass today. Episcope in such a setting would have been totally different from that exercised in London at the period in view. As a whimsical aside, the poem by E. L. Mascall, "The Ultra Catholic", has an apposite line: "Colonial prelates I employ from far off mission stations." E. L. Mascall, *Pi in the High* (London: The Faith Press, 1959).

[15] P. Anson, *The Call of the Cloister* (London: SPCK, 1955), revised edn 1964, p. 349.

[16] *Lessons on the Kingdom for the Little Ones of the Church of England*; *Stories about the Great King*; and *The Church Catechism Made Easy* (all London: Hayes, 1872).

[17] The "Penny Catechism" referred to by E. L. Mascall in the poem in note 15 above was very probably the unadulterated Roman Catholic version which had been circulating since early in the century. It is evident that Proby's revision had a wide circulation.

[18] *Carmarthen Weekly Reporter*, Saturday, 12 July 1873.

[19] *Western Times*, Friday, 12 February 1875.

[20] The census of 1881 places Proby at the address in Duncan Street. As a mildly amusing note, we know that he also visited Wells in 1880, perhaps on his way home from India. The *Wells Journal* of 30 September that year ran a column headed "Fashionable Arrivals at the Swan Hotel". Among the nobility and others mentioned there is "The Rev W. H. B. Proby".

[21] W. H. B. Proby, *The Annals of the Low Church Party in England: Down to the Death of Archbishop Tait*, vols 1 and 2 (London: Hayes, 1888). Hereafter referred to in the notes as Proby, *Annals*.

22 Ms. Letter from Thomas Shapter to W. H. B. Proby, 22 November 1881. Exeter Cathedral Library, ref. 536/Sha.

23 The term "Irvingites" has become a kind of shorthand for the Catholic Apostolic movement, but what actually emerged was neither founded nor anticipated by Edward Irving. In 1835, six months after Irving's death, the "Apostles" of the Catholic Apostolic Church, who had been selected by the prophetic utterances of members of the church, retired to Albury to order the worship and to formulate a testimony to be sent to world leaders and the heads of various religions. Two of the major themes were the imminent second coming of Jesus Christ and the unity of all those who had been baptized in the name of the Trinity.

24 Proby, *Annals*, p. iv.

25 Proby, *Annals*, pp. 229–30.

26 Proby, *Annals*, p. v.

27 W. Walsh was the author of *Secret History of the Oxford Movement* (1st edn, 1897), but in a subsequent work he specifically mentions Proby. W. Walsh, *A History of the Romeward Movement in the Church of England 1833 to 1864* (London: Nisbet, 1900), p. 5.

28 The dating of these events was given by the Revd C. Leech in his unpublished notes on the "Borcombe Homily".

29 Local oral tradition has it that W. H. B. Proby suspected a neighbour, living in Berry House on the opposite side of Vicarage Street, of spying on his wife as she walked in the grounds, so he raised the level of the wall. The neighbour's response was to build another storey on to his house!

30 *Exeter and Plymouth Gazette*, Friday, 23 September 1892.

31 *Taunton Courier and Western Advertiser*, Wednesday, 25 March 1895.

32 *Western Times*, Friday, 11 October 1895.

33 *Western Chronicle*, Friday, 18 October 1895.

34 See Chapter 7.

35 The 11th (North Devonshire) Regiment of Foot became the Devonshire Regiment in June 1881, at which time it absorbed the various Militia and Rifle Volunteer Companies of Devon. Colyton men served in the regiment throughout the Empire but chiefly in India and on the northern frontiers.

36 Interviews with the grandsons and a great nephew of the soldiers who served in the regiment still living in Colyton in 1990.

[37] The Palestine Exploration Fund had "a remit that fell somewhere between an expeditionary survey and military intelligence gathering", but its work in relation to biblical studies and understanding is clearly illustrated by the inaugural address by the Archbishop of York: "Our object is strictly an inductive inquiry. We are not to be a religious society; we are not about to launch controversy; we are about to apply the rules of science, which are so well understood by us in our branches, to an investigation into the facts concerning the Holy Land. No country should be of so much interest to us as that in which the documents of our Faith were written, and the momentous events they describe enacted. At the same time no country more urgently requires illustration ... Even to a casual traveller in the Holy Land the Bible becomes, in its form, and therefore to some extent in its substance, a new book. Much would be gained by ... bringing to light the remains of so many races and generations which must lie concealed under the accumulation of rubbish and ruins." Quoted in: Kathleen Stewart Howe, *Revealing the Holy Land: The Photographic Exploration of Palestine* (Berkeley, CA: University of California Press, 1997), p. 37.

[38] See Chapter 13.

[39] The South West Heritage Centre in Exeter has a considerable file of documents and letters relating to the Proby family. The collection includes letters from Louisa Proby, W. H. B. Proby's mother, dating from her childhood onwards; letters from his brother Charles, who died on his way home from the Crimea, and replies from his sister. There is much that was not germane to this work but which may be of interest to any who would research further into the Proby/Carysfort connection.

[40] South West Heritage Centre, Exeter. Faculty correspondence regarding the pews. Colyton faculty file.

[41] *The England and Wales Non-Conformist and Non-Parochial Registers 1567 to 1970* show that he was baptized in his full name of Harry De Spencer Kingdon. The suggestion that he added the De Spencer to add lustre to his name, put about by some of his later detractors, is therefore disproved.

[42] *The Gentleman's Magazine* XXXVII (1851), p. 182.

[43] National census 1861.

[44] South West Heritage Centre, Exeter: West Country Studies Library. Ref Colyton A31 Ms. dated August 1865.

[45] *The Field*, 10 January 1903.

[46] "All Things Bright and Beautiful", C. F. Alexander, 1848. Tunes: various composers, including W. H. Monk, Martin Shaw and Frederick Gore Ouseley.

[47] In his manuscript of *Colytonia: A Chapter in the History of East Devon*, G. E. Evans said of Kingdon in 1898 that he had not been connected with the Unitarian congregation since the ministry of Mr Taplin, which had ended in the 1870s.

[48] See the letter from E. C. Mortimer to S. L. Ollard in Appendix 1.

[49] G. W. Borlase, in J. F. Briscoe (ed.), *V. S. S. Coles* (London: Mowbray, 1930), p. 8.

[50] R. Bridges, "Memorial preface" to *The Poems of Digby Mackworth Dolben, edited with a memoir by Robert Bridges*, ed. Humphrey Milford (Oxford: Oxford University Press, 1911).

[51] V. S. S. Coles, *Recollections of Fifty Years of the Catholic Revival*. A paper read at the Exeter branch of the English Church Union and elsewhere afterwards. Reproduced in Briscoe, *V. S. S. Coles*, p. 159.

[52] Charles Gore, "Vincent Stuckey Stratton Coles, obituary", *The London Times*, July 1929.

[53] The later tensions between the Prayer Book Catholics and the users of the English Missal, although necessarily a part of the wider story, are not germane to this present exercise. However, it is worthy of note that Coles was a staunch defender of the rubrics and rules of the Prayer Book. "If he happened to be preaching in a strange church and caught only a distant glimpse of the Anglican Missal, then Stuckey would gird up his loins and denounce, rebuke and exhort with all the fervour of a Hebrew prophet." (Briscoe, *V. S. S. Coles*, p. 82).

[54] Briscoe, *V. S. S. Coles*, p. 13.

[55] *The Balliol College Register*, ed. E. Hilliard, printed for private circulation (Oxford: Oxford University Press, 1914), p. 66.

[56] Comment attributed to Fr Mackay. The Bullingdon Club is a private all-male dining club for Oxford University students. It is known for its wealthy members, grand banquets, and occasionally bad behaviour. Although in the time of Stuckey Coles the behaviour of members might have left much to be desired, both then and into the twentieth century their tailoring was exquisite—then. The Leander Club is a rowing club based in Remenham in Berkshire.

[57] See Appendix 1.

[58] A letter to J. F. Briscoe, reproduced in Briscoe, *V. S. S. Coles*.

59 T. Francis Bumpus, *An Historical London Church. A Record of Sixty-five Years' Life and Work in the Church and Parish of S. Matthias, Stoke Newington* (London: J. King, 1911), p. 20. (Author's note: elements of Bumpus' work should not be received entirely uncritically. His work, while extremely valuable, is understandably partisan and not always entirely accurate in detail.)

60 *Hampshire Advertiser*, Saturday, 5 January 1878.

61 J. T. Coleridge, *A Memoir of the Rev John Keble, late vicar of Hursley* (London: James Parker, 1880).

62 Among the visitors in 1861, in addition to the servants and immediate members of the family, were Hector Monro, a younger brother of Mrs Le Geyt, and Robert George Oxenham, a graduate of Exeter College, Oxford. Oxenham is mentioned here to illustrate the networking within clerical society of the time. He was the son of Nutcombe Oxenham, who had been incumbent of Modbury in Devon when Mamerto Gueritz was curate at Stoke Gabriel. Robert Oxenham went on to join the Bombay Civil Service and later retired to Heavitree in Exeter.

63 Bumpus, *An Historical London Church*, p. 22.

64 *Revue Anglo Romaine* 1 (1895), pp. 258ff.

65 *Revue Anglo Romaine* 1 (1895), p. 258.

66 *Revue Anglo Romaine* 1 (1895), p. 258.

67 Brett's qualifications are given in various ways in various sources. They should properly read: M.R.C.S. and L.S.A.L. A charter was given to the Royal College of Surgeons in London in 1803. A further charter, granted in 1843, gave it the title the Royal College of Surgeons of England. (A later reading of the acronym R.C.S.E. has been taken to refer to Edinburgh and Scottish qualifications, but this latter was not before 1851.) The initials L.S.A.L. refer to Brett's qualification as a Licentiate of the Society of Apothecaries of London, the equivalent of a degree in medicine, surgery and midwifery and not only, or even primarily, a licence to make and dispense medicines.

68 ... and thereby hangs a tale. John and Charlotte (Oxenborow) Reynolds appear to have had nine children. Their second son, Samuel, was the surgeon with whom Robert Brett went into practice in Stoke Newington. A slight anomaly appears in that the nonconformist and non-parochial registers show that John Reynolds baptized two of his daughters at Woolwich on 22 August 1824. They were Maria Hill Reynolds and Mary Reynolds. Maria's birth date is given as 1809 instead of 1811, but every other detail indicates that this was the same family. Again the mother's name is given as

Charlotte. These anomalies could simply be due to the sometimes idiosyncratic record-keeping around the turn of the eighteenth and nineteenth centuries . . . or not. John Reynolds died in 1851 having been Wesleyan minister of Loddon in Norfolk, some 30 miles from Diss. Charlotte, his wife, died in 1857. Notwithstanding their status as avowed Wesleyans, both were buried, as was their legal entitlement, by the Anglican curate of the parish in which they lived. Charlotte, their daughter, predeceased them in 1846, and her daughter, Eliza Fison, lived with the Bretts in Stoke Newington for several years.

69   John Shelton Reed, *Glorious Battle: The Cultural Politics of Victorian Anglo-Catholicism* (London: Tufton Books, 1998), p. 155. Reed states that Brett was a convert from (Wesleyan) nonconformity. This is unlikely, given Brett's upbringing. The most plausible explanation is a confusion between Brett and his wife Maria Hill (née Reynolds) Brett. She was undoubtedly raised as a Wesleyan.

70   *Post Office London Suburban Directory*, 1860.

71   *The Morning Chronicle*, Friday, 1 August 1851.

72   *John Bull*, 7 February 1874.

73   Bumpus, *An Historical London Church*, p. 28.

74   T. W. Belcher, *Robert Brett (of Stoke Newington): His Life and Work* (London: Griffith, Farran, Okeden & Welsh, 1889), p. 30.

75   Robert Brett published 16 such works. Among his publishers were James Burns, Mozely, Masters, Rivington's and James Parker. *The Power of the Catholic Faith: A Memorial (In loving remembrance of Maria Charlotte B)* was published privately in 1864.

76   Bumpus, *An Historical London Church*, p. 25.

77   Belcher, *Robert Brett*, p. 114. Letter reproduced in full.

78   *The Kentish Chronicle*, Saturday, 2 November 1867.

79   Belcher, *Robert Brett*, p. 248.

80   St Mary Hall was a medieval academic hall in Oxford linked with Oriel College from 1326 to 1545. It then became an independent institution but was re-incorporated into Oriel College in 1902.

81   John Keble to Robert Brett, Penzance, April 1864.

82   Bumpus states that Catherine was Robert Brett's youngest daughter, and this was repeated in newspaper reports of her death. However, the youngest child was Helen, who had been born in 1848 or 1849. Helen's name is spelt differently in almost every census up to and including 1891, ranging from Helen, to Healene (a misspelling),

to Eleanor and Elanor. In 1891, she was living with Mary and Frances, her sisters, in Hastings. Finally there is a registration of death, in Poplar in 1903, of an Eleanor Matilda Brett, born in Stoke Newington in 1848, aged 54. Shelton Reed, *Glorious Battle*, p. 301. (Footnote 39 to Chapter 8 notes the use of the soubriquet by Katherine Warburton, *Memories of a Sister of St. Saviour's Priory* (London: Mowbray, 1902))

[83]   Robert Brett, *An address to the Church Congress in Leeds on 10 October 1872 on "Church Comprehensiveness"*.

[84]   *Salisbury and Winchester Journal*, Saturday, 1 August 1857.

[85]   In this he was at one with Sabine Baring-Gould, whose obituary was published in the *New York Times* in June 1906. Baring-Gould died in 1924.

[86]   *The Bromyard News*, Thursday, 18 April 1889.

[87]   W. H. Monk was living at the house, Glebe Field, at the time of his death. His son Leonard advertised the sale of the house by private treaty in *The Globe*, Friday, 9 March 1894. This, fortuitously, leaves us a description of it: "formerly the residence of the late Dr. W.H. Monk, Mus.Doc. comprising three reception rooms (large drawing room with three manual organ by Willis) two hall-rooms, nine bedrooms, box and bath rooms, large kitchen, housekeepers room, and usual offices; coach house, stable and a coachman's room; large garden; suitable for a professional man or a religious or other institution; close to Clissold park and Parish Church." The possibility that a sisterhood or a school might want the property had clearly occurred to Leonard. Hope Isidore Monk, Leonard's mother, had died in January of that year.

[88]   It has been asserted that H. F. Lyte wrote his own tune for the hymn, but that appears to be lost. Perhaps it is hiding in a drawer somewhere waiting to be discovered by a historian of hymnody. Little did Monk realize that his tune would be sung annually from 1927 at the Football Association Cup Final, at the encouragement of King George V.

[89]   Ian Bradley, *Abide With Me: The World of Victorian Hymns* (London: SCM Press, 1997), p. 60.

[90]   Bradley, *Abide With Me*, pp. 60 and 263. A letter from Francis Murray to William Denton (Hymns Ancient & Modern Archives).

[91]   *The Guardian*, 20 and 27 October 1858.

[92]   William Purcell, *Onward Christian Soldier: A life of Sabine Baring-Gould, Parson, Squire, Novelist, Antiquary 1834–1924* (London: Longmans Green, 1957); Keith Lister, *"Half My Life": The Story of Sabine Baring-Gould and Grace* (Wakefield: Charwood

Press, 2002); J. E. Thomas, *Sabine Baring-Gould: The Life and Work of a Complete Victorian* (Stroud: Fonthill Media, 2015); Rebecca Tope, *Sabine Baring-Gould: The Man Who Told a Thousand Stories* (Dulles, VA: Praxis Books, 2017); Martin Graebe, *As I Walked Out: Sabine Baring-Gould and the Search for the Folk Songs of Devon and Cornwall* (Oxford: Signal Books, 2017).

93 William S. Baring-Gould, *Sherlock Holmes of Baker Street* (New York: Bramhall House, 1962).

94 *The Moor* was the fourth in King's series of books about Holmes and Russell. There are, at the time of writing, 16 novels and a goodly number of short stories. Her work may not be entirely to the liking of some Conan Doyle purists, but they are "ripping good yarns"!

95 Purcell, *Onward Christian Soldier*, p. 88. It should be noted that Purcell includes in the "second generation" category the Romanizers of the late 1840s and the Ritualists of the mid-50s and 60s. Other writers have used the term to describe men like Henry Parry Liddon, who retained much of the early restraint in liturgical externals. Purcell uses the term chronologically and embraces all post-Newman activity within it.

96 Purcell, *Onward Christian Soldier*, p. 134.

97 S. Baring-Gould, *Further Reminiscences 1867–71* (London: The Bodley Head, 1925), p. 18.

98 Baring-Gould, *Further Reminiscences*, p. 12.

99 Clergy Gazette, *Oxford Journal*, 11 November 1876.

100 *Somerset County Gazette*, August 1878, and *Exeter and Plymouth Gazette*, August 1878.

101 The *Western Daily Press*, *The Taunton Courier and Western Advertiser* and the *Exeter and Plymouth Gazette* among them.

A letter to S. L. Ollard from E. C. Mortimer

St Edmund Hall Archives

Richmond House
Colyton. Devon
Jan 9th 1909

Dear Vice-Principal.

This will be a very incoherent letter as I am writing in a room with my mother, a friend, two sisters & three brothers all talking on different topics, except one brother who is shouting a comic song, & one sister who is accompanying him. To begin with, I am extremely sorry not to have written before but I have been trying to get items out of my Grandfather & also things have been going with such a rush lately that I must confess to having forgotten my letter-writing duties. We have had four dances within the last five days & two or three to come yet, among other things. I am looking forward to the term as a rest-cure for the vac. Thank you so much for writing about the Librarianship; if I could count on it my money affairs would be as follows:

£
20 in Bank
132 to come from Boyd
25 Librarianship
15 to come from Cholmondeley Trust
82 Private Sources
20 Sons of Clergy Corporation
294

This has to last for the next eight terms, working out to £106.10 per year which is not princely but on which I might do possibly if I cannot get any elsewhere. The figures are not quite exact but quite approximate. I might get an extension of another £20 from the Corporation of the Sons of the Clergy & will write about it immediately. By the way there is £25 for the 4th year's librarianship which wd. make it £116 so it seems all right. Pardon the confusedness of this but the whole room has burst into a wild chorus from some oratorio in which the piano's plucky attempts to overcome the vocal section of the music fail hopelessly.

To turn to my Grandfather—he suffers from gout in his hand & asks me to say that he would be delighted to write if he could but cannot at present. His reminiscences are very sketchy & mostly quite personal but some of them may interest you; I have gathered them from him within the last few days but there are obviously many little incidents & details which he just cannot recal (sic) sufficiently to put in intelligible form.

Here goes—please skip judiciously where you get bored as may be the case where the interest is purely personal. I have put down a lot that is unnecessary in order to get a little continuity.

Up to the age of one my Grandfather had an adventurous career as he was born and baptized on the same day Jan 31st 1823 in Jativa[1] the city of the Borgias & then his father and mother had to flee the country to England as my great-grandfather's life was in danger under the new regime in Spain. King Alfonso was very much interested in my Grandfather when he came over after Princess Ena. He went to school in Plymouth up to the age of 13 & then became apprentice to a wine-merchant for seven years. At 20 he desired to go to Oxford with a view to Holy Orders & heard from Dr. Seaman of Colchester that there was a Society in Bristol formed to assist such as him. He, being absolutely poor at that time, applied to them & they paid all his expenses at S. Edmund Hall, whither he went in 1845 (Matriculating the year before.)

He worked very hard for honours, so hard that he did not join in 'Varsity life to any great extent, & broke down in health, necessitating his taking a Pass degree in 1848. (An interesting personal touch, that has nothing to do with the Hall, is that his first curacy was under the Rev. James Stratton Coles, a splendid worker & father of our mutual friend.) To come to the Hall in his time. The ordinary services were of course Mattins & Evensong with rare Eucharists. The Chapel altar was quite bare & all the services very plain indeed as the Vice-Principal, Mr Hill, was a rigid Calvinist. On one occasion after a 23/4 hours' sermon on the 17th Article[2] (Mr Hill's usual length!) he asked, according to custom, for biblical texts to illustrate his gloomy doctrine. Immediately one man blurted out "Who will have all men to be saved, & come to the knowledge of the truth"! (This enterprising youth was the Rev. F. G. Lee, author of a well-known book on Ritual which no doubt you know.) Poor Mr Hill struggled out of it somehow by saying that S. Paul was referring to different classes of people that should come to knowledge. The incident horrified everyone including my grandfather, as the Vice-Principal was a very lovable man & it was regarded as an unprecedented piece of rudeness on the part of Mr Lee! The undergraduates seem to have been a quiet & orderly set, for the most part brought up to very low ideas of the Church & very scanty knowledge of the Catholic Faith. Most of them would have called themselves Evangelicals, & were very little advanced in religious knowledge, with the exceptions of Mr Lee & Mr Norman & some others. He can well remember T. W. Morsman (sic) & Charles Voysey & a brother of the latter; the two Voyseys seem to have been a rather under-read & ignorant pair & not generally liked. Charles V. seems to have become a deist or something since, while Bousfield he can remember has become an Angel in the new Apostolic Church.[3] About 1847 a change came over the spirit of the Hall which from his words one would judge my Grandfather to have started. In the library one day he discovered Bp. Sumner's "Apostolical Preaching" which he read with very great interest as this was the first occasion on which the idea had occurred to him that S. Paul addressed all the baptized as regenerate. He passed the book on to his friends, including Morsman, Bousfield & Page & others to whom the occasion was absolutely the beginning of Catholic learning.

The man who seems to have had the best influence for good was called Haik, a B.A. & Hebrew Scholar & more of a Churchman than the majority. My Grandfather was well snubbed for joking on a Biblical sentence on one occasion by Haik, who expressed a hope that he would always remember the incident. There was a good deal of religious life among the undergraduates in the way of reading & prayer. The Principal was a Dr Thomson (sic) a 'Fellow of Queen's, who used to preach on Sunday mornings (he once preached a very Catholic sermon on "Thou art Peter") & generally came into the Hall once a week to hear essays read out. The only one my Grandfather can remember writing was on

"Patriotism". On weekdays, the Vice-Principal always read Mattins & Evensong but took duty elsewhere on Sundays. The men seem to have been very fond of sermons, & always went to the 'Varsity Sermon at S. Mary's. After that they often went to hear Gouldburn (of "Personal Religion" fame) preach at Holywell, & my Grandfather particularly remembers a sermon delivered there by Bp. Wilberforce. Also he had the keen pleasure of hearing Dr Pusey, in his first sermon after his suspension, resume his teaching just where he had left off.

He used to have the same rooms as I inhabit now, & especially remembers the cupboard in the corner, from the window of which he poured water once down the necks of people who had been disturbing his studies by their carousals in the rooms beneath.

One of the undergraduates in his time used to be elected Bible Clerk, & his duties were to read the first lesson (the second being read in rotation) & to say grace in Hall. The graces were rather terrifying: "Benedic nobis Domine Deus et his donis quae ex tua liberalitate sumpturi sumus per Jesum Christum Dominum nostrum" & "Agibus tibi gratias Domine Deus et Pater pro tot beneficiis quae ex tua benignitate largiter nobis (I forget the verb) per Jesum Xtum Dominum Nostrum." He was sconced once for getting tied up over "liberalitatis." He was Bible Clerk for one term in place of one Robins who vanished from the Hall one day & was heard no more of. At the end of the term he received an unexpected but none the less welcome cheque for £10.

There was no advanced asceticism in the Hall in his days. Fish was only given in Hall on Good Fridays, & then in addition to the ordinary dinner! The men had to attend Hall daily.

What is now the Common Room seems then to have been used as a Lecture Room. It was here during a lecture that my Grandfather suddenly fainted & was good for no work for a long time afterwards. Not, that is, until he was well out of his Oxford career.

There were two Scouts in his time, of which his was young and jolly & went by the name of Dick. The other was more staid. The marking for Chapel was undertaken by the Bible Clerk.

The man called Haik was very musical & got together several men to sing glees & such. Some got friends in from other colleges, & my Grandfather recollects Goss coming to one of the meetings with Sir Frederick Ouseley. He sang in the chorus of an oratorio given at Christchurch in aid of the victims of the Irish Potato Famine & remembers Dr Elvey, the conductor, stepping back for an impressive sweep & falling off the platform with nothing left to be seen but his wooden leg straight up & waving in distress.

The principal recreation at the Hall was walking, as there were no formal sports clubs at this period. My Grandfather went to call on a Magdalen man one day to take him out for a walk, & while waiting in the quad he was accosted by an imposing-looking Don who asked him what he was waiting for. This Don turned out to be the Proctor whom my Grandfather had never before met officially. Caps & gowns, it seems, had to be worn during the daytime then. My Grandfather managed to get up a four on the river but it never rowed in any race. He remembers it still with great enjoyment.

He remembers hearing a hot sermon against Mariolatry from Dr Jeune. One Easter vac. he had stayed up to work, & went to S. Peter's to Mattins, where he was immensely impressed by hearing the prayers intoned for the first time. He thought it a very beautiful innovation. The then Vicar was a Fellow of Merton & became a Bp. soon after. He was always very kind to my Grandfather.

The only person he knows to be alive now who used to be a friend of his at the Hall is the Rev. J. C. K. Saunders MA. of 7 Salisbury Rd. S. Jude's Plymouth. They used to be friends at Plymouth in their 'teens & spent much of their life together. He remembers him as a quiet, steady young fellow. Probably you could get some interesting details from him if you write.

I have set down all I can remember at present & it seems vilely written & put together, but you may be able to dig out of it a few bits of interest. The recollections of a man of eightysix are not likely to be very vivid & I am rather surprised at his getting out such a lot. He is quite pleased at your having the portrait of Mr Hill as he knows it will be valued as a relic of that time. I will try & get some more details about the Chapel.

Finally, would it be possible for me to go up on the Thursday (14th)? I have a friend going up on that day & there are a lot of things I want to arrange before term begins. I should be glad to have permission if possible.

Yours very truly

Ernest C. Mortimer.

PS. My Grandfather's name is the Rev. M. Gueritz B.A.

Notes

1   In Valencia.

2   *Of Predestination and Election.* There is an important collection of items relating to the lively ecclesiastical career of F. G. Lee in the Old Library of St Edmund Hall.

3   I.e., the Catholic Apostolic Church or "Irvingites". "Angel" was the designation of its bishops.

Gueritz in "E": A musical setting for the Holy Communion

HOLY COMMUNION.

Entroit.

VOICES FULL.

PSALM xxvi. 6, 8.

I ... will wash my hands in in-no-cen-cy, O Lord: ...

And so will I go to Thine Al ... tar,

TREBLES ONLY.

Lord, { I have loved the } Thy House, { and the } Thine honour dwelleth.
{ habitation of } { place where }

FULL UNISON.

Repeat first part.

Glo--ry be to the Father, and to the Son, And to the Holy Ghost;

(3)

As it { was in the begin- }{ ning, is now, and } over shall be, world with out end. A-men.

Repeat first part.

Kyrie.

No. 1. *After the 1st, 2nd, 3rd, and 7th, 8th, 9th Commandments.*

Lord, have mere-y up - on us, and in - cline our hearts to keep this law.

No. 2. *After the 4th, 5th and 6th Commandments.*

Lord, have mere-y up - on us, and in - cline our hearts to keep this law.

No. 3. *After the 10th Commandment.*

rall.

Lord, have mer-cy up - on us, and write all these Thy laws in our hearts, we beseech Thee.

BEFORE THE GOSPEL.

AFTER THE GOSPEL.

Glory be to Thee, O Lord. Thanks be to Thee, O God.

(4)

Credo.

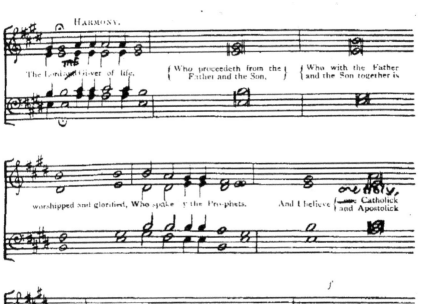

HARMONY.

The Lord and Gi-ver of life. {Who proceedeth from the Father and the Son,} {Who with the Father and the Son together is

worshipped and glorified, Who spake by the Prophets. And I believe {one holy, Catholick and Apostolick

f

Church. I acknowledge {one Baptism for the remission of} sins, And I look for the Resur-

rec-tion of the dead. And the life of the world to come, A-men.

Sursum Corda.

FULL. *f*

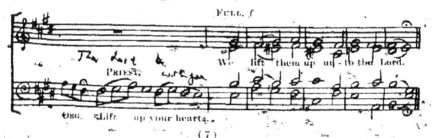

We lift them up up-to the Lord.

PRIEST. with joy

ORG. Lift up your hearts.

(7)

FULL. *f*

PRIEST.

It is sweet and right so to do.

Let us give thanks un-to our Lord God.

Sanctus.

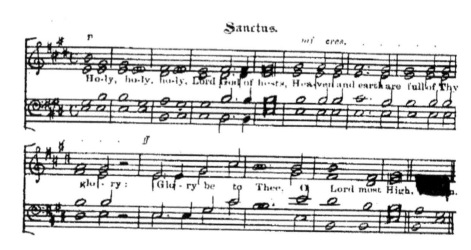

p   *mf* cres.

Ho-ly, ho-ly, ho-ly, Lord God of hosts, Heaven and earth are full of Thy

ff

glo-ry: Glo-ry be to Thee, O Lord most High.

Benedictus.

p Slow.   *mf*

Bless-ed, bless-ed, bless-ed is He that com-eth in the Name of the

Lord. Ho-san-na, Ho-san-na, Ho-san-na in the High-est.

(8)

Agnus Dei

O Lamb of God, that tak-est a - way the sins of the world, have mercy upon us.

PED.

O Lamb of God, that tak-est a - way the sins of the world, have mer-cy up - on us.

ORGAN.

O Lamb of God, that tak-est a-way the sins of the world, grant us Thy peace.

Gloria in Excelsis.

FULL p

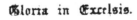

and in earth peace, good will towards men

PRIEST.

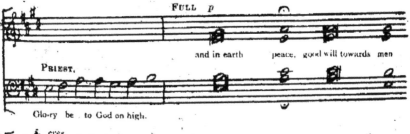

Glo-ry be to God on high.

cres.

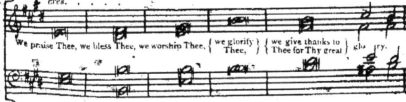

We praise Thee, we bless Thee, we worship Thee, { we glorify } { we give thanks to } glo-ry.
{ Thee, } { Thee for Thy great }

O Lord God, Heav'n-ly King, God the Fa-ther Al-migh-ty, {O Lord, the only begotten Son

Je-sus Christ: O Lord God, Lamb of God, Son of the Fa-ther,

that takest away the sins of the world.
Thou that takest away the sins of the world,
Thou that sittest at the right hand of God the Father, have mercy up - on us.

For Thou only art holy, Thou only art the Lord: Thou only, O Christ, with the Holy Ghost,

art most High in the glo-ry of God the Fa-ther. A-men.

AFTER THE BENEDICTION.

A - - men.

(10)

The Borcombe Homily

Written by W. H. B. Proby on 17 September 1909

TO MY FELLOW-PARISHIONERS
RESIDING IN THE NEIGHBOURHOOD
THE CHAPEL OF ST SIMON & ST JUI
BORCOMBE.

MY DEAR FRIENDS,—

I desire to say a few words to yo
about the above Chapel, in which the
Rector of Southleigh has kindly under
-taken, with the sanction of our Vicar
who is still your lawful Parish Priest,
to offer, from time to time, worship to
Almighty God, and to give Christian
teaching and exhortation, in the name
of the Lord, to those present.

And first, about the use of doing
such things. On entering the Chapel, you
will see at the east end, over the Altar,
what was our Lord Jesus Christ's *last
message* —BEHOLD, I COME AS A
THIEF. Some who have studied that Book
of the New Testament in which those words
are found are of opinion that the Lord
may fulfil them any day now, showing
Himself as *being come*. The message is
addressed to His Church —— to that
company of baptized people of which you all

I suppose) as well as myself are members; and of which the Church of England is the chief branch in this country. Now the use of the Chapel is that you may be helped forward in getting ready against the Lord's appearing, so as not to be taken by surprise.

May I remind you then that He Who sent the above message is no other than God the Son, the Second Person in the ever-blessed Trinity, One in Godhead with the Father and the Holy Ghost: that He took our nature, body, soul, and spirit, into oneness with Himself in the womb of the blessed Virgin, and was born, and grew up, and died upon the cross for our sins which He had been bearing, and was raised from the dead with a new spiritual life, and went up into heaven, and sent down from thence God the Holy Ghost, the Spirit of the Father and of the Son, to dwell for ever in the company of the Lord's disciples which we now call the Catholic Church, and to make them one body with the Lord Jesus Christ for their Head. Also, that when, in pursuance of His command, we were baptized (or christened as the expression is), God the Holy Ghost did so knit us on to the Lord, that the salvation which He wrought out becomes ours, and His resurrection-life becomes ours; and thus, in the power of that life, we become able to do, and speak, and think, as the limbs of His Body ought to do. And when He comes again (which I beg you always to remember, may be before you and I have time to die), He will wish to find us so living; fearing God and departing from evil; doing all the duties, first towards God and then towar our neighbours, which we learned (I sup -pose) in the Catechism.

Now it is with a view to these most desirable ends that this Chapel was built and that services in it are to be begun again. May I hope that all into whose hands these lines come will stir them -selves up to make use of it accordingly will kneel on their knees in the worshi of God; will join with all their heart in the prayers which will be offered; an with their voices also in the Amens and other parts of the service where the people are directed to join; and will gi the most earnest attention to the Word of God which will be read to them, and to the word which the Lord's ordaine priest and minister will deliver to them as from Him. I am sure that the Minist will be delighted to explain anything which I have said above, or wherein he also may have failed to make himself fully understood.

We must not think, however, that our offering of prayers, however hearty, makes up all the worship which our Maker expects at our hands. His perfect worship must have in it deeds as well as words; and we must not be content until there is celebrated, at the Altar in the Chapel, that chief deed which is our Christian Sacrifice — I mean, of course, the holy Eucharist. Our communion therein, too, is, according to New Testament teaching, the means by which our oneness with Christ, begun in our baptism, is to be kept up. It is important for us to remember that we are saved, not by hearing about Christ, or thinking about Christ, or even praying to Christ; but by being one with Him, and keeping our oneness up. — On all these points, however, I must refer you to that priest who will, with God's grace and help, minister among you.

I must add a word or two about money matters. Most good things in this world have to be paid for by those who would enjoy them; and God has so ordered things by His Providence, that this rule holds good

in matters of religion: in fact, a religion
which costs nothing is generally worth
nothing. Nor is it right or reasonable that
a clergyman should bear all the cost of
services by which other people are to be
benefitted. While then there will not be in
the Chapel any begging — any carrying
of a bag round, — I hope that every
grown person will place some money-
fering in that part of the offering-box
at the door which is devoted to Chapel
-expenses — such as washing linen, pro
viding oil, and perhaps coals, and
such like matters. These offerings will
from time to time be presented upon
the Altar to Almighty God, for Him to
take notice of ; as of course He will.

I remain

Your faithful Servant

& fellow- Christian

W. H. B. Proby.

Colyton House, Colyton
Sept. 17ᵗʰ 1909.

Curates, assisting clergy, missions and missioners

Name	Role	Dates	Notes
Kenelm Henry Smith	Ass't Curate and intended Headmaster of St Andrew's Collegiate School	1860–3 Subsequently at St Mary's Ely and Ely Cathedral as an assistant	Mrs K. H. (Frances) Smith was sister to Catharine and Mary Winter and with them gave the pulpit in 1878. K. H. S. returned from Ely to Colyton to marry her in 1867
Nettleton Balme Whitby	Ass't Curate	1867–8	
William. H. B. Proby	Hon. Ass't	Between 1866 and 1874	Irregular. At times extended periods. See Chapter 16.
J. W. Bennett	Curate in charge	Late 1868–70	Also rector of Markshall
D. J. Mackey	Ass't Curate	Late 1868–70	Ord. priest 1870
J. R. Vernon	Temp cover	Sept 1870	C. Stogumber
J. G. Dangar	Temp cover	30 June to 5 August 1871	Principal Exeter Training College
J. Edmondson	Temp cover	29 July to 29 August 1874	
Timothy G. Lynde	Temp cover	September 1874	C. St Leonard's Shoreditch

Name	Role	Dates	Notes
John Riley	Temp cover	October 1874	C. Sarawak, where Mamerto George was British Resident.
Jose Fortescue Gueritz	Ass't Curate	1876–9	Son
Walter Fell	Temp cover	December 1880	C. Sutton on Plym
C. J. Parsons	Ass't Curate	November 1882–January 1884	1893 R. Stockleigh English, Crediton
Reginald Arthur Mortimer	Ass't Curate	1884–9	Son-in-law
George Ellis	Ass't Curate	1889–90	
Albert A. Brookway	Curate in charge	1891	From New York
Arthur Sandbach	Ass't Curate	1892–5	D. 1892 P. 1894
I. J. Rosser	Ass't Curate	1892–6	C. at Colyford
H. F. G. James	Ass't Curate	1896–9	Prev C. Swymbridge w J. F. L. Gueritz
Ettrick Havelock Creak (misreported as Cheak)	Ass't Curate (Temporary Post)	1899–1900	In November 1900 Creak went to Madras as a chaplain in the Indian Army

Six Missions were held in Colyton from November 1875 to March 1878

Date	Name	Appointment held
7–14 November 1875	V. S. S. Coles	R. Shepton Beauchamp
	A. H. Drummond	
22–31 March 1876	V. S. S. Coles	R. Shepton Beauchamp
	H. J. Dodwell	
December 1876 Advent	J. Izod	C. Honiton
	H. A. Cartwright	R. Whitestaunton
	V. S. S. Coles	R. Shepton Beauchamp
February/March 1877 Lent	J. Izod	C. Honiton
	H. A. Cartwright	R. Whitestaunton
	C. H. Crooke	C. Membury
	W. P. C. Adams	R. Hawkchurch
December 1877 Advent	J. Izod	C. Honiton
	V. S. S. Coles	R. Shepton Beauchamp
	H. A. Cartwright	R. Whitestaunton
Lent 1878 *A series of sermons on Wednesdays in Lent*	V. S. S. Coles	R. Shepton Beauchamp
	J. Izod	C. Honiton
	H. A. Cartwright	R. Whitestaunton
	G. H. P. Barlow	V. Chardstock
	H. W. Thrupp	R. Musbury
	Mamerto Gueritz	V. Colyton

The Lent and Advent sermon series continued for many years

Mamerto Gueritz—A synoptic timeline

Year	Mamerto Gueritz and Colyton	Family and friends	The wider scene
1823	Birth in a convent at Jativa	Father, Jose, joins the Navarre Regiment	
1824	Taken to Barcelona by Antonia Josepha and thence to Alicante	Jose escapes to England via France. Antonia and Mamerto given safe passage to friends in Alicante	Jose discovers that Spanish veterans of the Peninsular War may receive a pension
1826	Antonia and Mamerto to England	Family reunited in London	
1828		Birth of sister Adelina	Repeal of the Test and Corporation Acts (Sacramental Test Act)
1828/9	Move with the family to Plymouth	Meets Dr Carne and joins the congregation of Charles Church	Catholic Emancipation Act
1830/1	Mamerto begins to study at Hampton House School in Plymouth	Constitutionalist rebellion gathers at Bayonne. Jose Gueritz joins General Mina	General Mina and his staff leave London for Bayonne Henry Phillpotts becomes Bishop of Exeter
1831		Birth of brother Edward Anselm Gueritz	
1832		Death of father, Jose, and baby brother, Edward	
1833			Church Temporalities (Ireland) Act. John Keble's Assize Sermon, "National Apostasy". The first 30 of *Tracts for the Times* published
1834			Twenty further *Tracts for the Times* issued
1836			Death of Richard Hurrell Froude

Year	Mamerto Gueritz and Colyton	Family and friends	The wider scene
1837/8	Apprenticed to W. H. Hawker, wine merchant. Also teaching in the parish school		
1839		Henry Parry Liddon to school in Lyme Regis	
1841			*Tract 90* published and the series brought to an end
1843	Full employment with W. H. Hawker		
1844	Study year with the Revd R. S. Field of Hatherleigh. Prep for university	Studies at Hatherleigh and Oxford paid for by "A Protestant Society for helping candidates for Holy Orders"	Bishop Phillpotts orders the wearing of the surplice in Exeter diocese. Bristol Church Union formed
1845	Matriculated to St Edmund Hall		Frederick Oakeley of Margaret Chapel suspended from ministry in the Church of England. Becomes a Roman Catholic. John Henry Newman also joins the Roman Catholic Church
1846		H. P. Liddon confirmed and later matriculates to Christ Church, Oxford	
1848	Graduation. Ordination as deacon in December. First curacy at Shepton and Barrington	Adelina governess to the children of Shepton Beauchamp parsonage	Bishop Phillpotts of Exeter refuses to institute George Cornelius Gorham to Bramford Speke. George Rundle Prynne goes to St Peter's, Plymouth. Lydia Sellon begins work in Devonport

Year	Mamerto Gueritz and Colyton	Family and friends	The wider scene
1849	In May, marriage to Anne Derby Lawrence, of Plymouth		
1850		Birth of Mamerto George Gueritz	The Judicial Committee of the Privy Council rule against Phillpotts in the Gorham case
1851	Return to Exeter diocese and a curacy at Brixham	Adelina to Glastonbury as governess to a GP's children	
1852	A curacy at Stoke Gabriel	Birth of Jose Fortescue Lawrence Gueritz	
1852/3	A "caretaker" curacy at Bigbury		
1853		Birth of Mary Louisa Gueritz	St Matthias, Stoke Newington consecrated
1855		Birth of Edward Peregrine Gueritz	The Hon Robert Liddell of St Paul's, Knightsbridge prosecuted for ritualism. Proceedings begun against Archdeacon Denison. Charles Lowder and others form the Society of the Holy Cross (SSC)
1856	A curacy at Yealmpton and a mastership at Yealmpton School	Birth of Henry Francis (Frank) Gueritz	
1857	Curate of St Mary's Penzance. Present at first midnight mass in Cornwall since the Reformation		F. G. Lee (*et aliorum*) founds Association for the Promotion of the Unity of Christendom. The 'Knightsbridge Judgement' affirms most of R. Liddell's practices. The Court of Arches overturns the judgement against Archdeacon Denison

Year	Mamerto Gueritz and Colyton	Family and friends	The wider scene
1858	A prime mover at the inaugural meeting of the Association of Church Choirs in Cornwall		First edition of *Directorium Anglicanum*—John Purchas
1859	Visits to All Saints Margaret Street begin	Birth of Antonia Anne Gueritz	St John's Hammersmith completed. The Saltash Bridge opened. Rail communication with London much eased
1860		Mamerto George to All Saints Margaret Street choir school	
1860	Presented to the incumbency of Colyton and perpetual curacy of Monckton. The railway arrives in Colyton	H. P. Liddon notes a "sister of Mercy" staying at the vicarage	Anti-ritualist riots at St George's in the East, London. Bryan King, Charles Lowder and Frederick G. Lee attacked. English Church Union formed
1861	Unitarian press attacks Gueritz for "High Church" activities		Worship in Colyton likened to that of St Paul's, Knightsbridge
1862	Open conflict with the Unitarians and the minister D. L. Evans		
1863	Gueritz protests to the Queen regarding the marriage of the Prince of Wales during Lent. Fury of local "Protestants"		St Alban's, Holborn completed
1864	The beginning of the dispute over the burial of Unitarian John Pavey	Legal proceedings taken against Gueritz	The case reported in the London papers

Year	Mamerto Gueritz and Colyton	Family and friends	The wider scene
1865	Bishop Phillpotts gives judgement. Gueritz reprimanded and ordered to pay costs		The Pavey case cited in debate in the House of Lords. F. G. Lee publishes enlarged edition of *Directorium Anglicanum*
1865		Adelina Gueritz and Samuel Bennett married in Colyton Church	The Church Association formed
1866	The ritual in Colyton becomes more "advanced". The reordering of pews first mooted	W. H. B. Proby returns to Colyton from the diocese of Brechin in Scotland. Gueritz and Proby burned in effigy on "Popeday Night"	
1867	Gueritz resigns the perpetual curacy of Monckton		The responsibility passed to John Mackarness of Honiton, later Bishop of Oxford
1867	Gueritz to London for a brief period of recuperation	Proby inflames local relationships over two funerals	
1868	Gueritz family to London Gueritz at St Matthias, Stoke Newington	Mamerto George leaves for Sarawak. Bishop Henry Jenner to Colyton for a confirmation. M. G. works with C. J. Le Geyt, Robert Brett and W. H. Monk	
1869	Guild of St Andrew fully operational A proposal for the reordering of pews defeated		Frederick Temple consecrated as Bishop of Exeter

Year	Mamerto Gueritz and Colyton	Family and friends	The wider scene
1870	Sunday afternoon services for children begun. The Society of the Holy Childhood formed. The Sisters of Our Lady of Compassion make a first appearance in Colyton. A branch of the Confraternity of the Blessed Sacrament established	Henry Parry Liddon made a canon of St Paul's Cathedral	Elementary Education Act passed. John Purchas, vicar of St James', Brighton tried in the Court of Arches. Confraternity of the Blessed Sacrament formed from earlier bodies.
1871	Full requiem in Colyton for G. Trevelyan. Gueritz visits Wallonie	Fortescue and Edward working as accountant's clerks in Hackney	The Church Association appeals against the existing Purchas Judgement and gains condemnation of all Purchas' practices
1872		Bishop Henry Jenner visits for the East Devon Choral Festival	Death of John Purchas
1873	New font in memory of John Snook		
1874	Disappearance of the sisterhood from Colyton. The Dorcas Society formed. The work of the district visitors expands	W. H. B. Proby opens an Irvingite chapel in King Street. First school board formed. The Elton family move to Colyton House from Whitestaunton. Death of Robert Brett of Stoke Newington	Public Worship Regulation Act passed (Repealed 1965)
1875	Parish Mission. Mamerto Gueritz appointed a Feoffee	Led by V. S. S. Coles	
1876	The proposal for the reordering of the pews defeated again. Advent Mission led by Mamerto	Jose Fortescue Gueritz ordained to the diaconate. V. S. S. Coles assisting	

Year	Mamerto Gueritz and Colyton	Family and friends	The wider scene
1877		Death of C. J. Le Geyt of Stoke Newington	Fr Tooth of St James', Hatcham imprisoned under the PW.R.A.
1878		Mary Louisa Gueritz and Reginald Mortimer married. Emigrate to New Zealand. Reginald ordained deacon	
1879		Jose Fortescue Gueritz ordained priest. Becomes rector of Templeton. Henry "Frank" Gueritz to New Zealand. Birth of Edith Mary, first child of Reginald and Mary Louisa Mortimer, in New Zealand	
1880	Mamerto Gueritz becomes chairman of the school board	Birth of John Lawrence Mortimer in New Zealand, the second child of Mary and Reginald Mortimer	Burial Laws Amendment Act. T. Pelham Dale of St Vedast's and R. W. Enraght of Bordesley imprisoned under the PW.R.A.
1881	Mamerto and Jose Fortescue exchange livings for a year		S. F. Green of Miles Platting imprisoned under the PW.R.A.
1882		Jose Fortescue married to Lucy Octavia Elton of Colyton House. Reginald Mortimer ordained priest	Death of Edward Bouverie Pusey
1883		Henry Frank Gueritz and Mamerto George home from NZ and Sarawak respectively. Birth of Aimee Winifred Mortimer in NZ. Birth of Reginald Mamerto Mortimer in NZ	

Year	Mamerto Gueritz and Colyton	Family and friends	The wider scene
1884		Death of Antonia Anne Gueritz. V. S. S. Coles presides at her requiem mass. Birth of Elton Lawrence Gueritz at Templeton. V. S. S. Coles, Librarian of Pusey Memorial. Mary Louisa and Reginald Mortimer return from New Zealand. Death of their infant son Reginald Mamerto. Death of Mamerto George in Borneo	Pusey Memorial opened in Oxford by the Bishop of Oxford, John Mackarness, previously of Honiton and Exeter Cathedral
1885		Jose Fortescue Gueritz elected Rural Dean of Tiverton	Edward King consecrated Bishop of Lincoln. Edward Bickersteth consecrated Bishop of Exeter
1886		Fortescue preferred to Swymbridge	
1887		Birth of Charles Mamerto, son of Fortescue and Lucy Octavia Gueritz	
1888	Outbreak of typhus in Colyton. Chapel of ease built in Colyford		Church Association begins attack on Edward King, Bishop of Lincoln
1889		Reginald Mortimer given the living of Roborough in North Devon. Death of W. H. Monk. Canon Liddon's last visit to Colyton	

Year	Mamerto Gueritz and Colyton	Family and friends	The wider scene
1890	Mamerto plagued by ill health. Resigns as precentor of the East Devon Choral Union		
1891	Travelling in Spain for two months		
1892	Influenza strikes in Colyton. Many of the "aged and infirm" die	Henry "Frank" Gueritz returns to Colyton having served two years as a lay reader in Shermanbury	
1893		W. H. B. Proby opens an Irvingite chapel at Pottlelake. Death of Charles Mamerto Gueritz at Swymbridge	
1893	The Church Lads' Brigade started in Colyton		
1896		Reginald Mortimer preferred to St Mary Major, Exeter	
1897	Mamerto and Anne Gueritz both seriously ill. Convalescent at St Mary Major		
1898	Faculty granted for the reordering of the church		
1899	Mamerto and Anne, golden wedding celebrations	Fortescue, Lucy and Elton Gueritz move to Scotland	
1900	Reordering complete. Bishop Edward Bickersteth presides at the opening celebration	Herbert Ryle to be Bishop of Exeter	Bishop Edward Bickersteth retires

Year	Mamerto Gueritz and Colyton	Family and friends	The wider scene
1901	Retirement of Mamerto in December		
1902		Death of Anne Derby Gueritz	
1904	Publication of the third edition of Mamerto's mass settings. Mamerto returns to Colyton to lodge with Mary Louisa in King Street	Death of Reginald Mortimer	
	Lodging with Adelina in Alexandra Terrace, Colyton		
1909		Fortescue and Lucy Gueritz move to Montrose	
1910			Death of Bishop Edward King
1912	Death of Mamerto Gueritz		

Bibliography

Primary sources

Colyton Parish File, South West Heritage Centre, Exeter.

Deposited records and papers. Ref PR 11 to 14. Mss correspondence.

The Minute Book of the Parish of Colyton (vestry meetings) 1861–1964.

The Feoffees Order and Minute Book 1760–1853.

Colyton Parish Magazine (from December 1894). Author's papers.

Colyton Parish Registers, South West Heritage Centre, Exeter (The records are maintained unbroken from 1538).

Exeter Cathedral Chapter Minute Books, Exeter Cathedral Archives.

Gueritz Family Papers, formerly in the possession of the late Rear Admiral E. Gueritz of Salisbury. Copies provided to the author. Includes letters, photographs and lithographs, Ms. accounts of the family history, newspaper cuttings and mementos. The papers are referred to in the endnotes according to the source (Gueritz or Mortimer), for example, G1, G2 and M1, and are in the author's papers. ECM. Ms. refers to a letter from E. C. Mortimer to the vice-principal of St Edmund Hall, S. L. Ollard. The original is in the St Edmund Hall archives.

National Census Returns, 1841–1901.

Penzance Parish File, Kresen Kernow (formerly Truro Record Office).

Rose, Ravenor E., Ms "History of Congregationalism in Colyton".

Seaward, Samuel Ms. description of Colyton c 1849. Author's papers.

Shapter, Thomas Ms. letter to W. H. B. Proby 22 November 1881, Exeter Cathedral Library ref. 536/Sha.

The Skinner Papers, a bequest to the Devon Record Office / South West Heritage Centre by A. J. P. Skinner, Colyton parish clerk.

United Parish Magazine to December 1894 (The parishes of Axminster, Awliscombe, Colyton, Combe Raleigh, Dalwood, Feniton, Hawkchurch, Honiton, Kilmington, Membury, Musbury, Seaton and Beer, and Shute).

Webb, B., "The Journal of Benjamin Webb 1819–85", Bodleian Library, Mss. Eng. Misc., d475, c406–43 and f97–9.

Theses

Chandler, M. J., "Church and Ministry in the Teaching of H. P. Liddon: A Study of his Theology and Pastoral Practice", PhD thesis, King's College, London, 1987.

Herring, G. W., "Tractarianism to Ritualism", DPhil thesis, Oxford University, 1984 (C5239–40 Bodleian Library, 2 vols).

Hoare, N. F., "The Community of Colyton and its Poor", MA thesis, University of Leicester, 1973.

Nelson, H., "The Law and the Lady: Consent and Marriage in Nineteenth-Century British Literature", DPhil thesis, Purdue University, 2015.

Orford, B. A., "Henry Parry Liddon: Correspondence on Church and Faith", PhD thesis, University of Wales, Bangor, 2000.

Official reports

Poor Law Commission, "Report on the Employment of Women and Children in Agriculture: Devon", 1843.

The Royal Commission on Ecclesiastical Discipline, Report 1904 (published 1906).

Published works

Alford, F. (ed.), *Life Journals and Letters of Henry Alford D.D.*, 2nd edn (London, Oxford and Cambridge: Rivingtons, 1873).

Allchin, A. M., *The Silent Rebellion: Anglican Religious Communities* 1845–1900 (London: SCM Press, 1958).

Anson, P. F., *The Call of the Cloister* (London: SPCK, 1955).

Barbe, L., *Francis Ysidro Edgeworth: A Portrait with Family and Friends*, tr. M. C. Black (Cheltenham: Edward Elgar Publishing, 2010).

Baring-Gould, S., *Further Reminiscences 1867–71* (London: The Bodley Head, 1925); *The Vicar of Morwenstow: A Life of Robert Stephen Hawker M.A.* (London: King, 1876).

Belcher, T. W., *Robert Brett (of Stoke Newington): His Life and Work* (London: Griffith, Farran, Okeden & Welsh, 1889).

Bennett, J. W. E., *The Old Church Porch*, vol. i 1854–5, vol. ii 1856–7, vol. iii 1858–9, vol iv. 1860–2 (London: Hayes).

Bertie, D. M., *Scottish Episcopal Clergy 1680 to 2000* (Edinburgh: Clarke, 2000).

Boggis, R. J. E., *The History of the Diocese of Exeter* (Exeter: Pollard, 1922).

Bolam, C. G. et al., *The English Presbyterians: From Elizabethan Puritanism to Modern Unitarianism* (London: Allen & Unwin, 1968).

Bradley, I., *Abide With Me: The World of Victorian Hymns* (London: SCM Press, 1997).

Brandreth, H. R. T., *Dr. Lee of Lambeth* (London: SPCK, 1951).

Bricknell, W. S., *The Judgement of the Bishops on Tractarian Theology* (Oxford: Vincent, 1845).

Briscoe, J. F., *V. S. S. Coles* (London: Mowbray, 1930).

Bumpus, T. F., *An Historical London Church: A Record of Sixty-five Years' Life and Work in the Church and Parish of S. Matthias, Stoke Newington* (London: J. King, 1911).

Burgon, J. W., *Lives of Twelve Good Men* (London: J. Murray, 1889).

Byles, C. E., *The Life and Letters of R. S. Hawker* (New York: The Bodley Head, 1906).

Cameron, A. T., *Religious Communities of the Church of England* (London: Faith Press, 1918).

Chadwick, O., *The Spirit of the Oxford Movement* (Cambridge: Cambridge University Press, 1990).

Chandler, M., *The Life and Work of Henry Parry Liddon* (Leominster: Gracewing, 2000).

Chandler, M., *An Introduction to the Oxford Movement* (London: SPCK, 2003).

Chanter, J. F., *The Bishop's Palace, Exeter and its Story* (London: SPCK, 1932).

Church, M. C., *The Life and Letters of Dean Church* (London: Macmillan, 1895).

Clutterbuck, I., *Marginal Catholics* (Leominster: Gracewing, 1993).

Coleridge, J. T., *A Memoir of the Rev. John Keble, M.A.* (Oxford: James Parker, 1880).

Courtenay, C. L., *Original Statutes of the Devon House of Mercy* (Private publication, 1893).

Cowie, L. & E., *That One Idea: Nathaniel Woodard and His Schools* (London: Woodard Corporation, 1991).

Davage, W. (ed.), *In This Sign Conquer: A History of the Society of the Holy Cross 1855–2005* (London: Continuum UK, 2006).

Davies, G. C. B., *Henry Phillpotts, Bishop of Exeter, 1778–1869* (London: SPCK, 1954).

Dawson, C., *The Spirit of the Oxford Movement and Newman's Place in History* (London: Saint Austin Press, 2001) (First published 1933).

Dickens, C., *Household Words* (London: Bradbury & Evans, 1850).

Evans, G. E., *Colytonia: A Chapter in the History of East Devon* (Liverpool: Gibbons, 1898). Published by private subscriptions.

Farmer, J., *Poems* (Private publication, 1901).

Goodwin, G. H., "Keble and Newman: Tractarian Aesthetics and the Romantic Tradition", *Victorian Studies* 30:4 (1987).

Gow, H., *The Unitarians* (London: Methuen, 1928).

Gresley, W., *Bernard Leslie: Second Part* (London: Masters, 1859).

Herring, G., *What Was the Oxford Movement?* (London: Continuum, 2002).

Herring, G., *The Oxford Movement in Practice* (Oxford: Oxford University Press, 2016).

Heygate, W. E., *Ember Hours* (London: Masters, 1857).

Hill, J. H., *The Religious Order* (London: Heinemann, 1973).

James, S., *The Cowley Fathers* (Norwich: Canterbury Press, 2019).

Johnstone, J. O., *The Life and Letters of Henry Parry Liddon DD* (London: Longmans Green & Co., 1904).

Jones, S., *England and the Holy See* (London: Longmans Green & Co., 1902).

Keble, J., *National Apostasy: Considered in a Sermon Preached in St. Mary's Church, Oxford Before His Majesty's Judges of Assize on Sunday July 14th 1833* (London: Mowbray, 1833) (Steventon: Rocket Press, 1983).

Keble, J., *The Christian Year* (London: Routledge & Sons, 1827).

Kelway, A. C., *Life of George Rundle Prynne* (London: Longmans Green & Co., 1905).

Ker, I., *John Henry Newman: A Biography* (Oxford: Clarendon, 1988).

Lach-Szmyrna, W. S., *A Church History of Cornwall and of the Diocese of Truro* (London, Plymouth and Truro: Stock, 1891).

Lee, F. G., *Directorium Anglicanum*, 2nd edn (London: Bosworth, 1867).

Lee, F. G. (ed.), *Essays on Reunion* (London: Hayes, 1867).

Lee, F. G., *The Validity of the Holy Orders of the Church of England* (London: Hayes, 1869).

Lee, F. G., *Glimpses in the Twilight: Being various notes, records and examples on the Supernatural* (Edinburgh and London: Blackwood, 1885).

Le Geyt, C. J., *On the Symbolism of the Ritual in the Church and the World* (London: Longmans, 1867).

Le Geyt, C. J., *Catholic Ritual in the Church of England: A Lecture Delivered at the Request of the Members of the Oxford Branch of the English Church Union, at the Music Room, Holywell, on Wednesday November 14, 1866* (Oxford: Mowbray, 1867).

Liddon, H. P., *Life of Edward Bouverie Pusey* (London: Longmans, 1894).

Little, B., *The Monmouth Episode* (London: Werner Laurie, 1956).

Littledale, R. F., *The North-side of the Altar: A Liturgical Essay* (London: Palmer, 1865).

Littledale, R. F., *Incense: A Liturgical Essay* (London: Palmer, 1866).

Mansel, P., *Pillars of Monarchy: An Outline of the Political and Social History of Royal Guards, 1400–1984* (London: Quartet Books, 1984).

Miles Brown, H., *The Catholic Revival in Cornish Anglicanism* (St Winnow: Private publication, 1980).

Millingen, J. G., *The History of Duelling*, vol. 1 (London: Bentley, 1841).

Mozley, A. (ed.), *The Letters and Correspondence of J. H. Newman* (London: Longmans, Green & Co., 1903) (2 vols).

Neale, J. M., *The History of Pues: A paper read before the Cambridge Camden Society on Monday, November 22, 1841* (London: Rivingtons and Cambridge: Stevenson, 1842).

Newland, H., *Three Lectures on Tractarianism* (London: Masters, 1852) (1855, 4th edn used).

Newman, J. H., *Apologia Pro Vita Sua* (London: Longmans, Green & Co., 1864) (London: Dent, 1942 edn used).

Nockles, P. B., *The Oxford Movement in Context* (Cambridge: Cambridge University Press, 1994).

Ollard, S. L., *A Short History of the Oxford Movement* (London: Mowbray, 1915).

Orme, N. (ed.), *Unity and Variety: A History of the Church in Devon and Cornwall* (Exeter: Exeter University Press, 1991).

Palmer, B., *Reverend Rebels: Five Victorian Clerics and Their Fight Against Authority* (London: Darton, Longman & Todd, 1993).

Perry, W., *The Oxford Movement in Scotland* (Cambridge: Cambridge University Press, 1933).

Polwhele, R., *The History of Devonshire in three volumes* (London: Cadell Johnson & Dilly, 1797).

Proby, W. H. B., *Lessons on the Kingdom for the Little Ones of the Church of England* (London: Hayes, 1872).

Proby, W. H. B., *Stories About the Great King* (London: Hayes, 1872).

Proby, W. H. B., *The Church Catechism Made Easy* (London: Hayes, 1872).

Proby, W. H. B., *Annals of the Low Church Party in England: Down to the Death of Archbishop Tait* (London: Hayes, 1888).

Pulman, G. P. R., *The Book of the Axe* (London: Longman, Green, Reader & Dyer, 1875) (Edn used: Bath: Kingsmead Reprints, 1969).

Purcell, W., *Onward Christian Soldier* (London: Longmans, 1957).

Purchas, J., *Directorium Anglicanum*, 1st edn, 1858.

Rainbow, B., *The Choral Revival in the Anglican Church 1859 to 1872* (London: Barrie & Jenkins, 1970).

Reed, J. S., *Glorious Battle: The Cultural Politics of Victorian Anglo-Catholicism* (London: Tufton Books, 1998).

Rees, E. A., *Old Penzance* (Private publication, 1956).

Robin, J., *The Way We Lived Then* (Aldershot: Ashgate, 2000).

Robin, J., "Prenuptial Pregnancy in a Rural Area of Devonshire in the Mid Nineteenth Century: Colyton 1851 to 1881", *Community Change* 1; "Illegitimacy in Colyton, 1851 to 1881", *Community Change* 2, occasional papers for the Cambridge Group for the History of Population and Social Structure.

Rowell, G., *The Vision Glorious* (Oxford: Oxford University Press, 1983).

Rowell, G. (ed.), *Tradition Renewed: The Oxford Movement Conference Papers* (Darton, Longman & Todd, 1986).

Russell, G. W. E., *Arthur Stanton, a Memoir* (London: Longmans, 1917).

Sandford, E. G. (ed.), *Frederick Temple, Archbishop of Canterbury* (London: Macmillan, 1906).

Shipley, O., *The Ritual of the Altar* (London: Longmans, 1878).

Stephenson, C., *Merrily on High* (London: Darton, Longman & Todd, 1972).

Thomas, J. E., *Sabine Baring-Gould: The Life of a Complete Victorian* (Stroud: Fonthill Media, 2015).

Thompson, F., *Lark Rise to Candleford* (Oxford: Oxford University Press, 1945).

Walke, B., *Twenty Years at St. Hilary* (London: Methuen, 1936).

Walsh, W., *A History of the Romeward Movement in the Church of England* (London: Nisbet, 1900).

Walsh, W., *A Secret History of the Oxford Movement* (London: Chas. J. Thynne, 1899).

White, R. G. C., *The Feoffees of Colyton 1596 to 1946* (Private publication, 1951).

Whitworth, W. A., *Quam Dilecta* (London: Wells, Gardner, Darton & Co., 1891).

Yelton, M., *Outposts of the Faith* (Norwich: Canterbury Press, 2009).

Milton Keynes UK
Ingram Content Group UK Ltd.
UKHW051850210324
439912UK00006B/11/J